COPYRIGHT

Simon Crawford Welch, PhD, brings a unique and multi-dimensional perspective to the conversation around personal growth, leadership, and societal challenges. His latest book, American Chasms: Essays on the Divided States of America, explores one of the most pressing issues of our time—the growing divisions within American society—through the lens of his extraordinary life experiences, global travels, and professional expertise.

A maverick thinker and global nomad, Simon's journey has taken him across the globe, allowing him to view life, people, and challenges through a broad and empathetic lens. From his early years in Ethiopia and Djibouti to his education in the UK and subsequent leadership roles in North America and Mexico, his path has been anything but conventional. His upbringing, shaped by cultural diversity, fostered a unique outlook on life that values innovation, perseverance, and the courage to reinvent oneself in the face of adversity. These qualities form the foundation of Simon's approach to leadership, critical thinking, and problem-solving—attributes that shine through in his writing.

Throughout his career, Simon has excelled in executive leadership roles across industries, from hospitality to digital marketing, always with a focus on transformational growth. As the former President & Chief Operating Officer of Diamond Resorts International, he oversaw a network of 160 resorts across 14 countries, steering the company through significant expansion. Later roles in Mexico, as President of Tesoro Resorts and Chief Sales & Marketing Officer of Royal Resorts, cemented his reputation as a visionary leader with a keen understanding of global markets and cultural dynamics.

Simon's unique life experiences have equipped him with a mental model that allows him to cut through noise, identify core issues, and offer practical solutions.

In American Chasms, Simon brings this skill to bear, dissecting the social, political, and cultural fractures in America with an emphasis on finding pathways toward understanding and unity. His analytical approach, combined with his deep sense of empathy, helps readers see these divides not just as problems, but as opportunities for growth and transformation.

Having lived in or visited over 100 countries, Simon's global outlook has been honed by years of travel, exposing him to diverse cultures and perspectives. This worldly wisdom, combined with his professional experience and academic background, gives him a rare ability to distill complex issues into actionable insights—whether they are about leadership, critical thinking, or societal challenges. His journey of reinvention, resilience, and innovation serves as a compelling reminder that the challenges we face—whether personal, professional, or societal—can be reframed as opportunities for profound growth.

Simon's writing is not just a reflection of his academic and professional prowess, but is also deeply personal. His experiences of facing financial struggles, overcoming personal loss, and parenting a special-needs child have shaped his understanding of resilience, empathy, and what it means to lead with integrity. In American Chasms, these life lessons permeate every page, offering readers not only a road-map to understanding America's divides but also practical advice on how to foster unity in an increasingly fragmented world.

Simon's work continues to inspire those around him, whether through his writings, his coaching, or his leadership at The Critical Thought Lab, an organization dedicated to fostering critical thinking and clarity of purpose. Through his extensive career and life experiences, Simon Crawford-Welch has consistently demonstrated his ability to help others navigate complexity with insight and integrity. In American Chasms, he offers readers the tools to confront and understand the divisions that threaten to pull us apart and, in doing so, provides hope for a more united future.

Why I Wrote This Collection of Essays

I did not set out to write a book. In fact, this collection of essays started as something much smaller—an outlet for my frustration, a way to organize my thoughts, and maybe even a conversation starter for the many debates I found myself immersed in with family, friends, and colleagues. Over time, it became clear that the debates weren't just casual disagreements; they were reflections of something deeper—a profound division in the way Americans, even the most educated among us, perceive and understand the key issues facing our society.

What disturbed me the most wasn't the diversity of opinion. I've always believed that disagreement when based on reason, facts, and empathy, is healthy in a democracy. The issue was that these discussions often felt shallow and uninformed—driven by five-second sound bites, repeated endlessly by 24-hour news channels, echo chambers on social media, and polarizing political rhetoric. These weren't ignorant people. In fact, many of them are some of the brightest minds I know—professionals, intellectuals, and creative thinkers. Yet, they were falling prey to misinformation, disinformation, and oversimplified narratives that distorted their understanding of critical issues.

The problem, as I see it, is that many of us have stopped engaging in real, intellectual discourse. Instead, we cling to emotionally charged rhetoric, misleading headlines, and confirmation bias—often without taking the time to dive deeper into the facts. We've become accustomed to quick judgments, polarized opinions, and the relentless demand for immediate answers, rather than taking the time to listen, learn, and engage in reasoned debate. This book, "American Chasms: Essays on the Divided States of America," is my response to that trend.

An Attempt to Bridge the Divide

The essays in this collection are not intended to preach or proselytize. They are certainly not designed to provide all the answers or to demand that readers align with a specific ideology. Instead, this book is an effort to encourage something that seems increasingly rare in our current social and political environment: thoughtful, informed, and objective discourse.

I'm aware that many of the topics I cover—fascism, wokeism, free speech, abortion rights, immigration, gun control, and climate change—are emotionally charged and highly divisive. But they are also important. These are the issues that define our political and cultural landscape, the issues that shape how we interact with one another, how we vote, how we live, and ultimately how we define ourselves as a nation. Whether we like it or not, these debates are not going away, and we must find a way to engage with them meaningfully.

Escaping the Echo Chambers

One of the greatest challenges of our time is the rise of echo chambers, where we surround ourselves with like-minded people who reinforce our existing beliefs and dismiss any conflicting viewpoints. This phenomenon, amplified by social media algorithms, partisan news outlets, and political tribalism, has turned nuanced debates into black-and-white binaries, leaving little room for understanding or compromise.

Take, for example, the debate over gun control, which has become synonymous with Second Amendment rights versus public safety. Or the heated arguments over abortion rights, framed as pro-life versus pro-choice with very little attention paid to the complexities that underlie both positions. These debates are presented as simple, binary choices when in reality, they are deeply complex, requiring a full understanding of the historical, social, economic, and legal contexts.

In my conversations with those around me, I often found that people were arguing based on emotion, rhetoric, and half-truths—not because they weren't smart or capable of deeper thinking, but because that's what the media environment had fed them. Instead of informed discussion, we were engaging in battles of shallow sound bites, hastily delivered arguments shaped by political agendas and fragmented media.

Why Facts Matter

What I aim to do with this book is to strip away the propaganda and talking points that have polluted our public discourse. The essays you'll find here— whether on race and policing, voting rights, climate change, or free speech—are rooted in facts, data, and historical context. I don't claim that the facts alone will solve our societal divisions, but I firmly believe that no meaningful discussion can happen without them.

We live in an era where misinformation spreads faster than the truth, where fake news masquerades as journalism, and where partisan platforms have turned news into entertainment. It is no longer enough to simply consume the information that aligns with your worldview. To be a responsible citizen, one must challenge those views, seek out multiple sources, and be willing to engage with uncomfortable truths.

Facts are not partisan, but their interpretation often is. A clear example is the debate over climate change. While the overwhelming scientific consensus supports the reality of human-caused global warming, the issue remains one of the most politically polarizing topics in America. It's not because the facts are disputed by the scientific community, but because those facts have been obscured, spun, and distorted by ideological interests.

Encouraging Intellectual Discourse

I wrote this book because I am tired of seeing smart people being swayed by simplistic narratives and emotional manipulation. We need to get back to a place where we can have real conversations—conversations that are rooted in a shared commitment to truth, understanding, and respect for opposing viewpoints. We need to reject the temptation of easy answers and embrace the complexity of the world we live in.

That's not to say that emotions don't have a place in our discussions—they absolutely do. Passion for justice, fairness, freedom, and equality has fueled some of the most important social movements in history. But emotion must be tempered by reason. When emotion and ideology take precedence over objectivity, we lose the ability to have productive conversations. We lose the ability to listen.

Through these essays, I hope to spark discussions that are fact-based and well-rounded, that go beyond partisan sound bites and ideological rigidity. I want to challenge readers—whether they are liberal, conservative, or somewhere in between—to confront their assumptions, question their sources of information, and engage in the kind of intellectual discourse that moves us forward, rather than deeper into division.

The Essays

The essays in this book cover a wide range of topics that illustrate the many divides in our country today. From the political—Fascism in America and The Rich-Poor Divide—to the social and cultural—The Dynamic and Evolving Debate Around Sexuality and Gender Roles and The Fragmentation of Religion in America—I explore the issues that are driving us apart and suggest ways to understand them in a more nuanced, fact-based way.

Each essay seeks to inform and educate, but also to provoke thought and reflection. Fascism in America, for instance, asks whether some of the warning signs of authoritarianism are already visible in our political system. The Dangers of Extreme Wokeism examines the unintended consequences of an overzealous push for social justice. The Demise of True Communication explores how our reliance on technology and short-form communication has degraded our ability to meaningfully engage with one another.

In other essays, I tackle free speech, gun control, race and policing, economic inequality, abortion rights, and voting integrity—all issues that dominate the American political landscape. These topics are controversial and emotionally charged, but they are also vital to the future of our democracy. By grounding these discussions in facts, I hope to move us away from polarization and toward a shared understanding of the challenges we face.

My Cognitive Bias

In writing this book, my goal has been to explore the critical issues dividing America today through an objective lens, rather than to push a particular political agenda or promote any single ideology. I recognize that, like anyone, I have my own cognitive biases and personal beliefs, but I have made every effort to set them aside in order to provide a fair, balanced, and factual examination of the topics at hand. My purpose is not to validate one perspective over another, but to foster an intellectual dialogue that encourages readers to engage with both sides of the argument.

It is far too easy, in today's polarized media environment, to retreat into echo chambers where only our own views are affirmed and opposing perspectives are dismissed. However, that approach doesn't help us solve the challenges we face as a society. Instead, it deepens the divide and discourages the nuanced thinking required to address complex issues. My intention with this book is to present the facts, as clearly and impartially as possible, so that readers can come to their own conclusions, fully informed by a broad spectrum of evidence and viewpoints.

That said, I fully acknowledge that complete objectivity is a challenging, if not impossible, goal. Everyone brings their own lenses of experience, beliefs, and biases to the table. I have tried to be self-aware of my own predispositions throughout the writing process, constantly questioning my approach and ensuring that I remain grounded in evidence, rather than rhetoric or personal conviction. Where possible, I have drawn from reliable sources, studies, and statistics, presenting both sides of each issue fairly and without distortion.

Ultimately, the goal of this book is to create a space for thoughtful discourse, not to take a side. I want readers to reflect deeply on the issues presented here, to engage in conversations that are based on reason and understanding, not on emotion, misinformation, or simplistic soundbites. Whether you identify more closely with one side of an argument or find yourself somewhere in the middle, I hope this book encourages you to look beyond the headlines and consider the complexities that define these debates. Only by embracing a full, objective understanding of the challenges we face can we begin to find real solutions.

The Way Forward

In writing these essays, my hope is not to convince you of any particular ideology or position. Rather, I hope to encourage you to think more critically about the complexity of the issues we're facing as a country. I want to promote a culture of intellectual curiosity, where we can engage with difficult questions without resorting to simplistic answers or knee-jerk reactions.

If there's one thing I've learned from my conversations with friends, family, and colleagues, it's that we are all capable of learning, growing, and changing our minds—if we are willing to listen to one another and engage with the facts. My goal with this book is to provide a foundation for those kinds of conversations, where facts are front and center, and where respectful, informed debate replaces the divisive rhetoric that has come to define too much of our public discourse.

We must move beyond the American chasms that divide us. It won't be easy, but if we can learn to communicate openly, listen thoughtfully, and challenge ourselves intellectually, I believe it's possible. This book is a small step in that direction.

Thank you for reading, and I hope these essays inspire you to approach the most difficult issues of our time with clarity, compassion, and curiosity.

A Final Note

I offer no apologies for the length and complexity of these essays. The topics discussed here are important and intricate, and they deserve far more than the oversimplified, five-second sound bites that we have grown accustomed to hearing on mass media and social media platforms.

In an era where attention spans are shrinking and information is increasingly filtered through biased, algorithm-driven newsfeeds, there is a tendency to reduce complex issues to shallow, surface-level takes. This book is meant to challenge that trend. It is for those who seek a deeper understanding, who are willing to engage with the nuances and complexities that cannot be captured in a headline or a tweet.

If you're comfortable forming your opinions based on fleeting sound bites and selective information fed to you by algorithms, then this book may not be for you. However, if you're ready to go beyond the noise and delve into thoughtful, in-depth exploration of significant issues, I invite you to read on. This is a space for reflection, not for shortcuts.

ACKNOWLEDGEMENTS

A Few Mentions

Acknowledgments are typically filled with the names of those who have had the patience to tolerate an author's idiosyncrasies throughout the process of writing a book. Without a doubt, my partner and 'human', Jamie, has been as patient as anyone could be during this time. She has been my North Star, and no words can fully convey my appreciation and love for her.

For me, the process of writing a book is driven by intellectual curiosity. I've often joked (only half-jokingly) that when I earned my PhD, I graduated fully prepared for life in the 13th century. By this, I mean that the more education I pursued, the more doors were opened, and the more I realized how little I truly knew. It's a vicious cycle: the more knowledge I gain, the greater my thirst for new learning and the desire to quench that thirst.

So, I owe a debt of gratitude to everyone who has encouraged my passion for acquiring new knowledge across a variety of fields.

My grandfather once told me, "Simon, the good Lord above gave you two ears and one mouth for a reason. Act accordingly."

He was a wise man, my grandfather.

Contents

AMERICAN CHASMS

Essays on the Divided States of America

How Political Rhetoric, Misinformation, and Media Fragmentation Are Tearing Society Apart

Divisiveness has always been a feature of American society to some degree, with disagreements over politics, religion, and cultural norms shaping the country's history. However, in recent years, the intensity of this division has reached new heights, leaving many to wonder if the social fabric of the nation is being irreparably torn apart. Political rhetoric is becoming more extreme, fueling a chasm that has led to increasing vitriol, hatred, and even violence. The role of misinformation, disinformation, and propaganda has been instrumental in exacerbating this divide, while the changing landscape of media consumption is further isolating Americans into ideological echo chambers. Together, these forces are creating a toxic environment where civil discourse seems nearly impossible, and the consequences are becoming dire for American society.

The Role of Political Rhetoric in Fanning the Flames

Political rhetoric in America has become increasingly hostile over the last two decades, as politicians and public figures adopt a more combative and aggressive tone. This shift has led to a significant increase in polarization, where compromise is viewed as weakness and opponents are vilified. Instead of fostering healthy debate, political rhetoric is now aimed at generating outrage and demonizing the other side, turning every disagreement into an existential battle.

A study by Pew Research Center highlights the growing ideological chasm in American politics. In 1994, only 16% of Democrats and 17% of Republicans had a "very unfavorable" view of the opposing party. By 2022, those numbers had skyrocketed to 57% and 63%, respectively (Pew Research Center, 2022). This polarization is further fueled by the way political leaders frame issues. Terms like "war on democracy," "enemy of the people," or "traitor" are used liberally in political discourse, inflaming tensions and making it difficult for people to view opponents as fellow citizens with legitimate concerns.

Furthermore, political rhetoric has increasingly incited violence. The rise of political violence, both in terms of threats and actual acts, has become alarmingly common. For example, the FBI reported a dramatic uptick in threats against elected officials in recent years, receiving about 9,600 threats in 2021 alone (FBI, 2022). The January 6, 2021 insurrection at the U.S. Capitol is a stark reminder of how political rhetoric, particularly around the "stolen election" narrative, can lead to real-world violence. Rhetoric that frames political disagreements as a zero-sum game, where one side must be utterly destroyed for the other to prevail, has contributed to a culture of hostility that often spills over into physical aggression.

Misinformation, Disinformation, and the Destructive Power of Fake News

While political rhetoric fans the flames of division, misinformation, and disinformation serve as the accelerants. Misinformation refers to false or misleading information shared without malicious intent, while disinformation is the deliberate spread of false information to deceive or manipulate people. Both have become pervasive in the digital age, largely due to the rapid spread of information on social media platforms and the rise of fake news.

A 2020 study by MIT found that false information spreads six times faster on social media than factual information (Vosoughi, Roy, & Aral, 2018). This is because fake news often plays to people's emotions, triggering reactions of anger or fear—emotions that make people more likely to share content. Social media algorithms, designed to prioritize engagement, tend to amplify such content, even if it's inaccurate. Platforms like Facebook, Twitter, and YouTube have been criticized for allowing misinformation to proliferate, from baseless conspiracy theories to misleading claims about elections and vaccines.

One of the most prominent examples of disinformation affecting American society is the 2020 presidential election. A report by the Election Integrity Partnership found that much of the misinformation surrounding the election came from high-profile political figures and media outlets. The false narrative that the election was "stolen" or "rigged" gained immense traction, despite the lack of evidence. According to a 2021 survey by Ipsos, nearly two-thirds of Republicans still believe the 2020 election was fraudulent (Ipsos, 2021). This widespread belief has contributed to a lasting erosion of trust in democratic institutions, leading to the Capitol riot and further entrenching divisions between political parties and their supporters.

In addition to political disinformation, the COVID-19 pandemic provided fertile ground for the spread of fake news. False information about the virus, its origins, and the efficacy of vaccines spread rapidly on social media platforms, leading to a polarized debate over public health measures. A 2021 study published in The Lancet found that misinformation about COVID-19 vaccines contributed to vaccine hesitancy, which in turn led to lower vaccination rates and higher rates of preventable death (Lancet, 2021). This illustrates how disinformation not only deepens societal divisions but can also have deadly consequences.

The Changing Landscape of Media Consumption: Fragmentation and Echo Chambers

The way Americans consume news has changed drastically in the last 15 years, contributing significantly to the growing division. Gone are the days when most Americans tuned into a handful of trusted news sources, such as the evening news on ABC, NBC, or CBS, or read the same major newspapers like The New York Times or The Washington Post. Today, the media landscape is highly fragmented, with individuals able to curate their news feeds based on their ideological preferences.

This phenomenon, often referred to as the "echo chamber effect," means that people are more likely to consume information that reinforces their existing beliefs while avoiding information that challenges them. Social media platforms like Facebook and Twitter play a significant role in this, as algorithms are designed to show users content that aligns with their previous interactions. The result is that people increasingly live in separate information bubbles, where they are exposed only to viewpoints that confirm their biases. A study by the Pew Research Center found that 79% of Republicans and 78% of Democrats reported that their views on political issues were deeply influenced by the news sources they consumed, with little overlap between the two groups (Pew Research Center, 2020).

The rise of hyper-partisan news outlets, such as Fox News on the right and MSNBC on the left, has also contributed to this fragmentation. These outlets often frame news stories in a way that serves their political agendas, further deepening the ideological divide. For example, a 2019 study by the Knight Foundation found that viewers of partisan media are more likely to hold extreme views and are less willing to engage in civil discourse with those who hold opposing beliefs (Knight Foundation, 2019). The ability to choose news sources that align with one's ideology has created a situation where Americans are not only disagreeing on how to interpret facts but are often operating from entirely different sets of facts altogether.

Furthermore, the rise of alternative media outlets and influencers on platforms like YouTube, podcasts, and even Substack has led to the proliferation of unverified, opinion-driven content masquerading as legitimate news. While the diversity of voices in media is valuable, it has also allowed for the rapid spread of propaganda and misinformation. Individuals can now easily access content that reinforces conspiracies or extreme ideologies without being exposed to any form of critical analysis or rebuttal.

The Impact of Divisiveness: Eroding Trust, Increasing Violence, and the Breakdown of Civil Discourse

The divisiveness in American society has far-reaching consequences, affecting everything from political stability to social cohesion and public safety. One of the most troubling outcomes is the erosion of trust in key institutions. As misinformation and disinformation spread, fewer people trust the media, the government, or even science. The Edelman Trust Barometer, an annual global survey, found that trust in institutions in the United States reached an all-time low in 2022, with only 39% of Americans expressing trust in the government, and 46% trusting the media (Edelman Trust Barometer, 2022). This erosion of trust makes it difficult to address national crises, from public health emergencies to threats to democracy, as people are less willing to believe experts or engage in collective action.

In addition to eroding trust, divisiveness has contributed to rising political violence. The Anti-Defamation League (ADL) reported a significant rise in extremist-related murders and violent incidents in the U.S. over the past five years, with 2021 seeing a notable increase in politically motivated violence (ADL, 2022). While violent acts by fringe extremists were once relatively rare, political divisions have mainstreamed violent rhetoric, making such acts more common. Online forums and social media networks have become breeding grounds for extremist groups that use disinformation to radicalize individuals, further increasing the risk of political violence.

The breakdown of civil discourse is another devastating consequence of divisiveness. People are becoming less willing to engage in meaningful conversations with those who hold opposing views, preferring instead to retreat into their ideological bubbles. A 2019 poll by Public Religion Research Institute (PRRI) found that nearly 75% of Americans believe the country is more politically divided than at any point in their lifetime, with many citing an inability to have constructive conversations with those who hold opposing views (PRRI, 2019). This lack of dialogue makes it difficult to find common ground on key issues, leading to gridlock in Congress and at the local level, where compromise is increasingly seen as a betrayal rather than a necessity for governance.

Addressing Divisiveness Before It's Too Late

The current state of divisiveness in America is unsustainable. The rising polarization, driven by toxic political rhetoric, rampant misinformation, and a fragmented media landscape, has pushed the country to a dangerous tipping point. This level of division is not only paralyzing the ability of institutions to govern effectively but also eroding social trust and fueling violence. If left unchecked, these forces will continue to tear at the social fabric of the nation, resulting in further fragmentation, instability, and even the possibility of civil conflict.

Healing these divides will not be easy, but it is essential for the future of American democracy and society. Achieving this requires a comprehensive, multi-layered strategy that tackles the root causes of division. This will involve reducing the vitriol in political discourse, fostering a more informed and media-literate populace, reforming how information is consumed, and encouraging the restoration of trust in institutions. Each of these areas presents unique challenges, but addressing them is necessary if the country hopes to rebuild the bridges of communication and cooperation that have been systematically dismantled over the past two decades.

Reducing the Vitriol in Political Discourse

The most immediate and visible source of divisiveness in America is the increasingly hostile political rhetoric. Political leaders, pundits, and media figures play an outsized role in shaping the tone of public debate, and in recent years, many have adopted a strategy of stoking anger and fear to energize their bases. This "us vs. them" mentality has transformed political opponents into existential enemies, making cooperation and compromise seem like moral failings rather than essential components of a functioning democracy.

Reducing this vitriol requires a shift in political culture, beginning with leadership. Political figures must be held accountable for the language they use and the impact it has on public discourse. This can start with stricter consequences for violent and inflammatory rhetoric. Social media platforms, political organizations, and even voters must demand more responsible communication from those in power. Encouragingly, some political leaders have begun to acknowledge the toxicity of the current climate. A bipartisan group of senators, for example, have recently called for "civility in politics," recognizing that without respectful dialogue, democracy itself is at risk.

Media organizations also have a responsibility to temper their coverage. In an era of 24-hour news cycles and click-driven content, there is a temptation to sensationalize and polarize issues to generate viewership. But this short-term strategy is undermining the long-term health of society. Networks, print media, and online platforms should prioritize balanced, fact-based reporting and provide more opportunities for nuanced discussions. Programs that promote thoughtful debates between individuals with differing viewpoints should be highlighted rather than just punditry that reinforces echo chambers.

Encouraging Media Literacy and Critical Thinking

One of the root causes of divisiveness is the spread of misinformation and disinformation, which have flourished in an environment of media fragmentation and declining trust in traditional news sources. Americans today are inundated with information from a variety of sources—social media, blogs, alternative news outlets, podcasts—many of which lack journalistic rigor or accountability. In this chaotic media environment, it has become increasingly difficult for people to distinguish between fact and fiction, and as a result, many fall prey to misleading narratives.

Addressing this requires a national effort to improve media literacy. Media literacy refers to the ability to critically analyze and evaluate media messages, understand the biases inherent in different sources, and discern credible information from misinformation. By fostering media literacy, citizens can become better equipped to navigate the complex media landscape and make informed decisions. Studies show that individuals with higher levels of media literacy are less likely to be influenced by fake news and propaganda (Vraga & Tully, 2021).

Educational institutions should play a pivotal role in this effort, integrating media literacy into school curricula from a young age. Courses that teach students how to critically evaluate information sources, fact-check claims, and understand the mechanisms of media production are essential in creating an informed and discerning citizenry. Media literacy programs can also be implemented in workplaces, libraries, and community centers, helping adults who may not have grown up with these skills.

At the same time, tech companies and social media platforms must also take greater responsibility for the content that circulates on their networks. While platforms like Facebook, Twitter, and YouTube have taken some steps to flag misinformation and remove harmful content, much more needs to be done. One potential solution is to develop algorithms that prioritize content from credible sources and penalize the spread of disinformation. Moreover, social media companies should be transparent about how their algorithms work and make their platforms more conducive to informed, meaningful discussions rather than outrage-driven interactions.

Media Reform and Breaking Out of Echo Chambers

One of the key drivers of divisiveness is the fragmentation of the media landscape, which has allowed Americans to retreat into ideological echo chambers where their existing beliefs are constantly reinforced and rarely challenged. This trend has been exacerbated by the rise of partisan media outlets and the way social media algorithms curate content. When people are only exposed to one-sided viewpoints, it becomes much harder to understand, empathize with, or even acknowledge opposing perspectives. This siloed consumption of news has fueled a distorted perception of reality, leading to heightened mistrust and hostility between different political and social groups.

Breaking out of these echo chambers will require structural changes in how media is consumed and presented. First, the major social media platforms need to rethink their algorithms, which are currently designed to maximize engagement, often by promoting content that triggers strong emotional reactions like anger or fear. A 2018 study from the University of North Carolina found that divisive content is more likely to go viral, and this is largely due to how platforms prioritize engagement over substance (Brady et al., 2018). If these platforms prioritized content that promotes understanding and dialogue instead, the spread of misinformation and vitriol could be reduced.

Second, it is crucial to support and expand media that is dedicated to thoughtful, unbiased reporting. Public broadcasting outlets like NPR and PBS, which are generally seen as less partisan than their commercial counterparts, offer a model for how news can be presented in a way that prioritizes fact over sensation. However, public broadcasting is underfunded in the United States compared to other democracies, and increasing investment in these institutions could help provide Americans with a reliable source of balanced news. Furthermore, encouraging the growth of independent, nonpartisan media outlets that prioritize long-form investigative journalism and nuanced debate could help counterbalance the sensationalism of cable news and social media.

Third, news consumers must be encouraged to diversify their media diets. Americans should be urged to seek out multiple perspectives and engage with news sources that challenge their views rather than simply reinforce them. Apps and tools that help people discover a range of credible news sources, across the political spectrum, could play a role in this. For example, the app Ground News provides a breakdown of how different media outlets, from left to right, cover the same story, allowing users to see how their news consumption might be biased. Such tools can empower individuals to break free from the echo chambers that are deepening division.

Restoring Trust in Institutions

Perhaps the most alarming consequence of America's growing divisiveness is the erosion of trust in institutions. Government, media, science, law enforcement, and even the judiciary are now viewed with suspicion by large segments of the population. This distrust undermines social cohesion, hinders effective governance, and leaves the country vulnerable to disinformation, conspiracy theories, and authoritarian impulses. Rebuilding trust in these institutions is essential if America is to overcome its current divisions.

One critical way to restore trust is through transparency and accountability. Government agencies, media organizations, and other institutions must be more transparent about their processes and decision-making. This is especially important in an era where "fake news" and conspiracy theories have taken hold. For example, government transparency in how elections are conducted, how votes are counted, and how public health policies are developed can help counteract the dangerous spread of misinformation. When people feel that they have access to accurate, credible information, they are less likely to fall prey to disinformation campaigns.

Public institutions must also demonstrate a commitment to accountability. This means acknowledging and addressing their failures. Whether it's the police, the media, or the federal government, institutions that are willing to hold themselves accountable, admit mistakes, and enact reforms are more likely to regain the public's trust. For example, the U.S. military's acknowledgment of past errors in civilian airstrikes in conflict zones, followed by clear actions to prevent future occurrences, is one way that institutions can show they are acting in good faith.

Lastly, efforts to combat corruption and conflicts of interest within institutions can help rebuild public confidence. According to a 2021 report from Transparency International, public perceptions of corruption in the United States have worsened significantly in recent years (Transparency International, 2021). Stronger measures to prevent corruption in government, business, and other sectors will go a long way in restoring faith in the country's institutions.

Fostering Civil Discourse and Encouraging Dialogue

To heal the divisions that plague the nation, Americans must rediscover the lost art of civil discourse—constructive, respectful dialogue where people with differing views listen to and learn from each other. This kind of discourse is the foundation of a healthy democracy, and without it, finding common ground on major issues becomes nearly impossible. Currently, the prevailing mode of communication, especially online, is combative rather than collaborative. Changing this will require a cultural shift, one that places a greater value on empathy, active listening, and compromise.

Educational institutions can play a key role in fostering these values. Programs in schools and universities that teach students how to engage in productive debates and conversations—rather than shouting matches—can cultivate a generation of citizens better equipped to handle political disagreements without descending into hatred or violence. This can be done through courses in rhetoric, communication, and ethics, where students are encouraged to explore different viewpoints and learn how to argue in good faith.

In the public sphere, platforms that encourage dialogue rather than division must be supported. This could include everything from community forums and town halls to online platforms designed to promote thoughtful discussions. Organizations like Braver Angels, which works to depolarize American society by facilitating dialogue between people from opposing political backgrounds, are examples of how civil discourse can be promoted on a national level.

A Path Forward: Unity Through Diversity of Thought

America's strength has always been its diversity—of thought, culture, and people. Yet, in recent years, this diversity has become a source of division rather than unity. To overcome the challenges of divisiveness, the country must learn to embrace the fact that disagreement is a normal and healthy aspect of a democracy. What matters is how those disagreements are handled. By fostering civil discourse, improving media literacy, reforming political and media systems, and holding institutions accountable, America can begin to bridge the widening chasm that threatens its future.

This path forward will require sustained effort from individuals, communities, institutions, and leaders alike. But history has shown that Americans are resilient and capable of transformation in the face of adversity. If the country can address its current divisions with honesty and humility, while recognizing the shared values and goals that unite its people, there is hope for a more cohesive, just, and prosperous future.

If left unaddressed, however, the divisions of today will become the crises of tomorrow. The time to act is now before it's too late.

Fascism & Wokeism in America

SECTION NO. 1

Fascism in America

Jason Stanley, in his book, "How Fascism Works: The Politics of Us and Them" outlines 10 key principles that fascist movements and leaders often use to manipulate societies, sow division, and consolidate power. Each of these principles is aimed at dividing society into "us" versus "them" and undermining democratic institutions and norms. Below is a detailed explanation of each principle and a discussion of how they might be apparent in today's society in the USA.

No. 1 — The Mythic Past

- **Description.** Fascist movements often create an idealized, mythic version of the past, portraying it as a golden age when society was "pure," unified, and strong. They claim that the nation has since been corrupted by outside influences or internal enemies, and that a return to this glorious past is necessary.

- **How It Works.** By romanticizing a fictional history, fascists play on nostalgia and national pride. This mythic past is often ethnically homogeneous and patriarchal, and fascists promise to restore that order by removing or suppressing groups they deem responsible for the decline.

- **Example.** Nazi propaganda glorified an idealized vision of Aryan society and blamed Jews, communists, and others for Germany's downfall after World War I.

- **Modern Example.** The slogan "Make America Great Again" (MAGA), popularized by Donald Trump, appeals to a vague sense of returning to a past when America was supposedly stronger, wealthier, and more unified. This past is often portrayed as a time when traditional values dominated, and immigrants and minorities had less influence.

- **Impact.** This rhetoric often overlooks or ignores the historical realities of inequality, racism, and oppression that existed in that "golden" past. It selectively romanticizes history while sidestepping progress that has been made in civil rights and social justice.

No. 2 — Propaganda

- **Description.** Fascist regimes rely on constant disinformation, lies, and distorted facts to control the narrative. The goal is not just to convince people of a false truth, but to confuse the public and undermine their trust in objective facts.

- **How It Works.** Propaganda creates an alternate reality in which the leader's version of events is the only acceptable truth. Even blatant lies, when repeated often enough, begin to shape public perception. In fascist regimes, state-controlled media or complicit private media help spread this disinformation.

- **Example.** Joseph Goebbels, the Nazi Minister of Propaganda, famously controlled the German media, spreading falsehoods about Jewish conspiracies and glorifying Hitler's policies.

- **Modern Example.** The rise of disinformation and fake news in the U.S., particularly through social media platforms, has created deep confusion about what is true and what is false. Figures on both the right and left have weaponized media to push their agendas, but a particularly notable example is the dissemination of conspiracy theories like QAnon, which falsely claim that a secret cabal controls the government.

- **Impact.** The spread of propaganda through various media outlets has sown distrust in mainstream media and democratic institutions. This confusion destabilizes the political landscape and allows certain leaders to manipulate public perception.

No. 3 — Anti-Intellectualism

- **Description.** Fascist leaders frequently attack intellectuals, experts, scientists, and academics, portraying them as out-of-touch elites or agents of foreign ideologies. They encourage people to trust their own instincts and emotions rather than relying on expertise or critical thinking.

- **How It Works.** By discrediting intellectuals and experts, fascists can create a reality where only the leader's interpretation of events and policies matter. This also allows fascist regimes to dismiss inconvenient facts (like scientific research or historical evidence) that contradict their narrative.

- **Example.** During the rise of Italian fascism, Mussolini openly mocked intellectuals and positioned himself as a man of action, in contrast to the "overly complex" arguments of scholars.

- **Modern Example.** There has been a growing distrust of experts and intellectuals, particularly regarding science and higher education. This has been seen in the denial of climate change, the anti-vaccine movement, and skepticism about public health measures during the COVID-19 pandemic.

- **Impact.** By undermining trust in experts, scientists, and educators, segments of the population have been swayed by emotional or politically motivated rhetoric rather than facts, leading to public health crises and an erosion of evidence-based policy-making.

No. 4 — Unreality

- **Description.** Fascist leaders create an environment where truth and reality are constantly under attack, making it difficult for the public to distinguish between fact and fiction. This erosion of truth is intentional and fosters confusion, making the population more susceptible to authoritarian control.

- **How It Works.** By bombarding people with conflicting information and conspiracy theories, fascists can cause a state of "unreality" where citizens become disengaged or cynical, believing that no information can be trusted. This paves the way for fascist leaders to step in as the sole arbiters of truth.

- **Example.** Modern-day disinformation campaigns, such as those in Russia, often flood social media with false narratives, undermining public trust in traditional news outlets and democratic institutions.

- **Modern Example.** The "Big Lie"—the false claim that the 2020 U.S. presidential election was stolen—is a prime example of creating an alternate reality. Despite numerous court rulings, recounts, and investigations affirming the election results, many political figures and media outlets continue to promote this false narrative.

- **Impact.** This alternate reality has eroded trust in the electoral process and contributed to events like the January 6th Capitol insurrection, where people acted on the belief that the election results were illegitimate. The rejection of objective reality threatens the foundations of democracy.

No. 5 — Hierarchy

- **Description.** Fascist ideologies promote strict social hierarchies where certain groups are considered inherently superior to others based on race, ethnicity, religion, or nationality. This belief system legitimizes discrimination and dehumanization of those lower on the hierarchy.

- **How It Works.** By asserting the natural superiority of one group, fascists justify unequal treatment, repression, and even violence against those they deem inferior. Fascist movements thrive on dividing society into clear "us" versus "them" categories.

- **Example.** The caste-like racial hierarchy in Nazi Germany, where Aryans were at the top and Jews, Romani people, and other minorities were considered inferior and targeted for extermination.

- **Modern Example.** While explicit racial hierarchies are no longer legal, implicit forms of hierarchy still persist in rhetoric that emphasizes white nationalism or white supremacy. Some movements and political figures advocate for policies that disproportionately affect minorities, such as voting restrictions targeted at communities of color.

- **Impact.** By promoting policies or cultural norms that benefit one group over others, these movements reinforce social and economic hierarchies, undermining equality and justice. Rhetoric that emphasizes the superiority of certain racial or cultural groups continues to divide the nation along racial lines.

No. 6 — Victimhood

- **Description.** Fascist leaders often claim that the dominant or "superior" group is under threat from outsiders, minorities, or other internal enemies. They portray this group as victims who are being persecuted or displaced by others, even when this narrative is completely false.

- **How It Works.** By stoking fear and paranoia, fascists create a sense of urgency for their followers. The "victimized" group is convinced that they must defend themselves from an existential threat, leading them to support extreme measures, such as violence or suppression of other groups.

- **Example.** In Nazi Germany, Adolf Hitler framed Germans as victims of Jewish conspiracies, communists, and other groups, despite there being no evidence of such threats.

- **Modern Example.** Certain political movements in the U.S. portray white Americans or Christian conservatives as being under siege by immigrants, minorities, or liberal elites. This sense of victimhood is often expressed in terms of a "war on Christmas," claims of reverse racism, or fears of being "replaced" demographically.

- **Impact.** This narrative fuels resentment and justifies extreme measures like immigration bans, voter suppression, and attacks on minority rights. It positions the dominant group as victims, despite holding the most social and economic power, and deepens societal divisions.

No. 7 — Law and Order

- **Description.** Fascist movements often use the rhetoric of "law and order" to justify the suppression of civil liberties and target marginalized communities. The promise of restoring law and order is usually aimed at cracking down on those perceived as threats to the traditional social order.

- **How It Works.** Fascist leaders frame their authoritarian measures as necessary to restore stability, often exaggerating or fabricating threats from minorities, immigrants, or political opponents. In doing so, they erode democratic norms and justify repressive policies.

- **Example.** Mussolini's fascist regime in Italy used "law and order" as a pretext for violent crackdowns on political opponents, unions, and anyone who opposed his dictatorship.

- **Modern Example.** The "law and order" rhetoric is frequently used to justify crackdowns on protests, especially those connected to movements like Black Lives Matter. In 2020, protests against police brutality were often framed as chaotic and dangerous, leading to calls for heavy policing and even military intervention.

- **Impact.** While "law and order" rhetoric can seem like a call for stability, it often results in over-policing of marginalized communities and the suppression of dissent. It can be used to justify draconian measures that violate civil liberties, particularly for minorities.

No. 8 — Sexism

- **Description.** Fascist regimes often glorify traditional gender roles, portraying women primarily as mothers and caretakers while promoting male dominance in public life and leadership roles. They emphasize a return to "natural" or "traditional" family values.

- **How It Works.** Fascists use sexism to control women's rights, restrict their autonomy, and reinforce patriarchal structures. By promoting a hyper-masculine culture, they further entrench the power dynamics that keep marginalized groups in submissive roles.

- **Example.** Nazi Germany promoted a very strict view of women's roles, emphasizing that women should focus on "Kinder, Küche, Kirche" (Children, Kitchen, Church), while men were encouraged to be soldiers and leaders.

- **Modern Example.** The U.S. has seen ongoing debates over women's reproductive rights, with movements advocating for the reversal of Roe v. Wade and the restriction of access to abortion. The rise of the "traditional family values" movement also emphasizes traditional gender roles, with women positioned primarily as mothers and caretakers.

- **Impact.** By promoting a return to traditional gender roles, these movements attempt to limit women's autonomy and restrict their roles in society. Efforts to control reproductive rights are a direct means of enforcing patriarchal control over women's bodies.

No. 9 — Anti-Urbanism

- **Description.** Fascists often portray urban centers as decadent, corrupt, and full of foreigners or other "undesirable" populations. In contrast, they romanticize rural life and traditional agricultural values as pure and virtuous.

- **How It Works.** By vilifying cities as hubs of diversity and progressive thought, fascists create a divide between "authentic" rural citizens and "degenerate" urbanites. This division helps them gain support from rural and conservative areas while demonizing the urban elite.

- **Example.** Fascist propaganda often paints urban intellectuals, artists, and cosmopolitan citizens as corrupt or out of touch with the "true" people, as seen in both Nazi Germany and Mussolini's Italy.

- **Modern Example.** There is often a rural versus urban divide in U.S. politics, where rural communities are portrayed as embodying "true American values," while cities are seen as hubs of liberalism, diversity, and corruption. This anti-urban sentiment often aligns with attacks on "coastal elites" and accusations that urban areas are disconnected from the "real" America.

- **Impact.** This rural-urban divide deepens polarization, fostering resentment toward diverse, progressive cities and bolstering populist rhetoric that pits rural "real Americans" against urban elites. It also exacerbates political and economic divisions.

No. 10 — Sodomy

- **Description.** Fascist regimes frequently target LGBTQ+ communities as immoral and subversive. They often frame the fight against "sexual deviancy" as part of their broader goal to restore societal purity and traditional family values.

- **How It Works.** By scapegoating LGBTQ+ individuals, fascists foster fear and hatred, distracting from broader societal issues. They may also use this as an excuse to implement draconian policies that curtail civil rights for everyone.

- **Example.** The Nazi regime specifically targeted homosexual men, persecuting and imprisoning them under the guise of maintaining moral and racial purity.

- **Modern Example.** Although LGBTQ+ rights have made significant strides in the U.S., there are still political and cultural forces that oppose these gains. Anti-LGBTQ+ rhetoric remains prevalent in certain circles, often framed as a defense of "traditional" family values. Politicians and religious groups continue to push back against gay marriage, transgender rights, and LGBTQ+ inclusion in schools.

- **Impact.** By positioning LGBTQ+ individuals as threats to societal morality, these groups try to limit their rights and reinforce traditional norms. The continued political battles over issues like transgender rights in sports and bathrooms reflect ongoing efforts to restrict LGBTQ+ freedoms.

So, all this begs the question, "Is America becoming a fascist society?"

The question is highly complex and depends on how one defines fascism and how closely one believes the U.S. is aligning with its characteristics. While the U.S. remains a functioning democracy with strong institutions, there are worrying trends that some experts, including philosophers like Jason Stanley, point out could be early warning signs of authoritarianism or fascist-like tendencies.

Key Considerations

No. 1 — Fascism as a Process, Not an Event

- Fascism is often not a single event but a process that happens gradually. Stanley and other scholars emphasize that fascist tendencies can emerge within democratic systems. This can happen through the erosion of democratic norms, manipulation of public opinion, and the use of fear, division, and nationalism to consolidate power.

No. 2 — Early Warning Signs in America

While the U.S. hasn't fully transitioned into a fascist state, some warning signs align with fascist techniques:

- **Propaganda and Misinformation.** The rise of fake news, disinformation, and the deliberate use of conspiracy theories (e.g., QAnon, the "Big Lie" about the 2020 election) mirrors fascist propaganda techniques. This leads to confusion about truth and reality, a hallmark of fascist systems.

- **Authoritarian Leadership Styles.** Some political figures, including former President Donald Trump, have been accused of using authoritarian rhetoric and tactics, such as attacking the press, questioning the legitimacy of elections, and promoting "law and order" to justify repressive policies.

- **Erosion of Trust in Institutions.** Distrust in institutions—the media, the judiciary, and the electoral system—has grown significantly. When leaders and their supporters question the legitimacy of institutions without evidence, it weakens democratic foundations.

- **Hyper-Nationalism.** Some segments of American politics have leaned into hyper-nationalistic rhetoric that glorifies a past (often one that erases historical injustices) and positions certain groups (often immigrants, minorities, or the LGBTQ+ community) as threats to the nation's purity and stability.

- **"Us vs. Them" Rhetoric.** Division has become a central theme in U.S. politics, with some leaders stoking identity-based conflicts (racial, religious, etc.) to energize their bases. This "us vs. them" rhetoric is a common feature of fascist movements, which seek to unite a group against an external enemy, whether real or imagined.

No. 3 — Differences Between the U.S. and Fascist Regimes

Despite these troubling trends, there are key differences between the U.S. and historical fascist regimes like Nazi Germany, Mussolini's Italy, or Franco's Spain:

- **Free and Fair Elections.** Despite concerns about disinformation and voter suppression, the U.S. continues to hold free elections, and in many cases, electoral integrity has been upheld (e.g., the peaceful transfer of power - arguably - in 2021 after the 2020 election).

- **Strong Institutions.** The separation of powers, independent judiciary, and free press still function as checks on authoritarian behavior. For example, the U.S. court system, even when challenged, has maintained its independence by dismissing baseless claims about election fraud.

- **Civil Liberties.** While civil liberties are under pressure in some areas (e.g., voter suppression laws or limitations on protest rights), Americans still enjoy freedom of speech, freedom of assembly, and a robust legal system designed to protect civil rights.

No. 4 — Polarization and Democratic Backsliding

The biggest current threat may be democratic backsliding rather than full-blown fascism. Democratic backsliding refers to the gradual erosion of democratic norms and practices, such as:

- **Partisan Gerrymandering.** Drawing electoral districts to entrench political power, making elections less competitive.

- **Voter Suppression.** Policies that disproportionately affect marginalized groups and limit their ability to vote (e.g., ID laws, purging voter rolls, reduced polling locations).

- **Polarization.** Extreme political divisions, where compromise becomes impossible, leading to governmental dysfunction and making the system vulnerable to authoritarian solutions.

No. 5 — Cultural and Political Divisions

Political and cultural divisions have deepened to the point where many Americans view their political opponents as enemies rather than as fellow citizens with different views. This level of polarization is dangerous because it can make authoritarian solutions seem more acceptable, especially if people feel the existing democratic system is failing to address their needs.

While the U.S. is not currently a fascist state, certain troubling authoritarian tendencies and political dynamics resemble elements of fascism, particularly in terms of propaganda, polarization, and democratic erosion. Whether the U.S. moves closer to fascism or pulls back depends on how political leaders, institutions, and the public respond to these trends.

In short, the U.S. is experiencing stress on its democratic foundations, and the rise of authoritarian rhetoric combined with deep polarization has created an environment where fascist-like tactics could gain more traction. However, strong institutions and civil society continue to serve as bulwarks against a complete descent into authoritarianism. The future direction will depend on whether Americans can resist these pressures and reinforce democratic values, or if they allow these trends to continue unchecked.

SECTION NO. 2

The Dangers of Extreme Wokeism in American Society Today

The term "wokeism" originated as a positive call for awareness and action around social injustices, particularly concerning race, gender, and identity. Over time, however, "extreme wokeism" has been critiqued for overreaching, leading to social, cultural, and political consequences that some argue are harmful to democratic discourse, free speech, and societal cohesion. While many of the core principles behind wokeism are rooted in promoting equality, extreme forms of wokeism can have unintended negative impacts on American society.

10 Key Dangers of Extreme Wokeism Today

No. 1 — Erosion of Free Speech and Open Debate

- **Description.** Extreme wokeism often involves rigid enforcement of politically correct language and viewpoints, which can discourage open dialogue and suppress dissenting opinions. Critics of extreme wokeism argue that "cancel culture"—the act of ostracizing individuals for expressing unpopular or politically incorrect opinions—creates a culture of fear where people are hesitant to speak freely.

- **Impact.** When free speech is constrained by fear of being socially or professionally canceled, democratic discourse suffers. Open debate and the exchange of diverse ideas are essential for progress, but extreme wokeism can create an environment where only certain viewpoints are deemed acceptable, and any deviation is met with harsh consequences.

No. 2 — Polarization and Division

- **Description.** Extreme wokeism often emphasizes identity politics—the prioritization of group identity (race, gender, sexuality, etc.) over individual characteristics. While identity politics aims to address legitimate grievances, taken to the extreme, it can foster tribalism and exacerbate divisions in society.

- **Impact.** Instead of promoting unity, extreme wokeism can deepen societal divides by encouraging people to view themselves primarily through the lens of oppression and victimhood. This "us vs. them" mentality can fracture communities, making it difficult to find common ground and foster social cohesion.

No. 3 — Cancel Culture and Public Shaming

- **Description.** The most visible manifestation of extreme wokeism is "cancel culture," in which individuals, organizations, or public figures are deplatformed, boycotted, or shamed for past statements, behaviors, or actions that are considered offensive or politically incorrect. Cancel culture can happen quickly on social media platforms, often without room for context, apology, or redemption.

- **Impact.** Cancel culture fosters an unforgiving environment where mistakes, even those made years ago, can lead to severe social and professional consequences. This creates a chilling effect on public discourse, as people fear being canceled for expressing nuanced or unpopular opinions. It also denies individuals the opportunity to learn from their mistakes and grow.

No. 4 — Reductionism and Over-Simplification

- **Description.** Extreme wokeism often reduces complex social issues to overly simplistic narratives based on oppressor vs. oppressed dynamics. While systemic injustice is a real and serious issue, reducing it to black-and-white terms without acknowledging nuances can lead to distorted solutions and policies.

- **Impact.** This reductionist approach can oversimplify complicated societal challenges, such as crime, education, or poverty, making meaningful, evidence-based reforms more difficult to implement. Over-simplification also alienates those who believe that solutions to inequality require nuanced and multifaceted approaches.

No. 5 — Suppression of Academic Freedom

- **Description.** In educational settings, extreme wokeism can lead to censorship of certain viewpoints or subjects, particularly in areas like literature, history, and sociology. Trigger warnings, safe spaces, and calls to decolonize curricula can, when taken to the extreme, limit the exposure of students to a broad range of ideas and intellectual challenges.

- **Impact.** By shielding students from controversial or challenging ideas, extreme wokeism undermines the educational mission of universities, which is to promote critical thinking and expose students to diverse perspectives. Intellectual rigor suffers when certain perspectives are deemed "too harmful" to be discussed or debated in academic settings.

No. 6 — Perpetuation of Victimhood

- **Description.** Extreme wokeism often encourages individuals to view themselves primarily as victims of systemic oppression, emphasizing grievances over personal agency. While addressing systemic injustices is crucial, perpetuating a victimhood mindset can be counterproductive, as it can diminish personal empowerment and the belief in one's ability to effect change.

- **Impact.** This focus on victimhood may discourage personal responsibility and self-empowerment, fostering learned helplessness and a reliance on external forces (e.g., the government or societal institutions) to solve problems. This can, in turn, stifle innovation, resilience, and personal growth.

No. 7 — Moral Absolutism and Intolerance

- **Description.** Extreme wokeism often embraces a form of moral absolutism, where issues are seen in black-and-white terms, with little room for compromise or nuance. Those who disagree with extreme woke ideologies are often labeled as complicit in oppression, and there is little tolerance for alternate viewpoints.

- **Impact.** Moral absolutism creates an intolerant society where people are judged harshly for expressing different opinions or for not aligning perfectly with progressive ideals. This rigidity can make it difficult to foster collaboration and dialogue, which are essential for meaningful social progress.

No. 8 — Identity Reductionism

- **Description.** Extreme wokeism tends to reduce people to their identities— such as race, gender, or sexual orientation—rather than seeing individuals as complex beings with unique experiences, opinions, and backgrounds. While recognizing identity is important, an overemphasis on identity categories can obscure individual differences.

- **Impact.** This focus on identity can lead to stereotyping and the assumption that all members of a particular group think, act, or experience the world in the same way. It can also result in essentialism, where the diversity of thought within communities is ignored or suppressed in favor of monolithic narratives.

No. 9 — Undermining Meritocracy

- **Description.** Extreme wokeism often promotes policies such as affirmative action and equity initiatives to address historical inequalities. However, when taken to the extreme, these efforts can sometimes prioritize identity-based quotas over merit or qualifications.

- **Impact.** This undermines the principle of meritocracy, where people are judged based on their abilities, achievements, and character. If merit is devalued in favor of meeting diversity metrics, it can lead to resentment, inefficiency, and, in some cases, a reduction in the quality of work or education.

No. 10 — Weaponization of Language

- **Description.** Extreme wokeism often involves the strict policing of language, demanding the use of specific terms and phrases that align with progressive ideals. The weaponization of language can manifest in the form of microaggression policies, pronoun enforcement, or bans on certain terms deemed offensive.

- **Impact.** While language matters, over-policing it can lead to social rigidity and fear of speaking freely. Constantly evolving rules on acceptable language can create confusion and alienation, making social interaction more fraught with tension. People may become more focused on avoiding offense than on fostering genuine dialogue and understanding.

While wokeism in its original form aims to raise awareness about important social issues and injustices, the dangers of extreme wokeism are clear. It can suppress free speech, deepen societal divisions, and foster a climate of fear and intolerance. At its worst, extreme wokeism promotes cancel culture, moral absolutism, and reductionist thinking, all of which are detrimental to a healthy, democratic society. While addressing issues of inequality and injustice is vital, it is important to ensure that these efforts do not come at the expense of open dialogue, critical thinking, and social unity.

Extreme wokeism, if unchecked, risks eroding the very freedoms it seeks to protect, making it essential to approach social justice with a balance of compassion and nuance, while allowing for a diversity of opinions and robust debate.

A Nuanced Look at "Wokeism" in American Society

Rather than stating that America is unequivocally becoming a "society of wokeism," it's important to examine the various ways that woke culture and progressive ideologies have influenced different sectors of American society:

No. 1 — Cultural and Social Change

- There has been a noticeable cultural shift in America, especially in media, education, and corporate environments, where there is a growing emphasis on diversity, equity, and inclusion (DEI). This shift has led to policies promoting the representation of marginalized groups, addressing historical injustices, and fostering awareness about systemic inequalities.

- Terms like "microaggressions," "privilege," and "intersectionality" have entered mainstream discussions, especially in academia and progressive spaces. Many companies now invest in implicit bias training and public institutions have adopted gender-neutral language to reflect more inclusive values.

- **Impact.** These changes have heightened awareness of issues affecting historically marginalized groups, such as racial minorities, LGBTQ+ communities, and women. However, critics argue that the intensity of these efforts can sometimes lead to over-correction or censorship, especially when it comes to freedom of speech and open debate.

No. 2 — Cancel Culture and Free Speech

- "Cancel culture" has become a significant aspect of what critics describe as extreme wokeism. It refers to the practice of publicly shaming or ostracizing individuals or organizations that have expressed controversial or politically incorrect views. High-profile figures—such as celebrities, academics, or politicians—can face professional or social backlash over past statements or actions that are deemed offensive.

- In some cases, books, movies, and other forms of media are being revisited or removed from circulation if they are considered insensitive by modern standards.

- **Impact.** Advocates argue that cancel culture is a way for marginalized groups to hold powerful figures accountable, while critics contend that it can lead to over-policing of opinions, stifling free speech, and a lack of nuance in public discourse. The rise of cancel culture has polarized the country, with many fearing that fear of being canceled has created a chilling effect, discouraging people from speaking openly on controversial issues.

No. 3 — Corporate and Institutional Responses

- Many corporations and institutions have adopted woke-friendly policies in response to social movements like Black Lives Matter or LGBTQ+ advocacy. From gender-neutral bathrooms to diversity quotas in hiring, businesses are increasingly adopting progressive values to stay aligned with public sentiment.

- Universities, too, have become places where woke ideals have taken hold, with a focus on inclusive language, safe spaces, and policies aimed at addressing social injustices within their communities.

- **Impact.** While these changes are seen by supporters as necessary steps to address long-standing inequalities, critics argue that these policies can sometimes feel performative or coercive, designed more to protect corporate or institutional reputation than to address deeper societal problems. Furthermore, there is concern that such measures might prioritize identity over merit or suppress dissenting viewpoints.

No. 4 —Political Influence

- Progressive politicians have championed many of the causes associated with wokeism, from criminal justice reform to climate action and gender equity. Some elements of the Democratic Party have embraced aspects of woke culture, while conservative politicians frequently criticize wokeism, framing it as an attack on traditional American values.

- Issues like critical race theory in schools, transgender rights, and debates over free speech vs. hate speech have become flash-points in the American political landscape, with politicians and pundits on both sides using wokeism as a rallying point for their bases.

- **Impact.** This has deepened the political polarization in the U.S., as debates over race, gender, and identity become central to national politics. While some see wokeism as a necessary push toward a more just society, others view it as divisive and authoritarian, leading to a backlash that contributes to the polarization of American politics.

No. 5 — Backlash and "Anti-Woke" Movements

- The rise of woke culture has sparked a significant backlash, particularly from conservative commentators, media, and politicians. Critics argue that extreme wokeism promotes censorship, victimhood culture, and moral absolutism, where individuals or groups are judged harshly for not aligning with progressive ideals.

- This backlash has led to the creation of "anti-woke" movements, where individuals push back against what they see as the overreach of woke ideology, especially in areas such as free speech, academic freedom, and personal liberties.

- **Impact.** These anti-woke movements have gained momentum, particularly in conservative states where laws have been introduced to restrict certain educational curricula or DEI initiatives that are seen as overly progressive. The push-back has further contributed to the cultural divide in the U.S.

Certainly, the U.S. is not uniformly a society of wokeism, but woke values and principles have certainly gained significant traction in key sectors like academia, corporate America, media, and politics. The influence of woke culture is particularly strong in urban, liberal areas and among younger, more progressive generations who prioritize issues of social justice, diversity, and inclusivity.

At the same time, there is significant resistance to extreme forms of wokeism from conservative and moderate voices, who view it as a threat to free speech, traditional values, and merit-based systems. This tension between progressive ideals and traditional values has contributed to the polarization of American society, where debates over identity, justice, and free expression have become deeply contentious.

SECTION NO. 3

Finding a Middle Ground

In today's polarized society, extreme ideologies on both ends of the political spectrum—fascism on the right and extreme wokeism on the left—are driving a wedge between citizens. What once was a landscape for diverse, constructive debate has now become an arena of hostility, where opposing sides view each other as existential threats. This growing division erodes the foundation of civil discourse, leaving little room for compromise, understanding, or mutual respect. To safeguard democracy, we must find a middle ground. Both extremes, though seemingly different, share a dangerous similarity: they suppress dissent, stifle free speech, and threaten the pluralism necessary for a healthy society. To move forward as a nation, we need to reject authoritarianism and ideological gate-keeping, while championing freedom of thought, open debate, and respect for differing viewpoints. Only by restoring a culture of balance and dialogue can we heal the divisions that are tearing at the fabric of our democracy.

The Dangers of Polarization

These two extremes—fascism on the right and extreme wokeism on the left—represent more than just political ideologies. They are reflective of a polarization that has taken root in American society, one that pushes people into opposing camps, where each side views the other not as fellow citizens but as existential threats to the nation. This polarization creates a toxic environment where middle ground, compromise, and civil discourse are seen as weaknesses rather than strengths.

Both fascism and extreme wokeism are, in their own ways, anti-democratic. Fascism seeks to concentrate power in the hands of a few, eliminating dissent through repression. Extreme wokeism, while emerging from a desire for social justice, risks eliminating dissent through cultural coercion. In both cases, the result is the same—freedom of thought, open debate, and the pluralism necessary for a healthy democracy are under threat.

The Need for a Middle Path

To move forward as a nation, we cannot allow ourselves to be trapped between these two extremes. Instead, we must seek a middle path that champions the democratic values of freedom, pluralism, justice, and respect for dissenting views. This path requires us to reject the authoritarian impulses of fascism while also pushing back against the dogmatic overreach of extreme wokeism. Only by finding common ground can we begin to heal the divisions that are tearing at the fabric of our society.

The Need for Balance — Finding Common Ground

At the heart of America's success as a democratic nation is its ability to accommodate a wide range of opinions and ideologies. This pluralism is one of our greatest strengths—our capacity to bring together people of different backgrounds, beliefs, and perspectives and work toward a common future. However, as extreme ideologies from both ends of the political spectrum—fascism on the right and extreme wokeism on the left—have gained traction, the space for nuanced discussion and common ground has diminished. The result is a society where polarization and conflict are the new normal. But this doesn't have to be our future. To heal our divisions, we must actively work to rebuild the middle ground, a space where balance, tolerance, and respect for differing opinions allow us to engage in productive, democratic dialogue.

Core American Values: The Common Thread

Regardless of political orientation, most Americans share certain core values— freedom, justice, equality, and opportunity. These values are embedded in the Constitution, the Declaration of Independence, and the very identity of what it means to be American. Yet, both fascism and extreme wokeism threaten to undermine these ideals, albeit in different ways.

- Fascism endangers the principles of freedom and pluralism by seeking to centralize power in the hands of an authoritarian regime that suppresses dissent and diversity of thought. This stifles the marketplace of ideas and diminishes the individual freedoms that are foundational to democracy.

- Extreme wokeism, on the other hand, undermines free expression by enforcing a rigid cultural orthodoxy, where any deviation from accepted norms is met with social punishment, ostracization, or "cancellation." In this context, ideological purity tests replace genuine dialogue, and cultural censorship prevails, effectively silencing voices that could otherwise contribute to constructive discussions.

Both extremes erode trust in democratic processes and institutions, whether through authoritarian suppression or ideological gate-keeping. But common ground exists, and it lies in our shared commitment to the principles that underpin our democracy: freedom of speech, the right to dissent, equality of opportunity, and the belief that everyone should have a fair shot at the American Dream.

Recognizing the Dangers of Extremes

One of the first steps toward moving forward is recognizing the dangers posed by both ends of the political spectrum. While they may appear to be polar opposites, the extreme ideologies of fascism and wokeism share certain characteristics that make them deeply troubling.

- **Suppression of Free Speech.** Fascism suppresses speech through state power, while extreme wokeism suppresses it through cultural coercion. In both cases, the result is the same: individuals who deviate from the dominant narrative are silenced, shamed, or excluded. Whether it's through government censorship or cancel culture, these dynamics stifle open debate, limit intellectual diversity, and erode the free exchange of ideas that is crucial to a healthy democracy.

- **Us vs. Them Mentality.** Both fascism and extreme wokeism thrive on creating binary divisions—the belief that society is composed of two warring factions: those who are "righteous" or "correct" and those who are "the enemy." In fascism, this often manifests in terms of nationalism, where loyalty to the state or leader is paramount, and outsiders or dissenters are demonized. In extreme wokeism, this often manifests through a moral hierarchy that punishes those who do not conform to rigid social or political standards, labeling them as morally inferior or irredeemable.

- **Erosion of Democratic Norms.** Both extremes show disdain for democratic norms. Fascist movements often seek to dismantle checks and balances, attack the press, and delegitimize free elections, undermining the foundations of democracy. On the other hand, extreme wokeism, while not necessarily attacking institutions directly, can lead to a culture where ideological purity and identity politics dominate, marginalizing voices that dissent and fostering a climate of fear rather than open discussion. In both cases, the ability to govern effectively through democratic processes is diminished.

Recognizing these shared dangers is crucial to understanding why we must reject extremism from both sides and work to rebuild a middle ground based on democratic principles and a commitment to the common good.

Mutual Responsibility: Upholding Democratic Norms

If America is to move beyond these extremes, we must each take responsibility for upholding democratic norms. This starts with recognizing that no single ideology has a monopoly on the truth. It's not about silencing those we disagree with or winning at all costs; it's about engaging with different viewpoints in a way that respects our shared humanity and common values.

From the right, there must be a rejection of authoritarian rhetoric and a commitment to preserving the institutions that safeguard our democracy, including a free press, an independent judiciary, and the integrity of elections.

From the left, there must be a recognition that free speech is vital for social progress and that the best way to counter harmful or regressive ideas is not through censorship or cultural exclusion, but through debate, education, and engagement.

Both sides must also be willing to engage in self-reflection. No political ideology is above critique, and all movements, no matter how well-intentioned, must be open to constructive criticism if they are to contribute positively to society. The moment any group believes itself to be the sole arbiter of truth is the moment it begins to undermine the democratic process.

The Role of Civil Discourse

A key element in finding common ground is the restoration of civil discourse. In recent years, political debates have become increasingly toxic, with individuals on all sides resorting to personal attacks, name-calling, and moral grandstanding rather than engaging in thoughtful dialogue. If we are to move forward as a nation, we must revive the art of respectful disagreement.

Civil discourse allows us to challenge each other's ideas without questioning each other's humanity. It encourages us to listen as much as we speak and to approach disagreements with a sense of curiosity and openness rather than defensiveness. By doing so, we can begin to bridge the gaps between our different worldviews and find practical solutions to the challenges we face as a nation.

Restoring trust in one another, and in the institutions that uphold democracy, will require a concerted effort to elevate the level of public debate. This means rejecting polarizing rhetoric and instead fostering conversations that are based on mutual respect, shared values, and a commitment to the truth.

A Shared Commitment to Balance

The dangers of both fascism and extreme wokeism are real, but they do not represent the entirety of American society. Most Americans fall somewhere in the middle, committed to a vision of freedom, justice, and equality that allows for diverse viewpoints and respectful debate. By recognizing the shared threats posed by both ends of the ideological spectrum, we can begin to rebuild the middle ground that is essential for a healthy democracy.

Finding balance is not easy, and it requires us to constantly reflect on our values and actions. But it is the only way forward if we are to protect the pluralism, freedom, and opportunity that define the American experiment. The next step in moving forward is to examine how we can protect free speech, foster open discourse, and resist the extremes that threaten the fabric of our democracy.

Reclaiming Free Speech and Open Discourse

One of the defining elements of a healthy democracy is the ability for citizens to freely express their ideas, debate issues, and challenge prevailing opinions without fear of censorship or reprisal. Free speech is not just a constitutional right—it is the lifeblood of any society that values individual liberty and intellectual diversity. Yet, today, both fascist and extreme wokeist forces are eroding this principle from opposite ends of the ideological spectrum. Moving forward as a nation requires us to reclaim free speech and promote a culture of open discourse that respects and values different perspectives.

No. 1 — The Importance of Free Speech for Democracy

At its core, free speech allows for the exchange of ideas, the critique of power, and the innovation necessary for a society to thrive. The First Amendment protects citizens from government censorship, but the principle of free speech goes beyond mere legality—it represents a commitment to dialogue, debate, and the marketplace of ideas.

In a democratic society, citizens must be able to express dissent and challenge authority without fear of retaliation. Free speech is what allows for the questioning of political leaders, the examination of social structures, and the advocacy for change. Without it, we lose the ability to address systemic issues and ensure that all voices are heard, especially those of marginalized groups. From the Civil Rights Movement to the fight for LGBTQ+ rights, progress has often depended on the courage of individuals who dared to speak out against injustice.

But for free speech to truly flourish, it requires more than just the absence of government censorship. It requires a culture that values openness, tolerance, and the exchange of ideas—a culture where even controversial or unpopular views can be expressed and debated. When free speech is stifled—whether by authoritarian regimes or by cultural gate-keeping—democracy itself is weakened.

No. 2 — Fascism's Attack on Free Speech

In fascist movements, free speech is one of the first casualties. Authoritarian regimes thrive on control—control of information, control of narrative, and control of the public's ability to challenge the status quo. Historically, fascist governments have employed censorship, propaganda, and intimidation to silence dissenting voices. The Nazi regime in Germany, Fascist Italy, and other totalitarian systems all relied heavily on the suppression of free speech to maintain power and control over the population.

Today, we see echoes of these tactics in some American political movements that seek to undermine trust in journalism, discredit academic institutions, and delegitimize elections. The labeling of journalists as "enemies of the people," the spreading of disinformation to destabilize democratic processes, and the promotion of conspiracy theories that create fear and division are all part of this broader attack on free speech. Such efforts aim to concentrate power in the hands of a few by eroding the public's ability to think critically and engage in meaningful discourse.

The dangers of this approach are clear. Without the ability to criticize or question those in power, corruption and abuse can flourish unchecked. The erosion of free speech under fascist movements doesn't just silence individual voices—it fundamentally weakens democracy, making it more difficult for citizens to hold their leaders accountable.

No. 3 — Extreme Wokeism's Cultural Censorship

On the other side of the spectrum, extreme wokeism poses its own threat to free speech, though the mechanisms are different. Instead of government-imposed censorship, extreme wokeism enforces a kind of cultural censorship, where individuals are socially or professionally ostracized for expressing views that are deemed unacceptable by the prevailing orthodoxy. The rise of cancel culture, where people lose their jobs, reputations, or social standing for expressing controversial or dissenting opinions, exemplifies this dynamic.

Extreme wokeism can foster a climate where only a narrow range of viewpoints is considered acceptable, and any deviation from these norms is met with swift punishment. In this environment, the fear of being "canceled" can lead individuals to self-censor, avoiding important conversations about race, gender, identity, and social justice for fear of being misunderstood, mis-characterized, or shamed.

While the aim of wokeism is often to advance social justice, when taken to the extreme, it can stifle free expression and create an intolerant atmosphere where individuals are not allowed to disagree or offer alternative viewpoints without risking social or professional retribution. This kind of cultural gate-keeping can be just as damaging to democratic discourse as state-imposed censorship. It narrows the range of acceptable debate and discourages the kind of intellectual curiosity and critical thinking that are necessary for a vibrant democracy.

No. 4 — Fostering Tolerance for Different Viewpoints

To reclaim free speech, we must foster a culture of tolerance for different viewpoints. This doesn't mean we need to agree with every idea or refrain from challenging those we find harmful or offensive. But it does mean we need to create spaces where people can express their thoughts without fear of being silenced or vilified.

- **Encouraging Open Dialogue.** Free speech works best when it is accompanied by a willingness to listen and engage in meaningful dialogue. Instead of reacting with outrage or dismissal, we should seek to understand the underlying reasons for different viewpoints, especially those with which we disagree. This doesn't mean endorsing hate speech or incitements to violence, but it does mean allowing room for debate on contentious issues, even when it's uncomfortable.

- **Learning from Dissent.** Disagreement and dissent are essential components of democracy. Throughout history, many of the ideas that we now take for granted as moral truths—such as the abolition of slavery, the expansion of women's rights, and the recognition of gay marriage—began as dissenting views. We must be willing to engage with dissenting ideas rather than suppressing them.

- **Respecting Intellectual Diversity.** Intellectual diversity is the foundation of progress. In science, philosophy, politics, and art, new ideas often emerge from those willing to challenge conventional wisdom. Encouraging diverse perspectives, rather than punishing people for holding unpopular views, helps create a more innovative and resilient society.

No. 5 — The Role of Media and Social Platforms

In the modern world, the role of media and social media platforms in shaping public discourse cannot be overstated. Unfortunately, both fascist movements and extreme wokeism have used these platforms to stoke division and spread disinformation. If we are to foster an environment of open discourse, media and social media companies must also play a role in promoting intellectual diversity rather than exacerbating polarization.

- **Breaking Out of Echo Chambers.** Social media platforms often reinforce echo chambers by feeding users content that aligns with their existing beliefs, thus reducing exposure to differing opinions. Platforms must take responsibility for promoting a broader range of viewpoints and ensuring that algorithms do not simply reinforce extremist views on either side.

- **Promoting Civil Discourse.** Both traditional and social media can help set the tone for civil debate. Instead of prioritizing clicks and sensationalism, media organizations should commit to factual reporting and balanced perspectives. They must recognize that their coverage has the power to shape public perceptions and therefore should prioritize informing rather than inflaming.

- **Combating Disinformation.** While fostering free speech is essential, we must also tackle the rampant disinformation that has eroded trust in democratic institutions and the media. Media outlets and tech companies must invest in tools and strategies to fact-check, debunk, and combat false narratives that seek to divide the public and destabilize democracy.

A Culture of Free Speech

Reclaiming free speech and open discourse is essential to the future of American democracy. Both fascist tendencies and extreme wokeism pose a threat to the free exchange of ideas, though they do so in different ways. One relies on authoritarian repression; the other, on cultural coercion. But the result is the same: narrowed dialogue, suppressed dissent, and a society where people are afraid to express their true beliefs.

If America is to move forward, we must commit to protecting free speech—not just as a legal right but as a cultural value. We must build an environment where individuals feel free to express their ideas, where dissent is welcomed as a path to progress, and where open dialogue replaces intolerance. Only by fostering a culture of free speech can we ensure that our democracy remains robust, vibrant, and resilient in the face of the challenges ahead.

Reviving the Middle Ground: The Case for Moderation

As the polarization in America deepens, it becomes harder to envision a political and social landscape where moderation is valued. Extremes—whether in the form of authoritarianism or extreme wokeism—thrive in environments where fear, anger, and division are amplified, leaving little room for dialogue, compromise, or practical solutions. To move forward, the United States must revive the middle ground—the space where pragmatism, nuance, and thoughtful debate can flourish.

Moderation does not mean abandoning strong principles or settling for weak, ineffective governance. Rather, it means embracing the idea that solutions to complex problems often require balance, compromise, and an understanding that no single ideology holds all the answers. Extreme positions on both the right and left lead to gridlock, societal breakdown, and a loss of faith in democratic institutions. If we are to make meaningful progress on the challenges we face—whether they be economic inequality, racial justice, or climate change—we must rediscover the value of moderation in our political discourse and policymaking.

No. 1 — The Dangers of Polarization

Polarization has become the defining feature of American politics. Both ends of the spectrum have pulled the country further apart, fostering a culture of tribalism where political opponents are seen not as fellow citizens but as existential threats. This environment of "us vs. them" erodes the very fabric of democratic society, as it discourages cooperation, respect, and the exchange of ideas.

- **The Far Right and Authoritarianism.** On the far right, we see the rise of authoritarian rhetoric, with leaders and movements advocating for strongman rule, the suppression of dissent, and xenophobic nationalism. This has led to the demonization of immigrants, minority groups, and political opponents. These authoritarian tendencies pose a direct threat to democratic norms, as they prioritize the concentration of power over individual rights and pluralism.

- **The Far Left and Extreme Wokeism.** On the far left, extreme wokeism has taken root, creating a climate where ideological purity is prioritized over open discourse. Cancel culture and moral absolutism have created an environment where dissenting voices are silenced, and individuals are ostracized for holding views that don't align with the dominant progressive narrative. This stifles debate and discourages people from engaging in discussions that might otherwise lead to greater understanding and social progress.

Both extremes push people to choose sides, leaving little room for the nuanced and thoughtful debate that democracy relies on. As polarization intensifies, it becomes increasingly difficult to find common ground or pursue policies that benefit the greater good rather than just one faction of society.

No. 2 — The Power of Pragmatism

Pragmatism—the belief that solutions should be based on what works, rather than on ideological purity—is often dismissed as weak or indecisive in today's polarized climate. But history shows that some of America's greatest achievements were born out of pragmatic leadership that sought to unite, rather than divide.

- **The Civil Rights Movement.** While the Civil Rights Movement was driven by the moral courage of its leaders, it was also deeply pragmatic. Dr. Martin Luther King Jr. and other leaders understood that achieving meaningful change required working within the system and building broad coalitions that included not just activists but also politicians, religious leaders, and ordinary citizens. The passage of the Civil Rights Act of 1964 and the Voting Rights Act of 1965 was the result of compromise, persistence, and a recognition that real progress often requires working with those who may not fully share your vision.

- **FDR's New Deal.** During the Great Depression, Franklin D. Roosevelt implemented the New Deal, a series of programs designed to stimulate economic recovery. These policies were not driven by ideological rigidity but by practical necessity. FDR's ability to bring together business leaders, labor unions, and political allies from across the spectrum was key to the New Deal's success, showing that bold, effective policy requires flexibility and collaboration.

Today, we need leaders and citizens who embrace pragmatism. The challenges we face—whether in healthcare, education, or climate change—are too complex to be solved by ideological extremes. Pragmatism allows for the flexibility and adaptability that democracy requires to function effectively. It encourages us to find workable solutions rather than demanding that our leaders adhere to dogma.

No. 3 — Rejecting False Binaries

One of the most destructive aspects of polarization is the belief that people must choose between two extremes—that you are either for or against a particular issue, with no room for middle ground or nuance. This is a false binary, and it limits our ability to engage with the complexity of real-world issues.

For example, the debate over policing and criminal justice reform is often framed as a binary choice between supporting law enforcement or advocating for defunding the police. In reality, many Americans believe we can pursue both public safety and police reform—strengthening law enforcement while also ensuring accountability, transparency, and justice in how policing is conducted.

Similarly, the debate over economic inequality is often framed as a choice between unregulated capitalism and socialism. But there is broad agreement among moderates that a middle path is possible, where capitalism can coexist with regulations and safety nets that ensure fairness and opportunity for all citizens.

Rejecting false binaries means embracing the complexity of the issues we face and recognizing that there are often multiple ways to address a problem. It means being open to solutions that incorporate the best ideas from across the political spectrum, rather than adhering to a rigid ideological framework.

No. 4 — Restoring Pragmatism in Politics

The revival of moderation in American politics requires the promotion of pragmatic leadership that focuses on solutions, not just rhetoric. Extremes on both sides of the aisle are often more concerned with winning ideological battles than with governing effectively. This has led to gridlock and stagnation in Congress, where partisan posturing takes precedence over addressing the real needs of the American people.

- **Bipartisanship as a Strength.** Some of the most important legislative achievements in American history have been bipartisan efforts. From Social Security to Medicare to the Civil Rights Act, many of the programs and policies that have shaped modern America were the result of compromise and cooperation between Democrats and Republicans. Restoring a sense of bipartisanship—where leaders work across the aisle to find solutions that benefit the country as a whole—will be key to overcoming the paralysis of polarization.

- **Focusing on Results, Not Ideology.** Politicians and leaders need to refocus on outcomes rather than ideological purity. In healthcare, for example, the debate shouldn't be about whether the solution is "capitalist" or "socialist," but whether it ensures access to affordable healthcare for all Americans. Similarly, the goal of economic policy should be to create opportunities for economic mobility and shared prosperity, regardless of whether the policies fit neatly into a conservative or progressive framework.

No. 5 — Rejecting Performative Politics

In today's political landscape, there is a growing emphasis on performative politics—the act of performing outrage, virtue, or ideological commitment for the sake of public approval rather than focusing on real policy solutions. Performative politics thrives on social media, where politicians and activists alike can gain instant validation for their stances, regardless of whether they are actually advancing meaningful change.

- **Focus on Substance.** Moving forward, America must reject performative politics in favor of substantive governance. This means electing leaders who are more interested in problem-solving than in virtue signaling. It also means creating a political culture where results matter more than headlines or social media "likes."

- **Rewarding Problem-Solvers.** Voters have a role to play in this as well. We must demand more from our leaders, supporting those who demonstrate a genuine commitment to finding solutions and working for the public good, rather than those who simply fuel division and outrage.

The Middle Ground as America's Strength

Reviving the middle ground does not mean abandoning principles or compromising on core values. It means recognizing that effective governance requires the ability to listen, engage, and work together with people who may hold different views. It means embracing moderation as a strength, not a weakness, and understanding that the future of American democracy depends on our ability to move beyond the extremes and focus on what unites us rather than what divides us.

Rebuilding Trust in Institutions

One of the most troubling consequences of the increasing polarization in America is the erosion of trust in our democratic institutions. Whether it's trust in elections, the judiciary, the media, or Congress, public faith in the systems that uphold democracy has declined dramatically in recent years. Both fascist tendencies on the right and extreme wokeism on the left have contributed to this erosion, attacking the credibility of institutions from opposite ends of the spectrum. For America to move forward, we must rebuild trust in these institutions, ensuring they remain credible, transparent, and accountable to all citizens.

No. 1 — The Erosion of Trust in Democratic Institutions

Over the last decade, public trust in American institutions has been steadily declining. According to a 2021 Gallup poll, only 39% of Americans expressed confidence in the presidency, and just 27% had confidence in Congress. Trust in the media, meanwhile, is at an all-time low, with only 16% of Americans expressing confidence in newspapers and 11% in television news. This erosion of trust is dangerous because it undermines the very foundations of democracy, leading people to question the legitimacy of elections, the fairness of the legal system, and the objectivity of the press.

This lack of trust has been exacerbated by movements on both the right and the left. On the far right, fascist rhetoric has sought to discredit democratic institutions by spreading disinformation about election fraud, attacking the independence of the judiciary, and framing the media as "the enemy of the people." On the far left, extreme wokeism has questioned the legitimacy of institutions like universities and cultural organizations, arguing that they are inherently oppressive or biased if they do not conform to specific ideological standards.

In both cases, these attacks weaken the public's faith in the ability of our institutions to function fairly and effectively. If people no longer trust that the courts are impartial, that elections are fair, or that the media is reporting the truth, the very fabric of democracy begins to unravel. Rebuilding this trust is essential to ensuring that America can move forward as a unified nation.

No. 2 — Restoring Faith in Democracy

To restore faith in our democratic institutions, we must focus on reforms that increase transparency, accountability, and accessibility while ensuring that these institutions remain independent and resilient in the face of political and ideological pressure.

- **Electoral Integrity.** One of the most pressing issues in rebuilding trust is ensuring the integrity of elections. Over the past several years, misinformation about voter fraud has contributed to a widespread belief among some Americans that our electoral system is rigged. This belief reached its zenith in the aftermath of the 2020 Presidential Election, leading to the January 6th Capitol insurrection, where a mob sought to overturn the results of a free and fair election. To rebuild trust in elections, we must ensure that they are transparent, secure, and accessible to all citizens. This can include measures like expanding voting access, investing in voter education, and ensuring that ballots are counted accurately and independently. Moreover, politicians and media figures must commit to honestly conveying election results and refraining from spreading false claims about fraud that undermine faith in the system.

- **Reforming Campaign Finance.** Another critical step in restoring trust is addressing the outsized influence of money in politics. Many Americans feel that their voices are drowned out by wealthy donors and corporate interests, leading to a belief that elected officials are more accountable to their funders than to the people they represent. Reforming campaign finance laws to limit the influence of dark money and increase transparency can help restore the public's faith that their government truly represents their interests.

- **Promoting Civic Engagement.** Restoring faith in democracy also requires re-engaging the public in the democratic process. Too often, cynicism about politics leads to disengagement, with citizens feeling that their votes don't matter or that the system is too corrupt to change. By promoting civic education and encouraging greater voter participation, we can help citizens understand how they can influence government and make their voices heard. Local involvement—whether through town halls, school boards, or community organizing—can give people a sense of ownership over their democracy and restore trust that they can enact change.

No. 3 — Restoring Trust in the Media

The media plays a crucial role in informing the public, holding the powerful accountable, and facilitating democratic discourse. Yet trust in the media has been severely compromised in recent years, with both sides of the political spectrum contributing to its delegitimization. On the far right, fascist rhetoric has branded the press as "fake news," undermining its ability to serve as a check on government power. On the far left, extreme wokeism has contributed to the rise of echo chambers where only ideologically aligned news is considered valid, creating a fragmented media landscape where people consume information only from sources that confirm their existing beliefs.

To rebuild trust in the media, we must work toward restoring its role as a neutral provider of facts and a forum for open debate.

- **Objectivity and Accountability.** Media organizations must prioritize objectivity and fact-based reporting over sensationalism. While editorializing and opinion pieces have their place, news outlets must clearly distinguish between news and opinion to avoid blurring the lines between facts and commentary. Additionally, media outlets must hold themselves accountable by correcting mistakes promptly and transparently when they occur.

- **Combatting Disinformation.** In the era of social media, disinformation spreads rapidly, often faster than corrections can keep up. Media organizations must invest in fact-checking and disinformation detection to counter the spread of false narratives. Furthermore, tech companies must take greater responsibility for the content on their platforms, implementing tools to identify and combat false claims without infringing on free speech.

- **Diversifying Perspectives.** One of the criticisms leveled at mainstream media—often by those on the right—is that it lacks diverse viewpoints and often reflects the perspectives of coastal elites rather than the experiences of people from different regions and backgrounds. To rebuild trust, media organizations should work to include a broader range of voices, ensuring that their reporting reflects the diversity of American life.

No. 4 — Strengthening the Judiciary

The independence of the judiciary is a cornerstone of American democracy. Yet, in recent years, the courts have increasingly become a battleground for partisan politics, with judicial appointments being framed in stark ideological terms. The perception that courts are no longer impartial arbiters of justice but are instead political tools used to advance specific agendas undermines public confidence in the legal system.

- **Depoliticizing Judicial Appointments.** To restore faith in the judiciary, we must work to depoliticize the process of judicial appointments. While judges are always likely to have personal ideological leanings, the focus should be on appointing individuals who demonstrate legal expertise, fairness, and a commitment to upholding the Constitution, rather than those selected solely for their political alignment. Encouraging bipartisan support for judicial nominees can help restore the perception of the courts as impartial institutions.

- **Promoting Transparency in the Courts.** Transparency in the judicial process is also key to rebuilding trust. Citizens need to understand how judicial decisions are made and feel confident that rulings are based on law, not political ideology. Ensuring that court proceedings are open to the public and that judicial opinions are clearly explained can help foster greater accountability.

No. 5 — Restoring Trust in Academia and Cultural Institutions

Universities, museums, and other cultural institutions have historically been viewed as spaces for intellectual exploration and open debate. However, in recent years, many have become battlegrounds in the culture wars. On the left, extreme wokeism has led to the rise of cancel culture in academic settings, where professors and students alike fear expressing dissenting views for fear of professional consequences. On the right, universities are often framed as bastions of left-wing indoctrination, leading to efforts to defund or delegitimize these institutions.

Restoring trust in academia and cultural institutions requires a commitment to intellectual diversity and academic freedom.

- **Encouraging Intellectual Diversity.** Universities should be spaces where students are exposed to a wide range of viewpoints, not just those that align with a particular ideology. Encouraging diverse perspectives in the classroom can help foster critical thinking and allow students to engage with different ideas in meaningful ways. Intellectual diversity should be viewed as a strength, not a threat, to academic integrity.

- **Protecting Academic Freedom.** Professors and researchers must be free to pursue their work without fear of retaliation for holding controversial or unpopular views. Academic freedom is essential to the pursuit of knowledge and the advancement of ideas. Universities should commit to protecting free speech on campus and resisting efforts to stifle debate.

Rebuilding Trust Through Transparency and Accountability

Rebuilding trust in American institutions will not happen overnight, but it is essential to ensuring the health and longevity of our democracy. Both fascist and extreme wokeist ideologies have contributed to the erosion of trust in different ways, whether through attacks on the media and elections or through the promotion of ideological conformity and cancel culture. Moving forward, we must work to restore faith in our institutions by prioritizing transparency, accountability, and diverse perspectives.

By strengthening the integrity of our elections, ensuring the independence of our judiciary, promoting a fact-based media, and defending intellectual freedom in our academic and cultural institutions, we can begin to rebuild the trust that is so essential to a functioning democracy. In the next section, we will explore what kind of leadership America needs to navigate these challenges and move toward a future defined by unity, compassion, and hope.

Leadership for the Future: Moving Beyond Extremes

As America navigates an increasingly polarized and complex landscape, the role of leadership becomes paramount. The challenges we face—from political division to economic inequality, climate change, and racial justice—cannot be overcome without strong, compassionate, and pragmatic leadership. Unfortunately, much of the leadership we have seen in recent years has been defined by division, fear, and ideological extremism. To move forward, we must embrace leaders who are willing to reject the extremes on both ends of the spectrum—whether it's authoritarianism or extreme wokeism—and instead prioritize unity, pragmatism, and a commitment to the common good.

America needs leaders who build bridges, not walls. Leaders who can inspire hope, not stoke fear. Leaders who understand that real change requires collaboration, compromise, and the ability to listen to diverse perspectives. This kind of leadership is not about winning at all costs or promoting ideological purity; it's about creating a future where all Americans feel represented, heard, and empowered.

No. 1 — The Role of Leaders in Uniting a Divided Nation

Unity is a word often invoked in political speeches, but rarely is it practiced in meaningful ways. In recent years, the political climate in the United States has been defined by a deep us vs. them mentality, where partisanship often takes precedence over problem-solving. Leaders on both sides of the political spectrum have at times resorted to polarizing rhetoric, exploiting divisions for short-term political gains rather than seeking ways to bring people together.

Moving forward, America needs leaders who recognize that unity is not about erasing differences or forcing everyone to agree. Rather, it is about building a sense of shared purpose, where people from diverse backgrounds, political affiliations, and life experiences can work toward common goals. These leaders must be able to articulate a vision that transcends partisan divides and focuses on the greater good.

- **Leaders Who Build Coalitions.** Effective leadership in the future will require the ability to build broad coalitions across political, racial, and socio-economic lines. These coalitions must be rooted in a commitment to democratic values—freedom of speech, equality, and justice—and a belief that everyone deserves a seat at the table. Leaders like Abraham Lincoln and Franklin D. Roosevelt were able to bring together disparate groups to work toward a common purpose, even in times of great national crisis. We need similar leaders today—those who see diversity as a strength and compromise as a necessary tool for progress.

- **Leaders Who Model Civil Discourse.** In an era where public debate has too often devolved into name-calling and personal attacks, we need leaders who model civil discourse and respect for opposing viewpoints. This doesn't mean avoiding difficult conversations or suppressing passionate debate, but it does mean engaging in discussions in a way that is respectful, productive, and focused on solutions rather than ideological victories. Leaders who can model this kind of discourse can help to set a tone for the nation that prioritizes listening over shouting, understanding over division.

No. 2 — Rejecting Performative Politics and Embracing Substance

One of the greatest challenges facing American leadership today is the rise of performative politics—a style of leadership that prioritizes optics and social media soundbites over substantive policymaking. Whether it's the embrace of culture wars to rally political bases or the use of social media platforms to score quick points with viral moments, performative politics often distracts from the real work of governing and solving problems.

- **Substance Over Soundbites.** Leaders who focus on substance rather than spectacle are those who prioritize policy over political theater. They recognize that real leadership is not about dominating the news cycle or gaining likes and retweets, but about crafting solutions that benefit the American people. This requires leaders who are willing to roll up their sleeves and engage in the hard work of policymaking—listening to experts, negotiating with political opponents, and making decisions that may not always be popular in the short term but are necessary for the long-term health of the country.

- **Governing with Integrity.** Performative politics also breeds a culture of cynicism and distrust among the public. When leaders prioritize their own political careers or personal brand over the needs of their constituents, it erodes public faith in government. Leaders who govern with integrity—who are transparent about their actions, who admit when they've made mistakes, and who consistently act in the public's interest—are essential to restoring trust in our democratic institutions. Integrity means putting the country before political gain and making decisions based on what is best for the American people, not just what is best for a political party or movement.

No. 3 — Embracing Compassionate and Inclusive Leadership

At a time when many Americans feel disconnected from their leaders, we need those who lead with compassion and empathy. Compassionate leadership doesn't mean being soft on tough issues—it means understanding that policy affects real people's lives, and that leadership requires listening to and caring for those who are struggling, marginalized, or left behind.

- **Empathy as a Core Leadership Trait.** Empathy is a quality that has too often been overlooked in politics, but it is essential to effective leadership. Leaders like Nelson Mandela and Mahatma Gandhi showed the world that leadership rooted in empathy has the power to heal divisions and bring people together in ways that authoritarian or purely pragmatic leadership cannot. American leaders must listen to the concerns of all citizens, not just their political base, and work to understand the lived experiences of people across the country—from rural farmers and urban activists to small business owners and minimum-wage workers.

- **Inclusive Leadership.** America's future leaders must also prioritize inclusion—ensuring that people of all backgrounds, races, genders, and socio-economic statuses are represented in government and have a voice in decision-making. Inclusive leadership recognizes that diversity is a strength, and that policies created with input from diverse communities are more likely to be effective and equitable. This includes not just ensuring diversity in political office, but also creating spaces where marginalized groups can participate fully in the democratic process.

No. 4 — Fostering Long-Term Vision and Solutions

One of the major weaknesses of modern American politics is the tendency to focus on short-term victories rather than long-term solutions. Leaders often prioritize policies that will yield immediate political gains—whether for the next election cycle or the next news cycle—rather than those that will benefit future generations. To move forward, we need leaders who are willing to take the long view, even when it means making difficult decisions that may not be immediately popular.

- **Addressing Systemic Issues.** Many of the problems America faces today—whether it's economic inequality, climate change, or racial injustice—are systemic in nature, meaning they require long-term planning and sustained effort to address. Leaders who focus on quick fixes or who cater to the loudest voices on social media are unlikely to bring about meaningful change. What we need are leaders who are willing to look beyond the next election and focus on policies that address the root causes of these issues, even if the benefits won't be seen for years or decades.

- **Investing in the Future.** Part of long-term leadership is about investing in the future. This means supporting policies that prioritize education, infrastructure, and sustainability. For example, addressing climate change requires investments in green energy and environmental protection— even when doing so may meet resistance from powerful interests or may not provide immediate economic benefits. Similarly, addressing wealth inequality requires a focus on education, job training, and affordable healthcare, all of which are long-term solutions that require foresight and commitment.

No. 5 — Courage to Stand Against Extremes

In a time of growing extremism—whether from authoritarianism on the right or extreme wokeism on the left—America's future leaders must have the courage to stand against these forces, even when it is politically risky. Courageous leadership means calling out extremism and holding firm to the principles of democracy, freedom of speech, and the rule of law, even when those principles are unpopular with certain factions.

- **Defending Democratic Values.** Leaders must be willing to stand up for democratic institutions and free speech in the face of threats from both extremes. This includes defending the independence of the judiciary, the integrity of elections, and the right to dissent—all of which are under threat from authoritarian movements on the far right. It also means resisting the cultural censorship and ideological purity tests that have become common in some corners of the far left, ensuring that universities, media, and cultural institutions remain places where diverse ideas can be freely expressed.

- **Promoting National Healing.** Courageous leaders must also work to heal the wounds that have been caused by political division and societal strife. This means acknowledging the pain and anger that many Americans feel, while also offering a path forward that prioritizes reconciliation over revenge, and hope over fear.

A New Kind of Leadership for a New Era

The challenges America faces today are significant, but they are not insurmountable. With the right kind of leadership—pragmatic, inclusive, and visionary—we can move beyond the extremes that threaten to tear us apart and build a future defined by unity, justice, and opportunity.

America's future leaders must be those who are willing to reject performative politics and fear-mongering, embrace compassion and empathy, and focus on long-term solutions that will benefit all Americans. Only then can we begin to address the deep divisions in our society and build a future where democracy, freedom, and hope remain at the center of American life.

THE DEMISE OF TRUE COMMUNICATION IN AMERICAN SOCIETY

A Sad Commentary on the Human Condition

It could be argued that communication - real, substantive communication - appears to be a dying art. The age of digital convenience has made exchanging information easier than ever, but this accessibility comes at a steep cost: the erosion of meaningful conversation. Instead of fostering intellectual exchange, social media platforms have fueled echo chambers, reduced discourse to sound bites, and prioritized emotion over critical thought. Debate is being demonized, and intellectualism is losing its place in public discourse. The consequences of this trend for American society and the human condition are far-reaching and deeply troubling.

The Role of Social Media in the Decline of Communication

While the internet has undoubtedly provided unparalleled access to information and connection, it has also facilitated the rise of platforms that incentivize shallow interaction. Social media, in particular, is structured to prioritize quick consumption over deep engagement. Tweets, posts, and stories offer users a way to interact with ideas, but only on a surface level. Research shows that the average attention span online has dropped to just 8 seconds, less than that of a goldfish (Microsoft Corp, 2015). This brevity can stifle the nuanced, reflective conversation that fosters true understanding.

Moreover, social media algorithms are designed to keep users engaged by feeding them content that aligns with their existing beliefs. According to a 2020 study by MIT's Initiative on the Digital Economy, social media algorithms significantly amplify misinformation and divisive content because such material tends to provoke stronger emotional reactions, driving higher engagement (Vosoughi, Roy, & Aral, 2018). The result? Users become more deeply entrenched in their ideological bubbles, reinforcing rather than challenging their existing perspectives.

This creates an environment where genuine debate is either absent or quickly devolves into vitriolic exchanges. When communication becomes primarily about reinforcing one's beliefs, rather than exploring or understanding opposing viewpoints, it ceases to be productive. A 2022 Pew Research study found that 64% of U.S. adults feel that social media has a mostly negative effect on the way people communicate, with the majority citing polarization and disinformation as key factors.

The Impact on the Human Condition

The demise of true communication has profound implications for the human condition. Meaningful interaction—whether it be dialogue with others or internal reflection—allows individuals to grow intellectually and emotionally. It enables empathy, broadens perspectives, and encourages critical thinking. When this interaction is diminished, we lose touch with our ability to understand the complexities of the world and one another.

One of the most alarming effects of this shift is the decline in empathy. Research by Dr. Sara Konrath at the University of Michigan shows that college students today are 40% less empathetic than they were 30 years ago, with the most significant drop occurring after the year 2000—just as social media began to gain prominence (Konrath, O'Brien, & Hsing, 2011). The ability to engage in thoughtful, in-person conversation is key to developing empathy, as it allows individuals to understand and relate to the emotions and experiences of others. When communication is reduced to short, impersonal interactions, this empathetic connection is weakened.

Furthermore, the reduced capacity for meaningful debate and intellectual exchange undermines the foundation of a healthy democratic society. Open dialogue and the free exchange of ideas are essential for addressing complex social, economic, and political challenges. As debate becomes more demonized and intellectualism is increasingly dismissed as elitism, public discourse becomes polarized and impoverished. The result is a society less capable of critical thinking and more prone to division, mistrust, and authoritarian tendencies.

Social media has become one of the most powerful forces shaping public discourse in modern America. While these platforms offer unparalleled access to information and connection, they also contribute significantly to the growing polarization of society. The root of this division lies in how social media algorithms curate content, creating echo chambers that reinforce existing beliefs and further entrench ideological divides. These echo chambers, perpetuated by algorithms designed to maximize engagement, have contributed to what may be the most divisive society in American history.

The Echo Chamber Effect

An echo chamber is an environment where individuals are exposed only to information and opinions that reinforce their pre-existing views, while dissenting perspectives are filtered out or marginalized. In the context of social media, this effect is driven by algorithms that curate users' feeds based on their behavior—what they like, share, and comment on. Social media platforms like Facebook, Twitter (now X), and YouTube use sophisticated algorithms to prioritize content that will keep users engaged, and research has shown that content which provokes strong emotional responses—such as outrage or fear—is more likely to capture attention and go viral.

A 2021 study from researchers at Stanford University found that political polarization in the U.S. has been accelerating over the past decade, largely fueled by social media's role in creating ideological silos (Boxell, Gentzkow, & Shapiro, 2021). The study pointed out that, while polarization has long existed, the advent of social media has made it easier for individuals to insulate themselves from opposing views and become more deeply entrenched in their own beliefs. The more we interact with content that aligns with our views, the more the algorithms feed us similar content, leading to an information bubble that shuts out diverse perspectives.

This echo chamber effect isn't confined to politics. It permeates discussions around cultural, social, and even scientific topics, as seen with the spread of misinformation and conspiracy theories about vaccines, climate change, and other critical issues. A study by MIT's Media Lab revealed that false news spreads on Twitter six times faster than true news, largely due to the emotional reactions it provokes (Vosoughi, Roy, & Aral, 2018). The more sensational or controversial the content, the more it is promoted by the platform's algorithms, perpetuating false narratives and deepening divisions.

The Most Divisive Society in American History?

While America has faced periods of extreme division in the past—most notably during the Civil War and the Civil Rights Movement—the current political and social climate is unique in that the divisiveness is being amplified and accelerated by technology. Social media has turned ideological differences into stark divides, pushing people further apart and fostering a "with us or against us" mentality.

This polarization is evident in the increased animosity between political parties. A Pew Research study from 2022 found that 72% of Republicans and 63% of Democrats view members of the opposing party as "immoral," a significant increase from just a decade ago (Pew Research Center, 2022). Furthermore, 60% of Americans believe that the other political party is "a threat to the nation's well-being." Such entrenched hostility has made it difficult for meaningful dialogue and compromise to occur, both in Congress and in everyday life. Many Americans now view their political opponents not just as wrong, but as dangerous, making cooperation nearly impossible.

The 2021 Capitol riot is perhaps the most vivid manifestation of this growing divide, with social media playing a critical role in organizing and amplifying the misinformation that fueled the event. Platforms like Facebook and Twitter were instrumental in spreading conspiracy theories and unsubstantiated claims about the 2020 election, further illustrating how echo chambers can escalate tensions to dangerous levels.

The Psychological and Social Costs of Division

The deepening of these echo chambers has profound psychological and social consequences. As people become more entrenched in their views, they are less likely to empathize with those who hold opposing beliefs. This lack of empathy can erode the social fabric, increasing distrust and hostility between groups. Harvard political scientist Robert Putnam's seminal work on social capital shows that social cohesion is essential for a functioning democracy (Putnam, 2000). When people lose the ability to communicate across differences, social trust declines, and society becomes more fragmented and less cooperative.

This polarization also contributes to rising anxiety, depression, and feelings of isolation. According to a 2018 survey by the American Psychological Association, 69% of Americans say that the future of the nation causes them significant stress, with many citing political and social divisions as a primary source of anxiety. Social media, which was initially heralded as a tool for connection, has ironically contributed to feelings of loneliness and alienation, as users find themselves siloed into homogeneous groups that reinforce rather than challenge their worldviews.

Remedies for Overcoming Divisiveness

Breaking out of these echo chambers and bridging the divide will require concerted efforts both on an individual and societal level. Some strategies for countering the effects of social media algorithms include:

On an Individual Level

- **Diversify Your Feed.** Make an intentional effort to follow people and sources with different political, social, and cultural views. By exposing yourself to a broader range of perspectives, you can avoid the trap of the echo chamber and develop a more nuanced understanding of issues.

- **Fact-Check Before Sharing.** Before sharing information online, especially if it provokes a strong emotional reaction, take the time to verify its accuracy. Websites like FactCheck.org and Snopes can help debunk misinformation and ensure that what you're consuming and sharing is factual.

- **Engage in Civil Dialogue.** Seek out conversations with people who hold different opinions, and practice listening with the intent to understand, not just to respond. Civil dialogue is key to breaking down the walls that social media algorithms help build.

On an Institutional Level

- **Algorithmic Transparency and Regulation.** Policymakers and social media companies must work together to promote transparency in how content is curated. Platforms should be required to disclose how their algorithms prioritize content and be held accountable for the role they play in fostering division. Some experts have called for "algorithmic audits" to ensure that social media companies are not prioritizing sensational or misleading content over truthful, meaningful discourse.

- **Promote Cross-Partisan Dialogue.** Educational institutions, civic organizations, and media outlets should create more opportunities for cross-partisan engagement. Public forums, debate programs, and media initiatives that emphasize listening to and understanding the "other side" can help break down the barriers created by social media echo chambers.

- **Encourage Ethical Design in Social Media.** Developers and tech companies need to think critically about how the design of their platforms affects public discourse. Encouraging long-form content, promoting discussions that foster understanding rather than conflict, and reducing the emphasis on "likes" and "shares" as the primary metric for engagement are potential steps in the right direction.

The decline of true communication is not just a technological or social issue; it is a threat to the very fabric of society. When dialogue is reduced to sound bites and intellectualism is dismissed, we lose the ability to think critically, empathize with others, and tackle the complex challenges facing our world. However, by making a conscious effort to engage in deeper, more meaningful communication—both as individuals and as a society—we can begin to reverse this trend. The future of American democracy, intellectualism, and the human condition may depend on it.

THE DECLINE OF HOPE IN AMERICAN SOCIETY

A Crisis of Cynicism and Victimhood

Hope, a fundamental force that has long driven progress, perseverance, and optimism, is rapidly diminishing in American society. Once considered a cornerstone of the "American Dream," hope is now being replaced by cynicism, frustration, and an increasingly prevalent victim mentality. In recent decades, the sense of optimism about the future has declined, leaving many Americans feeling disillusioned and disconnected from the possibility of a better tomorrow. This decline in hope is not just a fleeting trend - it is a profound and far-reaching issue that threatens to reshape the nation's collective psyche and future.

The Decline of Hope in Recent Decades

Studies have shown a significant decline in hope and optimism in the United States over the past several decades. According to a 2020 survey conducted by Gallup, only 42% of Americans said they felt hopeful about the future of the country, compared to 72% who said the same in the early 1970s (Gallup, 2020). Similarly, research by the University of Chicago found that in 2022, the percentage of Americans who described themselves as "very happy" hit a 50-year low, with only 14% of respondents feeling a strong sense of personal happiness (NORC, 2022).

This sense of hopelessness is often coupled with a growing cynicism toward institutions and a belief that personal efforts will make little difference. The Pew Research Center found that in 2022, just 20% of Americans had trust in the federal government, marking a steep decline from the 73% who trusted the government in 1958 (Pew Research Center, 2022). This erosion of trust in institutions has fostered a belief that the problems facing society are too large and complex for individual action to make a meaningful impact.

Additionally, the prevalence of a victim mentality has grown, as more people view themselves as powerless in the face of systemic challenges like inequality, racism, economic instability, and political corruption. While these issues are undoubtedly real and serious, the increasing tendency to see oneself as a victim of circumstances can lead to a sense of helplessness that further erodes hope. Psychologists have long warned that adopting a victim mentality can contribute to learned helplessness - a state where individuals believe they have no control over their lives, making them less likely to take proactive steps toward change (Seligman, 1972).

Why Hope Matters

Hope is not just an abstract feeling - it's a vital component of the human condition, driving resilience, ambition, and creativity. Psychologists define hope as a cognitive process that involves setting goals, developing strategies to achieve those goals, and maintaining the motivation to follow through (Snyder, 1994). Without hope, people are less likely to set meaningful goals, believe in the possibility of success, or persevere through adversity. Hope, in essence, gives individuals the psychological stamina to confront life's challenges and believe that the future can be better than the present.

On a societal level, hope fuels collective progress. Societies that are optimistic about the future are more likely to invest in education, innovation, and community-building. When people believe their efforts can lead to a better world, they are more inclined to participate in civic life, engage in social activism, and work toward long-term goals. In contrast, a society that lacks hope becomes stagnant, with citizens withdrawing from public life and becoming more insular, distrustful, and disengaged.

The loss of hope also has profound consequences for mental health. Numerous studies have shown that a lack of hope is closely tied to depression, anxiety, and even physical health problems. A study by researchers at the University of Michigan found that individuals with high levels of hope are 30% more likely to engage in healthy behaviors, such as exercising and avoiding smoking, than those with low levels of hope (Berg et al., 2007). Conversely, those who feel hopeless are more likely to experience chronic stress, which can lead to a host of health issues, including heart disease and weakened immune function.

Perhaps most alarmingly, the decline in hope has been linked to a rise in suicide rates. The Centers for Disease Control and Prevention (CDC) reported that between 1999 and 2021, the suicide rate in the United States increased by 33% (CDC, 2021). This tragic statistic underscores the severe impact of hopelessness on individual lives, as more people find themselves unable to see a way out of their despair.

Political Divisiveness and the Erosion of Hope

The divisive political environment in America has played a significant role in this erosion of hope. The hyperpolarization of political discourse has left many

Americans feeling as though the nation is deeply fractured, with no common ground to be found. Instead of healthy debate and compromise, political parties increasingly demonize one another, portraying every issue as an existential crisis. The constant barrage of negative news, political infighting, and sensationalist media coverage only exacerbates the sense that the country is in a state of irreversible decline.

A 2019 study by the American Psychological Association found that 69% of Americans feel that the future of the country is a significant source of stress, with political divisiveness being a major contributing factor (APA, 2019). As people become more entrenched in their political ideologies, they are less likely to believe that positive change is possible, particularly if they view the opposing party as an insurmountable obstacle. This environment of distrust and animosity makes it difficult for hope to flourish.

Furthermore, political leaders often use fear-based rhetoric to mobilize voters, reinforcing a narrative that the future is bleak unless drastic measures are taken. This creates a climate where hope is systematically undermined, as people are told that they must constantly be on guard against threats—whether they are real or imagined—rather than working toward a shared vision of a better future.

The Impacts of Declining Hope: Individual and Societal Consequences

The real-life impacts of declining hope are profound, affecting individuals, families, communities, and society as a whole. When hope diminishes, people begin to disengage from life, lose faith in their ability to effect change, and experience greater mental health struggles. This collective sense of despair, compounded by the erosion of trust in institutions, leads to significant social and economic consequences. Below, we delve deeper into the effects of this decline in hope, both at the individual and societal levels, highlighting the long-term risks if the current trends are not addressed.

No. 1 — Individual Impacts: Disengagement, Mental Health, and Destructive Behaviors

When people lose hope, their ability to envision a better future and to strive toward personal goals diminishes. Hope is crucial in motivating individuals to take action, persevere through challenges, and pursue their dreams. Without it, individuals are more likely to become disengaged, leading to a range of negative personal and psychological outcomes.

- **Mental Health Crisis.** A lack of hope is closely tied to rising rates of mental health disorders, particularly depression and anxiety. According to the World Health Organization (WHO), depression is now the leading cause of disability worldwide, affecting over 280 million people globally (WHO, 2021). In the United States, the National Institute of Mental Health reports that nearly 21 million adults experienced at least one major depressive episode in 2020, with rates particularly high among young adults aged 18-25 (NIMH, 2021). Depression is often characterized by feelings of helplessness, hopelessness, and a lack of control over one's circumstances— symptoms that are exacerbated by the eroding sense of hope in American society.

  The mental health toll is particularly severe among younger generations, who are facing economic uncertainty, political instability, and environmental crises, all of which contribute to a pervasive sense of dread about the future. A 2019 report from the American Psychological Association found that 91% of Generation Z (those born between 1997 and 2012) report experiencing significant stress about the future of the country, with many expressing anxiety over climate change, social justice issues, and financial security (APA, 2019).

- **Increased Suicide Rates.** One of the most alarming indicators of declining hope is the rising rate of suicide in the United States. The Centers for Disease Control and Prevention (CDC) reported that between 1999 and 2021, the U.S. suicide rate increased by 33%, with over 48,000 deaths by suicide in 2021 alone (CDC, 2021). Suicide is often the tragic result of individuals feeling that they have no way out of their despair, that their circumstances are unchangeable, and that there is no hope for a better future. This rise in suicide is especially pronounced among certain demographics, including middle-aged men and rural communities, where economic hardship and social isolation are common.

  Veterans, in particular, are one group severely affected by the loss of hope. The Department of Veterans Affairs reported that the suicide rate among veterans is significantly higher than that of the general population, with an average of 17 veterans dying by suicide every day (VA, 2021). Many veterans struggle with a sense of hopelessness after leaving military service, facing difficulties in finding employment, dealing with mental health issues like PTSD, and feeling disconnected from civilian life.

- **Substance Abuse and Destructive Behaviors.** A lack of hope can also lead to destructive coping mechanisms, such as substance abuse. When people feel that their future is bleak and out of their control, they are more likely to turn to drugs, alcohol, or other risky behaviors as a way of numbing their emotional pain. The opioid epidemic is a stark example of how hopelessness can drive people toward self-destructive paths.

In 2020 alone, more than 93,000 Americans died from drug overdoses, the highest number ever recorded in a single year (CDC, 2021). This epidemic has hit hardest in economically depressed regions, such as Appalachia and parts of the Midwest, where many people feel trapped by poverty, unemployment, and a lack of opportunities. These areas have been described as "deaths of despair" zones, where people increasingly turn to drugs and alcohol as a response to their perceived lack of future prospects (Case & Deaton, 2020).

No. 2 — Societal Impacts: Weakening Social Cohesion and Economic Decline

The decline of hope is not just an individual issue—it has widespread consequences for society as a whole. When large segments of the population lose faith in the future, it can weaken social cohesion, reduce civic engagement, and contribute to economic stagnation. Over time, a society that lacks hope becomes more fragmented, less innovative, and increasingly susceptible to social unrest.

- **Erosion of Social Trust and Civic Engagement.** Social trust—the belief that people in a society are generally trustworthy and that institutions are reliable—forms the backbone of a functioning democracy. Without trust, people are less likely to engage with others in meaningful ways, whether through political participation, community building, or collective problem-solving. The decline in hope is eroding this foundational trust in American society.

Research from the Pew Research Center shows that Americans' trust in each other and in key institutions has been steadily declining for decades. In 2022, only 32% of Americans said they trusted their fellow citizens to act in the best interest of the country, compared to 58% in 1974 (Pew Research Center, 2022). Similarly, trust in the federal government has plummeted to historic lows, with just 20% of Americans expressing trust in the government to do what is right most of the time (Pew Research Center, 2022). This lack of trust fosters a sense of cynicism and disengagement, as people feel that their efforts to contribute to society will not lead to meaningful change.

This decline in civic engagement is particularly evident in voter participation. While voter turnout surged during the highly polarized 2020 election, a long-term trend of political disengagement remains evident, particularly in local elections. Low voter turnout in non-presidential elections suggests that many Americans feel disconnected from the political process and disillusioned with the idea that their vote can make a difference.

- **Economic Stagnation and Reduced Innovation.** A society that lacks hope for the future is less likely to invest in long-term growth, innovation, and education. When people do not believe that their efforts will pay off, they are less likely to pursue higher education, start new businesses, or take risks that could lead to economic progress. This is particularly concerning in a rapidly changing global economy, where innovation and adaptability are key to maintaining competitiveness.

The economic impacts of declining hope are already evident in certain regions of the United States, particularly in areas that have been hit hardest by deindustrialization, automation, and globalization. In these areas, many workers have been left behind by the modern economy, with few opportunities for retraining or upward mobility. The result is a cycle of poverty and stagnation, where people feel trapped in low-wage jobs with little hope of advancement.

A study by economists Anne Case and Angus Deaton highlights this trend, pointing out that "deaths of despair"—deaths caused by suicide, drug overdose, or alcohol-related liver disease—are most prevalent in areas with limited economic opportunities (Case & Deaton, 2020). These regions often suffer from a lack of investment in education, infrastructure, and healthcare, further perpetuating the sense of hopelessness and economic decline.

- **Social Fragmentation and Polarization.** The decline in hope also contributes to increasing social fragmentation and polarization. When people lose faith in the future, they often retreat into tribal identities, seeking solace in groups that share their frustrations and fears. This can lead to heightened political polarization, as people become more entrenched in their ideological beliefs and less willing to engage with those who hold different views.

The rise of social media has exacerbated this trend, creating echo chambers where people are exposed only to information that reinforces their existing beliefs. The result is a more divided society, where common ground is increasingly difficult to find. Political polarization in America has reached a level not seen since the Civil War, with the country split into warring ideological camps that view each other not just as political opponents, but as existential threats.

According to a 2021 study by the American Psychological Association, nearly 70% of Americans reported that they feel the nation is more divided now than it has been at any point in their lifetime (APA, 2021). This growing sense of division fuels cynicism and hopelessness, as people become increasingly convinced that meaningful change is impossible in such a polarized environment.

All Is Not Lost: A Path Forward

Despite the challenges, all is not lost. The American spirit, characterized by resilience and a belief in the power of individuals to effect change, has not disappeared entirely. While hope may be waning, it can be rekindled with concerted efforts at both the personal and societal levels.

Rebuilding Hope at the Individual Level

- **Cultivate Gratitude and Optimism.** Psychological research shows that practicing gratitude and focusing on positive aspects of life can help boost hope and reduce stress. By consciously acknowledging the good things in our lives, we can shift our focus away from negativity and regain a sense of control over our circumstances.

- **Set Achievable Goals.** Hope thrives when people have clear, attainable goals. Even small successes can foster a sense of agency and momentum. Individuals can regain hope by breaking down larger aspirations into smaller, manageable steps and celebrating progress along the way.

- **Engage in Community.** Building connections with others and participating in local communities can help combat feelings of isolation and cynicism. Volunteering, joining community organizations, or simply fostering relationships with neighbors can remind individuals that they are part of something larger than themselves and that collective action can make a difference.

Rebuilding Hope at the Societal Level

- **Promote Political and Social Unity.** Political leaders, media outlets, and influencers must prioritize messages of unity and collaboration over division and fear. Creating spaces for respectful dialogue, compromise, and shared goals can help rebuild trust in institutions and show that progress is possible when people work together.

- **Invest in Education and Innovation.** Societies that invest in education and innovation tend to foster greater hope for the future. By funding programs that promote STEM education, renewable energy research, and job training for emerging industries, the United States can create new opportunities for its citizens and generate a sense of optimism about the future.

- **Address Systemic Inequities.** While it's important to cultivate hope at the individual level, systemic changes are also necessary to restore faith in the future. Policymakers must address economic inequality, racial disparities, and healthcare access to ensure that everyone has a fair chance to succeed. When people feel that the system is working for them, they are more likely to believe in the possibility of a better future.

Rebuilding Hope Through Collective Action

Rebuilding hope requires a multi-faceted approach, one that addresses both the individual and societal levels of despair. It begins with fostering a renewed sense of optimism, setting meaningful and attainable goals, and cultivating a culture of collective action. At its core, hope is a communal project: no one individual can restore it on their own, but by working together, societies can lift each other up. This collective nature of hope is critical—when people believe they are part of a larger effort to create positive change, they are more likely to feel empowered and less isolated.

At the individual level, we can start by engaging in practices that help restore personal hope. Setting small, realistic goals and achieving them, whether in education, work, or personal life, can build momentum and self-confidence. These small successes provide evidence that progress is possible, even in the face of challenges. This mindset can ripple outwards, encouraging others in one's community to pursue their own goals, creating a shared culture of optimism and perseverance.

At the societal level, institutions—schools, media, workplaces, government— can play a pivotal role in fostering hope. Rather than promoting fear, division, and cynicism, we must demand narratives of possibility and resilience. Politicians and public leaders must shift their rhetoric from apocalyptic warnings to messages of solidarity and progress. Media outlets must prioritize stories of innovation, success, and community-building, showing that positive change is possible even amid ongoing challenges.

The Importance of Purpose and Long-Term Vision

One of the reasons hope has declined in recent decades is the growing sense that people no longer feel connected to a larger purpose. Without a clear sense of direction or meaning, it becomes difficult to see how individual actions can contribute to a better future. Historically, movements like the civil rights era or the post-war economic boom gave Americans a sense of shared purpose and optimism. Today, however, many feel disconnected from the broader social fabric, focusing instead on immediate concerns, often driven by short-term thinking.

Rebuilding hope will require reclaiming a long-term vision. Americans must reconnect with the idea that the future is not preordained—it is something we actively shape through our actions, decisions, and collective will. This means embracing big, ambitious projects that inspire people to work together toward common goals. Addressing climate change, rebuilding infrastructure, advancing scientific research, and fostering economic opportunities in underprivileged communities can provide a renewed sense of national purpose and offer tangible proof that a better future is within reach. When people see that their efforts contribute to a larger cause, hope is restored, and pessimism is replaced with possibility.

Embracing Resilience: Learning from History

The challenges facing America today are great, but history has shown time and time again that Americans are resilient. From the Great Depression to the Civil Rights Movement, the country has faced moments of profound crisis and emerged stronger. The very fabric of American identity is woven with stories of perseverance, adaptation, and triumph over adversity.

During the Great Depression, for example, hope seemed all but lost as millions faced unemployment, poverty, and economic collapse. Yet, through collective action, innovative policies like the New Deal, and a shared commitment to rebuilding the nation, Americans managed to lift themselves out of despair. Similarly, the Civil Rights Movement of the 1960s demonstrated the power of hope in overcoming deep-seated systemic injustice. Despite overwhelming odds, activists persisted in their efforts, driven by the hope of a better, more equitable future. Their courage and conviction changed the course of history and laid the foundation for progress in the decades that followed.

These historical moments remind us that hope is not merely a passive feeling—it's an active, driving force that inspires people to take risks, make sacrifices, and work toward a vision of a better world. Just as previous generations fought for their futures, we must find the strength to confront our current challenges with hope and resilience.

Turning Crisis into Opportunity

While today's crises—whether they be political division, economic inequality, environmental degradation, or social injustice—are serious, they also present an opportunity to rebuild the nation's sense of hope. History tells us that moments of profound difficulty can also be moments of profound transformation. It is in times of crisis that societies are most capable of change, adaptation, and innovation.

Consider the potential that lies ahead: the fight against climate change, for instance, presents an unprecedented opportunity to transition to a sustainable, green economy. This effort could create millions of new jobs, foster technological innovation, and re-imagine entire industries. Similarly, addressing social and racial inequalities can lead to a more just and cohesive society, where everyone has an opportunity to thrive. The question is not whether we can rise to these challenges, but whether we will embrace the opportunity they present to rebuild hope in a better future.

Ensuring a Better Future for Our Children and Grandchildren

Perhaps the most important reason to rebuild hope is that the future belongs not to us, but to our children and grandchildren. The decisions we make today will determine the kind of world they inherit. If we allow hopelessness to persist, we risk leaving behind a society that is more fractured, more cynical, and more uncertain than the one we live in now. But if we take action to restore hope—if we invest in education, innovation, equity, and community—then we can leave behind a legacy of resilience, progress, and possibility.

The future may be uncertain, but uncertainty can be a source of power. It means that the future is not fixed—it is something we can shape and mold. If we choose hope, if we choose to believe in our collective capacity to solve problems and make progress, then we can create a world that is not just better for us, but for the generations that follow.

A Call to Action

Rebuilding hope is not a task for any one person or institution—it is a collective effort that requires the participation of all. Individuals, families, communities, schools, workplaces, media, and government all have a role to play. We must each take responsibility for fostering optimism, setting goals, and believing in the power of collective action.

At the community level, efforts to create safe, supportive, and inclusive spaces where people feel connected and empowered will help restore trust and hope. On a national level, political leaders must prioritize solutions that address the root causes of hopelessness—such as inequality, systemic injustice, and economic insecurity—while fostering a culture of empathy, collaboration, and shared purpose.

The challenges are great, but they are not insurmountable. By choosing hope and taking deliberate steps to restore it, we can pave the way for a brighter, more united, and more optimistic America. This is a future worth fighting for—a future where we leave behind a better world for our children and grandchildren, full of possibility, progress, and hope.

FREE SPEECH IN THE CONTEXT OF THE U.S. CONSTITUTION

Elon Musk's "Free Speech Absolutism"

Free speech is a foundational principle in the United States, enshrined in the First Amendment of the U.S. Constitution. The amendment states:

"Congress shall make no law... abridging the freedom of speech, or of the press..."

At its core, the First Amendment protects individuals from government censorship, ensuring the right to express opinions, share ideas, and engage in open discourse without fear of governmental reprisal. It is a cornerstone of American democracy, enabling citizens to criticize the government, advocate for social change, and contribute to the marketplace of ideas.

However, it's important to note that the First Amendment protects free speech from governmental interference - not from private entities or individuals. Private companies, social media platforms, and employers are not obligated by the Constitution to allow all forms of speech on their platforms or in their workplaces. Thus, while the First Amendment protects citizens from censorship by the government, it does not require private companies to provide an unrestricted platform for any and all speech.

Limits on Free Speech in the U.S.

While the First Amendment's protection of free speech is broad, it is not absolute. There are several well-established legal limits to free speech in the U.S., including:

- **Incitement to Violence.** Speech that directly incites imminent violence or lawless action is not protected (as established in Brandenburg v. Ohio in 1969).

- **Defamation.** False statements that damage someone's reputation (libel and slander) are not protected by the First Amendment.

- **Obscenity.** The government can regulate obscene material, though the legal definition of obscenity has evolved over time.

- **True Threats.** Direct threats of violence or harm toward others are not protected speech.

- **Commercial Speech.** Advertising or promotional speech can be regulated if it is misleading or false.

Given these limitations, the concept of "free speech absolutism"—the idea that all speech should be allowed, without any restrictions - would be a radical departure from how free speech is traditionally interpreted in American law.

Elon Musk's "Free Speech Absolutism": A Closer Look

Elon Musk has publicly positioned himself as a "free speech absolutist." He has repeatedly stated his belief that free speech is a fundamental right, and has even claimed that his acquisition of Twitter was driven by a desire to promote free expression and reduce censorship on the platform.

For example, in April 2022, Musk tweeted:

"By 'free speech', I simply mean that which matches the law. I am against censorship that goes far beyond the law."

However, despite this rhetoric, Musk's actions since acquiring Twitter/X have demonstrated that he is not a true free speech absolutist. In practice, Musk has repeatedly restricted speech on the platform, contradicted his own supposed principles, and made decisions that align more closely with corporate or personal interests than with an unwavering commitment to free expression.

Examples of Musk's Inconsistencies on Free Speech

- **Suspension of Journalists' Accounts.** In December 2022, Musk temporarily suspended the accounts of several prominent journalists from The New York Times, CNN, and The Washington Post, among others. These journalists had been covering Musk's handling of Twitter/X, including a controversy involving the tracking of his private jet. Musk claimed that these journalists had violated the platform's rules on "doxxing" by sharing real-time information about his location. While Musk has every right to establish and enforce platform rules, this action was seen by many as hypocritical, given his earlier statements about opposing censorship. Suspending journalists who were reporting on him—without clear evidence of wrongdoing - appears to contradict the values of free speech and open discourse that he had publicly embraced. Musk's reaction was viewed as thin-skinned and inconsistent with the idea of tolerating critical or uncomfortable speech, a key component of true free speech absolutism.

- **Blocking and Banning Users for Criticizing Musk.** In addition to suspending journalists, Musk has personally blocked and banned users who have been critical of him. Several high-profile accounts were suspended or silenced, often with little to no explanation. For example, the account @ ElonJet, which tracked Musk's private jet using publicly available flight data, was banned shortly after Musk acquired the platform, despite Musk previously saying he would allow it to remain online due to his commitment to free speech. This action directly contradicted his stance on allowing all legal speech. These decisions reveal that Musk's commitment to free speech appears to waver when it comes to speech that affects his personal interests or reputation. A true free speech absolutist would allow such speech to exist on the platform, even if it were personally inconvenient or uncomfortable.

- **Content Moderation and Government Influence.** After Musk took over Twitter/X, there were reports that the platform had adjusted its content moderation policies to comply with the demands of authoritarian governments. For example, in June 2022, Twitter agreed to block the accounts of critics of the Indian government at the request of Indian authorities. This included prominent journalists and activists who were speaking out against the government's policies. Allowing governments to dictate who can speak on a platform is the antithesis of free speech absolutism. A true free speech absolutist would resist government pressure and defend the rights of individuals to criticize authority. By capitulating to these requests, Musk showed that he is willing to censor speech when it is in his or his company's best interest.

- **Promotion of Paid Verification and Restriction of Non-Verified Speech.** Musk also introduced a paid verification system on Twitter/X, where users could pay for a blue check-mark, previously a symbol of verified public figures or organizations. While this change was framed as democratizing access to verification, it also led to a two-tiered system where those who could afford to pay for verification were given greater visibility and privileges on the platform. Non-verified users were algorithmically down-ranked or even restricted in some instances. This move undermines the principles of free speech, as it places wealth and status above the equal right to free expression. It restricts access to visibility and amplifies certain voices over others based on financial means, which contradicts the idea that everyone should have an equal platform for speech.

- **Censorship of Specific Topics or Content.** Despite his claim to allow all legal speech, Musk has selectively censored or restricted specific content on Twitter/X. For instance, certain content related to the ongoing conflict between Russia and Ukraine has been subject to removal or suppression, often at the behest of government entities or corporate interests. This selective enforcement shows that Musk's version of free speech is not as absolute as he claims, but rather flexible depending on the context and his own interests.

Why Elon Musk is Dangerous to American Society in the Context of Free Speech

Musk's selective enforcement of speech policies, his willingness to censor critics, and his control over one of the most important public forums for discourse in modern society raise serious concerns about his impact on free speech, democratic debate, and the marketplace of ideas in the U.S.

No. 1 — Centralized Power Over Public Discourse

One of the greatest dangers Musk poses to American society stems from the sheer amount of power he wields over public discourse. Twitter/X is not just another social media platform; it serves as one of the world's largest and most influential public squares. Politicians, journalists, activists, and everyday citizens use the platform to share information, debate ideas, and shape public opinion. The control of this platform by one individual with an erratic, unregulated, and self-serving approach to free speech creates an imbalance of power and undermines the very idea of democratic expression.

In a functional democracy, public discourse should be diverse, decentralized, and resistant to the whims of any one person. However, by owning and controlling Twitter/X, Musk holds enormous sway over who gets to participate in that discourse and what kinds of speech are amplified or silenced. His inconsistent policies and tendencies to ban critics—while claiming to be a defender of free speech—are a clear demonstration of how his control over such an influential platform threatens free expression. By dictating the rules of what is acceptable speech based on his own interests, Musk has the ability to shape and distort public conversations on critical topics like politics, elections, and social issues.

Moreover, Musk's history of promoting conspiracy theories, such as his retweet of a baseless claim regarding the attack on Paul Pelosi, shows that he has the power to fuel dangerous misinformation directly from his personal account. This blending of personal influence and platform control allows Musk to skew the marketplace of ideas in his favor, which is antithetical to the principles of democratic debate.

No. 2 — The Risk of Arbitrary and Inconsistent Censorship

Despite his claims of being a free speech absolutist, Musk's actions show that he is willing to engage in arbitrary censorship, which is perhaps even more dangerous than traditional, transparent moderation. In a system of established content moderation, there are clear rules about what constitutes prohibited speech (such as incitement to violence, hate speech, or harassment). However, under Musk's leadership, Twitter/X's rules have become inconsistent and capricious, with Musk often making decisions that serve his personal or business interests, rather than adhering to a principled stance on free speech.

Musk is willing to silence voices that are critical of him or that he finds personally uncomfortable. This arbitrary enforcement creates a chilling effect, where users are unsure which rules apply and fear they could be censored for reasons that seem capricious or self-serving. Such selective censorship, motivated by personal grievances, is a direct threat to the free exchange of ideas and undermines the credibility of Twitter/X as a space for open dialogue.

No. 3 — Amplification of Misinformation and Conspiracy Theories

Musk's leadership has also contributed to the amplification of misinformation and conspiracy theories on Twitter/X, making him a dangerous figure in the context of free speech. His personal behavior, combined with the platform's changing algorithms under his control, has led to a degradation of the quality of information circulating on the site.

Shortly after taking over Twitter/X, Musk began dismantling the company's content moderation teams and reversing bans on accounts that had previously been suspended for spreading misinformation, hate speech, and conspiracies. One of his first acts as CEO was to reinstate accounts that had been banned for spreading false information about COVID-19 vaccines, election fraud, and other debunked conspiracies. Under his leadership, content moderation rules have been relaxed, leading to a flood of harmful misinformation returning to the platform.

Even more concerning is Musk's own willingness to promote unverified or conspiratorial information. For example, in late 2022, Musk tweeted a conspiracy theory about the attack on Paul Pelosi, suggesting that it might have been a "false flag" operation or something more nefarious than it appeared. Although he eventually deleted the tweet, the damage was already done. Musk's actions gave credibility to a baseless and harmful conspiracy theory, which spread quickly through the platform and beyond.

This behavior is particularly dangerous because Musk is not just an ordinary user—he owns the platform. His tweets have a disproportionate impact on the discourse, and when he promotes misinformation, it lends credence to fringe narratives that can have real-world consequences. The spread of misinformation during the COVID-19 pandemic and the 2020 election demonstrates the dangers of allowing false information to proliferate unchecked. It can lead to public health crises, undermine democratic institutions, and foster social unrest.

No. 4 — Fostering Polarization and Extremism

Under Musk's leadership, Twitter/X has become a more polarized space, fostering extremism rather than encouraging dialogue. One of the most important aspects of free speech is the ability to bridge divides, engage in meaningful dialogue, and create an environment where differing viewpoints can coexist. Yet, by reinstating accounts that had previously been banned for inciting violence or spreading hate, Musk has allowed the platform to become a breeding ground for radical and extremist ideas.

Studies have shown that platforms that do not moderate extremist content tend to become echo chambers for more radical voices. The far-right, in particular, has benefited from Musk's policies, with several white nationalist and conspiracy-driven accounts returning to Twitter/X after being previously banned. For example, former President Donald Trump's account was reinstated, as were the accounts of figures like Alex Jones, known for promoting dangerous and harmful conspiracy theories. By allowing these voices to return to the platform, Musk has created an environment where extremism thrives and where the risk of real-world violence increases.

A study by the Anti-Defamation League (ADL) in 2022 found that there was a 61% increase in the use of hate speech on Twitter in the weeks following Musk's takeover. This kind of amplification of hate speech and extremism has dire consequences for society. The platform's lack of accountability and its role in spreading divisive rhetoric and misinformation can lead to increased political polarization, social unrest, and even violent acts.

No. 5 — Erosion of Public Trust in Social Media as a Forum for Free Speech

Musk's handling of Twitter/X also poses a threat to public trust in social media as a forum for free speech and democratic engagement. Platforms like Twitter were once seen as crucial spaces for grassroots activism, social movements, and the exchange of diverse viewpoints. However, Musk's arbitrary and self-interested approach to managing Twitter/X has eroded trust in the platform as a space for genuine free expression.

For instance, Twitter/X has been accused of bending to the pressures of authoritarian governments, such as in India, where it has complied with demands to block accounts critical of the ruling government. This willingness to capitulate to government pressure undermines the very principles of free speech that Musk claims to champion. If platforms like Twitter/X become spaces where free expression is only tolerated when it aligns with the interests of the powerful—be it Musk himself or authoritarian governments—then the integrity of social media as a democratic tool is fundamentally compromised.

Moreover, the introduction of paid verification systems, which grant privileges to users who can afford to pay for them, further distorts the democratic nature of the platform. By privileging wealth and status over equal access to speech, Musk has transformed Twitter/X into a space where certain voices are amplified based on their financial means rather than the merit of their ideas. This undermines the egalitarian promise of social media, where all users are supposed to have equal access to a public platform for free expression.

Why Musk Is Not a Free Speech Absolutist

Elon Musk's actions demonstrate that his self-professed "free speech absolutism" is more rhetorical than real. While he has made sweeping statements about the importance of free speech, his management of Twitter/X has revealed that he is willing to restrict speech when it suits his personal, business, or political interests. True free speech absolutism would require tolerating all forms of legal speech, regardless of personal impact, reputational risk, or external pressure.

A genuine free speech absolutist would defend speech that is critical of themselves, resist government attempts to limit expression, and avoid creating structures that privilege certain voices over others based on wealth or influence. Musk's selective enforcement of speech policies and willingness to silence critics show that his version of free speech is conditional and inconsistent with the principles of free speech absolutism.

Musk represents a dangerous force because he wields immense power over one of the most important platforms for public discourse, and he has demonstrated a willingness to use that power in ways that serve his personal and business interests rather than the public good. His selective enforcement of speech policies, promotion of misinformation, and willingness to allow extremists back on the platform are all serious threats to the principles of free speech, democratic debate, and social cohesion in American society.

If Musk's approach to free speech is allowed to become the standard for social media platforms, it could further degrade the quality of public discourse, deepen polarization, and make it more difficult for democratic institutions to function. Free speech in a democracy requires more than just the absence of government censorship—it requires a commitment to fairness, accountability, and the responsible management of platforms that shape public discourse. Unfortunately, Musk's actions suggest that he is more interested in wielding the power of free speech for personal gain than in fostering a truly open and democratic marketplace of ideas.

Understanding the Urban-Rural Divide in America

Introduction

The urban-rural divide in America has become one of the most defining—and troubling—features of contemporary society. More than just a difference in geography, this divide represents a widening chasm in political ideology, economic opportunities, access to resources, and cultural values. From the densely populated cities on the coasts to the wide-open expanses of rural heartland, the contrasts between urban and rural life have never been more pronounced. What was once a nuanced distinction has evolved into a full-blown fault line, reshaping national politics, influencing public policy, and driving social tensions to new heights.

Over the past few decades, urban centers have surged ahead economically, becoming hubs for technology, finance, and innovation. In contrast, many rural areas, once anchored by manufacturing, agriculture, and mining, have faced stagnation, job loss, and population decline. The resulting economic disparities have fueled a sense of alienation and resentment in rural communities, while urban residents often struggle to understand the unique challenges faced by their rural counterparts. This divide has manifested in political polarization, with urban areas trending more liberal and progressive, while rural regions have increasingly aligned with conservative movements.

But the urban-rural divide goes beyond politics and economics. It touches every aspect of American life—how people live, work, think, and interact with one another. It is reflected in the schools we attend, the jobs we pursue, the media we consume, and even the ways we understand our national identity. The divide raises critical questions: How can a nation so diverse in its geography and experiences find common ground? What can be done to bridge the gap and restore social cohesion?

Here, we explore the origins and evolution of the urban-rural divide, delve into its economic, political, and cultural dimensions, and examine its real-world impacts on American society. By understanding the roots of this growing separation, we can begin to consider solutions that address the concerns of both rural and urban America—ultimately working toward a more unified, inclusive future.

No. 1 — Historical Context of the Urban-Rural Divide

To fully understand the urban-rural divide in contemporary America, it's crucial to explore its historical roots. While differences between urban and rural areas have always existed to some degree, the current divide is the product of decades of economic, social, and political shifts that have transformed the American landscape.

The Agricultural Foundation of Early America

In the early years of the United States, the country was predominantly rural. Agriculture was the primary economic driver, and the vast majority of the population lived in small towns or rural areas. The political and economic elite were often landowners, and the rhythms of rural life were deeply intertwined with the nation's identity. Thomas Jefferson himself envisioned the ideal American citizen as a yeoman farmer—self-sufficient, independent, and virtuous.

During this period, the urban-rural divide was less pronounced. While cities like New York, Philadelphia, and Boston were growing as centers of trade and commerce, they were still relatively small, and rural America was seen as the backbone of the country. This balance, however, would soon begin to shift with industrialization.

The Rise of Industrialization and Urbanization

The Industrial Revolution, beginning in the late 18th century and accelerating throughout the 19th century, marked a significant turning point in the relationship between urban and rural America. As industries grew in cities, factories, railroads, and ports began to concentrate economic power in urban centers. Jobs in manufacturing, finance, and trade drew millions from rural areas to the cities, particularly during the massive wave of immigration in the late 19th and early 20th centuries.

Urban areas rapidly industrialized, transforming the economy and shifting the political and social center of gravity toward cities. Meanwhile, rural areas continued to rely on agriculture and natural resources, but they increasingly found themselves left behind as cities thrived on new industries. Urbanization during this period also brought about profound social changes, with cities becoming the loci of cultural diversity, innovation, and progressive politics. By contrast, rural areas tended to remain more socially conservative, rooted in traditional values and community structures.

The Post-World War II Era: Suburbanization and Economic Divergence

The period following World War II brought another major shift in the urban-rural dynamic. The rise of the suburbs, driven by the GI Bill, affordable housing, and the expansion of the highway system, saw millions of Americans move out of urban centers into newly developed suburban communities. While these suburban areas shared some of the characteristics of both urban and rural life, they were largely considered part of the growing urban sprawl that continued to reshape the economy and culture.

At the same time, rural areas began to experience economic decline. Advances in agricultural technology reduced the need for labor, and many manufacturing jobs—once a staple of rural economies—began to disappear as factories moved to cheaper locations overseas. The decline of coal, mining, and other extractive industries in rural areas led to high unemployment and poverty in many regions, especially in the American South and Midwest.

This economic divergence between urban and rural areas was further exacerbated by the rise of the knowledge economy in the late 20th and early 21st centuries. Cities became hubs for finance, technology, healthcare, and higher education, industries that favored a highly educated workforce. Rural areas, by contrast, struggled to adapt, with fewer opportunities for employment in these emerging sectors and lower access to educational and healthcare resources.

The Political Realignment of the Late 20th Century

As these economic shifts unfolded, they were accompanied by a political realignment that cemented the urban-rural divide we see today. Beginning in the 1960s, the Democratic Party, traditionally the party of the working class and rural America, began to align more closely with urban interests, particularly on issues such as civil rights, environmental protection, and labor unions. Meanwhile, the Republican Party increasingly courted rural voters by appealing to their cultural conservatism, religious values, and skepticism of government regulation.

This political realignment was solidified during the Reagan era in the 1980s, when rural America overwhelmingly supported conservative policies that emphasized deregulation, free-market economics, and traditional values. The urban-rural divide was now not only an economic and cultural divide but a deeply political one as well.

Globalization and the Modern Divide

In the late 20th and early 21st centuries, the forces of globalization and technological advancement have further widened the urban-rural divide. Cities have continued to benefit from global trade, innovation in technology, and an influx of immigrants, which have fueled economic growth and cultural vibrancy. Meanwhile, many rural areas, particularly in the Midwest and the South, have faced the hollowing out of industries, population loss, and economic stagnation.

The 2008 financial crisis exacerbated this divide, as urban areas—particularly those on the coasts—recovered more quickly, thanks in part to their diversified economies and access to capital. Rural areas, however, were slower to rebound, with many regions still struggling to regain pre-recession employment levels.

The historical context of the urban-rural divide shows that the current chasm between these two Americas is not new—it is the culmination of centuries of economic, social, and political changes. From the Industrial Revolution to the rise of the knowledge economy, urban and rural areas have diverged in their economic fortunes, cultural values, and political loyalties. Understanding this historical backdrop is critical to addressing the challenges of the present and bridging the divide that threatens the unity of American society.

No. 2 — Economic Differences: Decline of Industry vs. Growth of the Knowledge Economy

The urban-rural divide in America is perhaps most visibly expressed through economic disparities. Over the past several decades, the economic trajectories of urban and rural areas have diverged sharply, with cities reaping the benefits of globalization and the rise of the knowledge economy, while many rural areas have faced stagnation, job loss, and population decline. These economic differences not only shape the material conditions of urban and rural residents but also influence their political views, social mobility, and overall sense of opportunity.

The Decline of Traditional Industries in Rural America

Historically, rural America thrived on agriculture, mining, logging, and manufacturing, industries that formed the backbone of local economies and supported middle-class livelihoods. These industries provided stable, well-paying jobs for generations, creating strong communities where families could count on long-term employment in fields that didn't require advanced degrees. However, over the past several decades, many of these industries have declined dramatically, driven by several key factors:

- **Automation.** Advances in technology have significantly reduced the need for labor in industries such as agriculture and manufacturing. For example, modern farming equipment, combined with agribusiness consolidation, means fewer workers are needed to manage much larger farms. Similarly, manufacturing plants that once employed thousands of workers now require far fewer people due to automated processes and robotics. According to a report from the Brookings Institution, between 1980 and 2016, the number of manufacturing jobs in the U.S. dropped from 18.9 million to 12.2 million, with rural areas being hit hardest by these losses (Brookings, 2017).

- **Globalization.** The rise of globalization in the late 20th and early 21st centuries has seen many manufacturing jobs move overseas to countries with cheaper labor costs. The economic restructuring caused by trade agreements like NAFTA (the North American Free Trade Agreement) led to job outsourcing in industries like textiles, auto manufacturing, and electronics. Many rural areas that were once manufacturing hubs have been left without alternative industries to sustain their economies, contributing to high levels of unemployment and underemployment.

- **Decline of Resource-Based Industries.** Rural areas that once relied on natural resource extraction, such as coal mining, have also seen a sharp decline due to both market forces and environmental policies. The U.S. has shifted toward cleaner energy sources, and competition from cheaper natural gas has further diminished the coal industry. In states like West Virginia and Kentucky, entire communities have been devastated by the loss of coal jobs, leading to population decline and a shrinking tax base that makes it harder to support public services like schools and hospitals.

The combination of these factors has led to widespread economic distress in rural America. Many small towns and rural communities have experienced a steady exodus of young people in search of better opportunities in urban centers, leaving behind aging populations with fewer economic prospects. This outmigration further exacerbates the economic challenges faced by these areas, as businesses close, schools consolidate, and healthcare services become increasingly scarce.

The Rise of the Knowledge Economy in Urban Areas

In stark contrast to the struggles faced by rural America, urban centers have seen explosive growth driven by the rise of the knowledge economy. This new economic model, based on technology, finance, healthcare, education, and professional services, has transformed cities into hubs of innovation and prosperity. The concentration of high-tech industries in urban areas has created a dynamic economy that rewards education, creativity, and specialized skills.

- **Technology and Innovation.** Cities like San Francisco, New York, Boston, and Austin have become global centers for tech startups and innovation. The growth of industries like software development, biotechnology, and artificial intelligence has created a wealth of high-paying jobs in these cities, attracting young, educated workers from across the country. In 2020, the tech sector alone accounted for 10.5% of the U.S. GDP, much of which is concentrated in urban areas (CompTIA, 2021). This has contributed to the rising affluence of these cities, driving demand for real estate, luxury goods, and services.

- **Finance and Services.** The financialization of the economy has further concentrated wealth in urban centers. Cities like New York, Chicago, and Los Angeles are home to the country's largest financial institutions, law firms, and consulting companies, which have seen tremendous growth over the past several decades. These industries are heavily reliant on highly educated workers, leading to the proliferation of jobs that require advanced degrees and specialized skills. According to the Bureau of Labor Statistics, the top-paying jobs in the U.S. are increasingly in fields like healthcare, technology, and professional services—all of which are concentrated in urban areas.

- **Urban Migration.** The economic opportunities offered by cities have led to a significant migration of young people from rural areas to urban centers. This "brain drain" has further accelerated the economic divide between rural and urban America. Cities attract talent not only because of job opportunities but also because of access to amenities such as cultural institutions, public transportation, and higher education. This influx of young, educated workers has fueled the growth of the urban middle class and contributed to gentrification in many city neighborhoods.

Wage Gaps and Cost of Living

One of the most striking differences between urban and rural economies is the disparity in wages. According to data from the U.S. Bureau of Economic Analysis, the average wage in metropolitan areas is significantly higher than in non-metropolitan (rural) areas. For example, in 2021, the average wage in urban areas was $71,000, compared to just $48,000 in rural areas (U.S. Bureau of Economic Analysis, 2021). This wage gap reflects the concentration of high-paying jobs in cities, particularly in industries like technology, finance, and healthcare.

However, it's important to note that the higher wages in urban areas are often offset by the significantly higher cost of living. Housing prices in cities have skyrocketed in recent years, making homeownership unaffordable for many urban residents. According to the National Association of Realtors, the median home price in the U.S. in 2022 was $375,000, but in cities like San Francisco and New York, median home prices can exceed $1 million. Rent prices in cities have also surged, with many working-class families being priced out of urban centers and forced to move to suburban or exurban areas.

Rural areas, by contrast, offer a much lower cost of living, with affordable housing and fewer expenses for daily necessities. However, the lack of economic opportunities in rural areas often means that residents must contend with lower wages and limited upward mobility, making it difficult for families to build wealth or escape poverty.

Economic Mobility and Inequality

The economic divide between urban and rural areas also extends to social mobility and economic inequality. Urban areas, particularly those with strong job markets and access to education, offer greater opportunities for upward mobility. A study by economist Raj Chetty found that cities like San Francisco and Boston provide some of the highest rates of economic mobility, where children born into low-income families have a greater chance of moving up the income ladder (Chetty et al., 2018).

In contrast, rural areas often struggle with low social mobility. The lack of access to higher education, healthcare, and good-paying jobs means that many rural residents are trapped in cycles of poverty. This growing inequality between urban and rural areas has profound social and political implications, contributing to a sense of disenfranchisement and resentment in rural communities.

The economic differences between urban and rural America are stark and growing. While urban areas have thrived in the knowledge economy, rural areas have faced the decline of traditional industries and struggled to adapt to the changing economic landscape. This divide has far-reaching consequences for social mobility, political polarization, and the overall health of the nation's economy. Addressing these economic disparities will require targeted policies that address the unique challenges faced by both urban and rural communities, from job creation and education to infrastructure and healthcare. Understanding the roots of these economic differences is key to bridging the urban-rural divide and fostering a more equitable future for all Americans.

No. 3 — Political Polarization: Urban Liberalism vs. Rural Conservatism

The urban-rural divide in America is not just an economic or cultural phenomenon—it is also deeply political. Over the past few decades, political polarization has intensified, with cities becoming increasingly liberal and rural areas leaning more conservative. This divide has come to define much of American politics, influencing elections, policy decisions, and the overall tenor of national discourse. The sharp contrast in political beliefs between urban and rural areas reflects broader differences in values, priorities, and lived experiences, but it also exacerbates the sense of division that permeates American society today.

The Political Realignment of the 20th Century

Historically, the Democratic Party was once the party of rural America, particularly in the South, where farmers, laborers, and working-class whites formed the backbone of the party's electoral base. Conversely, cities were home to a mix of political affiliations, though they began to trend more progressive as the 20th century wore on, largely due to waves of immigration, union movements, and the rise of social welfare programs.

However, beginning in the 1960s and accelerating through the Reagan era, a political realignment took place. The Democratic Party increasingly aligned itself with progressive social issues, civil rights, and environmental policies that resonated with urban voters but alienated much of rural America. Rural voters, feeling that their interests were no longer being represented by the Democratic Party, shifted toward the Republican Party, particularly as Republicans began to emphasize free-market economics, cultural conservatism, and skepticism toward government regulation—values that aligned more closely with rural America's social and economic worldview.

This realignment became even more pronounced in the 1990s and 2000s, as the Republican Party's platform focused heavily on issues like gun rights, religion, and individual liberty—core concerns for many rural voters—while the Democratic Party continued to champion social justice, environmentalism, and multiculturalism, causes that resonated with urban voters. This growing divide set the stage for the political polarization that dominates today's landscape.

Urban Liberalism

Urban areas have become bastions of liberalism, with the majority of city dwellers supporting progressive policies on a wide range of social and economic issues. Cities tend to have more diverse populations, with higher concentrations of immigrants, people of color, LGBTQ+ individuals, and young professionals. This diversity often leads to greater support for policies that promote inclusion, civil rights, and government intervention in the economy.

- **Social Issues.** Urban voters are far more likely to support liberal positions on social issues like LGBTQ+ rights, abortion access, immigration, and racial justice. For example, a Pew Research Center study in 2020 found that 77% of urban Americans believe that same-sex marriage should be legal, compared to only 48% of rural Americans (Pew Research Center, 2020). Urban residents tend to prioritize policies that promote equality, diversity, and social justice, seeing these issues as essential to creating a fair and inclusive society.

- **Economic Policies.** On economic matters, urban voters generally favor government intervention to address inequality, provide social safety nets, and regulate industries. Cities, where income inequality is often starkly visible, tend to support progressive taxation, healthcare reform (such as Medicare for All), and policies aimed at reducing the cost of housing and education. For example, cities like New York and San Francisco have passed progressive housing policies to combat homelessness and rising rents, reflecting the priorities of urban voters who are concerned with economic justice.

- **Environmentalism.** Urban areas are also strongholds for environmental activism. With pollution and climate change directly affecting urban residents—whether through poor air quality, flooding, or heatwaves—there is strong support for policies aimed at reducing carbon emissions, transitioning to renewable energy, and protecting public lands. A 2021 Pew Research survey found that 76% of urban residents believe that addressing climate change should be a top priority for the government, compared to just 45% of rural residents (Pew Research Center, 2021).

Rural Conservatism

In contrast to cities, rural America has become a political stronghold for conservatism, particularly within the Republican Party. Rural voters tend to favor limited government, individual responsibility, and traditional values. The political priorities of rural Americans often reflect their way of life—focused on agriculture, small business, and self-reliance. Over the years, rural voters have increasingly aligned themselves with conservative positions on social, economic, and environmental issues.

- **Cultural Values.** Rural voters are generally more socially conservative, with stronger support for traditional family structures, religious freedom, and gun rights. Religion plays a key role in rural communities, with church attendance higher in rural areas compared to urban centers. This cultural conservatism translates into political support for policies that uphold religious values, oppose abortion, and protect the Second Amendment. For example, rural voters overwhelmingly support gun rights, with 73% of rural Americans opposing stricter gun laws, compared to 42% of urban Americans (Pew Research Center, 2017).

- **Economic Policies.** Rural voters are more likely to prioritize free-market economics and reduced government intervention. Many rural residents, particularly those working in agriculture or small businesses, see government regulations as burdensome and harmful to their livelihoods. They tend to oppose higher taxes, support deregulation, and advocate for personal responsibility over government welfare programs. Additionally, rural voters are often skeptical of policies that favor environmental regulations, which they see as threatening industries like farming, mining, and oil extraction that are crucial to their economies.

- **Distrust of Government and Urban Elites.** There is also a growing sentiment in rural America that urban elites, bureaucrats, and politicians in Washington, D.C., do not understand or care about the issues facing rural communities. This has led to a deepening sense of alienation and resentment, which has been skillfully leveraged by conservative politicians. Candidates like Donald Trump have capitalized on this sentiment, framing themselves as champions of "forgotten" rural Americans who feel left behind by globalization, cultural change, and what they see as the liberal agenda dominating urban areas. Trump's "America First" message resonated deeply with rural voters, particularly in the Midwest and South, who feel that urban elites benefit from policies that harm rural America.

The Consequences of Political Polarization

The urban-rural divide has contributed to some of the most profound political polarization in American history. This polarization is not just about differing opinions on policy; it is often characterized by deep distrust and hostility between urban and rural voters, each viewing the other as a threat to the American way of life. According to a 2020 survey by the Pew Research Center, 63% of Republicans (who tend to live in rural areas) and 56% of Democrats (who tend to live in urban areas) say that members of the opposing party are "immoral" (Pew Research Center, 2020). This moralization of politics has made compromise and dialogue increasingly difficult.

This polarization is reflected in voting patterns, with rural and urban voters supporting vastly different candidates and parties. In the 2020 presidential election, rural areas overwhelmingly supported Donald Trump, while urban areas voted decisively for Joe Biden. This stark contrast in voting behavior has led to electoral maps where the vast majority of the U.S. landmass is red (Republican) but the population centers in cities are blue (Democratic). This imbalance creates a sense of political disenfranchisement in both urban and rural voters, as each side feels its interests are being neglected by the other.

The political divide has far-reaching consequences for policy-making and governance. Gridlock in Congress, where representatives from rural and urban districts often have diametrically opposed priorities, has made it difficult to pass bipartisan legislation on key issues like healthcare, climate change, infrastructure, and immigration. The divide also influences state politics, with rural states often pushing for more conservative policies that may clash with the more progressive policies of urban areas within the same state.

The political polarization between urban and rural America is not just a matter of differing opinions—it reflects deeper economic, cultural, and social divides that have been growing for decades. Urban areas, with their liberal, progressive tendencies, and rural areas, with their conservative, traditional values, are increasingly living in separate political realities. This polarization threatens to undermine national unity, making it difficult to address shared challenges and find common ground. Moving forward, efforts to bridge the political divide will require recognizing the unique concerns and values of both urban and rural voters, and fostering dialogue that transcends partisan divides. If left unchecked, this polarization could continue to erode the functioning of American democracy.

No. 4 — Social and Cultural Differences: Values, Identity, and Media Consumption

The urban-rural divide in America is not just a political or economic phenomenon—it is deeply rooted in cultural and social differences that shape the everyday lives of Americans. The ways people live, the values they hold, the media they consume, and the identities they form all contribute to a widening gap between urban and rural communities. These social and cultural divisions create a profound sense of "otherness," where each side views the other through a lens of misunderstanding, distrust, and, at times, outright hostility. By exploring these differences in depth, we can better understand how the urban-rural divide shapes American society, further exacerbating the challenges of political polarization and economic disparity.

Cultural Values: Community, Tradition, and Modernity

One of the most striking differences between urban and rural America is the divergence in cultural values. These differences are often shaped by factors such as geography, religion, community structure, and levels of exposure to diversity.

Traditionalism vs. Progressivism

- Rural areas tend to be more traditional in their cultural values, often prioritizing family, community, religion, and patriotism. These values reflect a deep sense of continuity with the past, where maintaining long-standing traditions is seen as essential to preserving the fabric of society. Religion, especially Christianity, plays a significant role in shaping the social norms and cultural practices of many rural communities. According to a 2021 Pew Research study, 63% of rural Americans say that religion is very important to their lives, compared to only 32% of urban Americans (Pew Research Center, 2021). This strong religious foundation often leads to more conservative views on issues such as marriage, gender roles, and abortion.

- In contrast, urban areas tend to embrace more progressive values. Cities are typically more diverse in terms of ethnicity, religion, and lifestyle, fostering an environment where inclusivity, equality, and social justice are prioritized. Urban residents are more likely to support LGBTQ+ rights, gender equality, and immigration reform, and they tend to be more open to rapid social change. The same Pew Research study found that urban residents are more likely to describe their views as "liberal" or "progressive" and express support for secularism over religion in public life. For many urban dwellers, diversity and multiculturalism are seen as strengths that enrich society, while traditional rural values are sometimes perceived as outdated or intolerant.

Individualism vs. Communalism

- Rural America places a high value on community and personal relationships. Smaller, close-knit towns tend to emphasize interpersonal connections, with individuals more likely to know their neighbors and be involved in local institutions such as churches, schools, or volunteer organizations. This creates a strong sense of belonging and loyalty to the community, where individuals see themselves as part of a larger whole.

- Urban areas, by contrast, tend to emphasize individualism. In larger cities, people are more anonymous, and personal success is often prioritized over communal responsibility. With a focus on career advancement, innovation, and personal freedom, urban residents often lead more transient lives, moving from one city to another in pursuit of opportunities. While cities provide access to a wider range of social and cultural experiences, the fast-paced, competitive nature of urban life can also lead to a sense of isolation or disconnection from community.

Identity: Who We Are and How We See Ourselves

The urban-rural divide is also reflected in the way Americans form their identities—how they see themselves and how they perceive others. These identity differences can create a sense of tribalism, where people strongly identify with those who share their lifestyle, values, and experiences, while viewing those from different backgrounds with suspicion or animosity.

Urban Identity

- Urban residents often define their identity through diversity, progress, and education. Many urban dwellers see themselves as cosmopolitan, open-minded, and forward-thinking. Their identity is often shaped by their proximity to cultural institutions, universities, and businesses that are on the cutting edge of technology and social change. Urbanites tend to value tolerance and multiculturalism, celebrating the variety of experiences and perspectives that cities offer. This is particularly true in cities like New York, San Francisco, and Los Angeles, which are global hubs for art, fashion, finance, and technology.

- In cities, higher levels of education are common, and academic credentials are often a key part of one's identity. According to the U.S. Census Bureau, 44% of urban adults have a bachelor's degree or higher, compared to just 24% of rural adults (U.S. Census Bureau, 2021). This difference in educational attainment contributes to a sense of intellectual superiority that urban residents may feel toward rural America, leading to stereotypes that rural people are less educated or less informed.

Rural Identity

- In contrast, rural identity is often shaped by a strong sense of place, self-reliance, and connection to the land. Rural residents frequently take pride in their hard work, family ties, and the stability of their communities. For many, rural life represents a slower, more authentic way of living, one that is connected to the natural world and less dominated by the hectic pace of modern urban life.

- Patriotism and a sense of loyalty to the nation are also key components of rural identity. In rural areas, there is often a stronger sense of national pride and a belief in traditional American values, such as freedom, hard work, and individual responsibility. According to a Gallup poll in 2020, 76% of rural residents consider themselves "extremely proud" to be American, compared to 54% of urban residents (Gallup, 2020). This sense of patriotism is closely linked to rural America's support for the military, law enforcement, and the Second Amendment.

- However, rural identity is also shaped by a sense of marginalization. Many rural Americans feel left behind by the political, economic, and cultural elites of urban areas, leading to a feeling of resentment or alienation. They see urbanites as disconnected from the realities of rural life, and as imposing their values on the rest of the country without understanding the unique challenges that rural communities face. This resentment is often reinforced by media portrayals of rural people as "backward" or "uneducated," which further deepens the divide.

Media Consumption: Echo Chambers and the Reinforcement of Biases

One of the most significant drivers of the urban-rural divide is the way Americans consume media. In an era of media fragmentation, people are increasingly able to curate their news sources to reflect their political, cultural, and social beliefs, creating echo chambers that reinforce existing biases and fuel polarization.

Urban Media Consumption

- Urban residents tend to consume media from a wide variety of sources, but they are more likely to follow mainstream or progressive outlets like The New York Times, NPR, CNN, and The Washington Post. These outlets cater to an audience that tends to prioritize issues such as climate change, social justice, and international affairs. Urbanites are more likely to follow global news and political commentary from journalists and intellectuals who align with their progressive worldview.

- Social media platforms like Twitter, Instagram, and Reddit also play a significant role in shaping urban discourse. Urban residents often engage with influencers, thought leaders, and advocacy organizations that champion progressive causes. This media landscape creates a feedback loop where urban residents' beliefs and opinions are constantly reinforced by content that aligns with their worldview.

Rural Media Consumption

- In rural areas, media consumption tends to lean more conservative, with outlets like Fox News, Newsmax, and OANN being the primary sources of information. These networks often frame news in a way that resonates with the concerns and values of rural viewers, emphasizing issues such as immigration, national security, and traditional American values. Rural Americans are also more likely to listen to talk radio, where conservative hosts like Rush Limbaugh (prior to his passing) and Sean Hannity dominated the airwaves.

- Social media also plays a role in rural media consumption, but platforms like Facebook tend to be more popular than Twitter. Many rural residents use Facebook groups to connect with their communities and share local news, but these spaces can also become echo chambers for misinformation or conspiracy theories. During the COVID-19 pandemic, for example, misinformation about vaccines and government mandates spread rapidly in rural communities via social media, reinforcing skepticism and distrust of public health measures.

Impact of Fragmented Media

- The fragmented media landscape exacerbates the urban-rural divide by creating two distinct realities. Urban and rural residents often get their news from completely different sources, with little overlap in the issues that are covered or the perspectives that are presented. This contributes to a sense of polarization, where each side feels that the other is living in a completely different world. The lack of shared media experiences makes it more difficult for Americans to find common ground or even agree on basic facts.

- Misinformation and disinformation further deepen the divide. In rural areas, where access to broadband internet can be limited and local news outlets are dwindling, people are more vulnerable to the spread of false information on social media. Similarly, in urban areas, people are often exposed to information that reinforces their progressive values, creating a sense of moral superiority that alienates rural Americans.

The social and cultural differences between urban and rural America run deep, shaping not only how people vote and think but also how they see themselves and each other. From divergent values and identities to fragmented media consumption, the urban-rural divide reflects a growing sense of disconnect between two fundamentally different ways of life. This divide contributes to misunderstandings, stereotypes, and a lack of empathy, making it increasingly difficult for Americans to bridge the gap. To address this divide, it is crucial to foster greater dialogue and understanding, create shared media experiences, and recognize the common challenges facing both urban and rural communities.

No. 5 — Access to Resources: Healthcare, Education, and Infrastructure

One of the most tangible and impactful aspects of the urban-rural divide in America is the stark difference in access to critical resources such as healthcare, education, and infrastructure. These disparities not only exacerbate the economic and social challenges faced by rural communities but also deepen feelings of marginalization and resentment, fueling political polarization and social discord. While urban areas benefit from concentrated investment and a range of readily available services, rural communities often struggle with limited resources, fewer opportunities, and a lack of access to the modern infrastructure that is essential in today's globalized, technology-driven world.

Healthcare Disparities: A Crisis in Rural America

Access to quality healthcare is one of the most pressing issues facing rural America. The gap between urban and rural areas in terms of healthcare availability, affordability, and outcomes is wide and growing, contributing to significant public health challenges in rural regions.

Hospital Closures and Healthcare Access

- Rural America has been grappling with the closure of hospitals at an alarming rate. Since 2010, over 140 rural hospitals have closed in the United States, and many more are at risk of shutting down due to financial difficulties (North Carolina Rural Health Research Program, 2021). These closures leave residents without nearby emergency care, forcing them to travel long distances to receive treatment. In emergency situations, such as heart attacks or accidents, this delay in care can be life-threatening.

- Even where hospitals remain open, the availability of specialized care is limited. Many rural hospitals lack the resources to provide comprehensive care for conditions like cancer, diabetes, or mental health disorders, forcing patients to travel to urban centers for treatment. This is particularly challenging for low-income rural residents who may not have reliable transportation or the financial means to access care outside their community.

Shortage of Healthcare Professionals

- Rural areas face a significant shortage of healthcare professionals, including doctors, nurses, and specialists. According to the National Rural Health Association, there are only 30 physicians per 100,000 people in rural areas, compared to 53 physicians per 100,000 people in urban areas (National Rural Health Association, 2020). This shortage is exacerbated by the fact that fewer medical professionals are choosing to work in rural areas, where salaries are often lower, and the challenges of providing care are greater.

- The lack of healthcare providers also contributes to delays in care and poorer health outcomes. For example, rural residents are more likely to delay medical appointments or forgo preventive care due to the difficulty of finding a healthcare provider or the costs associated with long travel distances. As a result, rural Americans are more likely to suffer from chronic conditions like heart disease, diabetes, and obesity at higher rates than their urban counterparts.

Health Outcomes

- The combination of hospital closures, limited access to healthcare providers, and socioeconomic factors has led to worse health outcomes in rural areas. Rural Americans are more likely to die from preventable conditions such as chronic respiratory diseases, heart disease, stroke, and suicide. According to the Centers for Disease Control and Prevention (CDC), rural residents have a 23% higher mortality rate than urban residents (CDC, 2020).

- Mental health care is particularly inadequate in rural America. Rural areas face high rates of opioid addiction, alcoholism, and suicide, yet mental health services are severely lacking. Many rural counties have no licensed mental health professionals, making it difficult for residents to access treatment. The opioid epidemic has hit rural communities especially hard, with rural overdose death rates surpassing those in urban areas. The isolation, economic stress, and lack of healthcare infrastructure have all contributed to this crisis.

Educational Inequality: A Barrier to Opportunity

Access to quality education is another critical area where rural communities face significant disadvantages compared to their urban counterparts. The differences in funding, resources, and opportunities between rural and urban schools contribute to long-term disparities in educational attainment and economic mobility.

Underfunded Schools

- Rural schools are often underfunded compared to urban and suburban schools, leading to a lack of resources, outdated technology, and fewer extracurricular opportunities. Because school funding is largely tied to local property taxes, rural areas with lower property values have smaller tax bases, resulting in less funding per student. This underfunding can lead to larger class sizes, lower teacher salaries, and reduced access to specialized programs such as advanced placement (AP) courses, arts education, and vocational training.

- A report by the National Center for Education Statistics found that rural schools spend significantly less per student than urban schools, contributing to educational inequality. This funding gap makes it difficult for rural schools to attract and retain high-quality teachers, invest in modern facilities, or provide students with the tools they need to succeed in an increasingly technology-driven world.

Teacher Shortages

- Rural schools often struggle to recruit and retain qualified teachers. The lower pay, limited resources, and isolation of rural areas make it difficult to attract educators, particularly in specialized subjects like science, technology, engineering, and mathematics (STEM). The teacher shortage in rural areas disproportionately affects students' access to rigorous coursework and extracurricular activities, further limiting their opportunities for academic success and college readiness.

- According to the U.S. Department of Education, rural schools have a higher rate of unfilled teaching positions, and many rural districts are forced to rely on long-term substitutes or teachers who are teaching subjects outside their areas of expertise (U.S. Department of Education, 2021). This lack of consistency and specialization can hinder student learning and academic achievement.

Limited Access to Higher Education

- Rural students face significant barriers when it comes to accessing higher education. Many rural communities are located far from colleges and universities, making it more difficult for students to pursue post-secondary education without leaving home. Additionally, rural students are less likely to receive guidance on the college admission's process or financial aid, and they are more likely to face financial obstacles that prevent them from attending college.

- As a result, rural Americans are less likely to have a college degree compared to their urban counterparts. According to the U.S. Department of Agriculture, only 20% of rural adults hold a bachelor's degree or higher, compared to 34% of urban adults (U.S. Department of Agriculture, 2021). This educational gap has long-term consequences for economic mobility, as individuals without a college degree are more likely to earn lower wages and have fewer career opportunities.

Infrastructure Gaps: Roads, Broadband, and Public Services

Infrastructure is another area where the urban-rural divide is acutely felt. While cities benefit from robust transportation networks, modern utilities, and access to cutting-edge technology, rural areas are often left with outdated infrastructure that limits their economic development and quality of life.

Transportation and Roads

- Rural areas frequently struggle with poorly maintained roads, bridges, and transportation infrastructure. Many rural communities lack reliable public transportation, making it difficult for residents to access jobs, healthcare, and education. The decline of industries like coal and manufacturing, coupled with population loss, has left many rural areas without the tax revenue necessary to maintain or improve infrastructure.

- According to the American Society of Civil Engineers, rural roads and bridges are in worse condition than those in urban areas, with 15% of rural roads classified as in "poor" condition and 12% of rural bridges deemed structurally deficient (ASCE, 2021). This infrastructure deficit not only creates safety hazards but also limits economic development, as businesses are less likely to invest in areas without adequate transportation networks.

Broadband Internet Access

- One of the most significant infrastructure disparities between urban and rural areas is access to high-speed broadband internet. In today's digital economy, reliable internet access is essential for everything from education and healthcare to business and communication. However, millions of rural Americans still lack access to broadband, creating a "digital divide" that limits economic opportunities and social mobility.

- According to the Federal Communications Commission (FCC), approximately 22% of rural Americans lack access to broadband, compared to only 1.5% of urban Americans (FCC, 2021). This gap disproportionately affects rural students, who may not have access to online learning resources, and rural businesses, which may struggle to compete in an increasingly digital marketplace. Efforts to expand rural broadband access have been slow and underfunded, leaving many rural communities disconnected from the global economy.

Public Services

- Public services, such as emergency response, social services, and utilities, are often less available or reliable in rural areas compared to urban centers. Rural communities may have fewer police officers, firefighters, and emergency medical technicians (EMTs), leading to longer response times in emergencies. Similarly, services like garbage collection, water treatment, and public transportation are often limited or nonexistent in rural areas.

- This lack of infrastructure and services contributes to a lower quality of life for many rural residents, who must contend with fewer public amenities and greater distances between essential services. As a result, rural communities often feel neglected by state and federal governments, further reinforcing the sense of isolation and marginalization that characterizes the rural experience.

The disparities in access to healthcare, education, and infrastructure between urban and rural America highlight the profound challenges facing rural communities. The lack of adequate resources not only contributes to poorer health and educational outcomes but also limits economic development and social mobility. Addressing these gaps will require targeted investment in rural infrastructure, healthcare, and education to ensure that all Americans, regardless of where they live, have the opportunity to thrive. By narrowing the resource divide, we can begin to bridge the broader urban-rural divide and create a more equitable society for future generations.

No. 6 — The Role of Technology and Media in Shaping the Divide

The role of technology and media in shaping the urban-rural divide in America is both profound and far-reaching. In today's digital age, where information spreads faster and more widely than ever before, media consumption habits, the spread of misinformation, and access to technology have become major forces driving division between urban and rural communities. The fragmentation of the media landscape and the growing "digital divide" between areas with and without reliable access to high-speed internet further deepen the cultural, social, and political differences between urban and rural America. Understanding how technology and media contribute to this divide is essential to bridging the gap and fostering more informed, unified communities.

Fragmented Media Consumption and the Echo Chamber Effect

In the past, Americans across the country often turned to a few trusted news sources, such as national television networks or major newspapers, for their information. This shared media experience helped create a sense of collective understanding of national issues, even if interpretations of those issues differed. However, the rapid proliferation of digital media and the rise of social media platforms over the past two decades have transformed the way Americans consume news and information, leading to greater fragmentation.

The Rise of Partisan News Outlets

- As media consumption has become more specialized, many Americans have gravitated toward news outlets that reflect their political and ideological views. Urban and rural residents, in particular, tend to consume different types of media that reinforce their distinct worldviews. For example, urban Americans are more likely to consume media from progressive-leaning sources such as The New York Times, CNN, MSNBC, and NPR, while rural Americans are more likely to consume conservative-leaning sources such as Fox News, Newsmax, and OANN.

- This partisan divide in media consumption has contributed to the rise of "echo chambers," where individuals are primarily exposed to information that reinforces their existing beliefs. According to a 2020 Pew Research Center study, 70% of conservative Republicans said their primary news source was Fox News, while 65% of liberal Democrats said they relied on outlets like CNN and MSNBC (Pew Research Center, 2020). This selective exposure to partisan media reduces the likelihood of encountering opposing viewpoints and fosters polarization.

Social Media Algorithms and the Amplification of Division

- Social media platforms such as Facebook, Twitter, and YouTube have become key channels for news consumption, especially among younger Americans. However, the algorithms that power these platforms are designed to prioritize content that generates engagement—likes, shares, comments—often promoting sensational, divisive, or emotionally charged posts. This tendency to amplify polarizing content further entrenches ideological divides.

- Social media algorithms tend to create "filter bubbles," where users are primarily exposed to information that aligns with their pre-existing beliefs. A study by the Massachusetts Institute of Technology (MIT) found that false news and sensational stories spread six times faster on Twitter than factual information (Vosoughi, Roy, & Aral, 2018). These algorithms can lead to the spread of misinformation, conspiracy theories, and exaggerated narratives, especially in rural areas with limited access to alternative sources of information.

The Decline of Local News

- One of the most significant consequences of media fragmentation is the decline of local news outlets, particularly in rural areas. Over the past few decades, hundreds of local newspapers have closed, creating so-called "news deserts" where residents lack access to reliable, locally relevant information. According to a report from the University of North Carolina, more than 1,800 local newspapers have shut down since 2004, leaving large swaths of rural America without independent journalism (UNC School of Media and Journalism, 2020).

- The decline of local news has serious consequences for rural communities, which now rely more heavily on national or partisan news outlets for information. Without local journalists to cover the issues directly affecting rural residents, communities become more isolated and disconnected from broader societal debates. Additionally, the absence of local watchdog journalism allows misinformation and unchecked rumors to proliferate, further dividing communities.

The Spread of Misinformation and Disinformation

Misinformation and disinformation have become significant challenges in the digital age, contributing to the urban-rural divide by fostering distrust, conspiracy theories, and a distorted perception of reality. Misinformation refers to false or misleading information spread without malicious intent, while disinformation involves the deliberate spread of false information to deceive or manipulate. Both forms of false information are widespread online, particularly on social media platforms, where users can easily share content without verifying its accuracy.

Political Misinformation

- Political misinformation is a major driver of polarization, with rural and urban communities often consuming entirely different versions of political events. This was particularly evident during the 2020 U.S. presidential election, when widespread misinformation about voter fraud and election security led many rural voters to believe that the election had been "stolen" from Donald Trump. A survey conducted by Ipsos in 2021 found that 65% of rural Republicans believed that the 2020 election was fraudulent, compared to just 22% of urban Democrats (Ipsos, 2021).

- Disinformation campaigns, both foreign and domestic, have also targeted rural areas, exploiting cultural and political differences to sow division. Russian interference in the 2016 and 2020 elections, for example, used social media to spread divisive content aimed at inflaming tensions between rural conservatives and urban liberals.

Misinformation on Health and Science

- The COVID-19 pandemic provided a stark example of how misinformation can deepen the urban-rural divide, particularly on matters of health and science. Throughout the pandemic, false information about the virus, vaccines, and government responses spread widely on social media, leading to significant differences in public attitudes between urban and rural areas.

- Rural communities, in particular, were more susceptible to vaccine hesitancy and misinformation about the pandemic. A Pew Research Center study found that only 54% of rural Americans had received a COVID-19 vaccine by mid-2021, compared to 72% of urban Americans (Pew Research Center, 2021). Many rural residents were exposed to misinformation about vaccine safety or government overreach, which fueled skepticism and resistance to public health measures. The result was a higher rate of COVID-19 infections and deaths in rural areas compared to urban centers.

The Role of Alternative Media

- In the absence of reliable local news and due to the decline in trust in mainstream media, many rural Americans have turned to alternative media sources that cater specifically to their political and cultural views. These outlets, such as Newsmax and OANN, often promote conspiracy theories or false information that reinforces rural residents' distrust of urban elites, the federal government, and mainstream institutions.

- In contrast, urban Americans are more likely to rely on mainstream media sources, which tend to emphasize expert opinions, scientific consensus, and fact-checking. This divergence in media consumption leads to a situation where urban and rural Americans are not only exposed to different information but often fundamentally disagree on basic facts.

The Digital Divide: Unequal Access to Technology

One of the most significant challenges facing rural America is the digital divide—the gap in access to high-speed broadband internet between urban and rural areas. In today's digital economy, internet access is essential for everything from education and healthcare to business and communication. However, many rural communities lack reliable broadband infrastructure, putting them at a significant disadvantage in a world that increasingly relies on digital connectivity.

Limited Broadband Access in Rural Areas

- According to the Federal Communications Commission (FCC), approximately 22% of rural Americans do not have access to high-speed broadband, compared to just 1.5% of urban Americans (FCC, 2021). This lack of internet access limits opportunities for rural residents to participate in the digital economy, access online education and healthcare resources, or even engage with digital news and social media platforms.

- The digital divide exacerbates existing inequalities in education and healthcare, as rural students are often unable to participate in online learning or access remote healthcare services. During the COVID-19 pandemic, the lack of broadband in rural areas made it difficult for students to attend virtual classes, putting them at a further disadvantage compared to their urban peers. Similarly, telehealth services, which expanded rapidly during the pandemic, were less accessible to rural residents due to inadequate internet infrastructure.

Economic Consequences of the Digital Divide

- The lack of broadband access in rural areas has significant economic consequences. Many rural businesses, particularly small businesses and farms, struggle to compete in a digital marketplace where e-commerce and online marketing are essential. Farmers, for example, rely on high-speed internet to access real-time data on crop prices, weather conditions, and supply chain logistics, but many are unable to take advantage of these tools due to poor internet access.

- Moreover, the digital divide limits opportunities for remote work, which has become increasingly common in urban areas. As more companies offer remote work options, workers in urban areas with reliable internet access can take advantage of flexible job opportunities that rural residents often cannot. This further contributes to the economic and social isolation of rural communities.

The role of technology and media in shaping the urban-rural divide cannot be overstated. Fragmented media consumption, the spread of misinformation, and unequal access to broadband internet have all contributed to a growing sense of division between urban and rural Americans. These factors not only deepen cultural and political polarization but also limit opportunities for rural communities to thrive in an increasingly digital world. Addressing these challenges will require targeted efforts to expand broadband access, improve media literacy, and foster a more diverse, fact-based media landscape. Only by bridging the digital and informational gaps can we begin to heal the growing rift between urban and rural America.

No. 7 — Impact of the Divide on National Politics and Policy

The urban-rural divide in America has far-reaching implications for national politics and public policy. As the country becomes increasingly polarized along geographic lines, the differences in priorities, values, and lived experiences between urban and rural communities are shaping the policies debated in statehouses and on Capitol Hill. This divide is not just a reflection of differing opinions but represents a deeper structural challenge to the functioning of American democracy. It influences everything from electoral outcomes and legislative gridlock to the very issues that dominate the national conversation. Understanding the impact of the urban-rural divide on politics and policy is critical to addressing the growing divisions in American society.

Voting Patterns and Electoral Outcomes: Red States vs. Blue States

One of the most visible manifestations of the urban-rural divide is in voting behavior. The stark contrast in voting patterns between urban and rural areas has created an electoral map that is deeply divided along geographic lines. Cities, with their diverse populations and progressive values, overwhelmingly vote Democratic, while rural areas, with their more traditional values and economic concerns, consistently support Republicans. This political realignment has had profound effects on electoral outcomes and the overall balance of power in American politics.

Urban Areas as Democratic Strongholds

- Urban centers across the country have become bastions of liberalism, with a clear majority of voters supporting Democratic candidates in presidential, congressional, and local elections. In cities like New York, Los Angeles, Chicago, and Washington, D.C., Democrats often win by large margins, reflecting the progressive views of urban populations on issues such as social justice, immigration, climate change, and healthcare.

- In the 2020 presidential election, for example, Joe Biden won 91 of the 100 largest counties in the U.S., while Donald Trump overwhelmingly carried rural counties (Pew Research Center, 2021). This geographic polarization illustrates the growing disconnect between the priorities of urban voters, who are more likely to focus on issues like systemic inequality and environmental protection, and rural voters, who prioritize economic survival, agriculture, and traditional values.

Rural Areas as Republican Strongholds

- Conversely, rural America has increasingly shifted toward the Republican Party, reflecting a growing sense of disenfranchisement and cultural alienation. In 2020, Donald Trump won 85% of rural counties, underscoring the strong support for conservative values, skepticism of government intervention, and concerns over job loss in rural industries like manufacturing and agriculture (Pew Research Center, 2021).

- The political shift in rural areas has been driven by a combination of factors, including economic stagnation, distrust of urban elites, and resistance to social changes that are seen as more aligned with urban liberalism. Issues such as gun rights, religion, immigration, and a general belief in "small government" play a significant role in rural political identity. The sense that rural America is being "left behind" by the coastal cities and urban elites has been a key talking point for Republican politicians seeking to appeal to rural voters.

The Geographic Imbalance in Electoral College and Senate Representation.

- The Electoral College and Senate representation further highlight the political consequences of the urban-rural divide. The Electoral College system, which allocates votes based on states rather than population, gives disproportionate influence to rural states. States like Wyoming, North Dakota, and Vermont, which have small populations but a large land area, are awarded the same number of senators as populous states like California or New York. As a result, rural voters wield more political power relative to their numbers, often leading to election outcomes that reflect rural interests even when urban areas have larger populations.

- In the Senate, this imbalance is even more stark. Rural states with small populations have the same level of representation as heavily urbanized states, which creates a significant power differential in shaping national legislation. For example, rural states like Kentucky and West Virginia can punch above their weight in national politics, influencing legislation on healthcare, taxes, environmental regulations, and more, despite representing fewer people than large urban states. This structural imbalance can lead to frustrations among urban voters, who feel underrepresented in national politics despite their numerical superiority.

Legislative Gridlock: Competing Policy Priorities

The urban-rural divide also contributes to significant legislative gridlock in Congress. As representatives from urban and rural districts bring very different policy priorities to Washington, D.C., the ability to find common ground has become increasingly difficult. The resulting gridlock makes it harder to pass meaningful legislation on key issues that affect both urban and rural Americans, leading to frustration with the political system as a whole.

Divergent Policy Priorities

- Urban areas prioritize progressive policies that reflect the needs of densely populated, diverse, and economically dynamic communities. Issues such as affordable housing, public transportation, climate change, healthcare reform, and racial justice are central to the urban political agenda. Urban voters tend to support government intervention to address inequality, protect the environment, and provide social services. As a result, urban lawmakers push for policies like rent control, minimum wage increases, universal healthcare, and stricter environmental regulations.

- Rural areas, by contrast, often focus on issues that reflect the needs of smaller, more homogeneous communities that rely on traditional industries like agriculture, mining, and manufacturing. Rural lawmakers prioritize issues such as deregulation, tax cuts, gun rights, and protecting industries that are vital to rural economies. Rural voters tend to be skeptical of government intervention and favor policies that promote individual responsibility, religious freedom, and the preservation of traditional values.

- These competing policy priorities create a significant challenge in Congress, where lawmakers representing urban and rural districts struggle to agree on issues like climate change, healthcare, education, and taxation. For example, urban lawmakers may push for stricter environmental regulations to address climate change, while rural lawmakers resist such measures, arguing that they would harm rural industries like coal mining or farming. Similarly, debates over healthcare policy reveal deep divisions, with urban representatives advocating for expanded government programs like Medicare for All, while rural lawmakers oppose what they see as excessive government overreach.

Legislative Gridlock and Partisanship

- The urban-rural divide is one of the key drivers of legislative gridlock in Congress, where polarization between the two major parties has reached historic levels. According to a 2021 report by the Brookings Institution, Congress is more divided now than at any point in the past 50 years, with members of each party increasingly voting along strict partisan lines (Brookings Institution, 2021). This polarization is often driven by geographic divides, as urban Democrats and rural Republicans are elected by constituencies with vastly different views on major policy issues.

- The result is a legislative process that frequently stalls, with few opportunities for bipartisan compromise. Issues that require long-term, structural solutions—such as healthcare reform, infrastructure investment, and climate change—often fall victim to partisan bickering, as lawmakers from rural and urban areas struggle to agree on a path forward. This gridlock not only prevents meaningful policy change but also contributes to the public's growing frustration with the political system.

Cultural Conflicts and National Identity

The urban-rural divide also fuels cultural conflicts that have become central to national debates over American identity. As urban and rural Americans hold different views on issues such as immigration, race, religion, and gender, these cultural divides shape the broader national conversation and often lead to contentious policy battles.

Immigration

- Immigration is a key issue where urban and rural views diverge sharply. Urban areas, which tend to be more diverse and rely on immigrant labor, generally support policies that promote immigration and provide pathways to citizenship for undocumented immigrants. Cities like New York, Los Angeles, and Chicago are home to large immigrant populations and benefit from the cultural and economic contributions that immigrants bring.

- Rural areas, by contrast, often view immigration as a threat to their way of life and economic stability. Many rural voters fear that an influx of immigrants could take jobs away from American workers or change the cultural fabric of their communities. This sentiment has been skillfully exploited by politicians who frame immigration as a security threat, calling for stricter border enforcement and immigration restrictions. The result is a national debate that pits urban values of diversity and inclusion against rural concerns about cultural preservation and economic competition.

Race and Social Justice

- Urban and rural Americans also have different perspectives on issues of race and social justice. Cities are more likely to support movements like Black Lives Matter, which call for police reform and an end to systemic racism. Urban areas, where racial diversity is more common, tend to be more aware of and sympathetic to the struggles faced by minority communities. According to a 2020 Pew Research study, 74% of urban residents believe that racial discrimination is a major problem in America, compared to 49% of rural residents (Pew Research Center, 2020).

- Rural areas, which are often more racially homogeneous, tend to have less exposure to the challenges faced by minorities and are more likely to view social justice movements with skepticism. Many rural Americans believe that the focus on race is divisive and that the push for racial equity threatens traditional values. This cultural divide plays out in national debates over police reform, Confederate monuments, and affirmative action, with rural and urban lawmakers often at odds on how to address these issues.

Religion and Secularism

- Religion also plays a significant role in shaping the cultural divide between urban and rural America. Rural areas, particularly in the South and Midwest, are more likely to be religious, with church attendance and adherence to traditional religious values remaining strong. Many rural voters prioritize issues such as religious freedom, opposition to abortion, and the protection of "family values" in their political decision-making. This religious identity often aligns rural voters with conservative social policies and candidates.

- Urban areas, by contrast, are more secular, with lower rates of church attendance and a greater emphasis on individual rights and freedoms. Urban residents are more likely to support progressive policies on issues like LGBTQ+ rights, reproductive rights, and the separation of church and state. This difference in religious values contributes to the broader cultural divide between urban and rural America, with each side viewing the other as either overly dogmatic or morally permissive.

The urban-rural divide in America has profound implications for national politics and policy. It shapes voting behavior, contributes to legislative gridlock, and fuels cultural conflicts that define the national conversation. As urban and rural communities become increasingly polarized, finding common ground on critical issues becomes more difficult, leading to frustration with the political system and a growing sense of alienation. Addressing the challenges posed by the urban-rural divide will require efforts to bridge cultural, political, and economic differences, foster dialogue between disparate communities, and create policies that address the needs of all Americans—whether they live in bustling cities or small rural towns. Only by narrowing the gap between urban and rural America can the country move forward toward a more cohesive, functioning democracy.

No. 8 — Real-World Implications: Social Cohesion and the Future of Democracy

The widening urban-rural divide in the United States has far-reaching real-world implications, affecting everything from social cohesion to the stability of American democracy. The division between these two Americas is no longer just a matter of differing opinions or lifestyles—it is shaping the ways in which people engage with one another, trust institutions, and participate in democratic processes. As this divide grows deeper, the potential for lasting damage to national unity, civic engagement, and governance becomes more pronounced. If left unaddressed, the urban-rural divide threatens to erode the foundations of democracy itself by undermining trust, cooperation, and the idea of a shared national identity.

Erosion of Social Cohesion: Two Americas

Social cohesion—the sense of connection, trust, and solidarity within a society—is essential for a functioning democracy. When citizens feel that they share common values, experiences, and goals, they are more likely to work together to solve problems, engage in civil discourse, and support democratic institutions. However, the growing urban-rural divide has created two increasingly separate realities in America, weakening the bonds that hold society together.

Increasing Social Isolation

- Urban and rural Americans are living increasingly isolated lives, with fewer opportunities for meaningful interaction across geographic and cultural lines. According to a 2020 study by the Pew Research Center, 61% of urban residents say they rarely or never interact with people from rural areas, while 68% of rural residents say the same about urban dwellers (Pew Research Center, 2020). This lack of exposure to different perspectives reinforces stereotypes and misconceptions, making it harder for individuals to empathize with those who live in different environments.

- Social media, which could serve as a bridge between communities, often exacerbates this isolation by creating echo chambers where people are only exposed to information that aligns with their preexisting beliefs. As urban and rural Americans consume increasingly polarized media, their perceptions of each other become more distorted. Rural Americans may view cities as chaotic, crime-ridden places that are out of touch with "real" American values, while urbanites may see rural areas as backward, regressive, or resistant to change. These caricatures contribute to a growing sense of "us vs. them," undermining the possibility of meaningful dialogue.

Distrust and Polarization

- As social isolation increases, so does distrust. Urban and rural Americans often see each other as representing fundamentally different worldviews, leading to a breakdown in trust and cooperation. A 2021 study by the Public Religion Research Institute (PRRI) found that 73% of rural Republicans believe that urban Democrats hold values that threaten the American way of life, while 67% of urban Democrats feel the same about rural Republicans

(PRRI, 2021). This deep mistrust extends beyond politics to broader social and cultural attitudes, making it difficult to find common ground on even the most basic issues.

- The lack of trust is also reflected in attitudes toward institutions. Urban and rural Americans have vastly different levels of trust in key institutions like the federal government, the media, and science. Rural Americans tend to be more skeptical of these institutions, viewing them as dominated by urban elites who do not understand or represent their interests. This skepticism has been fueled by years of political rhetoric that frames rural Americans as being marginalized or left behind by globalization and technological change, while urban Americans are more likely to trust these institutions as key players in progress and social change.

Loss of a Shared National Identity

- One of the most troubling aspects of the urban-rural divide is the loss of a shared national identity. Historically, Americans have seen themselves as part of a common project—an experiment in democracy that values freedom, equality, and opportunity for all. But as urban and rural communities become more polarized, they are increasingly defining "American values" differently.

- Urban areas tend to embrace values such as diversity, inclusion, innovation, and global engagement. Rural communities, by contrast, prioritize tradition, self-reliance, patriotism, and localism. These differing definitions of what it means to be American have led to heated debates over issues like immigration, religious freedom, and national security. As a result, many Americans no longer feel that they are part of the same national project, which weakens the sense of unity and common purpose that is essential for a functioning democracy.

Impact on Democracy: Trust, Participation, and Governance

The urban-rural divide poses significant challenges to the future of American democracy, as it undermines trust in democratic institutions, depresses civic participation, and creates barriers to effective governance. Democracy thrives when citizens trust their leaders and institutions, feel that their voices are heard, and believe in the fairness of the system. When these conditions are not met, democracy falters.

Erosion of Trust in Democratic Institutions

- Trust in democratic institutions has been declining in both urban and rural areas, but the reasons for this erosion are often different. In rural areas, many residents feel that the federal government, media, and educational institutions are dominated by urban elites who are out of touch with their values and concerns. According to a 2022 Gallup poll, only 29% of rural Americans trust the federal government to do what is right, compared to 48% of urban Americans (Gallup, 2022).

- Urban Americans, on the other hand, tend to lose trust in institutions when they feel that their progressive values are being undermined by the disproportionate influence of rural voters, particularly in the Senate and Electoral College. They may view institutions like the Supreme Court or state governments as vehicles for imposing conservative policies that are out of step with urban priorities. This mutual distrust weakens the legitimacy of democratic institutions, making it harder to build consensus or pass meaningful legislation.

Voter Suppression and Disenfranchisement

- The urban-rural divide also affects the fairness and accessibility of the voting process. In recent years, there has been an increase in efforts to restrict voting access, particularly in rural areas and states where Republicans control the state legislature. Many of these efforts are justified by claims of preventing voter fraud, but critics argue that they disproportionately affect urban, minority, and lower-income voters who tend to vote for Democrats.

- Voter suppression tactics, such as strict voter ID laws, the closure of polling places in minority neighborhoods, and limits on early voting, have led to lower voter turnout in urban areas, where residents already face challenges like long wait times and limited access to transportation. On the flip side, rural areas may feel that expanding mail-in voting or allowing same-day registration creates opportunities for voter fraud, further undermining their trust in the system. These differing perspectives on voting rights deepen the divide and make it harder to ensure that elections are seen as legitimate by all Americans.

Polarized Policymaking and Gridlock

- The urban-rural divide also contributes to gridlock in policymaking, as representatives from urban and rural areas bring vastly different priorities to Washington, D.C. Urban lawmakers tend to focus on issues like climate change, healthcare reform, and social justice, while rural lawmakers emphasize deregulation, agriculture, and traditional values. This divergence in policy goals makes compromise difficult, particularly in a hyper-partisan political environment.

- Legislative gridlock has far-reaching consequences for the ability of the government to address pressing national issues. For example, rural areas may feel that their concerns about the decline of manufacturing, rising healthcare costs, or poor infrastructure are being ignored by urban lawmakers who are more focused on progressive causes. Conversely, urban areas may feel that rural lawmakers are obstructing progress on climate change, gun control, or police reform. The result is a Congress that struggles to pass meaningful legislation, leading to frustration and disillusionment among voters on both sides of the divide.

Decline in Civic Participation

- The erosion of trust in democratic institutions and the feeling that one's voice doesn't matter contribute to a decline in civic participation. This is particularly true in rural areas, where economic hardship and social isolation can lead to disengagement from political life. Rural Americans are less likely to vote, run for office, or participate in community organizations than their urban counterparts, contributing to a sense of political and social disenfranchisement.

- A study by the University of Wisconsin found that rural voters were 18% less likely to participate in local civic organizations than urban voters, a gap that has widened over the past decade (University of Wisconsin, 2021). This disengagement from civic life weakens democratic governance at the local level, where citizens traditionally have the greatest ability to influence policy and hold their leaders accountable.

The Future of Democracy: Bridging the Divide

The urban-rural divide poses serious challenges to the future of American democracy, but it is not an insurmountable problem. Addressing this divide will require a concerted effort to build trust, promote dialogue, and create policies that benefit all Americans, regardless of where they live. By fostering greater understanding between urban and rural communities, encouraging civic engagement, and ensuring fair representation, it is possible to strengthen democracy and create a more united nation.

Fostering Dialogue and Understanding

- One of the first steps in bridging the divide is fostering dialogue between urban and rural communities. Encouraging exchanges and conversations that promote mutual understanding can help dispel misconceptions and reduce the sense of "otherness" that drives polarization. Educational initiatives, cultural exchanges, and community-based programs that bring urban and rural Americans together can help rebuild social cohesion and trust.

- Media organizations can also play a role in fostering understanding by providing more balanced coverage of rural and urban issues. By highlighting common challenges—such as economic inequality, healthcare access, and education—rather than focusing on divisions, the media can help create a more nuanced picture of both urban and rural life.

Promoting Civic Engagement

- Rebuilding democracy requires reengaging citizens in the political process. Encouraging voter participation, particularly in rural areas, can help ensure that all voices are heard. Efforts to make voting more accessible—through measures such as expanding early voting, providing transportation to polling places, and reducing barriers to voter registration—can help increase turnout and reduce feelings of disenfranchisement.

- Similarly, promoting civic engagement at the local level can empower citizens to take an active role in shaping their communities. Initiatives that support local governance, community organizing, and public participation in decision-making processes can help restore faith in democracy and ensure that people feel their voices matter.

Addressing Policy Imbalances

- Policy solutions that address the specific needs of both urban and rural Americans can help bridge the divide. For example, investing in rural infrastructure, healthcare, and education can reduce economic disparities and create opportunities for rural communities to thrive. At the same time, addressing the challenges facing urban areas—such as affordable housing, public transportation, and climate resilience—can help ensure that urban residents feel their needs are being met.

- Policymakers must also find ways to create legislation that benefits both urban and rural constituents. This may require compromise on contentious issues, such as environmental regulations or tax policies, but finding common ground can help reduce the sense of competition and resentment between urban and rural communities.

The real-world implications of the urban-rural divide are significant and far-reaching, affecting everything from social cohesion to the functioning of democracy itself. As the divide grows wider, the potential for further polarization, distrust, and democratic decline becomes more acute. However, by fostering dialogue, promoting civic engagement, and addressing the policy imbalances that exacerbate the divide, there is hope for a more unified and inclusive future. Bridging the gap between urban and rural America is not only essential for the health of the nation's democracy—it is also key to building a society where all citizens feel valued, heard, and empowered to shape their collective future.

No. 9 — Bridging the Divide: What Can Be Done?

Addressing the urban-rural divide in America is a complex but necessary task if the country is to heal its deepening social, political, and economic fractures. While the gap between urban and rural areas has been widening for decades, there are steps that can be taken to bridge this divide and promote greater understanding, equity, and cooperation. Solutions will need to come from multiple fronts— government policy, grassroots initiatives, the media, and education. Only through targeted efforts to reduce economic disparities, foster dialogue, and increase access to resources can we begin to narrow the divide and build a more cohesive, united society. Here are some concrete measures that could help bridge the urban-rural divide.

Economic Development: Revitalizing Rural Communities

One of the most important steps in addressing the urban-rural divide is
revitalizing rural economies. Economic stagnation in many rural areas has been
a key factor in fueling resentment toward urban America, and without targeted
investment, the economic disparity will continue to grow.

Targeted Infrastructure Investment

- Infrastructure investment is essential for improving the economic prospects
  of rural America. Expanding access to high-speed broadband is a critical
  step. As of 2021, around 22% of rural Americans still lack reliable access
  to broadband internet, compared to just 1.5% of urban Americans (Federal
  Communications Commission, 2021). This lack of access limits rural
  participation in the digital economy, online education, and telemedicine.
  Federal and state governments can prioritize funding for rural broadband
  expansion to ensure that rural communities are not left behind in an
  increasingly digital world.

- Similarly, investment in transportation infrastructure is critical. Many rural
  areas suffer from poor road conditions and a lack of public transportation,
  which limits mobility and economic opportunities. Improved infrastructure
  could help rural residents access jobs, healthcare, and education while
  attracting businesses to rural areas. The bipartisan infrastructure bill
  passed in 2021, which includes funding for roads, bridges, and broadband
  expansion, is a step in the right direction, but ongoing investment is
  necessary.

Rural Job Creation and Retraining Programs

- The decline of traditional industries like manufacturing, mining, and
  agriculture has left many rural areas with few economic opportunities.
  Federal and state governments should invest in job creation and retraining
  programs that help rural workers transition to new industries. Programs that
  promote renewable energy (such as solar and wind power), healthcare, and
  technology jobs can help bring new industries to rural areas while providing
  workers with the skills they need to succeed in a changing economy.

- Expanding access to vocational training and community colleges in rural
  areas can also help rural residents acquire new skills and increase economic

mobility. Programs that offer incentives for businesses to invest in rural areas, such as tax breaks for hiring local workers or locating facilities in under-served regions, can also help stimulate job growth.

Support for Agriculture and Small Businesses

- Agriculture remains the backbone of many rural economies, but small farms often struggle to compete with large agribusinesses. Federal and state policies can support small and family-owned farms by promoting sustainable agriculture, expanding access to markets, and offering financial assistance for farmers adopting new technologies or environmentally friendly practices.

- Small businesses are vital to rural economies, and policies that provide grants, low-interest loans, and technical assistance to rural entrepreneurs can help create local jobs and spur economic growth. Initiatives that encourage local entrepreneurship, such as business incubators or rural innovation hubs, can help nurture new businesses and keep economic activity within rural communities.

Political and Electoral Reform: Promoting Fair Representation

The urban-rural divide has led to significant political polarization, with both sides feeling that their interests are not adequately represented in government. Reforms that promote fairer representation and encourage political cooperation could help reduce the sense of alienation felt by both rural and urban Americans.

Gerrymandering Reform

- Gerrymandering, the practice of drawing electoral districts to favor one political party, has exacerbated political polarization by creating "safe" districts where politicians are incentivized to cater to their party's base rather than working toward compromise. Gerrymandering disproportionately affects rural and urban voters alike by diluting the political power of certain communities. Implementing independent redistricting commissions to draw fair and competitive districts could lead to more representative outcomes and reduce polarization. Several states, including California and Michigan, have already adopted independent redistricting models with positive results.

Reform of the Electoral College and Senate Representation

- The Electoral College system, which gives disproportionate power to smaller, rural states, has created significant frustration among urban voters who feel underrepresented in national elections. Reforming or abolishing the Electoral College is a contentious issue, but exploring alternatives such as the National Popular Vote Interstate Compact could help ensure that every vote counts equally in presidential elections.

- Similarly, the over-representation of rural states in the Senate poses challenges to democratic representation. While changing the structure of the Senate would require a constitutional amendment, which is unlikely, reforms that encourage greater political cooperation across states, such as regional coalitions or more frequent town halls and dialogue between senators and constituents, could help bridge the divide.

Ranked-Choice Voting and Proportional Representation

- One way to reduce polarization and promote more moderate, consensus-driven candidates is through electoral reforms like ranked-choice voting or proportional representation. Ranked-choice voting allows voters to rank candidates in order of preference, which encourages candidates to appeal to a broader spectrum of voters rather than catering to extreme positions. Proportional representation, used in many European democracies, allocates seats in legislative bodies based on the proportion of votes each party receives, ensuring that a wider range of political views is represented.

- Implementing these reforms at the local, state, or federal level could help reduce the influence of partisan extremism and encourage more collaborative policymaking.

Media and Information: Combatting Misinformation and Fostering Dialogue

The fragmentation of media consumption and the spread of misinformation have contributed significantly to the urban-rural divide. Efforts to promote media literacy, improve the quality of news reporting, and foster dialogue between different communities could help reduce misunderstandings and polarization.

Promoting Media Literacy

- Media literacy programs should be expanded in schools and communities to help people critically evaluate the information they consume. Teaching individuals how to identify credible news sources, recognize misinformation, and understand the role of algorithms in shaping social media feeds can help reduce the impact of misinformation and disinformation.

- Media companies and social media platforms also have a responsibility to combat the spread of false information. Platforms like Facebook, Twitter, and YouTube should continue to refine their algorithms to reduce the spread of misinformation and promote credible sources. Fact-checking tools and transparent content moderation policies can help build trust in the media while empowering users to make informed decisions.

Revitalizing Local News

- The decline of local news outlets has left many rural communities without access to reliable, locally relevant information. Government and private initiatives should support the revitalization of local journalism, especially in rural areas. Grants, subsidies, and tax incentives could help fund local news organizations, while nonprofit models for journalism, such as community-owned newspapers or publicly funded news outlets, could provide sustainable alternatives.

- Local news plays a critical role in fostering social cohesion by covering issues that directly impact residents' lives. Rebuilding trust in local journalism can help counteract the effects of national media polarization and create a more informed, engaged electorate.

Encouraging Cross-Community Dialogue

- One of the most effective ways to bridge the urban-rural divide is to promote dialogue and understanding between different communities. Programs that bring together urban and rural residents to discuss shared concerns, such as economic inequality, healthcare, or education, can help break down stereotypes and foster mutual respect.

- Organizations like Braver Angels, which aim to depolarize American politics by facilitating respectful conversations between people with different political views, offer a model for how cross-community dialogue can reduce polarization. Expanding these kinds of initiatives at the local and national levels can help rebuild social cohesion and promote empathy across the divide.

Education and Cultural Exchange: Building Understanding

Education plays a key role in shaping perceptions, and efforts to promote cross-cultural understanding between urban and rural communities can help reduce the sense of division.

Expanding Civic Education.

- Civic education should be expanded in schools to teach students about the diverse experiences and perspectives of Americans living in different regions. Understanding the history and contributions of both urban and rural communities can help students appreciate the complexity of the American experience and foster empathy for people from different backgrounds.

- Curriculum reforms that emphasize critical thinking, civic engagement, and media literacy can help prepare the next generation of citizens to engage in informed, respectful political discourse.

Encouraging Cultural Exchange.

- Programs that encourage cultural exchange between urban and rural communities can help bridge the gap between different ways of life. For example, exchange programs that allow urban students to spend time in rural areas, or rural students to visit cities, can expose young people to different environments and broaden their perspectives.

- Organizations that facilitate exchanges between urban and rural businesses, nonprofit organizations, or local governments can also promote collaboration and mutual understanding. These exchanges can help individuals in both communities learn from each other's strengths and challenges, fostering a greater sense of national unity.

The urban-rural divide in America is a complex and multifaceted issue, but it is not insurmountable. Through targeted economic investment, political and electoral reform, media literacy, and efforts to promote dialogue and understanding, it is possible to begin bridging the gap between these two communities. While the challenges are great, the potential rewards are even greater: a more cohesive, equitable, and functional democracy where all Americans, regardless of where they live, have the opportunity to thrive and contribute to the country's future. By addressing the root causes of the urban-rural divide, we can build a society that values the diversity of experience while working together toward common goals.

Bridging the Urban-Rural Divide for a Stronger Future

The urban-rural divide in America is one of the most pressing and multifaceted challenges facing the nation today. It touches every aspect of society—from economics and politics to culture and social cohesion—and threatens to further polarize an already divided country. The divide is not just a matter of geography but of opportunity, access, values, and identity, creating two distinct Americas that increasingly struggle to understand and engage with one another.

As we've explored, the economic disparities between urban and rural communities have deepened over the past several decades, driven by the rise of the knowledge economy in cities and the decline of traditional industries in rural areas. Political polarization, fueled by fragmented media consumption and starkly different priorities, has left Congress gridlocked, and has pitted urban progressivism against rural conservatism in ways that make compromise difficult. Social and cultural differences, exacerbated by stereotypes, misunderstandings, and the spread of misinformation, have further eroded the sense of shared national identity that is vital for a functioning democracy.

However, while the divide may seem insurmountable, it is not without solutions. Bridging the gap between urban and rural America will require a concerted effort across multiple fronts—economic revitalization, political reform, media literacy, and cross-cultural dialogue. Investing in rural infrastructure, broadband access, education, and job creation will be critical to ensuring that rural communities can thrive in the 21st-century economy. Political reforms, such as addressing gerrymandering and promoting electoral systems that encourage cooperation rather than polarization, can help reduce the legislative gridlock that is deepening the divide. Media and information reforms, along with efforts to combat misinformation, can help create a more informed and connected populace. And fostering dialogue between urban and rural communities, whether through education, cultural exchange, or civic engagement, can help rebuild the social cohesion necessary for a healthy democracy.

Ultimately, the goal is not to erase the differences between urban and rural America but to build bridges of understanding, empathy, and cooperation. Both urban and rural communities bring valuable perspectives, experiences, and strengths to the national conversation. By recognizing these contributions and working together to address the challenges each group faces, we can create a more inclusive, equitable, and united society.

The future of American democracy depends on our ability to overcome the divisions that threaten to tear it apart. Bridging the urban-rural divide is not only a matter of economic or political necessity—it is a moral imperative. If we are to leave a better, stronger, and more cohesive society for future generations, we must act now to build the connections, understanding, and trust that will carry us forward. By addressing the root causes of the divide and fostering a spirit of collaboration, we can ensure that America remains a place where all its citizens, regardless of where they live, have the opportunity to contribute to the nation's shared success.

Decline, Diversity, and the Rise of Spirituality

Religion in America has long played a significant role in shaping the country's cultural and social landscape. For centuries, organized religion, particularly Christianity, has influenced American values, politics, and community life. However, in recent decades, America has witnessed a notable decline in participation in organized religion and a simultaneous diversification of religious beliefs and practices. The landscape of faith is no longer dominated by a single or even a few religions, but instead reflects a complex web of affiliations, spiritualities, and beliefs. This transformation carries profound implications for American society, individual values, and the human condition.

The Decline of Organized Religion

In recent decades, the United States has experienced a marked decline in participation in organized religion. This trend is most clearly reflected in the rise of the religiously unaffiliated, a group often referred to as "nones." According to a 2021 Pew Research Center study, around 29% of U.S. adults now identify as religiously unaffiliated, up from 16% in 2007 and 23% in 2016. This group includes atheists, agnostics, and individuals who describe themselves as "spiritual but not religious" (SBNR). Importantly, the rate of growth in this group is especially pronounced among younger Americans. The same Pew study shows that 40% of Millennials (born 1981-1996) and 36% of Generation Z adults (born after 1996) now identify as religiously unaffiliated, reflecting a stark generational divide when compared to older groups like Baby Boomers, only 16% of whom fall into this category.

Furthermore, regular attendance at religious services has steadily declined. A Gallup poll from 2020 found that, for the first time in eight decades of polling, less than 50% of Americans reported membership in a church, synagogue, or mosque. Specifically, church membership dropped from 70% in 1999 to just 47% in 2020. The decline in attendance is most prominent among younger people, with only 36% of Millennials reporting regular attendance at religious services, compared to 58% of Baby Boomers.

Factors Contributing to the Decline

A range of social, cultural, and historical factors has contributed to this growing disengagement from organized religion.

- **Changing Cultural Attitudes.** Over the past few decades, there has been a significant shift in social values, particularly regarding issues like gender equality, LGBTQ+ rights, and racial justice. Many organized religious institutions, particularly conservative denominations, have been slow to adapt to these changes or have maintained opposition to them. As a result, many younger Americans see traditional religious teachings as incompatible with the values of inclusivity, social justice, and personal autonomy. A 2019 PRRI (Public Religion Research Institute) study found that 65% of religiously unaffiliated Americans believe that religion "causes more harm than good" due to its perceived opposition to progressive social values.

- **Rising Skepticism of Religious Authority.** Another major factor is the growing skepticism toward institutional authority in general, and religious authority in particular. The information age, fueled by the internet and social media, has allowed individuals to access diverse viewpoints and question long-held beliefs, undermining the central authority of religious leaders. The ease of exploring alternative worldviews or criticisms of religious institutions has contributed to an erosion of confidence in traditional religious teachings. Additionally, religious institutions' involvement in political and cultural battles, particularly those relating to reproductive rights, gender roles, and LGBTQ+ rights, has alienated many Americans, especially younger generations. A 2016 Barna Group study revealed that 59% of Millennials who grew up in Christian churches left because they perceived the church as "too focused on politics."

- **Scandals and Abuse in Religious Institutions.** Scandals involving religious institutions have also played a significant role in eroding trust and participation. Most notably, the Catholic Church has been rocked by revelations of widespread sexual abuse by clergy members and subsequent cover-ups by church leadership. These scandals have deeply damaged the credibility of the church and driven many Catholics away. According to a Gallup poll from 2019, 37% of U.S. Catholics reported that they had questioned whether they should remain in the church in light of the sexual abuse scandals. The problem is not limited to the Catholic Church— allegations of abuse and corruption have also surfaced in Protestant denominations and other religious communities.

- **Rise of Secularism.** The broader trend of secularization, in which societies become more oriented toward rationalism, science, and individualism, has also contributed to the decline in organized religion. In the U.S., secularism has grown more prominent, and there is a decreasing societal expectation that individuals must affiliate with a religious group to be considered moral or upright. A 2020 Gallup survey found that 21% of Americans said they believed religion was "not very important" in their daily lives, a stark contrast to the 70% of Americans who considered religion to be "very important" in 1952.

- **Individualism and Spiritual Autonomy.** The increasing value placed on personal autonomy and individualism in American culture has made the rigid structures and communal expectations of many organized religions less appealing. In particular, younger people are less likely to adhere to doctrines that require conformity to specific beliefs or behaviors. Instead, they are more inclined to form their own spiritual identities, often blending elements from multiple religious or secular philosophies. A 2020 Pew study found that 64% of religiously unaffiliated Americans said they believe in God or a higher power, even if they don't identify with a formal religious institution, reflecting a shift toward personalized and individual forms of spirituality.

The Disconnect Between Organized Religion and Younger Generations

Much of the decline in organized religion can be attributed to a generational shift, with younger generations being far less likely to engage in traditional religious practices than their parents or grandparents. According to a 2018 Pew Research Center report, only 25% of Millennials and Gen Z adults attend religious services at least once a week, compared to 49% of Baby Boomers. Among the contributing factors is the perception that religious institutions are increasingly out of touch with modern life and the concerns of younger people.

A 2021 Springtide Research Institute survey found that 52% of young people (ages 13 to 25) believe religious institutions "ignore the issues and concerns" most relevant to them, such as climate change, social justice, and mental health. Additionally, 39% said they do not feel welcome in religious spaces, especially those that maintain conservative stances on issues like LGBTQ+ rights. This disconnect has led to younger Americans seeking meaning and belonging outside of traditional religious institutions, whether through activism, online communities, or alternative spiritual practices.

The Growth of Religious Diversity

As traditional Christian denominations have experienced a decline, the religious landscape in the United States has simultaneously become more diverse. Immigration, globalization, and an increasing openness to religious plurality have contributed to the growth of non-Christian religions, as well as new movements within Christianity itself. America, once seen as predominantly Protestant, now reflects a mosaic of faiths and practices, from Islam to Buddhism to new expressions of Christianity. This growing diversity has reshaped religious practices, attitudes toward faith, and even how Americans perceive spirituality.

Immigration and the Rise of Non-Christian Faiths

One of the primary drivers of religious diversity in America has been immigration. Since the 1965 Immigration and Nationality Act, which ended quotas that had disproportionately favored European immigrants, the United States has seen an influx of people from Asia, Latin America, the Middle East, and Africa— many of whom brought their distinct religious traditions with them.

- **Islam.** The Muslim population in the U.S. has grown significantly in recent decades. According to the Pew Research Center, in 2017, there were about 3.45 million Muslims in the United States, making up about 1.1% of the population. This represents a steady increase from 0.4% in 2007. Much of this growth is attributed to immigration from Muslim-majority countries such as Pakistan, Bangladesh, and the Arab world, as well as the increasing number of native-born converts to Islam, particularly among African Americans. The American Muslim community is now one of the most ethnically diverse religious groups in the country, with no single nationality or ethnic group holding a majority. As a result, Muslim institutions like mosques and schools are rapidly expanding to meet the needs of this growing population.

- **Hinduism.** Hinduism, another religion largely bolstered by immigration, has also seen significant growth. As of 2020, there are an estimated 2.23 million Hindus in the United States, a significant increase from previous decades. Most American Hindus trace their heritage to India, though the community also includes immigrants from Nepal, Sri Lanka, and Bangladesh. The Hindu population has made a visible cultural impact, with temples and cultural centers being built across the country, especially in states with large Indian immigrant populations such as California, New York, and Texas. Festivals like Diwali, once celebrated only in private, have grown in prominence and are now often publicly recognized, with some cities holding large-scale community events.

- **Buddhism.** The U.S. is also home to a growing Buddhist population, estimated to be around 3.6 million people as of 2020. The growth of Buddhism in America comes from two major sources: immigrants from traditionally Buddhist countries such as Thailand, Vietnam, Myanmar, and Japan, and a growing number of American converts. Over the past few decades, Buddhism has appealed to a segment of the American population that values mindfulness, meditation, and a non-theistic approach to spirituality. The mindfulness movement, popularized by figures like Thich Nhat Hanh and the Dalai Lama, has made Buddhist practices more accessible to the broader American public, blurring the lines between religious and secular practice.

- **Sikhism.** Sikhism, though still a relatively small religious group in the U.S., has seen significant growth due to immigration from India, particularly the state of Punjab. According to the Pew Research Center, there are approximately 500,000 Sikhs living in the United States as of 2021. Sikh communities have established Gurdwaras (Sikh temples) across the country, especially in states with large Indian immigrant populations like California. Sikhs have also become more prominent in American public life, with figures like Ravi Bhalla, the mayor of Hoboken, New Jersey, and Dalip Singh Saund, the first Asian American elected to Congress, bringing visibility to the Sikh community.

The Growth of New Christian Movements

Even as traditional denominations such as Mainline Protestantism and Roman Catholicism have faced declining membership, other forms of Christianity have experienced growth, often offering a more contemporary or charismatic approach to worship.

- **Pentecostalism and Evangelicalism.** One of the most significant trends within American Christianity has been the rise of Pentecostalism and Evangelicalism. Pentecostal churches, which emphasize spiritual experiences like speaking in tongues, healing, and prophecy, have grown steadily in the U.S. and worldwide. This movement's appeal lies in its emotional, participatory worship style and its focus on direct personal encounters with the divine. Pentecostalism has been particularly attractive to African Americans and Latino populations, many of whom have shifted from more traditional forms of Christianity to these dynamic congregations. According to the Hartford Institute for Religion Research, Pentecostal and charismatic churches, including the Assemblies of God and non-denominational charismatic movements, are some of the fastest-growing Christian groups in America.

- **Megachurches.** The rise of megachurches, defined as Protestant churches with more than 2,000 weekly attendees, is another notable development in American religious life. As of 2020, there are over 1,500 megachurches in the U.S., drawing millions of worshipers each week. These churches often offer a blend of traditional Christian teachings with contemporary music, multimedia presentations, and social activities, creating a dynamic and accessible worship environment. Notable examples include Lakewood Church in Houston, led by Joel Osteen, and Saddleback Church in California, led by Rick Warren. Megachurches frequently emphasize a positive, self-help-oriented version of Christianity, often referred to as the "prosperity gospel," which appeals to a wide demographic, including young families and suburban dwellers.

- **Non-Denominational Christianity.** There has also been a significant rise in non-denominational churches, which eschew formal affiliation with established Christian denominations. These churches often have flexible doctrines and worship practices that attract individuals who want to maintain their Christian faith without the perceived rigidity or bureaucracy of traditional denominations. According to Pew Research, non-denominational Christians now make up 6.2% of the U.S. population, up from 4.5% in 2007. These churches often focus on community, personal relationships with Jesus, and modern worship styles, creating an inclusive atmosphere for people seeking a more personal approach to their faith.

Indigenous and Neo-Pagan Religions

Another significant aspect of America's religious diversification is the rise of indigenous and neo-pagan traditions.

- **Native American Spirituality.** In recent years, Native American religious practices have experienced a resurgence, both within Indigenous communities and among non-Natives interested in earth-based spiritual traditions. Sacred rituals such as sweat lodges, vision quests, and the use of traditional medicines like peyote and tobacco are being revived and practiced across the country. Organizations like the Native American Church have been working to protect Indigenous religious practices, which often incorporate elements of Christianity alongside traditional beliefs. Native American spirituality, with its focus on environmental stewardship and connection to the land, has also influenced broader spiritual movements concerned with sustainability and ecological balance.

- **Neo-Paganism.** The Neo-Pagan movement, which encompasses a variety of modern religions such as Wicca, Druidry, and eclectic Paganism, has also been growing. These belief systems often center around nature worship, polytheism, and the practice of ancient or reconstructed rituals. According to a 2014 Pew Research study, the number of people practicing Wicca or other forms of Paganism has more than doubled since the early 1990s, with estimates suggesting there are up to 1.5 million practitioners in the U.S. Neo-Paganism appeals to individuals seeking spirituality outside of mainstream religion, offering a more individualized and often feminist or ecological approach to faith. The rise of witchcraft, astrology, and other esoteric practices among younger Americans, especially Millennials, is part of this broader shift toward alternative spiritual paths.

The Impact of Religious Diversity

The growing diversity of religious beliefs in the United States has reshaped how Americans engage with faith, creating a more pluralistic society. Interfaith dialogue and cooperation have become increasingly common, with organizations like the Interfaith Youth Core and the Parliament of the World's Religions working to foster understanding and collaboration among different religious communities. This diversity has also influenced politics, education, and public policy, as lawmakers and civic leaders must navigate the rights and needs of a broader range of faith groups.

At the same time, this religious diversity has raised challenges regarding social integration, religious freedom, and intergroup tensions. While many Americans are increasingly comfortable with religious diversity, surveys show that certain groups, particularly Muslims and atheists, still face significant prejudice and discrimination. According to a 2019 Pew Research survey, 42% of Americans say Muslims face "a lot of discrimination" in the U.S., a sentiment that has been heightened by political rhetoric and global events.

Overall, the increasing religious diversity in the U.S. reflects a broader trend toward a more pluralistic, multicultural society. This shift has both enriched the American religious landscape and posed challenges to the nation's foundational principles of religious freedom and equality.

The Rise of Spirituality

While organized religion has been in decline, many Americans are not abandoning faith or belief altogether. Instead, they are shifting toward spirituality, often in forms that do not involve traditional religious structures. This movement toward individualized, non-institutional forms of faith—commonly referred to as the "spiritual but not religious" (SBNR) phenomenon—has been growing rapidly over the past few decades. This trend emphasizes personal experiences, inner peace, and connections to something greater than oneself, while often rejecting the dogma, rituals, and authority associated with organized religions.

Growth in the "Spiritual But Not Religious" Population

The rise of spirituality in the U.S. is most visible in the increasing number of people who describe themselves as spiritual but not affiliated with any formal religious tradition. According to a 2021 Pew Research Center survey, 29% of U.S. adults identified as religiously unaffiliated, and within this group, a significant proportion consider themselves to be spiritual but not religious. Pew data from 2017 shows that 27% of Americans identified as SBNR, a substantial rise from 19% in 2012. Younger generations are especially likely to describe themselves this way, with 34% of Millennials and 40% of Generation Z adults (born after 1996) identifying as SBNR, according to the Springtide Research Institute's 2021 survey on youth spirituality.

What defines the SBNR population is their preference for exploring spirituality on their own terms, rather than through established religious authorities or institutions. Many people in this group maintain belief in a higher power or divine presence, even though they may not adhere to specific religious doctrines or practices. For instance, the 2021 Pew study found that 72% of religiously unaffiliated people believe in some form of spiritual force or higher power, even if they do not identify with traditional religious teachings.

Real-Life Examples of Spirituality in Practice

The rise of spirituality has taken many forms across the United States, from the increased popularity of meditation and yoga to the embrace of holistic wellness practices. These spiritual practices are often rooted in Eastern philosophies, New Age beliefs, or Indigenous traditions but are adapted to modern lifestyles, emphasizing personal well-being and mindfulness.

- **Meditation and Mindfulness Practices.** Meditation, particularly mindfulness meditation, has become a central practice for many Americans seeking spiritual fulfillment outside traditional religious settings. Influenced by Buddhist traditions, mindfulness practices focus on cultivating awareness, inner peace, and presence in the moment. The Centers for Disease Control and Prevention (CDC) found that 14.2% of U.S. adults reported practicing meditation as of 2017, up from 4.1% in 2012, indicating a substantial increase in interest.

  This surge in mindfulness practices is reflected in the rise of meditation centers, apps like Headspace and Calm, and corporate wellness programs across the country. Silicon Valley, for example, has embraced mindfulness as a key tool for mental clarity and stress management. Many companies, including Google, now offer mindfulness programs to their employees, with thousands attending mindfulness and meditation workshops each year. Schools across America, from elementary to high schools, have also begun integrating mindfulness programs to reduce student anxiety and increase focus, reflecting how spiritual practices are becoming mainstream in secular institutions.

- **Yoga as a Spiritual Practice.** Yoga, traditionally rooted in Hindu and Buddhist traditions, has evolved into a spiritual practice embraced by millions of Americans, often without the overt religious aspects. While many initially take up yoga for its physical benefits, it also serves as a gateway to a broader spiritual practice for many practitioners. According to a Yoga Alliance and Yoga Journal survey conducted in 2016, 36.7 million Americans practiced yoga, up from 20.4 million in 2012, demonstrating its growing popularity as a spiritual and wellness practice. Many yoga practitioners, while not adhering to organized religion, describe their practice as spiritual, finding meaning in the connection between mind, body, and spirit. The integration of yoga with spirituality is evident in the proliferation of yoga festivals, such as Wanderlust, held annually in multiple U.S. locations. These festivals draw large crowds seeking spiritual renewal, offering workshops that blend yoga, meditation, mindfulness, and even Buddhist-inspired philosophies. Yoga studios like YogaWorks and CorePower Yoga have also contributed to the rising trend of Americans embracing yoga not just as exercise, but as a path to spiritual growth.

- **The Influence of New Age Beliefs.** Another key facet of the rise of spirituality in the U.S. has been the resurgence of New Age beliefs, which emphasize personal spiritual experience, energy healing, and the interconnectedness of all life. Many people who identify as spiritual but not religious are drawn to practices such as crystal healing, astrology, tarot reading, and Reiki, all of which have seen a revival in recent years. A 2018 Pew Research Center study found that 60% of U.S. adults hold at least one New Age belief, such as belief in psychics, reincarnation, or astrology, indicating that these practices are no longer relegated to the fringes of society but are becoming increasingly mainstream.

For example, astrology has seen a significant revival, particularly among younger generations. The popularity of astrology apps like Co–Star and

The Pattern has surged, with millions of users regularly consulting their star charts for spiritual guidance. According to a 2019 survey by the National Science Foundation, 29% of Americans believe in astrology, a significant increase from the 23% recorded in 2010. This resurgence is also visible in the increasing number of astrology-based wellness businesses and spiritual influencers on social media platforms like Instagram and TikTok, where astrology, tarot readings, and energy healing are widely discussed and practiced.

- **Holistic Wellness and the Rise of Alternative Healing.** The rise of holistic wellness practices, which often incorporate spiritual elements, is another key aspect of America's shift toward spirituality. Practices like Reiki (a form of energy healing), sound baths, and the use of crystals for healing and balance have gained significant popularity. Holistic wellness is often associated with New Age spirituality and draws on various traditions, including Indigenous and Eastern practices.

One prominent example of this shift is the booming wellness industry in places like Sedona, Arizona, which has become a hub for spiritual retreats and alternative healing practices. Sedona's "energy vortexes" are believed by many to be powerful centers of spiritual energy, attracting people from across the U.S. for meditation, healing, and spiritual renewal. Similarly, major metropolitan areas such as Los Angeles and New York City have become centers for spiritual wellness, with numerous wellness studios offering services such as crystal therapy, sound healing, and Reiki to clients seeking spiritual balance and personal growth.

- **Digital Spiritual Communities.** The rise of the internet and social media has enabled the growth of digital spiritual communities, allowing people to explore and share spiritual ideas outside of traditional religious contexts. Platforms like YouTube, Instagram, and TikTok are filled with content on mindfulness, meditation, astrology, and other spiritual practices. These platforms allow spiritual seekers to connect with like-minded individuals, learn from spiritual influencers, and practice their beliefs in a virtual space.

For example, the #SpiritualTok community on TikTok has amassed billions of views, featuring content creators sharing advice on topics ranging from manifestation and tarot to healing trauma through spiritual practices. This democratization of spiritual knowledge has allowed millions of people to explore spirituality in ways that are accessible and adaptable to their personal needs, often without any formal religious affiliation. Online courses, virtual retreats, and guided meditation apps further contribute to the rise of digital spirituality.

Studies and Statistics on the Growth of Spirituality

Several studies reflect the increasing embrace of spirituality over religion in the U.S.:

- A 2017 PRRI (Public Religion Research Institute) survey found that 18% of Americans say they are spiritual but not religious, up from 12% in 2012. This growing demographic is especially prevalent among younger generations, with 22% of Millennials and 19% of Generation Z identifying as SBNR.

- A 2021 Springtide Research Institute study found that 51% of young people aged 13 to 25 reported that they are "spiritual in some way," and while only 31% of these young people attended traditional religious services regularly, many engaged in spiritual practices like meditation, yoga, or prayer on their own terms.

- According to a 2018 Pew study, 26% of Americans say they regularly feel a deep sense of spiritual peace and well-being, and 34% say they regularly feel a deep sense of wonder about the universe, highlighting the spiritual curiosity that persists even outside of organized religious frameworks.

The Impact of Spirituality on American Society

The rise of spirituality in America is having a profound impact on how individuals relate to themselves, each other, and the broader world. As more people seek meaning outside of traditional institutions, spiritual practices are filling the void that organized religion once occupied. Practices such as mindfulness and yoga are often used as tools to manage stress, improve mental health, and cultivate emotional well-being, reflecting a shift in the purpose of spiritual practices from communal worship to personal growth and healing.

Moreover, the rise of spirituality reflects broader societal trends toward individualism, with many Americans preferring to craft their own belief systems rather than adhere to pre-determined doctrines. This has led to a more pluralistic and tolerant society in which people are more open to diverse spiritual ideas and practices. However, it also presents challenges for community-building, as traditional religious institutions, which once provided a shared moral framework and social cohesion, play a diminishing role in public life.

The rise of spirituality in America is reshaping how individuals seek meaning, healing, and connection. While participation in organized religion declines, the spiritual needs of Americans remain strong, leading many to embrace practices that focus on personal experience, well-being, and inner peace. This shift reflects broader cultural trends toward individualism and self-exploration, marking a new chapter in the evolving religious landscape of the United States.

Impacts on Values and Society

The fragmentation of organized religion and the rise of diverse spiritual practices are having profound effects on American values, societal norms, and cultural cohesion. As fewer Americans participate in traditional religious institutions, and as the nation becomes more religiously diverse and spiritually individualized, the frameworks that once shaped moral and ethical values are evolving. This shift has significant implications for the way people view morality, community, politics, and social cohesion. While the decline of organized religion and rise of spirituality offer opportunities for increased inclusivity, personal autonomy, and pluralism, they also present challenges related to societal fragmentation, moral relativism, and the erosion of shared values.

The Shift from Collective to Individual-Centered Values

One of the most significant changes brought about by the decline of organized religion is the shift from community-centered to individual-centered values. Historically, religious institutions in the U.S. played a central role in fostering communal values, offering a shared moral framework and serving as social hubs. Religious congregations were often places where people came together not just for worship, but for education, charity, and social connection. As participation in these institutions has waned, the emphasis on individualism in American culture has grown stronger.

This shift has led to an increasing focus on personal fulfillment and self-expression, which aligns with broader societal trends emphasizing autonomy and choice. Many people today are less inclined to subscribe to rigid religious doctrines and instead choose to explore their own moral and spiritual paths. According to a 2018 Pew Research Center study, 56% of Americans believe that the "right thing to do" is based on personal experience and reasoning, rather than adhering to religious teachings or scripture. This reflects a growing trend toward moral individualism, in which people prioritize personal conscience over traditional, institutionalized notions of right and wrong.

The rise of spirituality over organized religion also speaks to this emphasis on the individual. Spirituality often prioritizes personal experience, subjective truth, and inner well-being. Practices like meditation, yoga, and mindfulness encourage individuals to look inward for guidance, rather than relying on external religious authorities. While this shift toward individual-centered values allows for greater personal freedom and diversity of belief, it also weakens the communal ties and shared moral compass that religious institutions once provided.

Erosion of Shared Moral Frameworks

As Americans increasingly move away from organized religion and toward individualized spirituality, society is experiencing a fragmentation of shared moral frameworks. Historically, religious institutions provided a common set of values that helped to shape laws, social norms, and ethical standards. In predominantly Christian America, concepts such as justice, charity, honesty, and family were often rooted in Biblical teachings and were widely accepted across political and cultural divides. However, as fewer people align with these religious institutions, the consensus on moral values is becoming more elusive.

This growing pluralism in moral beliefs has contributed to a rise in moral relativism, the idea that morality is subjective and can vary based on individual or cultural perspectives. While some see this as a positive development—promoting tolerance for different worldviews and the inclusion of previously marginalized voices—others worry that it could erode societal cohesion and make it more difficult to build consensus on key ethical issues. For example, debates around abortion, same-sex marriage, and assisted suicide have become increasingly polarized, with different groups drawing on competing moral frameworks to argue their positions.

The PRRI (Public Religion Research Institute) American Values Survey conducted in 2020 found that 60% of Americans believe that morality is "situational" and should adapt to the context, while only 40% believe in moral absolutes. This divide is reflected in political and social discourse, where disagreements over what constitutes a moral society have become a key driver of polarization. While shared religious values once provided a common ground for ethical debates, today's moral landscape is more fragmented, leading to greater conflict over issues such as reproductive rights, LGBTQ+ equality, racial justice, and environmental responsibility.

Changing Views on Social and Political Issues

As religion's role in shaping public morality has diminished, there has been a corresponding shift in societal attitudes toward various social and political issues. Historically, religious organizations, particularly conservative Christian groups, wielded significant influence over U.S. politics, often shaping policies on issues like abortion, marriage, education, and the role of government. However, as more Americans step away from religious institutions, views on these issues are increasingly informed by secular, progressive, or pluralistic values.

- **LGBTQ+ Rights.** One of the clearest examples of this shift is the rapid change in public opinion regarding LGBTQ+ rights. In the past, many religious groups, particularly evangelical Christians and conservative Catholics, opposed LGBTQ+ equality, arguing that it violated traditional religious teachings about marriage and gender roles. However, as religious influence has waned and new moral frameworks have emerged, public opinion has shifted dramatically. A Pew Research Center survey from 2023 found that 72% of Americans now support same-sex marriage, up from just 37% in 2007. This change is largely driven by younger, more secular Americans who prioritize individual autonomy and equality over traditional religious values.

- **Reproductive Rights.** Another area where changing values are evident is in debates around reproductive rights. While religious groups, particularly Catholics and evangelical Christians, have historically opposed abortion on moral grounds, public opinion has become more divided as religious affiliation has declined. According to the Pew Research Center, 61% of Americans believe abortion should be legal in all or most cases, with support strongest among those who identify as religiously unaffiliated or spiritual but not religious. The fragmentation of moral authority in

America has created deep divisions over how issues like abortion should be legislated, reflecting the broader tension between traditional religious beliefs and more secular, progressive values.

- **Environmentalism and Climate Change.** Interestingly, while religion's influence has waned in some areas, new spiritual and ethical frameworks have emerged to fill the void, particularly in relation to environmentalism. Many Americans, especially those who identify as spiritual but not religious, have embraced environmentalism as a form of moral and spiritual duty. The belief in the interconnectedness of all life, which is central to many Eastern and Indigenous spiritual traditions, has inspired a new wave of activism centered on protecting the planet. A 2021 Pew study found that 74% of Millennials believe that environmental protection is a moral issue, compared to 57% of Baby Boomers. This shift reflects how new moral frameworks, rooted in spirituality and global awareness, are taking the place of traditional religious teachings on stewardship and responsibility.

Social Isolation and the Decline of Community

The decline of organized religion and the rise of spirituality have also had profound effects on social cohesion and community life. For centuries, religious institutions served as important social hubs, providing a sense of belonging, support, and connection for their members. Churches, synagogues, and mosques not only facilitated worship but also offered opportunities for education, charity, and social interaction. As participation in these institutions declines, many Americans are experiencing a growing sense of social isolation and a loss of community.

A 2021 Gallup poll found that 47% of Americans reported feeling "somewhat or very lonely" on a regular basis, a sharp increase from previous decades. This trend is particularly acute among younger generations, many of whom have turned away from traditional religious communities but have not found equivalent sources of social connection. The same poll found that regular churchgoers were significantly less likely to report feelings of loneliness compared to those who never attend religious services, suggesting that the decline of organized religion may be contributing to the broader societal problem of isolation and disconnection.

In response to this growing social isolation, some Americans have turned to new forms of community that reflect the rise of spirituality and the decline of traditional religion. Spiritual gatherings such as meditation retreats, yoga festivals, and wellness workshops are becoming more popular, offering people a chance to connect with others who share their values and spiritual interests. Similarly, online communities centered around spirituality and wellness, such as those found on platforms like Instagram, TikTok, and Reddit, have provided new ways for people to find belonging and support, even if they don't participate in traditional religious congregations.

The Role of Religion in Public Life

The fragmentation of religious affiliation has also led to debates about the role of religion in public life. The First Amendment guarantees freedom of religion and the separation of church and state, yet for much of American history, religion— particularly Christianity—has played a significant role in shaping public policy and national identity. As religious diversity grows and fewer Americans identify with any one faith tradition, tensions have emerged over how much influence religious values should have in government, education, and public spaces.

For instance, debates about religious exemptions in healthcare, education, and business have become more contentious. Some religious groups seek exemptions from laws they view as violating their beliefs, such as mandates requiring healthcare providers to offer contraception or employers to recognize same-sex marriages. Others, particularly secular and religiously unaffiliated Americans, argue that such exemptions undermine civil rights and contribute to inequality. A 2019 PRRI survey found that 66% of Americans believe businesses should not be allowed to refuse service to LGBTQ+ individuals on religious grounds, reflecting growing discomfort with the idea of religious beliefs being used to justify discrimination.

Similarly, the ongoing debate over prayer in public schools and the display of religious symbols in government buildings reflects broader tensions about the role of religion in a pluralistic society. While some Americans see such practices as integral to the nation's heritage, others argue that they violate the principle of religious neutrality and alienate those who do not share the dominant faith.

The fragmentation of organized religion and the rise of spirituality are reshaping American society in significant ways. As more people embrace individualism and personalized spiritual paths, traditional moral frameworks are being replaced by a diversity of ethical viewpoints, creating both opportunities for inclusivity and challenges related to social cohesion. The weakening of religious institutions as social hubs has contributed to a rise in social isolation, while new forms of community and spirituality are emerging to fill the gap. At the same time, debates about the role of religion in public life are intensifying, reflecting broader questions about how to navigate a society where religious beliefs are increasingly pluralistic and individualized. As American values continue to evolve, the impact of these trends will shape the nation's cultural, political, and social landscape for years to come.

Controversies Around Religion and Institutions

As religious affiliation in the United States declines and becomes more fragmented, debates about the role of religion in public life and institutions have intensified. These controversies reflect deeper societal tensions about how to balance religious freedom with the rights and freedoms of others in an increasingly pluralistic and secular society. From religious exemptions in healthcare to the display of religious symbols in public spaces, these debates have significant implications for governance, law, education, and civil rights. They also highlight the ongoing challenge of upholding the First Amendment's guarantee of both religious freedom and the separation of church and state.

Religious Exemptions in Healthcare and Business

One of the most prominent and controversial areas where religion and institutions collide is in healthcare, particularly regarding religious exemptions to certain laws and policies. Religious groups, particularly conservative Christian organizations, have sought exemptions from healthcare mandates that they argue violate their beliefs, especially on issues like contraception, abortion, and LGBTQ+ rights.

- **Burwell v. Hobby Lobby (2014).** In one of the most significant legal battles over religious exemptions, the Supreme Court ruled in favor of Hobby Lobby, a Christian-owned craft store chain, allowing it to refuse to provide contraception coverage to its employees based on the owners' religious beliefs. The case was a challenge to the Affordable Care Act's (ACA) mandate that employer-provided health insurance plans cover contraception. The Court ruled that closely held corporations like Hobby Lobby could be exempt from the ACA's mandate if it violated the owners' religious beliefs, under the Religious Freedom Restoration Act (RFRA).

The Hobby Lobby decision sparked heated debate. Supporters of the ruling argued that it protected religious freedom, ensuring that business owners would not have to violate their deeply held beliefs. Critics, however, contended that the ruling allowed corporations to impose their religious views on employees, thereby limiting access to critical healthcare services, particularly for women. Moreover, this case set a precedent for broader religious exemptions in other areas, fueling concerns about the potential erosion of civil rights, particularly in relation to healthcare and LGBTQ+ rights.

- **Masterpiece Cakeshop v. Colorado Civil Rights Commission (2018).** Another landmark case involving the intersection of religion and business was Masterpiece Cakeshop, in which the Supreme Court ruled in favor of a Christian baker, Jack Phillips, who refused to create a wedding cake for a same-sex couple due to his religious beliefs. The Court's decision was narrow, focusing on the specifics of how the Colorado Civil Rights Commission had handled the case rather than creating a broad precedent about religious exemptions in business. Nonetheless, the case reignited debates about whether religious freedom should allow businesses to deny services to certain groups, particularly the LGBTQ+ community. Supporters of the ruling viewed it as a victory for religious liberty, allowing individuals to operate their businesses in accordance with their beliefs. Opponents, however, saw it as a license for discrimination, warning that such rulings could pave the way for businesses to deny services to marginalized groups under the guise of religious freedom.

- **Little Sisters of the Poor v. Pennsylvania (2020).** This case further expanded religious exemptions in healthcare. The Little Sisters of the Poor, a Catholic religious order, objected to the ACA's contraception mandate, arguing that even filling out the form to opt out of providing contraception coverage would make them complicit in providing birth control, which violated their religious beliefs. In a 7-2 decision, the Supreme Court ruled that the Trump administration could broaden the religious exemptions to the ACA, allowing religious organizations to opt out of the contraception mandate entirely.

This ruling, like Hobby Lobby, was hailed by religious freedom advocates as a win for protecting religious organizations from being forced to act against their beliefs. However, critics argued that the decision harmed women's access to healthcare, particularly low-income women, by allowing employers to deny contraception coverage. The broader issue raised by these cases is the extent to which religious exemptions can undermine public health policy and the rights of individuals who do not share the religious beliefs of their employers.

Prayer and Religious Symbols in Public Spaces

The question of whether religious symbols and practices should be allowed in public spaces and government institutions has long been a contentious issue in the U.S., with numerous court cases and public debates focused on the separation of church and state. As American society becomes more religiously diverse and secular, these controversies have only intensified.

- **Prayer in Public Schools.** One of the most enduring and controversial issues is the role of prayer in public schools. The Supreme Court's 1962 ruling in Engel v. Vitale, which prohibited state-sponsored prayer in public schools, has been a source of debate for decades. Despite this ruling, efforts to reintroduce prayer or religious instruction in schools continue to surface in various states, particularly in more conservative regions of the country. For example, in 2019, Florida passed a law requiring public schools to hold a daily moment of silence, which some critics saw as a backdoor attempt to reintroduce prayer into schools.

  Advocates for school prayer argue that removing prayer from schools has contributed to the moral decline of American society, and that students should have the right to express their religious beliefs freely. Opponents counter that public schools, as government institutions, should remain neutral on matters of religion, and that state-sponsored prayer violates the Establishment Clause of the First Amendment.

- **The Bladensburg Cross Case (2019).** The display of religious symbols on public property has also been the subject of intense legal battles. In The American Legion v. American Humanist Association (2019), the Supreme Court ruled that a large cross erected as a World War I memorial on public land in Bladensburg, Maryland, did not violate the Establishment Clause of the Constitution. The Court reasoned that the cross, while a religious symbol, had acquired a secular meaning over time as a symbol of sacrifice and remembrance.

This decision was seen as a significant shift in the Court's approach to religious symbols in public spaces. Supporters argued that removing the cross would be an unnecessary attack on religious tradition and history. Critics, however, warned that the ruling could open the door to more religious symbols being placed on public property, blurring the line between church and state.

- **Ten Commandments Displays.** Another recurring controversy is the display of the Ten Commandments on public property, particularly in courthouses and government buildings. Over the years, courts have delivered mixed rulings on the issue. For instance, in McCreary County v. ACLU of Kentucky (2005), the Supreme Court ruled that the display of the Ten Commandments in Kentucky courthouses violated the Establishment Clause because it was intended to promote a religious message. However, in Van Orden v. Perry (2005), the Court upheld the constitutionality of a Ten Commandments monument on the grounds of the Texas State Capitol, arguing that it served a secular purpose as part of a broader historical display.

These cases illustrate the ongoing struggle to define the boundaries of religious expression in public life. Supporters of such displays argue that the Ten Commandments are part of America's legal and moral heritage, while opponents contend that their presence in government buildings constitutes an endorsement of a particular religious tradition, thus violating the principle of religious neutrality.

Religious Education and Public Funding

The role of religion in education has been another major area of controversy, particularly regarding the use of public funds to support religious schools.

- **Espinoza v. Montana Department of Revenue (2020).** In this case, the Supreme Court ruled that states could not exclude religious schools from programs that provide public funding to private schools. The case arose when Montana created a tax credit program to support private school scholarships but prohibited the use of the funds for religious schools, citing the state's constitutional ban on public funding for religious education. The Supreme Court ruled that this prohibition violated the Free Exercise Clause of the First Amendment, allowing religious schools to receive public funds.

This ruling was seen as a victory for school choice advocates, particularly those in the religious community who argue that parents should have the right to send their children to religious schools with the help of public funds. However, critics, including advocates for church-state separation, warned that the decision could erode the wall between church and state, leading to increased government support for religious institutions. They argue that public funds should not be used to support schools that may promote religious doctrines or discriminate against students or staff based on religious beliefs.

- **Public School Curriculum and Religious Content.** In addition to funding religious schools, there have been numerous controversies surrounding the inclusion of religious content in public school curricula. For example, debates have arisen over the teaching of intelligent design (a concept related to creationism) in science classes. In Kitzmiller v. Dover Area School District (2005), a federal court ruled that teaching intelligent design in public school science classes was unconstitutional because it amounted to promoting religious beliefs under the guise of science education.

Similarly, battles over sex education in public schools often have religious undertones. Conservative religious groups frequently advocate for abstinence-only education, arguing that comprehensive sex education promotes values that conflict with their beliefs. However, public health advocates argue that abstinence-only programs are ineffective and deny students critical information about sexual health. These debates highlight the broader conflict between secular education and religiously motivated efforts to influence public school curricula.

Religious Freedom vs. Civil Rights

Another area of controversy where religion and institutions collide is in the tension between religious freedom and civil rights, particularly in relation to LGBTQ+ rights and gender equality.

- **Religious Freedom Restoration Act (RFRA) and State-Level Religious Freedom Laws.** The Religious Freedom Restoration Act (RFRA), passed by Congress in 1993, was intended to protect individuals from laws that substantially burden their free exercise of religion. However, in recent years, RFRA and similar state-level laws have been invoked in ways that have sparked significant controversy. In some cases, religious business owners and institutions have used RFRA to justify refusing services to LGBTQ+ individuals, such as in the Masterpiece Cakeshop case, or to deny contraception coverage, as in Hobby Lobby.

Many states have also passed their own religious freedom laws, which have been criticized as tools for legalizing discrimination. For instance, Indiana's 2015 Religious Freedom Restoration Act faced widespread backlash because it was seen as a way for businesses to discriminate against LGBTQ+ people. In response to public pressure, Indiana later amended the law to explicitly state that it could not be used to justify discrimination.

- **Transgender Rights and Religious Objections.** The growing movement for transgender rights has also clashed with religious beliefs, particularly in areas such as healthcare and education. Some religious healthcare providers, citing their beliefs, have refused to provide services related to gender transition, such as hormone therapy or gender-affirming surgeries. In education, controversies have arisen over the use of gendered facilities, with some religious schools and organizations objecting to allowing transgender students to use bathrooms or locker rooms that align with their gender identity. These conflicts illustrate the broader struggle to balance religious freedom with the rights of transgender individuals.

For example, in 2016, North Carolina's House Bill 2 (HB2), also known as the "bathroom bill," sparked national controversy by requiring people to use public bathrooms that correspond to their sex assigned at birth, rather than their gender identity. Religious groups supported the bill, arguing that it protected privacy and religious values. However, civil rights advocates condemned it as discriminatory and a violation of transgender individuals' rights.

The controversies surrounding religion and institutions reflect broader societal tensions as America becomes more religiously diverse, secular, and pluralistic.

While the U.S. Constitution guarantees both religious freedom and the separation of church and state, these principles are continually tested in a society where religious beliefs intersect with public life, healthcare, education, business, and civil rights. As these debates continue to evolve, they raise critical questions about how to balance religious freedom with the rights of others, how to maintain the separation of church and state, and how to navigate an increasingly complex and diverse religious landscape. The outcomes of these ongoing controversies will shape the future of religious liberty, equality, and pluralism in the United States.

The Human Condition and the Search for Meaning

The decline of organized religion and the rise of individualized spirituality in America have profound implications for the human condition, particularly as people continue to grapple with existential questions about life, death, purpose, and morality. Despite the decreasing influence of traditional religious institutions, the fundamental need for meaning, connection, and belonging persists. As human beings, we are innately driven to seek answers to life's most profound questions: Why are we here? What happens after we die? What gives life purpose? These inquiries are central to the human condition, and for much of history, organized religion provided frameworks for addressing them. Today, however, as fewer people turn to religion for answers, the search for meaning has shifted in new and diverse directions, with significant implications for both individuals and society.

The Decline of Religion and the Search for Meaning

For many centuries, organized religion provided a sense of meaning and structure to human life, offering not only spiritual guidance but also explanations for the mysteries of existence, ethical frameworks, and a sense of belonging. Major world religions such as Christianity, Islam, Judaism, Hinduism, and Buddhism presented comprehensive systems of belief that shaped how individuals understood their place in the universe and their responsibilities to others. However, with the rise of secularism, scientific advancement, and increasing skepticism toward religious authority, many people have turned away from these traditional belief systems, leaving a void that must be filled in new ways.

According to the 2021 Pew Research Center study, 29% of Americans now identify as religiously unaffiliated, a group that includes atheists, agnostics, and people who describe themselves as "spiritual but not religious" (SBNR). This shift indicates that while formal religious affiliation is declining, the search for meaning and a connection to something greater than oneself has not disappeared. In fact, many Americans continue to seek answers to life's existential questions, though increasingly outside the framework of traditional religion. The desire for meaning remains a fundamental part of the human condition, but the avenues through which people pursue it have diversified significantly.

The Rise of Spirituality and Individualized Meaning-Making

One of the most striking trends in the search for meaning is the rise of spirituality, often in highly individualized forms. People who identify as spiritual but not religious (SBNR) tend to reject the dogma, rituals, and hierarchies associated with organized religion, preferring instead to explore spirituality on their own terms. This shift reflects a broader cultural trend toward individualism and self-determination, where personal experience and inner fulfillment are prioritized over external authority.

For many in this group, practices like meditation, yoga, mindfulness, and energy healing have become pathways to spiritual connection and meaning. These practices are often drawn from Eastern traditions such as Buddhism and Hinduism, but they are adapted and secularized to fit contemporary Western lifestyles. For example, the mindfulness movement has its roots in Buddhist meditation practices, but it has been widely adopted in the U.S. as a tool for stress reduction, emotional regulation, and mental health. While not everyone who practices mindfulness identifies as spiritual, for many, these practices offer a way to connect with a deeper sense of self and the universe without the need for formal religious structures.

In addition to these practices, the New Age movement has seen a resurgence in recent years, with beliefs in astrology, crystals, energy healing, and manifestation becoming popular among those seeking spiritual meaning outside traditional religious frameworks. A 2018 Pew study found that 60% of U.S. adults hold at least one New Age belief, such as belief in psychics, astrology, or the healing power of crystals. These practices offer individuals a way to engage with the mysteries of the universe, explore their personal sense of destiny, and craft a narrative about their place in the world. In a rapidly changing, often uncertain world, such beliefs provide a sense of control, purpose, and connection to forces beyond the material realm.

The Role of Science and Secular Humanism

As traditional religious beliefs decline, many people are turning to science and secular humanism as sources of meaning and ethical guidance. Scientific advancements, particularly in fields like cosmology, biology, and neuroscience, have offered new ways of understanding the universe and the human experience. For some, science provides a sense of awe and wonder akin to spiritual experiences, as they explore the vastness of space, the complexity of life, and the mysteries of consciousness. Figures like the late physicist Carl Sagan and contemporary cosmologist Neil deGrasse Tyson have popularized the idea that scientific inquiry can inspire a "cosmic perspective" that connects individuals to the universe in profound ways.

Secular humanism, which emphasizes reason, ethics, and the inherent dignity of all human beings without reference to the supernatural, offers another path for those seeking meaning in a post-religious world. Secular humanists argue that humans can live fulfilling, meaningful lives by fostering empathy, pursuing knowledge, and working to improve the well-being of others. This approach aligns with the growing desire among many people to create meaning through service, social justice, and community involvement. A 2020 Pew Research Center study found that 65% of religiously unaffiliated Americans believe that one's purpose in life is to "help others" and contribute to society, suggesting that ethical engagement and social responsibility are central components of the search for meaning among those who do not adhere to traditional religions.

Community and Belonging in a Fragmented World

Despite the move away from organized religion, the desire for community and belonging remains a key part of the human search for meaning. Historically, religious congregations provided a built-in sense of community where people could connect with others who shared their values and beliefs. As participation in traditional religious communities declines, many people are seeking new forms of connection and community, often in ways that are less formal and more fluid.

One of the most prominent examples of this is the rise of spiritual retreats and wellness festivals like Wanderlust and Spirit Weavers Gathering. These events attract people from across the country who are looking for a sense of spiritual renewal, connection, and personal growth. At these gatherings, participants engage in workshops on mindfulness, yoga, energy healing, and other spiritual practices, while also building connections with like-minded individuals. Such events offer a sense of community and belonging that, for many, is reminiscent of religious gatherings, but without the doctrinal or hierarchical structures of traditional faith communities.

In addition, online communities have emerged as important spaces for people seeking spiritual connection and meaning. Social media platforms like Instagram, TikTok, and YouTube host vast communities of individuals sharing spiritual content, from guided meditations to tarot readings to discussions about astrology. These platforms allow people to explore their spirituality, connect with others, and build a sense of belonging, even in the absence of formal religious institutions. The rise of digital spirituality reflects a broader trend toward decentralized and democratized forms of meaning-making, where individuals can craft their own spiritual paths and find community online.

Existential Anxiety and the Crisis of Meaning

While the rise of spirituality and individualized belief systems provides new avenues for meaning-making, it also raises concerns about the potential for existential anxiety and a crisis of meaning in modern life. The decline of traditional religious institutions has left many without the clear answers and moral frameworks that organized religion once provided, leading some to feel adrift in a world that seems increasingly chaotic and uncertain.

A 2021 Gallup poll found that 55% of Americans reported feeling "a lot" of stress or worry in their daily lives, and 40% reported feeling frequent loneliness. These feelings are particularly pronounced among younger generations, many of whom have disengaged from traditional religious structures but have not found adequate replacements for the community, purpose, and existential certainty that religion once offered. For some, the decline of organized religion has led to a sense of moral relativism or nihilism, where the lack of shared values or meaning creates a vacuum of purpose.

Philosophers and psychologists, such as Viktor Frankl, have long argued that the search for meaning is central to human well-being. In his seminal work "Man's Search for Meaning," Frankl, a Holocaust survivor and psychiatrist, contended that humans are driven by the need to find purpose, and that the failure to do so leads to despair and existential suffering. In today's secular, pluralistic society, many individuals are struggling to find meaning in a world that no longer offers the clear, overarching narratives that traditional religion once provided.

The Future of the Search for Meaning

The search for meaning in America is likely to continue evolving in response to broader cultural, technological, and social changes. As organized religion continues to decline, new forms of spirituality, science, and secular humanism will play an increasingly important role in how people understand their place in the world. However, the challenge will be to ensure that these new forms of meaning-making provide the same sense of purpose, connection, and ethical guidance that religion once did, while also adapting to the diverse and rapidly changing needs of modern society.

In the absence of traditional religious frameworks, many will continue to turn to personal spiritual practices, community involvement, and scientific inquiry as sources of meaning. At the same time, the rise of mental health awareness and wellness culture suggests that the search for meaning will increasingly focus on personal well-being and emotional health, blending elements of spirituality, psychology, and self-care. Whether through meditation, social justice work, or the pursuit of knowledge, the need for meaning will remain a defining aspect of the human condition, driving individuals to seek answers to life's most profound questions in new and innovative ways.

While the role of organized religion may be declining, the search for meaning is as vital as ever. As individuals navigate an increasingly complex and fragmented world, they will continue to explore new spiritual paths, ethical frameworks, and forms of community that address their deepest existential needs. This ongoing search will shape the future of American culture and society, as people redefine what it means to live a meaningful, fulfilling life in the 21st century.

The Future of Religion, Spirituality, and Meaning in America

The fragmentation of religion in America, marked by the decline of traditional organized religious participation and the rise of diverse spiritual practices, reflects deep and ongoing shifts in the cultural, social, and moral landscape of the country. While fewer Americans are affiliating with established religious institutions, the human search for meaning, purpose, and connection remains as strong as ever. However, this search is increasingly taking place outside the confines of conventional religious frameworks, with individuals crafting their own belief systems, exploring new spiritual paths, and seeking answers to life's profound questions through personalized, often eclectic practices. This transformation presents both opportunities and challenges for American society in the years to come.

The Rise of Individualism and Personal Autonomy

The rise of individualized spirituality and secularism reflects a broader cultural trend toward personal autonomy and self-determination. Many Americans now seek spiritual fulfillment on their own terms, rejecting the authority and dogma of traditional religious institutions in favor of a more personal and flexible approach to belief. Practices like meditation, yoga, mindfulness, and astrology allow individuals to cultivate a sense of connection to something greater than themselves while avoiding the hierarchical structures that characterize organized religion.

This shift toward individualism has positive implications for personal freedom and inclusivity. It allows for a more pluralistic society where people are free to explore different spiritual and moral paths without feeling constrained by traditional doctrines. It also fosters an environment where diverse beliefs can coexist, creating opportunities for interfaith dialogue, cross-cultural understanding, and new forms of community-building. The increasing visibility and acceptance of practices drawn from non-Christian traditions—such as Buddhism, Hinduism, and Indigenous spiritualities—further enrich America's religious and cultural tapestry.

At the same time, however, the move toward individualism raises important questions about the future of social cohesion. With fewer people participating in shared religious practices and adhering to common moral frameworks, society risks becoming more fragmented. The traditional role of religious institutions in fostering community, offering moral guidance, and providing a sense of belonging is weakening, and it remains unclear whether new spiritual practices or secular ideologies can fully replace these functions. The rise of loneliness and social isolation, particularly among younger generations, suggests that while personal autonomy offers freedom, it can also lead to disconnection in an increasingly atomized world.

Challenges of Moral Relativism and Social Fragmentation

The fragmentation of religious belief also brings with it the challenge of moral relativism. In a world where fewer people subscribe to universal religious teachings, society is increasingly characterized by a diversity of moral viewpoints. While this pluralism allows for greater tolerance and respect for different lifestyles and beliefs, it can also lead to conflict, particularly when it comes to defining societal norms and laws. As Americans become more divided on key ethical issues—such as reproductive rights, LGBTQ+ rights, and healthcare—the lack of a shared moral framework can make it difficult to achieve consensus on matters of public policy.

The erosion of traditional religious authority has also contributed to growing political and cultural polarization. In the absence of shared religious values, political ideologies have often taken their place as the primary sources of identity and moral guidance. This dynamic is evident in the increasing alignment of religious identity with political affiliation, particularly in the context of evangelical Christianity's close relationship with conservative politics. Conversely, the rise of secularism and spirituality among younger generations has often aligned with progressive causes, creating deeper divisions between religious conservatives and secular progressives. These cultural divisions, while not new, have become more entrenched, as religious and moral pluralism makes it harder to find common ground on issues of national importance.

The Ongoing Human Search for Meaning

Despite the challenges posed by religious fragmentation and moral pluralism, the search for meaning remains central to the human condition. Whether through religion, spirituality, science, or secular humanism, people continue to seek answers to existential questions about life, death, and purpose. This fundamental drive is unlikely to diminish, even as traditional religious structures continue to lose influence. Instead, new forms of meaning-making will continue to emerge, reflecting the diversity of beliefs and values in modern society.

For some, this search will involve exploring ancient spiritual traditions, adapting them to contemporary needs and contexts. Practices like mindfulness and yoga, once rooted in specific religious traditions, have become tools for personal growth and emotional well-being, offering a way to address the stress and uncertainty of modern life. Others will turn to science and secular philosophies to find meaning in the pursuit of knowledge, ethics, and social justice. Secular humanism, with its emphasis on reason, empathy, and the inherent dignity of all people, offers a compelling alternative to traditional religious morality, especially for those who seek to live meaningful lives without belief in the supernatural.

Meanwhile, religious diversity will continue to shape the American experience. The rise of Islam, Hinduism, Buddhism, and other non-Christian faiths, as well as the resurgence of Indigenous spiritual practices and New Age beliefs, will add to the rich mosaic of belief systems coexisting in the U.S. These developments offer opportunities for new forms of interfaith dialogue and cooperation, as people from different backgrounds and traditions come together to address shared concerns, such as climate change, inequality, and human rights.

The Role of Institutions in a Pluralistic Society

As religion and spirituality become more diverse, American institutions—particularly schools, workplaces, and government bodies—will be tasked with navigating this pluralism in ways that respect both religious freedom and the rights of others. Controversies over religious exemptions in healthcare, education, and business will likely continue, raising important questions about how to balance the rights of religious groups with the rights of marginalized communities, such as women and LGBTQ+ individuals. The principle of church-state separation, while still foundational, will be increasingly tested as new religious and spiritual movements intersect with public life.

Moreover, institutions will need to find ways to foster community and a sense of belonging in a society where traditional religious communities are in decline. As more people move away from religious congregations, new forms of civic engagement, volunteerism, and social networks will be essential for building social cohesion. Public institutions, from schools to workplaces, may need to play a greater role in fostering spaces for dialogue, mutual understanding, and collective purpose.

The Future of Religion and Spirituality in America

Looking ahead, it is clear that the religious landscape in America will continue to evolve in response to changing cultural, social, and technological forces.

While organized religion is likely to play a diminished role in the lives of future generations, spirituality, ethics, and the search for meaning will remain central to human existence. Whether through new spiritual movements, secular humanism, or emerging forms of community engagement, Americans will continue to seek ways to live meaningful lives and address the moral and existential challenges of their time.

The future of religion and spirituality in America will be shaped by a delicate balance between personal autonomy and communal responsibility, between individual meaning-making and the need for shared values. As society becomes more religiously diverse and spiritually fragmented, the challenge will be to create spaces where different belief systems can coexist, where individuals can find both personal fulfillment and a sense of belonging, and where the pursuit of meaning remains at the heart of the human experience.

In conclusion, the fragmentation of organized religion and the rise of spiritual diversity mark a significant transformation in American society. While this shift offers new opportunities for personal growth, freedom, and inclusivity, it also presents challenges related to moral consensus, social cohesion, and the role of religion in public life. As Americans continue to navigate these changes, the ongoing search for meaning—whether through religion, spirituality, or secular pursuits—will remain a defining feature of the human condition. The ways in which individuals and institutions respond to these challenges will shape the future of American values, culture, and community in profound ways

The Dynamic and Evolving Debate

In recent years, America has witnessed a profound shift in the understanding and discussion of gender roles, sexuality, and identity. What was once considered fixed and unchangeable—ideas about what it means to be a man or a woman, the role of gender in society, and the boundaries of sexuality—has become a fluid and ever-changing discourse. This transformation has sparked heated debates, cultural conflicts, and legal battles across the country, affecting everything from education to sports, healthcare, and public policy. Central to these discussions are questions about identity, pronouns, and what truly constitutes a man or a woman. These issues challenge deeply ingrained societal norms and evoke strong emotional responses on all sides of the debate.

The Evolution of Gender Roles and Sexuality

Traditionally, gender roles in America were largely defined by biological sex: men were expected to exhibit traits such as strength, assertiveness, and leadership, while women were often associated with nurturing, care-giving, and emotional support. These roles were underpinned by heterosexual norms, where relationships between men and women followed a prescribed pattern of marriage, family-building, and gender-specific duties. For most of the 20th century, these gender expectations were seen as natural and immutable.

However, the latter half of the 20th century—fueled by feminist movements, the sexual revolution, and growing LGBTQ+ advocacy—saw a gradual but significant unraveling of these traditional norms. The Women's Liberation Movement of the 1960s and 1970s, for example, challenged restrictive gender roles and called for women's rights to work, vote, and have control over their own bodies. Meanwhile, the Gay Rights Movement sought to normalize same-sex relationships and challenge laws that discriminated against LGBTQ+ individuals. Together, these movements laid the groundwork for today's more complex and inclusive understanding of gender and sexuality.

In contemporary America, gender is increasingly viewed not as a binary but as a spectrum. Terms like non-binary, gender-queer, and gender-fluid have entered the mainstream, representing identities that fall outside traditional male and female categories. Similarly, sexuality is now recognized as existing on a spectrum, with individuals identifying as gay, lesbian, bisexual, pan-sexual, or asexual, among other orientations. A 2021 Gallup poll found that 5.6% of U.S. adults identify as LGBTQ+, a significant increase from 4.5% in 2017, reflecting growing awareness and acceptance of diverse sexual identities. Among Generation Z (born between 1997 and 2012), that number is even higher, with nearly 21% identifying as LGBTQ+.

The Pronoun Debate: Identity and Language

One of the most visible and contentious aspects of the evolving discussion around gender in America is the debate over pronouns. The pronoun issue is about much more than just grammar—it represents a fundamental shift in how society understands and respects individual identity, particularly for people who do not identify strictly as male or female. For many, adopting new pronouns or using gender-neutral pronouns like they/them is a critical way of affirming gender identity and challenging traditional binary conceptions of gender. However, the pronoun debate has sparked significant controversy, particularly among those who feel it challenges biological realities or infringes on freedom of speech. This debate has played out in schools, workplaces, social media, and the legal system, reflecting deeper tensions about identity, autonomy, and societal norms.

The Rise of Gender-Neutral Pronouns

The growing visibility of non-binary and gender-nonconforming people has brought gender-neutral pronouns to the forefront of public discourse. While English has long used "he" and "she" as gender-specific pronouns, many individuals who do not fit within the traditional male-female binary have advocated for the use of they/them as singular, gender-neutral pronouns. This practice has gained considerable traction in recent years and is now widely accepted in many institutions, media outlets, and online platforms. In 2019, Merriam-Webster named "they" as its Word of the Year, recognizing the word's growing use as a singular, non-binary pronoun.

Other alternatives to "he" and "she" have also emerged, including neopronouns like ze/zir, xe/xem, and ey/em, which are used by some individuals who feel that traditional pronouns do not adequately represent their gender identity. These neopronouns have yet to achieve the same level of mainstream acceptance as "they/them," but their existence reflects the desire among some people to have language that more fully captures their personal experience of gender.

According to a 2021 Pew Research Center survey, 1.6% of U.S. adults identify as transgender or non-binary, and nearly 35% of Generation Z say they know someone who uses gender-neutral pronouns. This figure highlights a generational divide: younger Americans are far more likely to encounter and accept gender-neutral pronouns, while older generations are less familiar or comfortable with these changes. Pew's data also shows that 56% of U.S. adults now believe that society should accept the use of gender-neutral pronouns, though this support is far from universal.

The Significance of Pronouns for Gender Identity

For many transgender, non-binary, and gender-nonconforming individuals, pronouns are more than just a grammatical preference—they are a critical aspect of their identity. Using the correct pronouns is seen as a sign of respect, acknowledgment, and validation of a person's gender. For transgender individuals who have transitioned, being addressed with their chosen pronouns is an affirmation of their authentic self, while mis-gendering (using the wrong pronouns) can be deeply hurtful and even traumatic. A 2021 study published by the Journal of Adolescent Health found that transgender and non-binary youth who are consistently referred to by their correct pronouns experience significantly lower rates of depression and suicide compared to those who are mis-gendered. This underscores the psychological importance of pronoun recognition for gender-diverse individuals.

At the heart of the pronoun debate is the question of self-determination. Advocates for gender-neutral pronouns argue that every person has the right to define their own identity and that society should adapt its language to reflect and respect that identity. This argument is based on the idea that language shapes social reality and that by recognizing a broader spectrum of gender identities, society becomes more inclusive and equitable. In this sense, the pronoun debate is not just about language but about recognizing and affirming the human dignity of individuals who do not conform to binary gender norms.

Resistance to Pronoun Changes: Free Speech and Biological Reality

While the use of gender-neutral pronouns has gained support in many sectors, it has also sparked significant resistance, particularly from those who see it as a challenge to free speech, biological science, or traditional values. One of the most common arguments against mandated use of gender-neutral pronouns is that it infringes on freedom of speech. Critics argue that compelling individuals to use certain pronouns, especially those that do not align with their understanding of biological sex, constitutes a form of ideological coercion. This argument gained national attention with the controversy surrounding Canada's Bill C-16, passed in 2016, which added gender identity and expression to the country's Human Rights Code. While the bill was intended to protect transgender and non-binary people from discrimination, critics, including academic and psychologist Jordan Peterson, claimed that it would force individuals to use gender-neutral pronouns or face legal consequences, though no such cases have yet occurred under the law.

In the United States, concerns about free speech have surfaced in several high-profile cases. In Shawnee State University, a professor named Nicholas Meriwether filed a lawsuit after being reprimanded for refusing to use the preferred pronouns of a transgender student, citing his religious beliefs. In 2021, the 6th U.S. Circuit Court of Appeals ruled in favor of Meriwether, arguing that the university had violated his free speech rights. This case highlights the ongoing tension between protecting the rights of transgender and non-binary individuals and safeguarding freedom of expression, particularly when personal beliefs or religious convictions are involved.

Another major source of resistance to gender-neutral pronouns comes from individuals who believe that gender is fundamentally tied to biological sex. Many opponents of gender-neutral pronouns argue that terms like "man" and "woman" are rooted in physical, anatomical differences and that attempting to redefine these terms based on identity rather than biology undermines scientific realities. This view is often associated with gender-critical feminists, sometimes referred to as TERFs (trans-exclusionary radical feminists), who argue that recognizing transgender women as women erases the distinct experiences of biological women and undermines sex-based protections for women, especially in areas like healthcare, education, and sports.

This debate over biology versus identity extends into legal and political spheres. Several states, including Tennessee and Florida, have introduced legislation that seeks to restrict the use of gender-neutral pronouns in schools, particularly when addressing students who are under 18. Proponents of these laws argue that children should not be exposed to what they see as radical gender ideology, while opponents view such measures as harmful to transgender and non-binary youth, who often rely on schools as spaces where their identities are affirmed.

Pronouns and Public Policy

The pronoun debate has increasingly moved from social discourse into the realm of public policy, with significant implications for schools, workplaces, and public institutions. Many organizations, from universities to corporations, have adopted policies requiring the use of preferred pronouns in official communications and employee interactions. Schools, in particular, have become a battleground in the pronoun debate, as educators navigate the legal and ethical complexities of respecting students' gender identities while balancing parental rights and community standards.

In 2021, the Biden administration introduced new policies that allow people to select X as a gender marker on their U.S. passports, offering a non-binary option in official documentation for the first time. This move was praised by LGBTQ+ advocacy groups as a step toward greater inclusivity and recognition of diverse gender identities. However, critics argued that allowing individuals to choose their gender on official documents undermines the clarity and reliability of these records. Some states, including California and New York, have also introduced gender-neutral options on driver's licenses and birth certificates, reflecting the growing movement toward official recognition of non-binary and gender-nonconforming individuals.

In schools, the use of gender-neutral pronouns has become a contentious issue, particularly as more students come out as transgender or non-binary at younger ages. According to a 2020 Trevor Project study, 27% of LGBTQ+ youth use pronouns that fall outside the traditional male-female binary. Schools across the country have responded by implementing policies that require teachers and staff to use students' preferred names and pronouns, even if they differ from the student's legal name or sex assigned at birth. While many educators support these policies as a way to foster a safe and supportive learning environment, others have raised concerns about whether parents should have more control over how schools handle gender identity issues.

In some cases, these policies have led to significant backlash. In Virginia, for example, a high school teacher was fired for refusing to use a transgender student's preferred pronouns, citing his religious beliefs. The case became a flash-point in the broader national debate about gender identity and religious freedom, and the teacher ultimately sued the school district, with the case being closely watched by both LGBTQ+ advocacy groups and religious freedom organizations.

Pronouns in the Digital Age

The rise of social media has amplified the pronoun debate, with platforms like Twitter, Instagram, and TikTok becoming arenas for discussions about gender identity and language. Many social media platforms now allow users to display their pronouns in their profiles, a practice that has become increasingly common as a way to signal support for transgender and non-binary individuals. For many young people, particularly those in Generation Z, sharing pronouns is seen as an essential part of building an inclusive online community.

At the same time, social media has also amplified the backlash against gender-neutral pronouns. Influential conservative figures and commentators have taken to platforms like YouTube to criticize what they see as "forced" use of pronouns, framing it as an imposition of radical gender ideology. This rhetoric often appeals to audiences who feel that their values or beliefs are being marginalized in favor of progressive ideologies. The viral nature of these debates has contributed to a culture war over language and identity, with each side feeling that their perspective is under attack.

The Future of the Pronoun Debate

The pronoun debate is likely to continue evolving as society grapples with questions about identity, language, and the rights of individuals. As more people embrace non-binary and gender-nonconforming identities, the use of gender-neutral pronouns is likely to become more widespread and normalized, particularly among younger generations. However, resistance to these changes will likely persist, particularly from those who view the redefinition of gender and the use of alternative pronouns as a threat to free speech or biological truths.

Ultimately, the pronoun debate is about more than just language—it is a reflection of deeper societal changes around gender, identity, and inclusion. How society chooses to navigate this issue will have lasting implications for the rights and recognition of transgender and non-binary individuals, as well as for broader conversations about autonomy, respect, and equality. As new policies are implemented and legal battles continue, the pronoun debate will remain a key battleground in the ongoing struggle to define and defend individual identity in an increasingly diverse and complex world.

What Constitutes a Man or a Woman? Scientific and Societal Dynamics

At the heart of the ongoing debates about gender identity is a fundamental and deeply contested question: What constitutes a man or a woman? For centuries, this question was thought to have a clear answer, with sex being viewed as a straightforward biological binary. People were generally classified as male or female based on their anatomy, chromosomes, and reproductive systems. However, in recent decades, this binary understanding of gender has been increasingly challenged by scientific discoveries, social movements, and personal lived experiences, leading to a more nuanced and complex understanding of what it means to be a man or a woman.

The conversation is now shaped by multiple perspectives—biological, psychological, and sociocultural—each contributing to the broader debate about how society defines gender. These differing views have significant implications for everything from legal rights and healthcare to sports and education, fueling ongoing cultural conflicts.

The Biological Perspective: Chromosomes, Hormones, and Anatomy

For much of modern history, biological sex has been understood in terms of chromosomes, hormones, and anatomy. Traditionally, someone with two X chromosomes (XX) was classified as female, while someone with one X and one Y chromosome (XY) was classified as male. This binary view of sex has been reinforced by the physical traits typically associated with these chromosomes: individuals with XX chromosomes generally develop female reproductive organs (ovaries, uterus), while individuals with XY chromosomes generally develop male reproductive organs (testes).

Additionally, hormones like testosterone and estrogen have been considered primary drivers of physical and behavioral differences between men and women. Testosterone, which is more prevalent in males, is associated with traits like muscle mass, deeper voices, and body hair, while estrogen, more prevalent in females, is linked to menstruation, breast development, and other secondary sexual characteristics.

However, the biological story is far more complex than the XX/XY binary suggests. While chromosomes, hormones, and reproductive anatomy are important markers of biological sex, they do not always align neatly into two distinct categories. Intersex individuals—those born with physical or chromosomal characteristics that do not fit typical definitions of male or female—constitute around 1.7% of the population, according to estimates from the Intersex Society of North America. Intersex people may have ambiguous genitalia, atypical chromosomal patterns (such as XXY or XO), or hormone levels that do not conform to typical male or female patterns.

Moreover, research has shown that sex and gender involve a complex interplay of biological, genetic, and environmental factors. Some scientists argue that focusing solely on chromosomes and anatomy to define gender oversimplifies the diversity of human experiences. Dr. Anne Fausto-Sterling, a biologist and gender studies scholar, has argued for a more expansive understanding of biological sex, proposing that we think of sex along a spectrum rather than as a binary.

The Psychological and Identity-Based Perspective: Gender as a Social Construct

While biological sex refers to the physical characteristics associated with being male or female, gender is increasingly understood as a distinct concept, often framed as a social construct that reflects how individuals identify themselves and how society expects people to behave based on their perceived sex. Many contemporary scholars and activists argue that gender is not determined solely by biology but is shaped by cultural, social, and individual factors.

For example, Judith Butler, a philosopher and gender theorist, has argued that gender is something we "perform" rather than something we inherently are. According to Butler, gender norms and roles are perpetuated through repeated behaviors and social expectations, and as such, they can be deconstructed and redefined. In this view, being a man or a woman is not about adhering to a fixed biological template but about aligning one's identity and expression with the roles and characteristics that society associates with masculinity or femininity.

This perspective has become especially relevant in discussions about transgender individuals, who experience a disconnect between their biological sex and their gender identity. For transgender people, transitioning—whether through hormone therapy, surgery, or simply social transition (changing one's name, pronouns, and appearance)—is often a way to align their physical presentation with their internal sense of self. According to the American Psychological Association (APA), gender identity is a deeply ingrained sense of being male, female, or something else, and it may not necessarily correspond with biological sex.

A 2021 Trevor Project survey found that 42% of LGBTQ+ youth identify as transgender or non-binary, indicating that younger generations are increasingly rejecting the binary framework of male and female in favor of more fluid and inclusive understandings of gender. This shift reflects a growing recognition that gender is not fixed at birth but can evolve over time based on personal experience and identity. In fact, the World Health Organization (WHO) defines gender as a "socially constructed" concept that varies across different cultures and periods in history, further supporting the idea that gender is not biologically determined.

Societal Dynamics: Traditional Views vs. Evolving Concepts

While there is growing recognition of gender diversity, the question of what constitutes a man or a woman remains a deeply polarizing issue in American society. Many Americans, especially those with more conservative or religious views, believe that gender is inherently tied to biological sex and that deviating from this binary undermines moral and social order. For them, the biological categories of male and female are not just scientific facts but are also divinely ordained or deeply rooted in natural law. According to a 2022 Pew Research Center survey, 54% of Americans believe that a person's gender is determined by their biological sex at birth, while 44% believe that gender can be different from biological sex.

This cultural divide is reflected in heated debates over public policy, particularly regarding the rights and recognition of transgender individuals. For example, many states, particularly in the South and Midwest, have introduced or passed legislation that restricts access to gender-affirming healthcare for minors or limits the ability of transgender individuals to change the gender markers on their legal documents. Supporters of these measures argue that biological sex is immutable and that recognizing gender identity over biology creates confusion, especially for children and adolescents.

In contrast, advocacy groups such as the American Medical Association (AMA) and the American Academy of Pediatrics (AAP) support access to gender-affirming care, including hormone therapy and puberty blockers for transgender youth, citing numerous studies that show such treatments significantly improve mental health outcomes for transgender individuals. A 2021 study published in the Journal of the American Medical Association (JAMA) found that transgender youth who received puberty blockers or hormone therapy had lower rates of depression, anxiety, and suicidal thoughts compared to those who did not receive such care. This reflects a growing medical consensus that gender identity, rather than biological sex alone, should be considered when determining a person's gender.

The Legal and Political Implications

The question of what constitutes a man or a woman has significant legal implications, particularly in areas such as employment, healthcare, and education. In 2020, the Supreme Court's landmark decision in Bostock v. Clayton County ruled that the Civil Rights Act of 1964 protects employees from discrimination based on sexual orientation and gender identity. This ruling was celebrated as a major victory for transgender rights, as it expanded federal protections against discrimination in the workplace. However, it also provoked backlash from religious groups and conservative lawmakers who argue that such decisions undermine religious freedoms and biological realities.

The debate has also extended to issues like bathroom access and participation in sports. Several states have introduced "bathroom bills" that require individuals to use public restrooms corresponding to their biological sex rather than their gender identity. These laws have sparked fierce protests from LGBTQ+ advocates, who argue that such measures not only discriminate against transgender individuals but also pose safety risks by forcing them to use facilities that do not align with their gender identity. A 2018 UCLA School of Law study found that 70% of transgender individuals reported experiencing verbal harassment, physical assault, or being denied access when attempting to use restrooms that aligned with their gender identity.

Gender in Sports: Fairness vs. Inclusion

The participation of transgender women (those assigned male at birth but who identify as women) in women's sports has emerged as one of the most contentious aspects of the debate over what constitutes a man or a woman. Supporters of transgender inclusion argue that transgender women should have the right to compete according to their gender identity, emphasizing the importance of equality and the right to participate in public life without discrimination. However, critics claim that transgender women retain physical advantages from male puberty, such as greater muscle mass and lung capacity, even after transitioning, which they argue creates unfair competition in women's sports.

This debate came to a head with the case of Lia Thomas, a transgender swimmer who competed on the University of Pennsylvania's women's swim team after transitioning. In 2022, Thomas won the NCAA Division I national championship in the women's 500-yard freestyle, sparking a media firestorm. Critics argued that Thomas had an unfair advantage due to her male puberty, while supporters emphasized that she had followed all NCAA rules, including undergoing hormone replacement therapy to lower her testosterone levels.

A 2021 Gallup poll found that 62% of Americans believe that transgender athletes should only be allowed to compete on teams that correspond with their biological sex, while 34% believe they should be allowed to compete according to their gender identity. This divide highlights the tension between fairness and inclusion—a key issue in the ongoing debate about how to define gender in competitive environments.

Conclusion: The Ongoing Evolution of Gender Identity

The question of what constitutes a man or a woman is no longer simply a matter of biology but a complex intersection of science, identity, culture, and politics. As society continues to evolve, the understanding of gender is becoming more fluid and inclusive, recognizing the diversity of human experiences beyond the traditional male-female binary.

While biological factors like chromosomes, hormones, and anatomy remain important, they are increasingly seen as just one part of a broader picture that includes psychological, social, and cultural dimensions. The ongoing debate reflects deeper societal shifts, with younger generations more likely to embrace a spectrum of gender identities and older generations more likely to adhere to binary definitions rooted in biological sex. As legal battles, political debates, and cultural conversations continue to unfold, the definition of what it means to be a man or a woman will remain central to the ongoing re-imagining of gender roles and identity in America.

Men in Women's Sports: A Heated Debate

One of the most contentious and visible aspects of the broader gender identity debate is the issue of transgender women (individuals assigned male at birth who identify and live as women) participating in women's sports. This issue strikes at the core of long-standing ideas about fairness, equality, and the role of biological differences in athletic competition. While advocates argue that transgender women should have the right to compete according to their gender identity, opponents claim that male puberty gives transgender women inherent physiological advantages that undermine fair competition in women's sports.

This debate has escalated in recent years, with high-profile cases and legislative efforts bringing national attention to the issue. The controversy raises fundamental questions about what it means to ensure fairness in sports and how to balance the rights of transgender athletes with concerns about competitive integrity. The consequences of this debate have far-reaching implications, not only for athletes but also for the broader conversation about gender, inclusion, and equity in public life.

The Case of Lia Thomas: A Turning Point in the Debate

A key flash-point in the debate over transgender athletes in women's sports was the case of Lia Thomas, a transgender swimmer at the University of Pennsylvania. Thomas, who began competing in NCAA Division I women's swimming after undergoing hormone replacement therapy (HRT), became the first openly transgender athlete to win an NCAA national championship in March 2022, claiming victory in the 500-yard freestyle event.

Before transitioning, Thomas had competed on the men's swim team for three years, with moderate success. After transitioning, she began competing in the women's division and quickly drew attention due to her performance. While Thomas followed NCAA guidelines, which require transgender women to undergo at least one year of HRT to lower testosterone levels, her success reignited the debate over whether transgender women retain physiological advantages, such as increased muscle mass, bone density, and cardiovascular capacity, even after transitioning.

Critics argued that Thomas's previous experience competing in men's swimming and the physical changes resulting from male puberty gave her an unfair advantage over cisgender women (those whose gender identity aligns with their sex assigned at birth). For example, former Olympic swimmer Nancy Hogshead-Makar, a vocal advocate for women's sports, expressed concerns about fairness, stating that allowing transgender women to compete in female categories "robs women of opportunities."

Supporters of Thomas, however, emphasized the importance of inclusivity and the right of transgender individuals to participate in sports that align with their gender identity. They pointed out that Thomas had complied with the NCAA's regulations on hormone therapy, which are designed to create a level playing field. Many also argued that focusing on Thomas's success ignores the broader context in which transgender athletes often face significant challenges, including discrimination and barriers to participation.

Thomas herself acknowledged the complexities of the debate, but maintained that her participation in women's sports was in line with both NCAA rules and her identity. In an interview with Sports Illustrated, she stated, "I just want to show trans kids and younger trans athletes that you're not alone."

The Science Behind the Debate: Do Transgender Women Have a Physical Advantage?

At the heart of the debate over transgender women in women's sports is the question of whether male puberty confers lasting physiological advantages that hormone therapy cannot fully mitigate. Male puberty typically leads to increased muscle mass, bone density, and lung capacity, all of which are considered advantages in many sports. Critics of transgender women's participation in women's sports argue that even with testosterone suppression, these advantages persist, making competition inherently unfair.

A 2020 study published in the British Journal of Sports Medicine examined the impact of hormone therapy on transgender athletes, finding that while transgender women's muscle mass and strength do decrease after one year of hormone therapy, they often remain higher than that of cisgender women. The study suggested that a one-year period of hormone therapy may not be sufficient to fully eliminate the performance differences between transgender women and cisgender women. This study has been frequently cited by those arguing for restrictions on transgender women's participation in women's sports.

On the other hand, supporters of transgender inclusion argue that the issue is more nuanced. Not all sports rely on the same set of physical attributes, and factors such as skill, strategy, and endurance also play critical roles in athletic success. Furthermore, transgender athletes who undergo hormone therapy often face significant physical challenges, including muscle loss and changes in stamina. Proponents of transgender inclusion, such as the advocacy group Athlete Ally, argue that sports organizations should focus on creating inclusive policies that balance fairness with the need to protect transgender athletes' rights to participate in sports according to their gender identity.

The scientific debate is far from settled, with ongoing research into how hormone therapy and other medical interventions affect athletic performance in transgender athletes. However, the complexity of this issue has made it difficult to find a consensus that satisfies both sides of the debate.

Legislative Responses: State-Level Bans and Federal Discussions

In response to the growing controversy, several states have passed or proposed legislation aimed at restricting transgender women from competing in women's sports. Idaho was the first state to pass such a law in 2020 with the Fairness in Women's Sports Act, which bars transgender women from participating in female athletic teams in public schools and colleges. The law is currently being challenged in federal court by the American Civil Liberties Union (ACLU), which argues that the ban is unconstitutional and discriminatory.

Since then, numerous states, including Florida, Texas, Mississippi, and Tennessee, have passed similar laws banning transgender women from participating in women's sports at the K-12 and collegiate levels. These laws often argue that the inclusion of transgender women undermines the integrity of women's sports and puts cisgender female athletes at a disadvantage. Florida Governor Ron DeSantis, when signing the state's bill into law in 2021, said, "In Florida, girls are going to play girls' sports and boys are going to play boys' sports," framing the law as a way to protect opportunities for female athletes.

At the federal level, the issue has sparked significant debate as well. In 2021, President Joe Biden signed an executive order aimed at preventing discrimination based on gender identity, including in school sports. This directive, which is based on the Bostock v. Clayton County Supreme Court ruling (which extended civil rights protections to LGBTQ+ individuals), could potentially lead to legal challenges to state laws that ban transgender athletes from competing according to their gender identity.

In Congress, the issue remains highly divisive. Republican lawmakers have introduced the Protection of Women and Girls in Sports Act, which would amend Title IX to explicitly require athletes to compete based on their biological sex. Title IX is a federal law passed in 1972 that prohibits sex-based discrimination in education programs and activities, including sports. Supporters of the bill argue that it would preserve the original intent of Title IX by ensuring that female athletes have equal opportunities. Opponents, however, contend that such a measure would violate the rights of transgender athletes and reinforce harmful stereotypes.

High School and Collegiate Sports: A Patchwork of Policies

The question of transgender participation in sports is especially contentious at the high school and collegiate levels, where different states and governing bodies have adopted widely varying policies.

The National Collegiate Athletic Association (NCAA) allows transgender women to compete in women's sports after one year of testosterone suppression. However, individual states and universities have the authority to impose their own rules. The NCAA has voiced its support for transgender athletes, stating in 2021 that the association "firmly and unequivocally supports the opportunity for transgender student-athletes to compete in college sports."

At the high school level, policies vary dramatically. Some states, like California and New York, have implemented policies that allow transgender students to participate in sports according to their gender identity without requiring medical intervention or hormone therapy. In contrast, states like Texas and Florida have passed laws mandating that students participate in sports based on the sex listed on their birth certificate, regardless of their gender identity or whether they have undergone hormone therapy.

This patchwork of policies has led to confusion and legal challenges, particularly for athletes who may find themselves eligible to compete in one state but banned in another. As transgender participation in sports continues to spark controversy, it seems likely that more states will pass legislation, resulting in further polarization and litigation.

The Broader Implications: Fairness, Inclusion, and the Future of Sports

The debate over transgender athletes in women's sports raises critical questions about how society defines fairness and inclusion in the context of gender identity. For advocates of transgender inclusion, allowing athletes to compete according to their gender identity is a matter of civil rights and equality. They argue that transgender individuals, like everyone else, deserve the opportunity to participate in sports without facing discrimination. They also point out that banning transgender athletes from women's sports could have devastating psychological effects, contributing to higher rates of depression, anxiety, and suicide among transgender youth.

Opponents, however, emphasize the need to protect competitive fairness and ensure that female athletes have a level playing field. For them, the inclusion of transgender women in women's sports raises concerns about the erosion of sex-based categories in athletics and the potential for biological advantages to distort competition. These concerns, they argue, are not rooted in prejudice but in the desire to preserve the integrity of women's sports, which were historically marginalized and only recently gained equal footing with men's sports through laws like Title IX.

Both sides of the debate raise valid concerns about how to balance the rights of transgender athletes with the need to maintain fairness in competition. As more transgender athletes seek to participate in elite and amateur sports, organizations will be forced to continually reevaluate their policies and practices. This ongoing debate will shape the future of sports, gender identity, and public policy in the United States for years to come.

The debate over transgender women in women's sports is a microcosm of the larger societal conversation about gender identity, fairness, and inclusion. As more transgender athletes step into the spotlight, the need for thoughtful, evidence-based policies that respect both the rights of transgender individuals and the integrity of competitive sports becomes more urgent. However, finding a balance between these competing interests will not be easy. With strong opinions on both sides, and with laws and policies in flux across the country, the issue of transgender participation in women's sports will likely remain a highly charged and evolving topic in the years ahead.

194 | AMERICAN CHASMS: THE DIVIDED STATES OF AMERICA

Impact on America's Value System

The evolving conversation around gender identity, sexuality, and participation in sports is not just about individual rights or policies—it strikes at the core of America's value system, challenging long-held beliefs about gender roles, fairness, and societal norms. Over the past several decades, the U.S. has undergone significant shifts in how these concepts are understood, and the debates surrounding issues like transgender rights and the inclusion of gender-diverse individuals have become key battlegrounds in a larger cultural conflict. These changes are reshaping the moral and ethical landscape of the country, forcing Americans to grapple with questions about identity, equality, and what it means to live in a truly inclusive society.

The impact on America's value system is multifaceted, affecting everything from religion, politics, and education to how Americans understand freedom, equality, and individualism. The debates over issues such as transgender participation in women's sports, the use of gender-neutral pronouns, and access to gender-affirming healthcare are emblematic of deeper divisions in the country. These conflicts reveal a growing tension between progressive values that emphasize inclusivity and diversity and traditional values that stress biological realities and gender binaries.

The Tension Between Traditional and Progressive Values

Historically, American society was shaped by Judeo-Christian values, which emphasized heteronormativity, binary gender roles, and clear distinctions between men and women. These values were reflected in everything from marriage and family structures to education and employment. For centuries, men and women were expected to adhere to specific roles: men were typically seen as breadwinners and leaders, while women were often expected to take on domestic and care-giving responsibilities. These traditional gender norms were widely accepted across the political spectrum and were considered the foundation of a stable society.

However, beginning in the mid-20th century, social movements such as second-wave feminism, the civil rights movement, and LGBTQ+ activism began challenging these rigid definitions. Feminists fought for gender equality, demanding that women be allowed to pursue careers, gain reproductive rights, and have equal access to education. LGBTQ+ activists, particularly following the

Stonewall Riots of 1969, sought to break down the social and legal barriers that prevented individuals from expressing their sexual orientation and gender identity freely.

As these progressive movements gained momentum, they began to fundamentally reshape American society's value system. Gender roles became more fluid, and there was a growing recognition that people's identities could not be fully captured by traditional categories like "male" or "female," "straight" or "gay." This shift toward inclusivity and personal freedom culminated in significant legal milestones, such as the legalization of same-sex marriage in 2015 with the Obergefell v. Hodges Supreme Court decision and the expansion of civil rights protections to LGBTQ+ individuals in the 2020 Bostock v. Clayton County decision.

These changes have been embraced by many Americans, particularly younger generations. According to a 2021 Gallup poll, 72% of Americans support same-sex marriage, up from just 37% in 2007. Additionally, 56% of Americans believe that society should accept transgender people, reflecting a growing tolerance for gender diversity. Younger generations are even more likely to hold these views, with 82% of Generation Z supporting LGBTQ+ rights, compared to 61% of Baby Boomers. This generational divide highlights how rapidly American values around gender and sexuality have evolved in recent decades.

However, this progressive shift has also generated significant backlash, particularly among conservatives, religious groups, and individuals who hold more traditional views about gender and sexuality. For many, the redefinition of gender and the acceptance of non-binary identities represents a rejection of biological reality and an erosion of the moral fabric of society. They argue that by breaking down traditional gender roles, society risks undermining institutions like marriage and family, which they believe are the bedrock of social stability.

This tension is reflected in ongoing political battles. Conservative politicians and religious organizations have increasingly positioned themselves as defenders of traditional values, opposing policies that they see as promoting "gender ideology" or undermining religious freedom. Issues like transgender participation in sports, the use of gender-neutral pronouns, and access to gender-affirming healthcare have become rallying points for conservative activists, who frame these debates as part of a broader cultural war over the future of America's value system.

The Role of Religion in Shaping Gender and Sexuality Debates

Religion continues to play a significant role in shaping America's discussions around gender and sexuality, particularly among those who oppose the recent shifts toward gender diversity. For many religious conservatives, gender is seen as divinely ordained, with clear roles for men and women based on biblical teachings. According to traditional Christian theology, men and women are created by God with distinct purposes, and attempts to redefine gender are viewed as contrary to God's design. This belief has fueled opposition to policies that promote transgender inclusion or the use of gender-neutral language.

For example, evangelical Christian leaders and organizations such as the Family Research Council and Alliance Defending Freedom have been vocal opponents of transgender rights, often framing the debate as a matter of protecting religious liberty. They argue that requiring individuals or institutions to use gender-neutral pronouns or accommodate transgender individuals in gender-specific spaces—such as bathrooms, shelters, or sports teams—violates their religious beliefs. In some cases, these religious groups have successfully challenged laws protecting transgender rights, citing the First Amendment as the basis for their opposition.

The Catholic Church has also expressed opposition to gender identity policies. In 2019, the Vatican issued a document titled "Male and Female He Created Them," which rejected the notion that gender identity can be separated from biological sex. The document described efforts to promote gender diversity as part of an "ideological colonization" and called for a reaffirmation of traditional gender roles. Catholic schools and institutions in the U.S. have often resisted implementing policies that support transgender students, leading to legal disputes and public backlash.

This religious perspective stands in stark contrast to the views of more progressive religious communities, such as Unitarian Universalists, Reform Jews, and many mainline Protestant denominations, which have embraced LGBTQ+ inclusion and gender diversity as part of their commitment to social justice. These groups argue that supporting transgender rights and gender inclusivity aligns with their spiritual values of compassion, equality, and dignity for all individuals. The existence of these competing religious perspectives reflects the broader cultural divide over the redefinition of gender roles in America.

The Political Polarization of Gender and Sexuality

The evolving conversation around gender roles and sexuality has further polarized the American political landscape, becoming a key issue in the broader culture wars. Political debates over LGBTQ+ rights, particularly transgender rights, have been sharply divided along partisan lines, with Democrats generally supporting policies aimed at inclusivity and Republicans advocating for the preservation of traditional gender norms.

This divide is particularly evident in the realm of state legislation. Since 2020, several conservative-leaning states have introduced or passed laws restricting transgender rights, particularly concerning participation in sports and access to gender-affirming healthcare for minors. In Texas, Governor Greg Abbott signed legislation that prohibits transgender girls from competing in women's sports, framing the law as a way to "protect women's sports from unfair competition." Similarly, states like Arkansas and Mississippi have passed laws banning gender-affirming treatments for transgender minors, arguing that children are too young to make such life-altering decisions.

On the other hand, states with more progressive governments, such as California, New York, and Oregon, have implemented policies that support transgender inclusion and protect the rights of gender-diverse individuals. For instance, California's Gender Recognition Act allows individuals to select a third gender option on official documents, such as driver's licenses and birth certificates, making it one of the most progressive states in terms of legal recognition of non-binary and transgender identities.

At the national level, President Joe Biden has positioned himself as a staunch advocate for LGBTQ+ rights. On his first day in office, Biden signed an executive order aimed at preventing discrimination based on gender identity and sexual orientation. His administration has also pushed for the passage of the Equality Act, which would amend the Civil Rights Act of 1964 to prohibit discrimination based on sexual orientation and gender identity in a wide range of areas, including employment, housing, education, and public accommodations. However, the Equality Act has faced fierce opposition in the Senate, where Republicans argue that it would infringe on religious liberties and force institutions to adopt practices that conflict with their beliefs about gender and sexuality.

This political divide has deepened the polarization around gender and sexuality in the U.S., making it a flash-point in broader debates about civil rights, individual freedoms, and societal values. As both sides of the political spectrum continue to emphasize these issues in their platforms, it is clear that the debate over gender identity and roles will remain a central issue in American politics for years to come.

Redefining Fairness, Equality, and Freedom

The impact of the gender debate on America's value system is not limited to legal and political battles—it also touches on deeply held beliefs about fairness, equality, and freedom. For many progressives, the push for transgender and non-binary inclusion represents a continuation of the broader civil rights movement, extending the principles of equality and non-discrimination to all individuals, regardless of gender identity. From this perspective, true fairness means recognizing and accommodating the diversity of human experience, including gender diversity. For example, policies that allow transgender individuals to use the restroom or compete in the sports category that aligns with their gender identity are seen as necessary steps toward a more just and equitable society.

However, for those who hold more traditional views, fairness is about protecting the rights of biological women and ensuring that they are not disadvantaged by policies that prioritize gender identity over biological sex. This is particularly evident in the debate over transgender women competing in women's sports, where critics argue that transgender women retain unfair advantages due to male puberty. They contend that policies allowing transgender women to compete in women's sports undermine the progress that women have made in gaining equal opportunities in athletics, a cornerstone of Title IX, the federal law that prohibits sex-based discrimination in education.

These conflicting definitions of fairness highlight the broader challenge of balancing individual rights with collective responsibilities in a diverse society. As America continues to grapple with questions about gender identity, the need to find common ground—while respecting differences—will be critical to maintaining social cohesion and fostering a culture of mutual respect.

Conclusion: The Future of America's Value System

The debate surrounding gender roles, sexuality, and identity in America is reshaping the nation's value system in profound ways, challenging long-standing assumptions about what it means to be a man or a woman, how society defines fairness, and the boundaries of individual rights versus collective responsibility. What began as a gradual shift toward inclusivity in the mid-20th century has, in the 21st century, transformed into a wide-reaching, polarizing conflict, affecting all levels of society—from laws and policies to personal relationships and social expectations.

At the heart of this transformation is a clash between progressive values that seek to redefine gender and sexuality as fluid and individual, and traditional values that hold onto biologically based, binary definitions of gender. The impact of these changes goes beyond personal identity; they affect the very fabric of American culture, including concepts of freedom, fairness, and equality—values that are deeply embedded in the national psyche. How these values are interpreted and prioritized in the coming years will shape the nation's legal system, education, healthcare, sports, and public life.

A Redefinition of Freedom and Equality

The shift in how Americans understand gender and sexuality is inherently tied to broader questions about freedom and equality. For those advocating for greater rights and recognition of transgender and non-binary individuals, freedom is about the right to express one's identity without fear of discrimination, exclusion, or violence. It is about expanding the concept of individual autonomy to encompass the ability to define one's gender and live authentically, even if that identity does not conform to traditional norms.

The drive for equality has similarly expanded. Historically, movements for racial and gender equality in America were focused on securing equal rights under the law for marginalized groups. Today, the movement for LGBTQ+ rights, particularly the rights of transgender individuals, is seen as an extension of this broader struggle for equality. The Equality Act, which seeks to amend the Civil Rights Act of 1964 to prohibit discrimination based on sexual orientation and gender identity, is a clear example of this push to ensure that all individuals, regardless of their gender identity, are afforded the same legal protections and opportunities.

However, this redefinition of freedom and equality faces opposition from those who fear that these changes come at the cost of religious liberty, free speech, and biological fairness. For many conservatives, the notion of freedom is deeply intertwined with the right to uphold personal and religious beliefs, including the belief that gender is biologically determined. They argue that policies requiring the use of gender-neutral pronouns, allowing transgender individuals to use bathrooms corresponding to their gender identity, or permitting transgender women to compete in women's sports force individuals and institutions to act against their convictions. In their view, this represents an infringement on their freedom of conscience and expression.

The question of equality is also hotly contested. While progressives argue for the inclusion of transgender individuals as a matter of equality, traditionalists contend that doing so undermines the equal opportunities of cisgender women, particularly in the context of sports and women-only spaces. For many conservatives, the struggle to protect women's rights under Title IX—fought over decades—risks being diluted if transgender women are allowed to compete in women's sports or access spaces originally created to protect biological women from discrimination.

The Role of Institutions in Navigating Change

America's public institutions—schools, workplaces, religious organizations, and government bodies—have been thrust into the center of this cultural debate, often serving as battlegrounds where the future of the country's value system is fought. In schools, the inclusion of gender identity in sex education, the right of students to use their preferred pronouns, and the participation of transgender athletes in high school sports have all become highly contentious issues. Some states, like California and New York, have embraced progressive policies that seek to support and protect transgender and non-binary students, while others, like Florida and Texas, have passed laws limiting discussions of gender identity in schools or banning transgender athletes from competing in girls' sports.

These differing policies reflect the broader polarization in American society. Schools, once viewed as neutral spaces for education, have become key arenas where debates about gender roles, sexuality, and societal norms play out. Teachers, administrators, and students alike find themselves grappling with how to balance inclusivity with parental rights, free speech, and religious freedom.

Similarly, the workplace has become another flash-point in the evolving conversation around gender. Many companies, especially in liberal-leaning industries like tech and media, have adopted policies that require employees to respect their coworkers' gender identities, including the use of gender-neutral pronouns and recognition of non-binary identities. Corporate America, in general, has embraced a more inclusive stance on LGBTQ+ rights, with many companies celebrating Pride Month and implementing policies to support transgender employees.

However, these shifts have not been without resistance. Some workers and employers, especially in more conservative industries or regions, view these changes as compelled speech or ideological coercion. Lawsuits involving employees who have been disciplined for refusing to use gender-neutral pronouns or for expressing views critical of transgender inclusion underscore the challenges of navigating a changing workplace culture. These cases highlight the tension between creating an inclusive environment for transgender employees and respecting the religious or personal beliefs of others.

The Evolution of Sports and Gender Identity

One of the most visible arenas where the evolving understanding of gender is being contested is in the world of sports. The debate over transgender athletes' participation in women's sports has become emblematic of the broader societal conversation about gender, fairness, and inclusivity. The case of Lia Thomas, the transgender swimmer who won the NCAA Division I national championship, brought this issue into the national spotlight, but it is just one of many instances where the rights of transgender athletes have been challenged.

Supporters of transgender inclusion in sports argue that denying transgender athletes the right to compete according to their gender identity is discriminatory and violates their right to participate fully in public life. They point to the fact that transgender athletes are often marginalized and face significant barriers to participation, including discrimination, stigma, and harassment.

However, opponents contend that allowing transgender women to compete in women's sports undermines the principle of fair competition, particularly in physical sports where the physiological effects of male puberty—such as greater muscle mass and lung capacity—may give transgender women an advantage. This debate has led to the passage of state laws that ban transgender women from competing in women's sports, as well as lawsuits challenging these laws on the grounds of discrimination. The future of these legal battles will have far-reaching implications not only for sports but for how society defines gender-based rights and fairness.

The Future of America's Value System

As the country navigates this complex cultural landscape, it is clear that the ongoing debates over gender identity, sexuality, and societal roles are redefining America's value system in real time. The tension between traditional and progressive values, between biological determinism and gender fluidity, reflects a broader struggle over the future of American identity.

While younger generations are more likely to embrace gender diversity, inclusivity, and fluid definitions of identity, older generations—and those with more conservative or religious beliefs—are pushing back against these changes, arguing that they threaten the foundations of American society. This generational divide, coupled with regional and political differences, suggests the conflict over gender and sexuality will continue to shape America's political, cultural, and legal landscape for years to come.

At the heart of this debate is the question of how America defines freedom, equality, and individual rights. As society becomes more diverse, and as traditional institutions face pressure to adapt to new understandings of gender and identity, the challenge will be to create a framework that respects both individual autonomy and collective values. Finding common ground, while respecting deeply held beliefs on all sides, will be essential for maintaining social cohesion in an increasingly polarized world.

Ultimately, the future of America's value system will depend on how successfully the country can navigate these tensions and create a society that is inclusive, equitable, and fair for all of its citizens. As the debate over gender roles, identity, and sexuality continues to unfold, America will be forced to confront the limits and possibilities of its commitment to freedom, justice, and equality in a diverse and changing world.

The Divisive Debate Surrounding the Second Amendment and Mass Shootings

Few issues in contemporary American society generate as much heated debate and emotional division as gun control. At the heart of this debate are two seemingly irreconcilable views: those who advocate for stricter gun control measures to reduce gun violence, especially in the wake of repeated mass shootings, and those who see gun ownership as a fundamental right enshrined in the Second Amendment of the U.S. Constitution, essential for personal protection and the defense of liberty. As mass shootings continue to plague the nation, the debate over gun control intensifies, raising difficult moral, legal, and political questions.

Here, I present both sides of the argument, delves into the prevalence and impact of mass shootings in the United States, compares America's approach to gun control with other countries, and explores the complex moral issues underlying current gun control policies.

The Argument for Stricter Gun Control

Advocates for stricter gun control argue that the proliferation of guns in the U.S. has led to an epidemic of gun violence, culminating in numerous mass shootings that have shattered communities and left families devastated. They argue that tighter regulations on firearms, including bans on certain types of weapons, universal background checks, and red-flag laws, are necessary to prevent further loss of life.

No. 1 — Mass Shootings: A Tragic Pattern

Mass shootings have become a disturbingly common phenomenon in the United States, sparking national debates, grief, and outrage. Defined by the Gun Violence Archive (GVA) as incidents where four or more people, excluding the perpetrator, are shot in a single event, these tragic events have left deep scars on communities across the country. Despite making up only a small fraction of overall gun deaths, mass shootings generate significant media attention and highlight the broader issue of gun violence in America. Their frequency, coupled with their devastating impact, has led to calls for urgent reforms in gun control policy. Statistical trends and studies offer insight into the growing prevalence of mass shootings and their effects on American society.

The Rise in Mass Shootings

Over the past few decades, mass shootings in the United States have escalated in both frequency and lethality. According to data compiled by the Gun Violence Archive, the number of mass shootings has increased dramatically in recent years. In 2014, the U.S. saw 273 mass shootings. By 2022, that number had ballooned to more than 600 mass shootings, averaging nearly two per day. This sharp rise has raised alarms about gun violence and fueled the national debate over gun control.

A report from the Federal Bureau of Investigation (FBI) tracking active shooter incidents also highlights a troubling trend. According to the FBI, the number of active shooter incidents—defined as shootings in which a perpetrator attempts to kill people in a populated area—rose from 20 incidents in 2016 to 61 in 2021, an increase of over 200% in just five years. Moreover, the lethality of these events has increased: in 2021 alone, these active shooter events resulted in 103 deaths and 140 injuries.

High-Profile Mass Shootings

Several high-profile mass shootings in recent years have drawn national attention and renewed demands for stricter gun control laws:

- Uvalde, Texas (2022): One of the deadliest school shootings in U.S. history occurred at Robb Elementary School in Uvalde, Texas, where an 18-year-old gunman killed 19 children and 2 teachers. The shooting raised questions about school safety, law enforcement response, and how the shooter obtained two AR-15-style rifles legally.

- Buffalo, New York (2022): In a racially motivated attack, a gunman opened fire in a supermarket located in a predominantly Black neighborhood, killing 10 people. The shooter had espoused white supremacist beliefs online, leading to discussions about the role of hate speech and social media in radicalizing individuals.

- Las Vegas, Nevada (2017): The Route 91 Harvest Festival became the site of the deadliest mass shooting in modern U.S. history when a gunman opened fire from a hotel room, killing 58 people and injuring hundreds. The shooter used multiple firearms, including bump stocks, which allow semi-automatic weapons to fire at rates similar to fully automatic weapons, raising debates about firearm accessories and regulations.

- Sandy Hook, Connecticut (2012): One of the most tragic mass shootings in U.S. history occurred at Sandy Hook Elementary School, where 20 children and six staff members were killed. The shooter used an AR-15-style rifle to carry out the massacre. The aftermath of Sandy Hook led to national outrage and prompted then-President Barack Obama to propose sweeping gun control measures, including universal background checks and a renewed assault weapons ban, although these efforts ultimately failed in Congress.

These mass shootings, and others like them, have left deep scars in the affected communities and have led to waves of public outcry. Each incident prompts renewed calls for reform, yet federal action on gun control has remained limited, in part due to political gridlock and strong opposition from gun rights groups.

Statistical Trends and Studies on Mass Shootings

Mass shootings in the U.S. are occurring more frequently and claiming more lives. According to a 2022 study by the National Institute of Justice (NIJ), the frequency of mass shootings has tripled since the early 2000s. Between 1966 and 2019, there were 166 mass shootings in the U.S., with an average of 2.5 mass shootings occurring per year from 1966 to 2000. However, from 2000 to 2019, that number jumped to 7.2 mass shootings per year. The study attributes this increase to a combination of factors, including the proliferation of firearms, easy access to high-capacity weapons, and social isolation.

In terms of lethality, data from the Gun Violence Archive shows that mass shootings have become more deadly. In 2019, mass shootings resulted in 211 deaths, a number that rose to 343 deaths in 2022. This trend is particularly concerning given that many mass shooters are able to acquire weapons legally, often without undergoing rigorous background checks due to loopholes in existing laws.

Additionally, the Centers for Disease Control and Prevention (CDC) reports that gun deaths overall reached record levels in 2021, with nearly 49,000 firearm-related deaths across the U.S. Of these deaths, mass shootings account for a small percentage, but their high profile and devastating nature amplify their impact on the national psyche. The New England Journal of Medicine published a study in 2022 showing that firearms have overtaken motor vehicle crashes as the leading cause of death for children and adolescents, highlighting the significant toll that gun violence takes on young Americans.

Factors Contributing to the Rise of Mass Shootings

- **Easy Access to Firearms.** One of the key factors cited in the rise of mass shootings is the relative ease with which Americans can access firearms, particularly high-capacity weapons like AR-15-style rifles. The U.S. has more guns per capita than any other country in the world, with approximately 120 guns for every 100 people. According to the Pew Research Center, about 44% of U.S. households own at least one firearm. Many mass shooters legally acquire their guns, taking advantage of loopholes such as the gun show loophole or private seller exemptions, which allow them to bypass background checks.

- **Mental Health and Social Isolation.** While gun access is a critical factor, mass shootings are often linked to mental health issues and social isolation. Studies show that many mass shooters exhibit signs of mental health struggles, including depression, narcissism, and suicidal ideation. A 2021 report from the Secret Service's National Threat Assessment Center found that most mass shooters experience a significant personal crisis before carrying out their attacks, including job loss, family conflict, or social isolation. However, experts caution against oversimplifying the role of mental illness, noting that only a small percentage of people with mental health issues engage in violence.

- **Copycat Effect and Media Attention.** The role of media coverage in mass shootings is another factor frequently discussed. The copycat effect refers to the tendency for mass shootings to inspire others, particularly when perpetrators receive widespread media attention. A 2016 study in the journal PLOS ONE found that mass shootings are contagious, meaning one mass shooting increases the likelihood of others occurring within a short period. This phenomenon is often linked to the intense coverage and notoriety that shooters receive, which can inspire others seeking similar attention or "fame."

- **Political Polarization.** The inability to enact meaningful gun control measures in response to mass shootings is also a reflection of deep political polarization. Gun rights advocates, led by organizations like the National Rifle Association (NRA), argue that restricting access to guns infringes on Second Amendment rights and would not effectively prevent violence.

Meanwhile, gun control advocates argue that common-sense measures like universal background checks, assault weapons bans, and red flag laws could prevent many of these tragedies. The resulting deadlock in Congress has made it difficult to pass federal legislation, even in the wake of highly publicized mass shootings.

The Broader Impact of Mass Shootings

The impact of mass shootings extends far beyond the immediate loss of life. Survivors, first responders, and entire communities are often left grappling with the emotional and psychological effects of these tragedies. Studies show that survivors of mass shootings frequently experience post-traumatic stress disorder (PTSD), anxiety, and depression. Families of victims are left mourning the loss of loved ones, often with little closure as they navigate the legal and political aftermath.

The broader societal impact of mass shootings also includes a growing sense of fear and insecurity. Many Americans now consider mass shootings to be an ever-present risk in public spaces such as schools, shopping malls, movie theaters, and places of worship. In a 2019 Gallup poll, 48% of Americans said they feared being a victim of a mass shooting, a significant increase from previous years.

Mass shootings have also led to changes in behavior, with schools conducting regular active shooter drills and communities investing in more robust security measures. These responses reflect the growing perception that mass shootings are no longer rare events, but a regular feature of American life.

Mass shootings represent a tragic and persistent pattern in the United States, claiming hundreds of lives each year and leaving lasting scars on survivors and communities. The rise in frequency and lethality of these shootings has prompted urgent calls for reform, with advocates pushing for stricter gun control measures to stem the tide of violence. However, political polarization, legal challenges, and cultural attitudes toward firearms continue to hinder progress on this issue. As the debate over how to address mass shootings continues, the question remains: how can America prevent these tragedies while balancing individual rights with public safety? The answer may require a reevaluation of the nation's approach to guns, mental health, and community resilience.

No. 2 — Policy Proposals: Addressing Access to Guns

In the ongoing debate over how to curb gun violence in the United States, a variety of policy proposals have emerged that aim to reduce the number of mass shootings and overall gun deaths. Advocates for gun control argue that addressing easy access to firearms, especially to high-powered weapons like semi-automatic rifles, is a critical first step in reducing the frequency and lethality of gun violence. These proposals include implementing universal background checks, reinstating an assault weapons ban, enacting red flag laws, and closing loopholes that allow individuals to purchase firearms without adequate oversight. Despite widespread public support for many of these measures, political gridlock, cultural resistance, and lobbying by gun rights organizations have stymied meaningful reform at the federal level. Below are the key policy proposals being discussed, along with their potential impact on gun violence in the U.S.

Universal Background Checks

One of the most widely supported gun control measures is the implementation of universal background checks. Current federal law requires background checks for individuals purchasing firearms through licensed dealers, but it does not extend to private sales, such as those that occur at gun shows, through online platforms, or in person-to-person sales. This loophole allows individuals who may not pass a background check—such as those with criminal records, histories of domestic violence, or serious mental health issues—to purchase firearms without undergoing the vetting process.

Public Support and Effectiveness

Polls consistently show that universal background checks are one of the most popular gun control measures among Americans, with a 2021 Pew Research Center survey revealing that 84% of U.S. adults—including 77% of Republicans and 91% of Democrats—support requiring background checks for all gun buyers. Many gun owners also support this proposal, viewing it as a common-sense safeguard that helps keep guns out of the hands of dangerous individuals without infringing on the rights of law-abiding citizens.

Research suggests that universal background checks can be effective in reducing gun violence. A 2019 study published in the Journal of General Internal Medicine found that states with universal background checks for all gun sales had 15% lower firearm homicide rates compared to states without such laws. Additionally, Centers for Disease Control and Prevention (CDC) data shows that states with more comprehensive background check laws tend to have lower rates of gun-related deaths, including homicides, suicides, and accidental shootings.

Legislative Proposals

Several bills aimed at expanding background checks have been introduced in Congress over the past decade. Most notably, the Bipartisan Background Checks Act of 2021 (H.R. 8) was passed by the House of Representatives but stalled in the Senate. This bill sought to close the gun show loophole by requiring background checks for all firearms sales, including private transactions. The bill also included exemptions for transfers between family members and temporary loans of firearms for hunting, sporting events, and self-defense.

Opponents of universal background checks argue that such measures could lead to the creation of a national gun registry, which they fear could be used by the government to track and potentially confiscate firearms. However, proponents of the legislation emphasize that the bill explicitly prohibits the creation of a federal firearms registry and focuses solely on preventing individuals who pose a risk to public safety from acquiring guns.

Assault Weapons Ban

Another prominent policy proposal involves reinstating a federal ban on assault weapons and high-capacity magazines. These firearms are often the weapon of choice in mass shootings because they allow shooters to fire multiple rounds in rapid succession, inflicting mass casualties in a short period. High-capacity magazines, which hold more than the standard number of bullets, allow shooters to fire continuously without stopping to reload. The most infamous mass shootings, such as those in Las Vegas (2017), Sandy Hook (2012), and Orlando (2016), involved the use of semi-automatic rifles like the AR-15, often equipped with high-capacity magazines.

Historical Context and Public Opinion

The U.S. had a federal Assault Weapons Ban (AWB) from 1994 to 2004, which prohibited the manufacture, transfer, or possession of certain semi-automatic firearms deemed "assault weapons" and banned magazines that could hold more than 10 rounds of ammunition. Studies conducted after the expiration of the ban showed mixed results regarding its impact on overall gun violence. According to a 2004 Department of Justice study, the effects of the ban on reducing gun deaths were difficult to measure, in part because assault weapons accounted for a small percentage of total gun crimes. However, the study did find that the ban had a notable effect on reducing the use of these weapons in mass shootings.

Since the ban expired, the frequency of mass shootings involving semi-automatic rifles has increased significantly. A 2019 study published in the Journal of Trauma and Acute Care Surgery found that mass shootings involving assault weapons accounted for 85% of fatalities in mass shootings with six or more victims. The study concluded that a renewed assault weapons ban could reduce the lethality of mass shootings, saving lives in the process.

Public opinion on assault weapons bans is more divided than it is on background checks, but a significant portion of Americans still support such measures. A 2021 poll by Morning Consult found that 57% of Americans support banning assault-style weapons, with sharp partisan divides: 83% of Democrats were in favor, compared to just 31% of Republicans.

Legislative Proposals

In recent years, several bills have been introduced in Congress to reinstate the assault weapons ban. One notable example is the Assault Weapons Ban of 2021, introduced by Senator Dianne Feinstein. The bill would prohibit the sale, transfer, manufacture, and importation of military-style assault weapons, including semi-automatic rifles with certain features such as pistol grips, folding stocks, and detachable magazines capable of holding more than 10 rounds.

Critics of the ban argue that many of the firearms targeted by the legislation are popular for hunting and sport shooting, and that banning them infringes on the rights of responsible gun owners. Gun rights advocates also contend that the ban focuses too heavily on cosmetic features rather than the actual functionality of the weapons, and they argue that most gun crimes are committed with handguns, not rifles. However, proponents emphasize that while assault weapons account for a small percentage of overall gun crimes, they are disproportionately used in mass shootings and allow shooters to inflict maximum damage in a short time.

Red Flag Laws

Red flag laws, also known as Extreme Risk Protection Orders (ERPOs), are another key policy proposal aimed at preventing individuals who pose a risk to themselves or others from accessing firearms. These laws allow family members, law enforcement officers, or healthcare providers to petition a court to temporarily remove firearms from individuals who are deemed to be a danger. Red flag laws are seen as a proactive measure to prevent gun violence, particularly in cases involving individuals with mental health issues, histories of domestic violence, or suicidal ideation.

Public Support and Effectiveness

Red flag laws have garnered widespread public support, with many Americans seeing them as a balanced approach that respects gun ownership while addressing clear and present dangers. According to a 2019 Quinnipiac University poll, 77% of Americans support the implementation of red flag laws, including 60% of gun owners. The bipartisan nature of support for these laws makes them one of the most politically feasible gun control measures.

Studies show that red flag laws can be effective in reducing certain types of gun violence. A 2018 study published in the Annals of Internal Medicine examined the effects of Connecticut's red flag law, which was enacted in 1999. The study found that the law prevented approximately one suicide for every 10 to 20 firearms seized. Similarly, a 2020 report from the American Psychiatric Association found that red flag laws can help prevent both mass shootings and suicides, which account for nearly 60% of all gun deaths in the U.S.

Legislative Proposals

As of 2022, 19 states and the District of Columbia have passed some form of red flag law. However, there is no federal red flag law, and efforts to pass one have faced opposition from gun rights advocates who argue that these laws could lead to abuse or false reports, resulting in the unwarranted confiscation of firearms. Critics also raise concerns about due process, arguing that red flag laws allow for the seizure of firearms before the individual in question has had an opportunity to defend themselves in court.

In response to these concerns, many states have built due process protections into their red flag laws. For example, the petition must be supported by evidence, and the individual has the right to a hearing to contest the removal of their firearms. In some cases, the orders are limited to a specific period (such as one year) and can be renewed only if the individual is still deemed a threat.

Closing the Gun Show Loophole

The so-called gun show loophole refers to the ability of individuals to purchase firearms at gun shows or through private sellers without undergoing a background check. While licensed dealers are required to perform background checks, private sellers—who are not licensed—are not subject to the same requirement, which allows for unregulated sales. This loophole has been widely criticized by gun control advocates, who argue that it creates a backdoor for individuals who would otherwise be prohibited from purchasing firearms due to criminal records, mental health issues, or restraining orders.

Public Support and Legislative Proposals

Closing the gun show loophole has been a longstanding goal of gun control advocates, and it is one of the central elements of proposals for universal background checks. Public support for closing the loophole is strong, with a 2020 Pew Research Center survey showing that 79% of Americans support requiring background checks for private sales and gun show purchases.

Several bills have been introduced in Congress to close the gun show loophole. Most notably, the Bipartisan Background Checks Act of 2021 (H.R. 8) would require background checks for all gun sales, including those at gun shows and between private parties. The bill passed the House of Representatives but has stalled in the Senate, where it faces opposition from Republican lawmakers and gun rights groups like the National Rifle Association (NRA).

Opponents argue that closing the loophole would place an undue burden on private sellers and infringe on individuals' rights to transfer firearms to family members or friends without government oversight. However, proponents argue that the loophole undermines the effectiveness of the existing background check system and allows dangerous individuals to bypass the law.

No. 3 — Moral Considerations: A Question of Public Safety

For gun control advocates, the moral imperative is clear: saving lives must take precedence over unfettered access to firearms. The frequent mass shootings, gun suicides, and daily acts of gun violence across the U.S. make it clear that the current level of gun access comes with an unacceptable human cost. Gun control supporters argue that the government has a responsibility to protect its citizens from harm and that regulating access to dangerous weapons is a key part of that duty.

From this perspective, owning a gun is not an absolute right but a conditional one—one that should be balanced against the collective right to public safety. For them, the sheer number of gun deaths in America is a failure of the current system, and reforming gun laws is an urgent matter of social justice and human dignity.

The Argument for Gun Rights and Second Amendment Protections

On the other side of the debate, gun rights advocates fiercely defend the Second Amendment, which they believe guarantees an individual's right to own and carry firearms. For them, guns represent not just a tool for personal protection but a safeguard against tyranny and a symbol of individual freedom. They argue that gun control measures, particularly those that restrict access to firearms, infringe on fundamental rights and may not effectively reduce crime or violence.

The Second Amendment: A Fundamental Right

The Second Amendment to the U.S. Constitution, ratified in 1791, states: "A well-regulated Militia, being necessary to the security of a free State, the right of the people to keep and bear Arms, shall not be infringed."

For gun rights advocates, this language affirms the right of individuals to own firearms for a variety of purposes, including self-defense, hunting, and the prevention of government overreach. Organizations like the National Rifle Association (NRA) argue that the right to bear arms is essential to American liberty and that attempts to curtail this right represent a slippery slope toward authoritarianism.

Many gun rights advocates believe that the founding fathers intended for citizens to have access to firearms to protect themselves against government tyranny. From this perspective, any form of gun control is viewed as not only unnecessary but also unconstitutional.

Guns for Self-Defense: A Personal Security Issue

Gun rights advocates often emphasize the importance of firearms for self-defense, particularly in a country where crime remains a concern. According to the Centers for Disease Control and Prevention (CDC), there are between 60,000 and 2.5 million defensive gun uses (DGUs) each year in the United States, though estimates vary widely depending on the source and methodology used.

For those who believe in the right to carry firearms for self-protection, gun ownership is seen as an equalizer, particularly for vulnerable populations such as women or individuals living in high-crime areas. They argue that responsible gun owners, through concealed carry or home defense, are able to protect themselves and their families in situations where law enforcement may not be able to respond in time.

Gun rights supporters also point out that criminals do not follow laws, meaning that even if stricter gun regulations were in place, those with bad intentions would still find ways to access firearms. In their view, gun control only disarms law-abiding citizens, leaving them defenseless against criminals who would flout the law.

Opposition to Assault Weapons Bans

While gun control advocates often call for a ban on assault weapons, gun rights supporters reject the notion that these weapons should be singled out for restriction. Many argue that the term "assault weapon" is poorly defined and politically charged, as it refers primarily to the cosmetic features of firearms rather than their function. For example, an AR-15, often targeted by gun control advocates, is a semi-automatic rifle—meaning it fires one round per trigger pull, just like many handguns that are not typically included in calls for bans.

Gun rights advocates argue that banning certain types of guns based on appearance or perceived lethality is both ineffective and arbitrary. They point out that most gun crimes, including homicides, are committed with handguns, not rifles, and that banning "assault weapons" would have a minimal impact on overall gun violence rates.

Furthermore, many gun owners argue that the Second Amendment was not designed to protect hunting rifles but to ensure that citizens have access to the same kinds of weapons that would allow them to resist tyranny or defend themselves against threats. In this view, banning semi-automatic rifles infringes on a fundamental aspect of the Second Amendment.

Moral Considerations: Individual Rights and Personal Freedom

For gun rights supporters, the moral argument centers on the sanctity of individual rights and the belief that people should have the freedom to protect themselves, their families, and their property. They argue that self-defense is a basic human right, and that gun ownership is a means of ensuring that right, especially in an unpredictable world where threats can arise from both criminal elements and government overreach.

In their view, restricting gun ownership infringes on personal freedoms and undermines the libertarian principle that the government should not interfere in the private lives of citizens unless absolutely necessary. For gun rights advocates, the problem is not guns themselves but bad actors, and the solution lies in better law enforcement, mental health care, and community engagement—not in restricting gun ownership for millions of law-abiding Americans.

No. 4 — Gun Control in America vs. the Rest of the World

The United States stands apart from most other developed nations when it comes to gun control and gun violence. With more guns than people, a powerful gun lobby, and a deeply ingrained culture of gun ownership tied to the Second Amendment, the U.S. faces unique challenges in addressing gun violence. In contrast, many other countries have responded to gun-related tragedies with swift and decisive legislative action, significantly reducing gun violence over time. By examining what has worked—and what hasn't—both in the U.S. and abroad, we can gain a deeper understanding of how different approaches to gun control have succeeded or failed to prevent mass shootings and reduce overall gun deaths.

Gun Control in America: A Patchwork of Laws and a Cultural Divide

In the United States, gun control is primarily regulated at the state level, resulting in a patchwork of laws that vary significantly across the country. States like California and New York have some of the strictest gun laws, including waiting periods, background checks, assault weapon bans, and restrictions on high-capacity magazines. Meanwhile, states like Texas and Florida have more permissive laws, allowing for open carry, concealed carry, and fewer restrictions on gun purchases. This patchwork system has made it difficult to implement a cohesive national strategy to reduce gun violence, and critics argue that lax laws in one state can undermine the efforts of neighboring states with stricter regulations.

At the federal level, major pieces of gun control legislation include the Brady Handgun Violence Prevention Act (1993), which established background checks for gun buyers from licensed dealers, and the now-expired Federal Assault Weapons Ban (1994-2004), which prohibited the manufacture and sale of certain semi-automatic firearms and high-capacity magazines. While these laws have had some impact, they have been criticized for loopholes and limited enforcement. For instance, private gun sales at gun shows or online are not subject to the same background check requirements as sales from licensed dealers, a loophole that has been exploited by people who would otherwise be barred from purchasing firearms.

Moreover, efforts to pass new federal gun control measures have repeatedly stalled in Congress, largely due to political polarization and lobbying from groups like the National Rifle Association (NRA). While public support for gun control measures like universal background checks is high—84% of Americans, according to a 2021 Pew Research Center survey—opposition from gun rights advocates has kept meaningful reform at bay.

International Comparisons: What Has Worked?

When we compare the U.S. to other countries, it becomes clear that stricter gun control laws have worked to significantly reduce gun violence in nations that have implemented them. Countries like Australia, New Zealand, Canada, and the United Kingdom offer case studies in how comprehensive, nationwide regulations can curb gun deaths, including mass shootings. Here's a closer look at how these countries have addressed gun violence and the impact of their policies.

Australia: Comprehensive Reform and a Buyback Program

Australia is often cited as one of the most successful examples of gun control in the world. In 1996, a mass shooting in Port Arthur, Tasmania, left 35 people dead and 23 injured. The massacre was a national turning point, leading to an overwhelming public demand for reform. In response, the Australian government, led by conservative Prime Minister John Howard, passed the National Firearms Agreement (NFA). This legislation included several key provisions:

- **Ban on semi-automatic rifles and shotguns.** The NFA banned certain categories of firearms, particularly semi-automatic rifles and shotguns, which were seen as particularly dangerous for mass shootings.

- **Gun buyback program.** The government instituted a mandatory buyback program, which resulted in the collection and destruction of approximately 650,000 firearms, nearly one-third of the country's total civilian firearms.

- **Licensing and registration requirements.** The NFA established strict licensing requirements for all gun owners. To obtain a firearm license, individuals had to demonstrate a genuine reason for owning a gun (self-defense was not considered a valid reason). Guns were also required to be registered with the government.

- **Waiting periods and background checks.** The law instituted a mandatory 28-day waiting period for all gun purchases, as well as thorough background checks.

The results were dramatic. In the decade following the passage of the NFA, Australia saw a 59% reduction in gun-related homicides and a 65% reduction in gun-related suicides. Since the reforms, Australia has not experienced another mass shooting on the scale of Port Arthur. The reforms also contributed to a broader cultural shift, with Australians increasingly seeing gun ownership as a privilege, not a right.

However, the NFA was not without controversy. Some rural Australians, particularly farmers and sports shooters, opposed the reforms, arguing that they restricted their access to firearms necessary for work or recreation. Despite this, the overwhelming public support for the changes, combined with the dramatic reduction in gun violence, has made the NFA one of the most successful gun control measures in history.

New Zealand: Swift Action After Christchurch

Another case study in effective gun control reform comes from New Zealand, which was traditionally known for its relatively permissive gun laws. However, in March 2019, a gunman opened fire in two mosques in Christchurch, killing 51 people and injuring dozens more. The perpetrator used semi-automatic weapons that had been legally obtained.

In response, Prime Minister Jacinda Ardern acted swiftly, introducing a package of gun control measures within weeks of the attack. These included:

- **Ban on military-style semi-automatic weapons.** The government banned all military-style semi-automatic rifles, similar to those used in the Christchurch shooting.

- **Gun buyback program.** Like Australia, New Zealand introduced a gun buyback program, collecting more than 56,000 firearms.

- **Stricter licensing laws.** The new laws also tightened licensing requirements, raising the age limit for purchasing guns and strengthening background checks.

New Zealand's swift and decisive response to the Christchurch shootings won international praise, and the country has not experienced another mass shooting since the reforms. However, like Australia, the reforms were not without opposition. Some gun owners argued that the government's response was too hasty and that the buyback program did not offer sufficient compensation for the guns surrendered. Still, the broad public support for gun control in the wake of the tragedy ensured the reforms were passed with little political resistance.

United Kingdom: Tight Controls After Dunblane and Hungerford

The United Kingdom has some of the strictest gun control laws in the world, largely in response to two mass shootings: the Hungerford massacre in 1987 and the Dunblane school shooting in 1996.

- **Hungerford (1987).** A gunman armed with semi-automatic rifles killed 16 people in the town of Hungerford. In response, the UK government passed the Firearms (Amendment) Act 1988, which banned semi-automatic rifles and required shotguns to be registered.

- **Dunblane (1996).** After a gunman killed 16 children and their teacher at a primary school in Dunblane, Scotland, the UK passed the Firearms (Amendment) Act 1997, which banned the private ownership of handguns. This was followed by another amendment in 1998 that extended the ban to all handguns, with few exceptions for certain sporting events.

The result has been a dramatic reduction in gun violence. Today, the UK has one of the lowest rates of gun-related deaths in the world, with fewer than 1 gun homicide per million people per year. In comparison, the U.S. has around 12 gun-related deaths per 100,000 people annually. The UK's approach to gun control demonstrates how sweeping legislative action, combined with strict enforcement, can effectively eliminate the risk of mass shootings and significantly reduce gun deaths.

Canada: Incremental but Effective Reform

Canada, a country that shares a long border with the United States, has taken a more incremental approach to gun control but has still seen significant results. After a mass shooting at École Polytechnique in Montreal in 1989, where a gunman killed 14 women, Canada passed the Firearms Act in 1995, which required gun owners to register all firearms and obtain licenses. This law also imposed restrictions on handguns and semi-automatic weapons.

While Canada's gun laws are not as restrictive as those in the UK or Australia, they are significantly stricter than in the U.S. The country requires all gun buyers to pass background checks that assess criminal, mental health, and domestic violence records. Additionally, the use of firearms for self-defense is heavily restricted.

Following a mass shooting in Nova Scotia in 2020, where 22 people were killed, the Canadian government implemented further restrictions, including a ban on 1,500 models of assault-style firearms. Canada's approach to gun control has contributed to a low rate of gun violence, with only 0.5 gun-related homicides per 100,000 people, compared to the U.S.'s rate of 4.12 per 100,000.

Why Has Gun Control Worked in Other Countries but Not in the U.S.?

While countries like Australia, the UK, and Canada have succeeded in reducing gun violence through stringent gun control measures, the U.S. faces a number of unique challenges that have made similar reforms more difficult to implement.

- **Cultural Attachment to Guns.** The U.S. has a deep cultural attachment to firearms, rooted in its history of frontier expansion, self-reliance, and individual liberty. Guns are seen by many Americans not only as tools for self-defense but as symbols of personal freedom. This cultural attachment is reflected in the Second Amendment, which gun rights advocates see as a constitutional guarantee of their right to own and carry firearms. In contrast, countries like the UK and Australia do not have the same cultural or constitutional attachment to gun ownership, making gun control measures more politically feasible.

- **The Power of the Gun Lobby.** The National Rifle Association (NRA) and other gun rights groups wield significant political power in the U.S. Through lobbying, campaign donations, and grassroots mobilization, these groups have successfully blocked or watered down efforts to pass stricter gun control laws. The NRA's influence is particularly strong among Republican lawmakers, many of whom view any form of gun control as a slippery slope toward government overreach.

- **Political Polarization.** The U.S. is deeply divided along political lines, and gun control is one of the most polarizing issues. While Democrats overwhelmingly support measures like universal background checks and bans on assault weapons, Republicans generally oppose such measures, framing them as infringements on personal liberty. This polarization has made it difficult to pass meaningful reforms at the federal level, even in the wake of high-profile mass shootings.

- **The Sheer Number of Guns.** The U.S. has an estimated 393 million civilian-owned firearms—more guns than people. This makes any attempt to reduce gun violence through buyback programs or bans far more challenging than in countries like Australia or New Zealand, where the total number of guns was much smaller. Critics of U.S. gun control measures argue that with so many guns already in circulation, restrictive laws will not prevent determined individuals from obtaining firearms through illegal means.

What Hasn't Worked in Other Countries?

While countries like Australia and New Zealand have seen great success in reducing gun violence, it's important to acknowledge that gun control is not a one-size-fits-all solution, and there are limits to what it can achieve.

In some countries, gun control measures have faced significant challenges. For instance:

- **Mexico** has some of the strictest gun laws in the world, yet it suffers from extremely high levels of gun violence, largely due to the influence of drug cartels and the illegal trafficking of firearms, often from the United States.

This highlights the fact that gun control laws must be coupled with effective enforcement and efforts to tackle illicit trafficking to be truly effective.

- **South Africa,**which has strict gun control laws, still experiences high levels of gun violence due to socio-economic factors like poverty, inequality, and weak law enforcement. This underscores the idea that gun control alone is not a silver bullet—addressing broader societal issues is also crucial to reducing violence.

No. 5 — Lessons for the United States and the Path Forward

The comparison between the United States and other countries highlights the potential effectiveness of strict gun control measures in reducing gun violence and preventing mass shootings. Nations like Australia, New Zealand, the United Kingdom, and Canada have all implemented comprehensive reforms that have demonstrably reduced gun-related deaths, particularly in the wake of high-profile tragedies. Their experiences provide valuable lessons about the role of strong legislative action, government intervention, and cultural shifts in addressing gun violence. However, while these countries offer models for success, the U.S. faces a unique set of challenges that complicate the adoption of similar policies.

At its core, the issue of gun control in America is not only a political and legal debate but a deeply cultural and ideological one. The Second Amendment is seen by many Americans as a symbol of individual liberty, self-reliance, and protection from tyranny. This cultural attachment to guns is deeply embedded in American history, making efforts to pass sweeping reforms more difficult than in other countries. Unlike Australia or New Zealand, where gun ownership is often viewed more pragmatically, many Americans consider gun ownership a fundamental right, intertwined with personal freedom and the concept of American identity. This cultural difference is a key reason why gun control measures that have worked elsewhere may not easily translate to the U.S.

Political polarization in the U.S. is another significant barrier to comprehensive gun control reform. Gun rights advocacy groups like the National Rifle Association (NRA) wield substantial influence over legislators, particularly in conservative-leaning states, where gun ownership is seen as a way of life. The NRA has successfully mobilized millions of gun owners and lobbyists to oppose gun control measures, portraying them as threats to constitutional freedoms. This resistance, combined with a deeply divided Congress, has led to gridlock at the federal level, where even widely supported measures like universal background checks struggle to gain traction. In countries like Australia and the U.K., political consensus on gun control was more easily achieved, especially in the aftermath of mass shootings that shocked the nation. In contrast, despite the staggering number of mass shootings in the U.S., political compromise has been elusive.

Another major obstacle to implementing the kinds of sweeping reforms seen in other countries is the sheer scale of gun ownership in the United States. With an estimated 393 million firearms in civilian hands—more than one for every person in the country—any effort to reduce gun violence would need to address the enormous number of guns already in circulation. This makes measures like buyback programs or bans on certain types of firearms more logistically and politically challenging than in places like Australia, where the number of civilian-owned guns was significantly lower before its reforms.

The U.S. also faces the issue of gun trafficking, both domestically and across borders, particularly with Mexico, where many firearms used in violent crimes originate from the U.S. Even with stricter gun control laws in place, the prevalence of illegal guns in circulation complicates efforts to curb gun violence. Therefore, any successful gun control strategy would need to include measures to combat the illegal arms trade and close loopholes that allow guns to be sold without background checks, such as the gun show loophole and private seller exemptions.

One key takeaway from the international examples is that while gun control laws are essential, they must be part of a holistic approach to reducing violence. Countries that have successfully reduced gun deaths have coupled stricter gun laws with investments in mental health care, community support, and social services. For instance, mass shootings are often carried out by individuals experiencing severe personal crises or mental health issues. A comprehensive strategy in the U.S. would need to focus not only on regulating gun ownership but also on identifying and addressing the root causes of violence, including mental health issues, social isolation, and economic inequality.

In this regard, the U.S. faces a two-pronged challenge: addressing the immediate issue of gun access while also tackling the broader societal factors that contribute to gun violence. This means expanding access to mental health care, improving intervention strategies for at-risk individuals, and creating programs to strengthen community bonds and reduce social alienation. Studies show that red flag laws, which allow authorities to temporarily remove firearms from individuals deemed to be a threat to themselves or others, are effective in preventing suicides and certain types of gun violence. Expanding such measures, while ensuring due process protections, could be a vital part of the solution.

The U.S. must also navigate the delicate balance between individual rights and public safety. For many gun owners, the right to own firearms is not just a matter of personal protection but a safeguard against potential government overreach and a way to ensure personal autonomy. This is a deeply held belief that cannot be easily dismissed. As such, any successful gun control reform in the U.S. must acknowledge the importance of the Second Amendment while making a compelling case for the collective good—arguing that reducing gun violence benefits all Americans, including gun owners.

The challenge, then, is not only passing effective legislation but also changing the narrative around gun control. Public opinion has shifted over the years, with a majority of Americans now supporting measures like universal background checks, bans on assault weapons, and restrictions on high-capacity magazines. However, for these measures to gain widespread acceptance, proponents of gun control need to engage with gun owners and communities that feel threatened by such reforms, emphasizing that responsible gun ownership and reasonable regulations are not mutually exclusive.

No. 6 — The Path Forward: A Multifaceted Approach

As the U.S. looks to the future, the path to reducing gun violence will likely involve a multifaceted approach that includes:

- **Comprehensive Background Checks.** Closing loopholes in the current system, such as the gun show loophole, and ensuring that all gun sales— whether through licensed dealers or private sellers—are subject to rigorous background checks.

- **Red Flag Laws.** Expanding the use of red flag laws that allow law enforcement and family members to temporarily remove guns from individuals who pose a threat to themselves or others, while safeguarding civil liberties through judicial oversight.

- **Assault Weapons Ban.** Reinstating a ban on military-style assault weapons and high-capacity magazines, which are often used in mass shootings.

This ban could be coupled with a buyback program, similar to those seen in Australia and New Zealand, to reduce the number of these firearms in circulation.

- **Mental Health and Social Services.** Investing in mental health care, crisis intervention, and community programs to address the root causes of violence, particularly for individuals who may be at risk of committing mass shootings.

- **Cultural Shifts.** Engaging in national dialogue to shift the cultural perception of gun ownership from an unrestricted right to a responsible privilege. This may involve public awareness campaigns, education on gun safety, and efforts to reduce the stigma around mental health treatment.

- **Enforcement of Existing Laws.** Strengthening the enforcement of existing gun laws, including cracking down on illegal gun trafficking and ensuring that states comply with federal regulations related to background checks and firearm sales.

Gun control is one of the most emotionally charged and divisive issues in the United States, and finding common ground will not be easy. However, the experiences of other countries show that meaningful reform is possible and that lives can be saved with the right combination of legislative action, cultural change, and community support. The key for the U.S. will be to craft a uniquely American solution that respects the country's historical and constitutional context while addressing the urgent need to reduce gun violence.

For real progress to be made, stakeholders on both sides of the debate—gun control advocates and gun rights supporters—will need to come together and acknowledge the validity of each other's concerns. By focusing on practical, evidence-based solutions and fostering a spirit of compromise, the U.S. can begin to address the epidemic of gun violence and work toward a safer future for all its citizens.

The path forward will require not only legislative action but also a willingness to change the narrative around gun ownership, recognizing that with rights come responsibilities, and that protecting public safety is a shared goal. Only through collaboration and understanding can the U.S. hope to prevent further tragedies and build a more just and secure society.

RACE AND POLICING IN AMERICA

Navigating Racial Justice, Police Reform, and Systemic Inequality

Introduction

The intersection of race and policing in America has been a deeply contentious and painful issue for decades, but it was the tragic killing of George Floyd in 2020 that reignited a national and global conversation about systemic racism, police misconduct, and racial injustice. Floyd's death, captured on video, showed a white police officer kneeling on Floyd's neck for nearly nine minutes while he gasped for air and pleaded for his life. This incident sparked mass protests not only across the United States but also around the world, as millions of people demanded accountability, justice, and significant reform in law enforcement.

Floyd's killing was not an isolated event. It followed a long line of high-profile cases involving police violence against Black Americans, including the deaths of Breonna Taylor, Michael Brown, and Tamir Rice, among others. These cases have become symbols of the broader racial disparities that exist in the American criminal justice system and the often fraught relationship between police and communities of color. The rise of the Black Lives Matter (BLM) movement, which began in response to the 2013 acquittal of Trayvon Martin's killer and grew in prominence after the police killings of unarmed Black individuals, brought these issues into sharper focus.

The debate over how to address racial inequality and police misconduct is as divisive as it is urgent. On one side are calls for sweeping reforms, including efforts to "defund the police" and re-imagine public safety by diverting resources away from law enforcement and toward social services, mental health support, and education. On the other side are concerns about maintaining law and order, with opponents of defunding arguing that reducing police funding could lead to a rise in crime and leave communities—especially marginalized ones—more vulnerable to violence and disorder.

At the same time, the national debate on Critical Race Theory (CRT)—a framework that examines how systemic racism is embedded in legal and social institutions—has become another flash-point. CRT's critics argue that it is divisive and should not be taught in schools, while its proponents insist that understanding the legacy of racism, particularly in policing, is essential for addressing and dismantling systemic inequality.

The issue of race and policing is therefore multifaceted, encompassing questions about justice, equality, public safety, and education. This article explores the historical context, the current debates over police reform, and the broader societal implications of this ongoing struggle for racial justice in America. As the nation grapples with these deeply rooted issues, the path forward remains uncertain but essential for building a more just and equitable society.

The Killing of George Floyd and the Rise of the Black Lives Matter Movement

The George Floyd Case

On May 25, 2020, George Floyd, a 46-year-old Black man, was killed by a Minneapolis police officer, Derek Chauvin, during an arrest. The arrest occurred after a store clerk suspected Floyd of using a counterfeit $20 bill. What followed was an event that became the catalyst for one of the largest racial justice movements in modern history. Chauvin, a white police officer, kneeled on Floyd's neck for 9 minutes and 29 seconds while Floyd lay handcuffed and prone on the ground, repeatedly saying, "I can't breathe."

The entire encounter was captured on video by a bystander and quickly went viral, sparking outrage across the country and internationally. The graphic footage of Floyd's final moments showed Chauvin's apparent indifference as Floyd pleaded for air, lost consciousness, and eventually died. The images of Floyd's death served as a visceral reminder of long-standing racial disparities in American law enforcement and a broader pattern of police violence against Black people.

Floyd's death was not just another case of police brutality—it was the tipping point in a country already grappling with its legacy of racial injustice. The fact that Floyd's killing occurred in broad daylight, with multiple witnesses, and yet took place over nearly 10 agonizing minutes, deeply shocked the American public. This prompted an intense national conversation about race, police accountability, and the institutional forces that allow police violence to persist, particularly in communities of color.

The Resurgence of Black Lives Matter

Floyd's killing was a significant catalyst for the resurgence of the Black Lives Matter (BLM) movement, which was originally founded in 2013 in response to the acquittal of George Zimmerman in the fatal shooting of Trayvon Martin, an unarmed Black teenager in Florida. BLM has since become a global movement advocating for an end to systemic racism, particularly as it manifests in law enforcement and the criminal justice system. In the wake of Floyd's death, the movement saw an unprecedented swell of support and participation.

Protests erupted in Minneapolis just hours after Floyd's death and quickly spread across the United States, with demonstrations occurring in all 50 states. These protests were overwhelmingly peaceful, with millions of people taking to the streets to demand justice for Floyd and other victims of police violence, including Breonna Taylor (killed in Louisville, Kentucky) and Ahmaud Arbery (killed while jogging in Georgia). The BLM protests grew into one of the largest social movements in American history, with estimates from The New York Times suggesting that more than 26 million people participated in protests across the U.S. during the summer of 2020.

The protests also spread globally, with demonstrations taking place in countries such as Canada, the United Kingdom, France, Germany, Brazil, and South Africa. In many of these places, protesters drew parallels between Floyd's killing and their own countries' struggles with racial injustice, colonialism, and police violence. The movement became a powerful call for solidarity among oppressed groups worldwide.

Calls for Racial Justice and Police Accountability

At the heart of the protests were calls for justice and accountability. Demonstrators demanded not only that the officers involved in Floyd's death be held responsible but also that structural changes be made to prevent similar tragedies in the future. The rallying cries of "No justice, no peace" and "Say his name" became symbolic of the broader demand for systemic change, including addressing racial disparities in policing and the criminal justice system.

The Minneapolis Police Department was quick to fire Chauvin and the other three officers involved in the incident, but protesters continued to demand Chauvin's arrest and conviction. In a rare moment of accountability, Chauvin was arrested and charged with second-degree murder, third-degree murder, and manslaughter. His trial, which took place in early 2021, ended in a landmark conviction—Chauvin was found guilty on all charges and sentenced to 22.5 years in prison.

While Chauvin's conviction marked a significant legal victory for racial justice advocates, it was not seen as the end of the fight. Many viewed it as one step in a much larger movement for comprehensive police reform and racial justice. Floyd's death reinvigorated discussions about the use of force by police officers, the lack of accountability for misconduct, and the broader question of whether police departments, in their current form, could be reformed at all.

Global Impact and Continuing Protests

The protests following Floyd's death were notable for their scale, diversity, and intensity. In many cities, people from all races, ethnicities, and socioeconomic backgrounds joined together to demand change. In cities like New York, Los Angeles, Atlanta, Portland, and Washington, D.C., large-scale protests sometimes lasted for weeks, bringing attention to longstanding issues of racial injustice in policing. The sheer size of the protests underscored the frustration and anger felt by many Americans over the repeated killings of Black people by police officers without accountability.

In addition to the protests, Floyd's death sparked broader discussions about systemic racism in institutions beyond policing, including education, healthcare, housing, and employment. Companies, universities, and cultural institutions began addressing their own roles in perpetuating racial inequality, leading to a wave of statements, diversity initiatives, and donations to racial justice organizations.

Globally, the BLM movement spurred action on racial justice issues in countries like the UK, where protesters called for the removal of statues of colonial figures and police reform in the wake of deaths like that of Mark Duggan, a Black man shot by London police in 2011. In France, demonstrations focused on the treatment of Black and Arab minorities by French law enforcement, reigniting the case of Adama Traoré, a young Black man who died in police custody in 2016. The global response to Floyd's death made clear that issues of racial inequality and police brutality were not confined to the U.S.

A Lasting Legacy

The killing of George Floyd, and the protests that followed, forced America—and much of the world—to confront deep-rooted issues of racial inequality, especially in law enforcement. While Floyd's death brought renewed urgency to the Black Lives Matter movement and led to some changes, such as the removal of Confederate statues and the creation of police reform commissions in several cities, the broader question of how to address systemic racism in policing remains unresolved.

Floyd's legacy continues to influence the national conversation on race and justice. His death sparked a widespread movement that demanded not just accountability for individual acts of police violence but a complete rethinking of how law enforcement operates, particularly in marginalized communities. The slogan "Defund the Police", a rallying cry for some activists, reflected the growing belief that policing needed to be fundamentally re-imagined and that resources should be redirected toward addressing the root causes of crime—poverty, mental health, education, and housing.

As the nation continues to grapple with these issues, the events of 2020 have left an indelible mark on the fight for racial justice in the U.S. Floyd's death became a symbol of the broader struggle against racial inequality, and the protests that followed forced an urgent reckoning with how America treats its Black citizens. While the full scope of change remains uncertain, the George Floyd protests have undeniably shifted the conversation and laid the groundwork for future efforts to achieve racial justice and police reform.

The Debate: Defund the Police vs. Law and Order

In the wake of George Floyd's death, one of the most polarizing issues to emerge from the nationwide protests was the debate over how to address systemic issues in policing. Central to this discussion was the call by some activists to "defund the police", a slogan that became a lightning rod for controversy. While for some, this phrase represented a clear demand for reallocating police funds toward community-based services, for others, it was interpreted as a dangerous call to dismantle law enforcement altogether. Opponents of defunding emphasized the need for law and order, arguing that weakening police departments could lead to an increase in crime and leave vulnerable communities without adequate protection.

This debate highlights the deep divisions in American society over the role of policing, public safety, and how to address the racial disparities in law enforcement. Below, we explore both sides of this contentious issue and the potential solutions being proposed.

Defund the Police: What Does It Really Mean?

The call to "defund the police" gained national prominence during the protests that followed George Floyd's killing, but the concept itself has deep roots in various social justice movements. At its core, defunding the police means reallocating or redirecting a portion of police budgets toward other public services that address the root causes of crime, such as mental health care, housing, education, and social work. Proponents argue that police departments are often tasked with handling situations—such as mental health crises, homelessness, or domestic disputes—that could be better managed by professionals trained in those areas.

Re-imagining Public Safety

Advocates of defunding the police do not all agree on what the end goal should be, but many emphasize re-imagining public safety in a way that prioritizes community well-being over punitive measures. Rather than responding to every social problem with law enforcement, they propose creating a broader network of services that could address the underlying issues that contribute to crime. For example, a person experiencing a mental health crisis would not be confronted by armed officers but by trained social workers or mental health professionals. Similarly, homelessness or substance abuse would be addressed through supportive housing and rehabilitation services rather than through criminalization.

In this model, the role of the police would be reduced, focusing on serious crimes such as violent offenses, rather than responding to low-level issues like minor traffic violations or non-violent misdemeanors. The underlying belief is that many current police responsibilities could be shifted to other professionals who are better equipped to handle specific situations without escalating them into violent encounters.

The Case for Reallocating Police Budgets

The push to defund police departments is rooted in a critique of the disproportionate funding given to law enforcement compared to other critical social services. In major cities like New York and Los Angeles, police budgets make up a significant portion of municipal spending, often outstripping investments in housing, healthcare, education, and youth programs. Advocates argue that by redirecting even a small percentage of police budgets to these areas, cities could address the root causes of crime and reduce the need for policing in the first place.

A 2020 analysis by Bloomberg found that major U.S. cities allocated between 20% and 45% of their total discretionary funds to police departments, often at the expense of social services. Advocates for defunding argue that over-policing and militarization of law enforcement have done little to reduce crime in marginalized communities but have contributed to widespread mistrust of the police, particularly among Black and Latino populations.

Case Studies: Reallocation in Action

Some cities have already begun experimenting with reallocating police funds to community services:

- **Minneapolis.** In the wake of George Floyd's killing, Minneapolis City Council voted to redirect $8 million from the police department to fund initiatives such as violence prevention, mental health crisis response, and social services. These changes aim to reduce reliance on police while still ensuring public safety.

- **Los Angeles.** The city cut $150 million from its police department's budget and redirected the funds to services for marginalized communities, including mental health programs, housing for homeless individuals, and education.

- **Austin, Texas.** In 2020, Austin City Council voted to reallocate about $150 million from the police budget to fund community services, including a family violence shelter, mental health first responders, and substance abuse programs.

While these experiments are still in the early stages, they represent a broader trend of cities reconsidering how their resources are distributed. However, defunding the police remains a controversial and divisive issue, with many questioning the long-term effects of such policies on public safety.

Opposition to Defunding: The Case for Law and Order

On the other side of the debate are those who argue that defunding the police is a dangerous approach that could jeopardize public safety, particularly in high-crime areas. Opponents of defunding emphasize the need for law and order, arguing that police presence is critical to maintaining safety and protecting communities from crime. For these critics, the focus should be on reforming police departments rather than reducing their budgets or shrinking their roles.

The Fear of Rising Crime

One of the most frequently cited concerns about defunding the police is the potential for rising crime rates. Opponents argue that reducing police budgets could weaken law enforcement's ability to prevent and respond to crime, leaving communities vulnerable. In the aftermath of the George Floyd protests, many cities did see an uptick in violent crime, particularly homicides. According to the Federal Bureau of Investigation (FBI), the U.S. saw a 30% increase in murders in 2020, the largest single-year rise since the agency began tracking these figures in 1960.

Critics of defunding point to these statistics as evidence that reducing police presence and resources could make cities less safe. They argue that while systemic reform is necessary, slashing police budgets in the short term will do little to address the complex factors driving crime, such as poverty, inequality, and gang violence.

The Importance of Community Policing

Many opponents of defunding the police advocate for community policing as an alternative reform strategy. Community policing emphasizes building stronger relationships between law enforcement and the communities they serve. The goal is to foster trust, reduce the likelihood of confrontational encounters, and encourage cooperation between the police and residents in preventing crime.

Proponents of community policing argue that defunding police departments could undermine these efforts, as fewer resources would be available to invest in training, outreach, and crime prevention programs. Instead of defunding, they call for greater investment in police training on de-escalation tactics, implicit bias, and cultural sensitivity to reduce instances of police violence and rebuild trust with marginalized communities.

The Push for Police Reform

Opponents of defunding also argue that rather than reducing police budgets, the focus should be on reforming police departments to ensure greater accountability, transparency, and oversight. Some of the key reform proposals include:

- Banning choke-holds and other dangerous restraints commonly used by police officers.

- Limiting qualified immunity, which shields police officers from civil lawsuits, making it easier to hold them accountable for misconduct.

- Requiring body cameras for all officers and ensuring the footage is publicly accessible in cases of police violence.

- Creating civilian oversight boards to investigate police misconduct and recommend disciplinary actions.

Many of these reforms have broad public support. A 2020 Pew Research Center survey found that 92% of Americans support requiring police officers to wear body cameras, and 75% support the creation of civilian oversight boards. These proposals reflect a desire to improve policing practices without significantly reducing the resources available to law enforcement.

Middle Ground: Reform, Not Defund?

The debate over defunding the police versus maintaining law and order is often presented as a binary choice, but many experts and policymakers are advocating for a middle ground. This approach emphasizes the need for significant police reform while maintaining an adequate police presence to ensure public safety. Proposals for reform often include better police training, improved accountability, and the creation of alternative response teams for situations where armed officers may not be necessary.

For example, cities like Denver have implemented programs where mental health professionals or crisis intervention teams are dispatched to non-violent incidents involving mental health crises or substance abuse, reducing the need for police intervention in situations where force could escalate tensions. These programs aim to complement traditional law enforcement rather than replace it.

Systemic Racism and Police Reform

The killing of George Floyd and the rise of the Black Lives Matter (BLM) movement not only reignited a debate about individual cases of police misconduct but also focused attention on the larger issue of systemic racism in American law enforcement. Systemic racism refers to the ingrained racial biases and disparities present in institutions such as the criminal justice system, which disproportionately affect people of color, especially Black Americans. When it comes to policing, systemic racism manifests in practices like racial profiling, over-policing in minority neighborhoods, and the disproportionate use of force against Black and Latino individuals. These issues have sparked ongoing debates over how to address racial inequality in policing and the criminal justice system, as well as what forms of police reform are necessary to achieve racial justice.

Understanding Systemic Racism in Policing

Systemic racism in law enforcement goes beyond the actions of individual officers; it refers to the policies, practices, and structures within the policing system that perpetuate racial inequality. These institutional biases are deeply rooted in American history and have evolved over time, often reinforcing racial hierarchies. The origins of policing in the United States can be traced back to practices like slave patrols in the South, which were designed to control and surveil Black populations. Over time, these systems of racial control were adapted to new forms, including Jim Crow laws, redlining, and the modern-day war on drugs, which disproportionately targeted Black and Latino communities.

One of the most glaring examples of systemic racism in policing is the racial disparities in arrests, incarceration, and police use of force. Black Americans are nearly three times more likely to be killed by police than white Americans, according to data from the Mapping Police Violence project. Additionally, Black individuals are more likely to be stopped, searched, and arrested by police, even though studies have shown that they are no more likely to be carrying contraband or engaged in criminal activity than their white counterparts.

Racial disparities in policing are also evident in the enforcement of minor offenses, such as marijuana possession. Despite roughly equal usage rates between Black and white Americans, Black individuals are almost four times more likely to be arrested for marijuana possession, according to the ACLU. These disparities fuel a broader cycle of criminalization, poverty, and disenfranchisement in communities of color, where aggressive policing often leads to negative long-term social and economic consequences.

The Use of Force and Police Accountability

One of the most pressing concerns in the conversation about systemic racism in policing is the disproportionate use of force against Black and Latino communities.

High-profile cases, such as the deaths of Eric Garner, Michael Brown, Philando Castile, and Breonna Taylor, highlight how routine police encounters can escalate into fatal incidents, often with little accountability for the officers involved.

A 2020 study published in the Proceedings of the National Academy of Sciences found that Black men are 2.5 times more likely than white men to be killed by police during their lifetime. This disparity in police use of force is not confined to fatal encounters but extends to non-lethal incidents as well, such as the use of tasers, batons, and pepper spray. The disproportionate use of force contributes to a broader distrust of police in communities of color, where officers are often seen as agents of surveillance and control rather than protection.

One of the central challenges in addressing police violence is the lack of accountability for officers who use excessive force. The legal doctrine of qualified immunity protects police officers from civil lawsuits, making it difficult for victims or their families to seek justice for wrongful deaths or injuries caused by police. Critics argue that qualified immunity shields officers from consequences, even in cases of egregious misconduct, perpetuating a culture of impunity within law enforcement. While some reforms have been proposed to limit the scope of qualified immunity, there has been significant resistance from police unions and lawmakers who argue that such changes could hinder officers' ability to do their jobs effectively.

Police Reform: Efforts and Proposals

In response to the demands for justice and an end to systemic racism in policing, a variety of reform efforts have been proposed and implemented at both the local and national levels. These reforms aim to address the underlying causes of racial disparities in policing and create a more equitable and accountable system. Some of the most prominent reform proposals include:

- **Use of Force Standards.** Many advocates are pushing for national standards that govern the use of force by police officers. These standards would include clear guidelines on when officers can use force and require officers to employ de-escalation techniques before resorting to physical force. Some proposals include banning choke-holds, like the one used on Eric Garner in 2014, and prohibiting the use of no-knock warrants, like the one that led to Breonna Taylor's death. At the federal level, the George Floyd Justice in Policing Act, passed by the House of Representatives in 2021, aimed to establish national use-of-force standards, restrict qualified immunity, and create a national registry of police misconduct. While the bill passed the House, it faced opposition in the Senate, particularly over provisions related to qualified immunity and federal oversight of local police departments.

- **Body Cameras and Transparency.** One of the most widely adopted reforms in recent years has been the use of body cameras by police officers. Body cameras are intended to provide an objective record of police interactions and have been shown to reduce incidents of excessive force when officers know they are being recorded. A 2017 study by the University of Cambridge found that officers wearing body cameras were less likely to use force and that complaints against officers decreased significantly. However, body cameras alone are not a panacea. In some high-profile cases, such as the shooting of Andre Hill in Ohio, body camera footage did not prevent the officer from using deadly force. Moreover, there are concerns about how body camera footage is managed, particularly in terms of ensuring that the public has access to the footage in cases of police violence.

- **Civilian Oversight and Independent Investigations.** Another key reform proposal involves the creation of civilian oversight boards that can investigate allegations of police misconduct and recommend disciplinary action. In many cities, police departments have historically conducted internal investigations into officer misconduct, leading to concerns about a lack of transparency and accountability. Civilian oversight boards, on the other hand, are independent bodies that provide an additional layer of accountability. While some cities, like Chicago, New York, and Los Angeles, have established civilian oversight boards, their effectiveness has been mixed. Critics argue that these boards often lack the authority or resources to hold officers accountable and that police unions have been successful in limiting the scope of their powers. For civilian oversight boards to be effective, advocates argue, they must have the power to conduct independent investigations, subpoena officers, and recommend sanctions.

- **Ending Qualified Immunity.** As mentioned earlier, the legal doctrine of qualified immunity is one of the biggest obstacles to holding police officers accountable for misconduct. Under qualified immunity, officers are shielded from civil liability unless it can be shown that they violated a "clearly established" constitutional right. In practice, this legal standard is so high that it has become difficult for victims of police violence to successfully sue officers, even in cases where their rights were violated. Calls to end or reform qualified immunity have gained traction in the wake of high-profile cases of police misconduct. Advocates argue that removing this legal shield would create more accountability by making it easier to hold officers personally liable for their actions. Opponents, including many police unions, argue that eliminating qualified immunity would discourage officers from taking necessary action in dangerous situations, fearing that they could be sued for their split-second decisions.

Reallocating Resources and Re-imagining Public Safety

While some reform efforts focus on improving existing police practices, others advocate for a more fundamental rethinking of public safety. The Defund the Police movement, discussed earlier, calls for reallocating funds from police departments to social services, mental health programs, and community-based interventions that address the root causes of crime. The idea is that by investing in education, housing, and healthcare, cities can reduce the need for aggressive policing and improve public safety in a more holistic and equitable way.

In cities like Portland and San Francisco, there have been efforts to shift resources from police departments to alternative crisis response teams that are trained to handle situations involving mental health crises, homelessness, or substance abuse. These programs aim to reduce the number of encounters between law enforcement and individuals in crisis, thereby reducing the likelihood of violence.

Resistance to Reform and the Role of Police Unions

Despite widespread calls for reform, efforts to change police practices have faced significant resistance, particularly from police unions. Unions wield considerable power in negotiating contracts that often include protections for officers accused of misconduct. These protections can include extended waiting periods before officers can be questioned after a shooting, limits on the use of body camera footage, and the ability to appeal disciplinary actions through binding arbitration.

Critics argue that police unions have been a major obstacle to accountability and reform. In many cities, union contracts have made it difficult to fire officers with a history of misconduct or to implement changes to department policies. Union leaders often argue that these protections are necessary to ensure that officers are treated fairly and that they are not unjustly punished for doing a difficult and dangerous job.

Critical Race Theory (CRT) and Policing

As the national conversation on race, policing, and justice evolved in the wake of George Floyd's death, a new front in the debate emerged: Critical Race Theory (CRT). Originally an academic framework for understanding how systemic racism is embedded in legal and social institutions, CRT has become one of the most controversial and divisive issues in contemporary American discourse. Its application to policing and the broader criminal justice system has fueled heated debates about how racial history and inequality should be taught, understood, and addressed in public life.

Supporters argue that CRT is essential for identifying and dismantling the institutional structures that perpetuate racial disparities in policing. They believe that without addressing these deeper, systemic issues, efforts at police reform will be limited and superficial. Meanwhile, opponents contend that CRT is divisive, paints law enforcement and society in a negative light, and promotes an overly pessimistic view of America's progress on race. The debate over CRT, much like the larger discussion of race and policing, has become a political flash-point, particularly in schools, law enforcement training, and public policy.

What is Critical Race Theory?

Critical Race Theory (CRT) originated in the late 1970s and early 1980s as a framework for examining the ways in which racism and racial inequality are not simply the product of individual bias or prejudice, but are also embedded in the structures, laws, and institutions of society. CRT scholars, including legal academics like Derrick Bell, Kimberlé Crenshaw, and Richard Delgado, argued that systemic racism has deep historical roots that continue to shape legal systems and public policies today.

At its core, CRT posits that racism is a structural problem—not merely an individual one. This means that even well-meaning policies can result in racially disparate outcomes because the legal and social institutions they are built upon are influenced by centuries of racial oppression. CRT emphasizes that law and legal institutions are not neutral but have often played a central role in reinforcing racial inequalities.

Some of the core concepts of CRT include:

- **Institutional Racism.** The idea that institutions—such as the criminal justice system—create and enforce laws and policies that have disproportionate negative effects on people of color, regardless of intent.

- **Intersectionality.** Coined by Kimberlé Crenshaw, this concept refers to the interconnectedness of social categories like race, gender, and class, and how these overlapping identities result in compounded experiences of discrimination or privilege.

- **Counter-Narratives.** CRT encourages the use of storytelling, especially from marginalized perspectives, to challenge dominant narratives that often ignore or minimize the role of racism in shaping societal outcomes.

When applied to policing, CRT argues that the disproportionate violence and policing of Black and Latino communities are not accidental or the result of a few "bad apples." Rather, they are outcomes of historical legacies and systems that have criminalized Blackness and embedded racial hierarchies into the very fabric of law enforcement.

CRT and Policing: How Systemic Racism Shapes Law Enforcement

Policing is one of the key areas where CRT is applied to examine how structural racism manifests in everyday life. Proponents of CRT argue that modern policing, especially in marginalized communities, cannot be fully understood without recognizing the historical context of how police forces were formed and the role they have played in maintaining racial hierarchies. From the slave patrols in the South, which were tasked with controlling enslaved Black populations, to the enforcement of Jim Crow laws, law enforcement has long played a role in racial oppression.

According to CRT scholars, today's racial disparities in policing—including racial profiling, the over-policing of minority neighborhoods, and the disproportionate use of force against Black and Latino people—are not merely the result of individual officers' biases, but are symptomatic of deeper institutional structures that prioritize control and punishment over rehabilitation or community safety. Even policies that appear race-neutral, such as stop-and-frisk practices or drug enforcement laws, often have disproportionate impacts on communities of color.

Racial Profiling and Mass Incarceration

One of the key areas where CRT has focused attention is on the practice of racial profiling. This is when law enforcement targets individuals for suspicion of crime based on their race or ethnicity rather than any specific behavior. CRT scholars argue that racial profiling is a clear example of how institutionalized racism operates within law enforcement. Research consistently shows that Black and Latino drivers, for instance, are more likely to be stopped, searched, and arrested than white drivers, even though they are no more likely to be in possession of illegal items.

This racial bias extends into the broader criminal justice system, where mass incarceration disproportionately affects people of color. The U.S. imprisons a higher percentage of its population than any other country in the world, and Black Americans are incarcerated at nearly five times the rate of white Americans. CRT argues that this disparity is not simply a reflection of differences in criminal behavior, but the result of laws and policies—like the War on Drugs—that disproportionately target communities of color.

The Backlash Against CRT in Policing and Education

Despite its academic origins, CRT has become a political flash-point, with significant opposition to its teachings, particularly in the realm of public education and law enforcement training. Critics of CRT argue that it promotes a divisive view of race relations and suggests that America is inherently racist. This backlash has led to legislative efforts in several states to ban CRT from being taught in schools, and has sparked a broader national debate over how race, history, and policing should be understood and taught.

The Push to Ban CRT in Schools

As the conversation about CRT expanded beyond academia and into the public sphere, conservative lawmakers in states like Texas, Florida, and Idaho moved to restrict the teaching of CRT and related concepts in public schools. These laws, often framed as efforts to prevent "divisive" or "anti-American" teachings, argue that CRT misrepresents American history and teaches children to view themselves and others primarily through the lens of race. Opponents of CRT argue that it encourages a victim mentality among people of color and unfairly paints white Americans as oppressors.

One of the most vocal critics of CRT, conservative commentator Christopher Rufo, has described CRT as a form of "cultural Marxism" that seeks to fundamentally transform American institutions by focusing on race and victimhood. This argument has resonated with many on the political right, who see CRT as a threat to traditional values and an attack on the notion of American exceptionalism.

CRT and Law Enforcement Training

The controversy over CRT has also extended to the realm of police training. In some cases, efforts to incorporate concepts like implicit bias training or anti-racism workshops for police officers have been met with resistance, with critics arguing that these programs amount to CRT by another name. In June 2021, Florida Governor Ron DeSantis signed legislation banning state agencies, including police departments, from using training materials that incorporate CRT, arguing that they promote division rather than unity.

Opponents of CRT-inspired training in law enforcement argue that it unfairly paints police officers as racially biased or complicit in systemic racism. They contend that focusing too heavily on race could undermine morale in police departments and create further divisions between officers and the communities they serve.

The Case for CRT: Addressing Historical and Structural Inequalities

Supporters of CRT argue that banning it, whether in schools or police training programs, is a way of silencing important conversations about racial inequality and policing. They assert that CRT is essential for understanding how historical injustices, such as slavery, segregation, and discriminatory laws, continue to shape the present-day realities of law enforcement and the criminal justice system. Without acknowledging these historical legacies, they argue, it is impossible to develop meaningful reforms that address the root causes of racial disparities in policing.

Proponents also emphasize that CRT is not about dividing people along racial lines, but about understanding the structural barriers that prevent true equality. By examining how laws, policies, and institutions perpetuate inequality, CRT provides a framework for addressing racial disparities in areas like policing, housing, and education. They argue that CRT encourages a deeper, more nuanced understanding of race in America, one that recognizes both the progress made and the work that still needs to be done to achieve racial justice.

The Broader Implications of the CRT Debate

The debate over CRT extends beyond policing into broader discussions of racial justice, education, and public policy. The controversy over how race and history should be taught in schools and addressed in law enforcement is part of a larger cultural conflict over what kind of country America is, and what it aspires to be. The question at the heart of the CRT debate is whether acknowledging and addressing systemic racism will bring about healing and progress, or whether it will create further divisions and polarization.

As cities and states grapple with police reform, the debate over CRT will likely continue to influence discussions about race, policing, and how America confronts its history of racial inequality. For now, CRT remains a powerful yet polarizing lens through which the nation's struggles with systemic racism—particularly in law enforcement—are being examined.

Critical Race Theory provides a framework for understanding the deep and enduring connections between race, law, and power in American society. As applied to policing, CRT sheds light on how systemic racism influences law enforcement practices and how racial disparities in policing are part of broader institutional inequalities. While the backlash against CRT has dominated recent political discourse, its proponents argue that CRT offers a necessary and transformative lens through which to address racial justice and police reform.

Ultimately, the future of policing—and of the broader conversation about race in America—may depend on whether the country chooses to engage with the difficult truths that CRT highlights, or whether it seeks to ignore or suppress these conversations in the name of avoiding discomfort or division. Whatever the outcome, the debate over CRT will continue to shape discussions about systemic racism and the future of policing in the U.S. for years to come.

Public Perceptions and Media Coverage

The debate surrounding race, policing, and systemic racism in the United States is not only shaped by policy discussions but also by public perceptions and media coverage. The ways in which police brutality, racial justice protests, and calls for reform are portrayed in the media have a significant impact on how the public understands and responds to these issues. In many cases, media framing and public opinion have fueled political polarization, shaping the national discourse on law enforcement, race, and justice.

The killing of George Floyd in 2020 and the subsequent resurgence of the Black Lives Matter (BLM) movement revealed deep divisions in how Americans view the role of policing, with significant differences based on race, political ideology, and geographic region. While some Americans demand radical changes to the criminal justice system, others call for stronger support of law enforcement and prioritize public safety over reform. This section examines the role of media in shaping public perceptions of race and policing, the impact of viral moments in galvanizing support for racial justice, and how Americans' views on these issues vary across different demographic groups.

The Role of Media in Shaping the Debate

The media plays a pivotal role in how issues related to policing and racial justice are framed and understood by the public. Coverage of high-profile incidents of police violence—such as the killings of George Floyd, Breonna Taylor, and Eric Garner—has brought national attention to the problem of police brutality, sparking waves of protests and calls for reform. However, the way the media covers these incidents can vary widely depending on the outlet, contributing to differing narratives about the scope of the problem and how it should be addressed.

Traditional Media

Traditional media outlets, including major television networks, newspapers, and radio stations, have a significant influence on public opinion about policing and race. However, their coverage of police violence and racial justice movements often varies depending on their editorial stance and political leanings. For example:

- Liberal-leaning outlets, such as The New York Times, CNN, and MSNBC, tend to focus on issues of systemic racism, police misconduct, and the need for comprehensive reform. They often highlight the stories of victims of police violence and provide extensive coverage of Black Lives Matter protests, framing them as part of a broader struggle for civil rights and justice.

- Conservative-leaning outlets, such as Fox News, The Wall Street Journal, and The Daily Caller, tend to emphasize concerns about law and order, the protection of police officers, and the potential dangers posed by anti-police rhetoric. They often frame Black Lives Matter protests as violent or chaotic and stress the importance of maintaining a strong police presence to ensure public safety.

The differences in media coverage contribute to polarized perceptions of racial justice movements and the role of policing. For example, while liberal outlets might focus on the peaceful aspects of BLM protests, conservative outlets may highlight instances of looting or violence, creating two starkly different narratives of the same event.

Social Media and Viral Moments

In addition to traditional media, social media platforms such as Twitter, Facebook, Instagram, and TikTok have become powerful tools for shaping public opinion on race and policing. The viral spread of videos showing police violence, such as the footage of Derek Chauvin kneeling on George Floyd's neck, has been instrumental in mobilizing protests and creating widespread outrage. These platforms allow ordinary citizens to bypass traditional media gatekeepers and share their own experiences and perspectives on racial injustice.

Social media has also played a key role in amplifying the voices of activists and organizations like Black Lives Matter, allowing them to reach a global audience and organize mass protests. The hashtags #BlackLivesMatter, #SayHerName, and #DefundThePolice have become rallying cries for those demanding accountability and reform.

However, social media platforms are also breeding grounds for misinformation, disinformation, and polarization. Viral videos that highlight police misconduct can provoke outrage, but without full context, they may sometimes lead to misunderstandings or incomplete narratives. Additionally, social media algorithms often reinforce users' preexisting beliefs by showing them content that aligns with their views, contributing to echo chambers where users are less likely to encounter differing perspectives.

The Influence of Viral Incidents

Viral incidents of police violence have had a profound impact on how Americans view the issue of policing and racial justice. The video of George Floyd's death, in particular, became a symbol of the broader problem of police brutality and racial inequality in the U.S. According to a Pew Research Center poll conducted shortly after Floyd's killing, 67% of Americans supported the Black Lives Matter movement, with many expressing outrage at Floyd's death and a desire for systemic change in policing.

Similarly, the deaths of Breonna Taylor, who was shot and killed by police in her own home during a botched raid, and Ahmaud Arbery, a Black man shot by white vigilantes while jogging, became flash-points for national conversations about race and justice. The media coverage of these incidents, along with the viral spread of videos related to them, helped bring attention to systemic racism and the need for police reform.

However, the media's coverage of these events also sparked backlash in some quarters, with critics accusing the media of sensationalizing these incidents and fueling anti-police sentiment. Conservative commentators, in particular, have pointed to the "war on cops" narrative, arguing that the media's focus on police misconduct creates a dangerous environment for law enforcement officers.

Polarization and Public Opinion

Public opinion on issues of race and policing is deeply divided, with stark differences based on race, political affiliation, age, and geography. The debate over police reform, defunding the police, and the role of systemic racism in law enforcement has polarized Americans, with many holding opposing views on how best to move forward.

Differences by Race

One of the most significant divides in public opinion is along racial lines. According to a 2021 Gallup poll, 78% of Black Americans believe that the criminal justice system treats people unfairly based on race, compared to only 40% of white Americans. Similarly, 84% of Black respondents said they had little or no confidence that police officers who commit misconduct will be held accountable, compared to 47% of white respondents.

Black Americans are also far more likely to support efforts to defund the police or reallocate police budgets to social services. In contrast, white Americans are more likely to express concerns about rising crime rates and the need for law and order. These differing perspectives are shaped by the lived experiences of racial groups, with many Black Americans experiencing disproportionately higher rates of police stops, arrests, and use of force.

Differences by Political Affiliation

Political affiliation is another major factor in how Americans view the issue of race and policing. According to a 2020 Pew Research Center poll, 88% of Democrats said police need to make major changes to address systemic racism, compared to only 30% of Republicans. Similarly, 75% of Democrats supported reducing police funding to reallocate resources to other social services, while only 15% of Republicans agreed.

Republicans tend to focus more on concerns about public safety and support for law enforcement, with many arguing that police reform should not come at the expense of reducing crime. Conservative media outlets and politicians have amplified these concerns, emphasizing the importance of maintaining strong police forces to combat crime and protect communities.

Age and Geography

Age also plays a role in shaping public opinion on policing and race. Younger Americans, particularly Generation Z and Millennials, are more likely to support Black Lives Matter and advocate for systemic police reform. According to a YouGov poll conducted in 2020, 62% of Americans under 30 expressed support for defunding the police, compared to just 29% of Americans over 65.

Geographic differences are also significant. In urban areas, where police-community relations tend to be more strained, there is more support for reform and reallocating police budgets. In rural areas and smaller towns, however, where crime rates are often lower and police are more integrated into community life, support for the police remains strong, and the idea of defunding is met with more resistance.

Impact of Public Opinion on Policy

Public opinion and media coverage have a profound impact on shaping policymaking at both the local and national levels. In cities where protests were large and sustained, such as Minneapolis, Los Angeles, and New York, local governments have responded by implementing police reforms, reallocating budgets, and creating task forces to address police misconduct. For instance, Minneapolis—the city where George Floyd was killed—voted to redirect $8 million from its police department to fund initiatives such as mental health response teams and community-based violence prevention.

At the national level, the pressure from activists and public opinion led to the introduction of the George Floyd Justice in Policing Act in 2020. The bill, which passed the House but stalled in the Senate, sought to ban choke-holds, end qualified immunity, and establish national standards for police conduct. However, the polarized nature of public opinion on policing has made it difficult to achieve broad, bipartisan support for more sweeping reforms at the federal level.

Comparative International Approaches to Policing

As the United States continues to grapple with issues of racial justice and police reform, looking at how other countries with diverse populations address policing can offer valuable insights. Nations like the United Kingdom, Canada, and New Zealand have taken different approaches to law enforcement that may serve as models for more equitable, community-oriented policing in the U.S. These countries face their own challenges with racial disparities, but their efforts to promote transparency, accountability, and community engagement in policing offer potential lessons for reforming the U.S. criminal justice system.

This section examines the approaches taken by the U.K., Canada, and other countries, focusing on key areas such as de-escalation practices, community-based policing, and systemic accountability. It also discusses the challenges they face, and what the U.S. might learn from their successes and limitations.

The United Kingdom: Emphasizing De-Escalation and Accountability

The United Kingdom has long been recognized for its approach to policing, particularly its emphasis on de-escalation and the limited use of firearms by police officers. One of the most striking differences between U.S. and U.K. policing is the fact that most British police officers do not carry firearms during their daily patrols. This reflects a broader philosophy of policing that emphasizes conflict resolution and de-escalation rather than immediate use of force.

De-Escalation and Training

In the U.K., police officers undergo extensive training in non-violent conflict resolution, including techniques for de-escalating potentially dangerous situations. British police are trained to use communication and negotiation skills to defuse confrontations, particularly in situations involving individuals with mental health issues or those who are intoxicated. This training is complemented by the use of specialized crisis intervention teams that respond to incidents involving vulnerable populations.

The effectiveness of de-escalation training can be seen in the relatively low number of fatal police shootings in the U.K. In 2021, for example, British police officers discharged their firearms in only five incidents, compared to the United States, where police shootings occur daily. This difference reflects not only the lower prevalence of firearms among the general population in the U.K. but also the prioritization of minimizing the use of deadly force.

Police Accountability and Oversight

The U.K. also has a robust system of police accountability that could provide useful insights for U.S. reform efforts. The Independent Office for Police Conduct (IOPC) oversees complaints against police officers and conducts investigations into incidents of police misconduct or excessive use of force. The IOPC operates independently of police departments, ensuring that investigations are transparent and not influenced by the internal politics of law enforcement agencies.

Additionally, body cameras are widely used by police officers in the U.K., and footage is made available to independent oversight bodies in cases where complaints are lodged. This system helps to maintain public trust by ensuring that allegations of misconduct are taken seriously and investigated thoroughly.

Lessons for the U.S.

The U.S. could benefit from adopting some of the U.K.'s practices, particularly in the areas of de-escalation training and independent oversight. By investing in training that prioritizes conflict resolution and non-violent interventions, U.S. police departments could reduce the number of fatal encounters with civilians, particularly in situations where deadly force is not necessary. Additionally, establishing independent oversight bodies similar to the IOPC could help improve accountability and transparency in U.S. law enforcement, building greater trust between police and communities.

However, it is important to recognize that while the U.K. has made significant strides in reducing the use of force, it still faces challenges with racial disparities in policing. Black and ethnic minority communities in the U.K. are more likely to be stopped and searched by police under the controversial stop-and-search policy, raising concerns about racial profiling. This highlights the fact that even countries with strong de-escalation and accountability practices must continue to address the systemic biases that influence policing outcomes.

Canada: A Focus on Community Policing and Indigenous Relations

Canada offers another valuable case study in policing and racial justice. The country's approach to law enforcement has traditionally emphasized community policing, which focuses on building relationships between police officers and the communities they serve. Community policing is rooted in the idea that public safety is best achieved when law enforcement works collaboratively with community members to solve problems, prevent crime, and address the root causes of violence.

Community Policing

In Canada, many police departments have adopted the principles of community policing as a core part of their strategy. This approach involves police officers working closely with neighborhood leaders, social workers, and community organizations to understand the unique challenges faced by local populations. By establishing relationships with community members, police officers can develop a better understanding of the social dynamics that contribute to crime, allowing them to focus on preventive measures rather than reactive enforcement.

Community policing also helps to reduce the adversarial relationship between police and civilians, particularly in marginalized communities. In cities like Toronto and Vancouver, police departments have established specialized units to work in areas with high concentrations of immigrants, refugees, and people of color, with the goal of building trust and reducing tensions.

Addressing Indigenous Relations

Canada has made notable efforts to address its history of systemic racism and violence against Indigenous peoples. For decades, Indigenous communities in Canada have faced significant challenges with law enforcement, including high rates of police violence, discrimination, and over-incarceration. In response, the Canadian government has undertaken a series of initiatives aimed at improving relations between police forces and Indigenous populations.

One such effort is the development of Indigenous-focused policing models, such as the First Nations Policing Program, which provides funding for Indigenous communities to create their own police forces. These forces are designed to be culturally sensitive and community-led, allowing Indigenous leaders to have a greater say in how law enforcement is conducted in their communities. These programs have had mixed results, with some achieving success in building trust, while others face challenges due to underfunding and a lack of resources.

Lessons for the U.S.

The U.S. could learn from Canada's emphasis on community policing and efforts to engage marginalized groups in law enforcement practices. By adopting similar models of community-based policing, U.S. police departments could work more collaboratively with communities of color, reducing tensions and fostering stronger relationships. Additionally, initiatives like Canada's First Nations Policing Program could offer inspiration for similar efforts in the U.S. to address the unique challenges faced by Native American communities, who often experience high levels of police violence and incarceration.

However, it is important to recognize that Canada's system is not without flaws. The country still struggles with racial disparities in policing, particularly in the treatment of Black Canadians and Indigenous peoples. Recent investigations into police conduct in Indigenous communities have revealed ongoing issues of discrimination and excessive use of force, showing that Canada's approach to racial justice in policing remains a work in progress.

New Zealand: Embracing Restorative Justice

New Zealand provides another compelling example of a country working to address racial inequalities in its criminal justice system, particularly through the use of restorative justice practices. Like Canada, New Zealand faces significant challenges with its Indigenous population, the Māori, who are disproportionately affected by policing and incarceration.

Restorative Justice

Restorative justice is a key element of New Zealand's approach to criminal justice reform, particularly in its efforts to address the over-policing and over-incarceration of Māori individuals. Restorative justice focuses on repairing the harm caused by criminal behavior rather than solely punishing the offender. This approach involves bringing together the victim, the offender, and members of the community to discuss the impact of the crime and agree on a resolution that allows the offender to make amends.

Restorative justice has been shown to reduce recidivism rates and foster greater community cohesion, particularly in Indigenous communities. For Māori offenders, the opportunity to engage in restorative justice practices—often within a cultural framework—has helped reduce the reliance on incarceration and build stronger community bonds.

Lessons for the U.S.

The U.S. could explore the implementation of restorative justice models, particularly for non-violent offenses, as a way to reduce incarceration rates and address racial disparities in the criminal justice system. Restorative justice emphasizes accountability and healing, rather than punishment, and could be particularly effective in addressing the underlying social factors that contribute to crime. By focusing on rehabilitation and reconciliation, the U.S. could take a more holistic approach to justice, especially in communities disproportionately affected by harsh policing and sentencing practices.

Challenges of Applying International Models to the U.S.

While these international examples offer valuable lessons, it is important to acknowledge that translating these models to the U.S. context presents challenges. The U.S. has a much larger, more diverse population and a uniquely complex history of racial inequality and policing. Moreover, the decentralized nature of U.S. law enforcement—with more than 18,000 police departments operating independently—makes implementing national reforms more difficult than in countries with more unified policing structures.

Additionally, the cultural attachment to firearms and the Second Amendment in the U.S. makes adopting policing practices from countries like the U.K., where police rarely carry guns, a challenge. Any approach to reforming U.S. policing must take into account the distinct cultural, legal, and historical factors that shape American law enforcement.

While there are challenges in adopting international models of policing in the U.S., countries like the U.K., Canada, and New Zealand provide valuable examples of how to approach racial justice and police reform. From the U.K.'s emphasis on de-escalation and accountability to Canada's focus on community policing and Indigenous relations, these countries offer insights into how law enforcement can be re-imagined to foster greater trust, reduce violence, and address systemic inequalities.

By learning from these models, the U.S. can explore new ways to balance public safety with racial justice, ensuring that policing serves all communities equitably and effectively. While the path to reform will require significant political will and cultural change, these international examples demonstrate that meaningful change is possible, and that rethinking how police engage with communities can lead to safer, more just outcomes for all.

Future Directions: Where Do We Go From Here?

The issues of race, policing, and systemic racism are deeply entrenched in the social, political, and cultural fabric of the United States. The tragic killing of George Floyd and the subsequent resurgence of the Black Lives Matter (BLM) movement brought the long-standing struggle for racial justice back into the national spotlight, forcing America to confront the uncomfortable realities of police violence and racial inequality. These events not only amplified calls for police reform but also prompted a larger conversation about how race, justice, and public safety are understood and addressed in American society.

As we have explored throughout this article, the debate surrounding race and policing is multifaceted, deeply divisive, and emotionally charged. On one side, reform advocates push for systemic changes, including efforts to defund or re-imagine police departments, introduce independent oversight, and implement community-based safety models. They argue that addressing the root causes of crime—poverty, mental health issues, housing insecurity—will reduce the need for police intervention, particularly in communities of color that have historically borne the brunt of over-policing and excessive force.

On the other side, opponents of defunding the police emphasize the importance of law and order, arguing that reducing police budgets could lead to an increase in crime and leave vulnerable communities without protection. They maintain that the answer to police misconduct lies in reforming rather than dismantling police departments, with a focus on improving training, accountability, and transparency.

This debate is compounded by the role of media coverage and public perception, which shape how Americans view policing and racial justice. Traditional and social media play pivotal roles in framing these discussions, often reinforcing preexisting political and cultural divides. While some media outlets amplify calls for justice and reform, others focus on concerns about public safety and the potential consequences of defunding law enforcement.

A Complex and Evolving Debate

The struggle to balance public safety with racial justice is at the heart of the national debate. Although many police departments have introduced reforms—such as body cameras, de-escalation training, and bans on choke-holds—these efforts are seen by many as insufficient to address the deep-rooted nature of systemic racism within law enforcement. Meanwhile, legislative attempts to pass comprehensive reform at the federal level, such as the George Floyd Justice in Policing Act, have stalled due to political polarization and opposition from various stakeholders, including police unions and conservative lawmakers.

The debate over Critical Race Theory (CRT) has further complicated the conversation. CRT has become a flash-point in the broader discussion of how race, policing, and history are taught and understood in public life. While proponents argue that CRT is essential for addressing the historical and structural inequalities that perpetuate racial disparities in policing, opponents see it as divisive and harmful, claiming it promotes a negative view of law enforcement and American society. The controversy surrounding CRT has only intensified the polarization of the public discourse on race and policing.

Key Takeaways and Lessons from International Models

Looking at how other countries—such as the United Kingdom, Canada, and New Zealand—approach policing offers valuable lessons for the U.S. These nations have adopted strategies that prioritize de-escalation, community engagement, and restorative justice while reducing reliance on aggressive policing tactics. Although there are significant cultural and structural differences between these countries and the U.S., their efforts demonstrate that reforms aimed at improving police accountability and reducing racial disparities can lead to more equitable outcomes.

For example, the U.K.'s focus on de-escalation training and limiting the use of firearms by police officers highlights the importance of conflict resolution in reducing fatal encounters. Canada's emphasis on community policing and engaging marginalized groups, such as Indigenous communities, shows that building trust between police and the public can create safer and more just outcomes. New Zealand's use of restorative justice to address criminal behavior within Indigenous populations provides a framework for rehabilitation and healing, rather than punishment, which could be particularly effective in addressing the racial disparities that exist in the U.S. criminal justice system.

Challenges and Obstacles to Lasting Reform

Despite the progress that has been made, significant challenges remain in the U.S. effort to reform policing. One of the greatest obstacles is political polarization, which has made it difficult to reach consensus on even modest reforms. On the left, some activists demand bold, systemic changes, such as defunding or abolishing the police, while on the right, many argue that any effort to reduce police funding or alter policing strategies would undermine public safety. This polarization is exacerbated by media outlets that present highly partisan views, reinforcing the divide between communities that support police reform and those that prioritize law and order.

Another major obstacle to reform is the power of police unions, which have successfully resisted efforts to introduce greater accountability for police officers. These unions often negotiate contracts that protect officers from disciplinary action, make it difficult to investigate misconduct, and allow officers with histories of abuse to remain on the job. For any meaningful reform to take place, lawmakers and reform advocates will need to navigate the political power of police unions while finding ways to implement greater transparency and accountability within police departments.

Additionally, the public perception of rising crime—whether or not supported by actual data—has made many Americans wary of reducing police presence in their communities. Although crime rates remain lower than the historic highs of the 1990s, the perception of increasing violence has led some voters to prioritize traditional law enforcement approaches over reform efforts, particularly in cities where violent crime has spiked in recent years.

The Path Forward: Building a Just and Equitable Future

Despite the challenges, there is reason for optimism. The protests and national conversations of the past few years have made it clear that the status quo is untenable and that there is widespread support for police reform, even if there is disagreement about how to achieve it. While more radical ideas like defunding the police remain polarizing, there is broad consensus on the need for reforms that improve accountability, reduce excessive force, and address systemic racism.

A path forward could involve a multi-faceted approach that combines elements of community-based safety, alternative crisis response teams, and targeted police reform. By expanding mental health services, social safety nets, and community-driven solutions to address the root causes of crime, cities can reduce the need for traditional law enforcement in non-violent situations. At the same time, police departments must undergo serious reforms to ensure that officers are held accountable for misconduct and that the use of force is minimized.

Some Key Areas For Reform Include

- Improving transparency and accountability through the use of body cameras and civilian oversight boards.
- Reforming qualified immunity to allow for greater legal accountability of police officers involved in misconduct.
- Expanding de-escalation and bias training to ensure that officers are equipped to handle complex situations without resorting to violence.
- Investing in community programs that address social inequities such as housing, education, and healthcare to prevent crime before it occurs.

Finally, any effort to reform policing in the U.S. must include a focus on racial justice. This means acknowledging the long history of racial disparities in law enforcement and working to dismantle the policies and practices that have disproportionately harmed Black and Latino communities. Achieving racial justice in policing will require not only changes to how police officers are trained and held accountable but also broader efforts to address the social and economic inequalities that fuel crime and tension between law enforcement and marginalized communities.

Toward a Safer and More Just Society

The future of policing in America is at a crossroads. The events of recent years have exposed the deep flaws in the current system and the urgent need for reform. While there is no simple solution to the complex issues of systemic racism and police violence, the national conversation has laid the groundwork for meaningful change. Whether through legislative action, community-based safety models, or alternative approaches to public safety, the path forward will require a commitment to both accountability and equity.

The challenge will be to find a way to balance public safety with justice—to create a system of policing that protects all communities while respecting the rights and dignity of every individual. This will require cooperation between lawmakers, law enforcement agencies, activists, and communities, as well as a willingness to rethink old models of policing in favor of more holistic, just, and effective approaches.

As America continues to reckon with its history of racial injustice and its future in law enforcement, the hope is that the country can move toward a system that truly reflects the values of justice, equality, and safety for all.

Navigating One of the Nation's Most Divisive Issues

Introduction: The Immigration Debate in America

Immigration has long been a defining feature of the United States, often described as a "nation of immigrants." From the early European settlers to the waves of newcomers from Latin America, Asia, and Africa, immigrants have played an essential role in shaping American society, culture, and economy. However, while immigration has contributed to the country's diversity and strength, it has also been a deeply divisive issue—one that has sparked intense debates about national identity, security, and what it means to be American.

In recent years, immigration has become one of the most polarizing topics in U.S. politics, with sharp divides over how to handle the growing number of immigrants arriving at the U.S.-Mexico border, the fate of millions of undocumented immigrants already living in the country, and the role of immigration in the nation's future. The debate over immigration policy touches on fundamental issues such as border security, economic competition, and humanitarian responsibilities, making it an issue that resonates with both progressive and conservative values in different ways.

The 21st century has seen immigration emerge as a flash-point in American political discourse. The Trump administration's hardline stance, epitomized by the construction of a border wall, travel bans, and family separations, galvanized both supporters and opponents of stricter immigration controls. Meanwhile, the Biden administration has sought to reverse many of these policies, with varying degrees of success, while facing ongoing challenges at the southern border and pressure from both sides of the political spectrum.

At the heart of the immigration debate are several key questions: How should the U.S. balance national security with the desire to remain a welcoming nation for immigrants and refugees? What is the best way to manage the undocumented population, many of whom have lived in the U.S. for decades? And how does immigration fit into the broader discussion of American identity and the values the nation seeks to uphold?

This essay delves into the complexities of the U.S. immigration debate, exploring both historical and contemporary perspectives. It will present the arguments from both sides of the issue, examine the role of immigration in American politics and society, and highlight the human impact of immigration policies. Finally, it will consider what the future of immigration in America might look like, given the ongoing tensions and the need for comprehensive reform. As the country navigates these complex and emotionally charged issues, finding a path forward requires balancing compassionate policy with pragmatic solutions that address the realities of a changing world.

Immigration in America is not just a policy issue; it is a reflection of the nation's values, its history, and its future. Understanding the different dimensions of the immigration debate is crucial for anyone seeking to grasp the broader social and political forces shaping America today.

Historical Context of Immigration in America

The United States has always been a country built by immigrants. From its founding, waves of people from different parts of the world have arrived on its shores in search of freedom, opportunity, and a better life. Immigration has shaped the demographic, cultural, and economic landscape of the nation, making it a melting pot of diverse cultures and experiences. However, while America is often celebrated as a "nation of immigrants," the history of immigration is also marked by periods of exclusion, discrimination, and heated debates over who should be allowed to enter and settle.

Immigration as a Pillar of American History

Immigration to the United States began in the colonial era, with European settlers, primarily from England, establishing the first colonies. Over time, the U.S. became a destination for people fleeing political persecution, economic hardship, and religious intolerance from across the globe. The 19th century saw millions of immigrants arriving from countries like Ireland, Germany, Italy, and Eastern Europe, many of them drawn by the promise of economic opportunity and freedom.

The Industrial Revolution in the 1800s created a booming economy that needed a large labor force, and immigrants were crucial to building America's infrastructure, from the transcontinental railroads to factories and mines. In addition to European immigrants, Chinese laborers were instrumental in building the railroads in the West, though they would later face severe discrimination.

This period of open immigration contributed significantly to the country's expansion and growth, but it also gave rise to nativist sentiment and anti-immigrant policies. The influx of immigrants from diverse regions led to cultural tensions, particularly as new arrivals were often blamed for social problems or economic competition. The idea of America as a "melting pot" was both a source of national pride and anxiety.

Historical Tensions and Anti-Immigrant Sentiment

While the U.S. has long welcomed immigrants, there have also been periods of intense backlash and exclusionary policies targeting specific groups. Anti-immigrant sentiment has ebbed and flowed throughout American history, often driven by fears of economic competition, racial and cultural differences, and concerns about national security.

One of the earliest examples of this backlash was the passage of the Chinese Exclusion Act of 1882, the first major law that restricted immigration based on nationality and race. The act specifically targeted Chinese laborers, who were blamed for lowering wages and taking jobs from American-born workers. It banned Chinese immigrants from entering the U.S. and prevented Chinese nationals already in the country from becoming citizens. This law remained in effect for more than 60 years and marked the beginning of an era of racially discriminatory immigration policies.

In the early 20th century, the U.S. implemented further restrictions, such as the Immigration Act of 1924, which established quotas that severely limited immigration from Southern and Eastern Europe, while nearly banning immigration from Asia. These quotas reflected widespread nativist fears that the cultural and racial makeup of the country was being threatened by the influx of immigrants who were seen as racially inferior or culturally incompatible with Anglo-Saxon norms.

The Red Scare of the 1920s and the post-World War II period saw increased suspicion of immigrants, particularly those from countries with communist or socialist regimes. This led to stricter immigration controls and a growing emphasis on national security. However, during the same period, the U.S. also served as a refuge for those fleeing war and political persecution, particularly after World War II, when the U.S. accepted thousands of displaced persons and refugees from Europe.

The Changing Face of Immigration

Immigration patterns in the U.S. shifted dramatically in the second half of the 20th century, following the passage of the Immigration and Nationality Act of 1965. This law abolished the discriminatory national origins quota system and opened the door to a new era of immigration from Latin America, Asia, and Africa. The 1965 act fundamentally reshaped the demographic makeup of the U.S. by allowing more immigrants from regions that had previously been heavily restricted.

Since then, immigration from Latin America, particularly from Mexico and Central America, has increased significantly, driven by factors such as economic instability, political turmoil, and violence in home countries. Similarly, immigration from countries like China, India, the Philippines, and Vietnam has grown, with many immigrants coming for educational and employment opportunities.

The rise in immigration from these regions has brought significant cultural and economic benefits, but it has also contributed to renewed tensions and debates over issues like illegal immigration, assimilation, and the cultural impact of a more diverse population. By the 21st century, debates about immigration had shifted from concerns about European immigrants to questions about Latin American and Asian immigration, leading to new political battles over border security, undocumented immigrants, and refugee policy.

Immigration and Economic Growth

One constant throughout American history has been the important role immigrants have played in the nation's economic growth. Immigrants have often filled labor gaps in key sectors of the economy, such as agriculture, construction, technology, and healthcare. During the Industrial Revolution, immigrants provided the labor force needed to build infrastructure, while in the modern era, immigrants have been central to the growth of the tech industry and other high-skill sectors.

At the same time, immigrants have founded some of America's most successful companies. For example, Sergey Brin, a co-founder of Google, was an immigrant from the Soviet Union, and Elon Musk, the founder of Tesla and SpaceX, immigrated to the U.S. from South Africa. These stories underscore how immigrants have contributed to American innovation and entrepreneurship throughout the country's history.

Periods of Reform and Restriction

Throughout American history, the country's immigration policies have oscillated between periods of openness and restriction, often influenced by changing economic, political, and social dynamics. In addition to the 1965 Immigration Act, other major reforms included the Immigration Reform and Control Act (IRCA) of 1986, which granted amnesty to millions of undocumented immigrants but also sought to strengthen border security and impose sanctions on employers who hired undocumented workers.

More recently, the immigration debate has centered on issues such as undocumented immigration, the rise of DACA (Deferred Action for Childhood Arrivals), and the push for comprehensive immigration reform, which has repeatedly stalled in Congress. Each of these debates reflects the broader tension between America's identity as a nation of immigrants and the political and social challenges that immigration can create.

The Current Immigration Landscape

Immigration remains one of the most contentious issues in American politics today, with debate swirling around how to handle the large and diverse population of immigrants coming into the United States. These discussions encompass a range of interconnected topics, including border security, asylum seekers, refugees, and undocumented immigrants. While immigration has always been a complex and multifaceted issue, recent years have brought heightened focus on specific policies and practices, particularly at the southern border, as well as questions about the overall impact of immigration on the U.S. economy, culture, and national security.

This section will explore the current immigration landscape in the United States, highlighting key statistics, policies, and ongoing challenges, and will provide an overview of the significant debates surrounding legal and undocumented immigration, border security, and refugee policy.

Key Statistics: Immigration by the Numbers

Immigration patterns have changed significantly over the past few decades, reflecting shifts in the global economy, conflict, and environmental factors. As of 2021, there were approximately 47 million foreign-born individuals living in the United States, making up roughly 14% of the total U.S. population. This is a dramatic increase from just 4.7% in 1970. Today, immigrants in the U.S. hail from a wide variety of countries, with Mexico, India, China, and the Philippines representing some of the largest sources of immigrants.

- **Legal immigration.** The U.S. continues to admit large numbers of legal immigrants each year. In 2019, about 1 million people were granted legal permanent residency (green cards), most of whom were sponsored by family members already living in the U.S. The family-based immigration system accounts for the majority of legal immigrants each year, followed by employment-based visas, and immigrants admitted on humanitarian grounds such as refugees and asylum seekers.

- **Undocumented immigration.** Estimates suggest there are about 11 million undocumented immigrants currently residing in the U.S., many of whom have lived in the country for years, if not decades. These individuals include those who entered the country illegally and those who overstayed visas. About half of the undocumented population is concentrated in California, Texas, Florida, and New York, where they work in industries like agriculture, construction, and hospitality.

- **Asylum seekers and refugees.** In recent years, the U.S. has seen a significant increase in asylum seekers, particularly from Central America and Mexico, fleeing violence, political instability, and economic hardship. The number of refugees resettled in the U.S. dropped sharply under the Trump administration, which imposed severe restrictions, but has begun to increase under the Biden administration. For Fiscal Year 2021, the Biden administration set the refugee admissions cap at 62,500, signaling a return to previous levels after a historic low of 18,000 under Trump.

Key Policies and Laws: An Evolving Framework

The current immigration landscape is shaped by a patchwork of laws and policies that address various aspects of legal immigration, border control, asylum, and undocumented immigrants. These policies have evolved over the decades, often in response to political pressures, economic needs, and international crises.

Deferred Action for Childhood Arrivals (DACA)

One of the most significant immigration policies in recent years has been the Deferred Action for Childhood Arrivals (DACA) program, implemented under the Obama administration in 2012. DACA provides temporary protection from deportation for certain undocumented immigrants who were brought to the U.S. as children, commonly known as "Dreamers." The program also grants eligible individuals work permits, allowing them to live and work in the U.S. legally. However, DACA does not provide a pathway to citizenship, and the status of the program remains uncertain.

In 2017, President Donald Trump attempted to end DACA, sparking legal battles and widespread protests. Although the Supreme Court blocked the Trump administration's efforts to terminate the program in 2020, DACA's future remains uncertain as Congress has yet to pass a permanent solution. President Joe Biden has expressed support for Dreamers and urged Congress to pass legislation that would create a pathway to citizenship for DACA recipients.

The Immigration Quota System and Visa Programs

The U.S. operates under a quota system that limits the number of immigrants allowed from each country. This system, established by the Immigration and Nationality Act of 1965, has been a major point of contention in recent debates over comprehensive immigration reform. Critics argue that the quotas are outdated and do not reflect the current global migration patterns or the U.S. economy's need for labor in certain sectors.

In addition to family-based immigration, the U.S. admits immigrants through employment-based visas. The H-1B visa program, for example, allows U.S. employers to hire highly skilled foreign workers in specialized fields such as technology, engineering, and medicine. While this program helps fill gaps in the labor market, it has been criticized for enabling companies to exploit foreign labor, sometimes at the expense of American workers. The annual cap on H-1B visas has also been a point of contention, with some arguing it should be expanded to allow more skilled immigrants into the country.

Temporary Protected Status (TPS)

Another important aspect of U.S. immigration policy is Temporary Protected Status (TPS), which allows individuals from countries experiencing armed conflict, natural disasters, or other extraordinary conditions to remain in the U.S. for a limited time. In recent years, TPS has been granted to people from countries like Haiti, El Salvador, and Venezuela due to ongoing crises in those nations. However, TPS does not offer a path to permanent residency or citizenship, and the Trump administration sought to end TPS protections for several countries, a move that was challenged in court.

Border Security and the Southern Border

Border security, particularly at the U.S.-Mexico border, has been one of the most politically charged elements of the immigration debate in recent years. Under the Trump administration, border security became a central issue, culminating in the push for a border wall and the zero-tolerance policy, which led to the widely criticized family separations at the border. The construction of the border wall became a symbol of the hardline stance on immigration enforcement, although much of the wall was never completed.

The handling of migrants at the southern border continues to be a major challenge for the Biden administration. Thousands of migrants, including large numbers of asylum seekers, attempt to cross the southern border each year, many fleeing violence and poverty in Central America. The administration has struggled to manage the surge of migrants, particularly unaccompanied minors, leading to criticism from both immigration advocates, who want more humane treatment and a pathway to asylum, and conservatives, who argue that the Biden administration's policies encourage illegal immigration.

The Remain in Mexico policy, also known as the Migrant Protection Protocols (MPP), which forced asylum seekers to wait in Mexico while their cases were processed, was implemented under Trump and widely criticized for subjecting vulnerable migrants to dangerous conditions. The Biden administration sought to end the policy, but legal battles have complicated efforts to fully dismantle it.

Ongoing Debates and Challenges

The immigration debate in the U.S. is far from settled. Key issues, such as how to handle the undocumented population, how to reform the legal immigration system, and how to balance security with humanitarian responsibilities, remain deeply contentious. Both sides of the political aisle agree that the current immigration system is broken, but there is little consensus on how to fix it.

Comprehensive Immigration Reform

Efforts to pass comprehensive immigration reform have repeatedly stalled in Congress, with the most recent significant effort occurring in 2013, when the Gang of Eight—a bipartisan group of U.S. senators—introduced a reform bill that would have provided a pathway to citizenship for undocumented immigrants while also increasing border security. Although the bill passed the Senate, it died in the House of Representatives.

Today, the debate over immigration reform is as polarized as ever. Democrats generally advocate for a path to citizenship for undocumented immigrants, including DACA recipients and those with TPS, as well as reforms to legal immigration to address visa backlogs and family reunification. Republicans, on the other hand, often focus on border security, enforcing immigration laws, and restricting immigration to protect American jobs.

Balancing Security and Humanitarian Concerns

One of the biggest challenges facing U.S. policymakers is how to balance the need for national security with humanitarian obligations to refugees and asylum seekers. The U.S. has long served as a beacon of hope for those fleeing persecution and violence, but rising numbers of migrants at the southern border, along with concerns about human trafficking, drug cartels, and terrorism, have fueled demands for stronger border control.

The Biden administration, like its predecessors, has struggled to find the right balance. On the one hand, the administration has sought to reverse many of Trump's hardline immigration policies, restoring DACA, raising the refugee cap, and halting border wall construction. On the other hand, Biden has faced criticism from immigration advocates for continuing to detain migrants and deporting many asylum seekers under Title 42, a public health law enacted during the COVID-19 pandemic to prevent the spread of the virus.

Arguments for and Against Immigration

Immigration has been a defining feature of America's national identity, but it is also one of the most hotly debated and divisive issues in contemporary politics. The debate surrounding immigration policy is characterized by two competing visions of America's future: one that views immigration as a vital source of economic growth, cultural enrichment, and humanitarian responsibility, and another that raises concerns about security, economic competition, and the preservation of national identity.

The Case for Immigration

Economic Contributions

One of the strongest arguments in favor of immigration is the vital role that immigrants play in driving economic growth and filling labor shortages in key industries. Immigrants make up a significant portion of the U.S. workforce and contribute to various sectors, including agriculture, construction, healthcare, and technology. Without immigrant labor, many of these industries would face serious workforce deficits, which could lead to higher consumer prices and reduced economic productivity.

- **Filling labor gaps.** Immigrants, particularly those with lower levels of formal education, often take jobs that native-born Americans are less willing to perform, such as seasonal agricultural work, hospitality, and domestic services. These sectors rely heavily on immigrant labor, and without it, many businesses would struggle to function efficiently. For example, the U.S. agricultural industry has historically depended on immigrant workers for harvesting crops, a job that is labor-intensive and difficult to fill with domestic workers alone.

- **Skilled immigration.** On the other end of the spectrum, highly skilled immigrants contribute to the U.S. economy by driving innovation and technological advancement. Immigrants hold a significant share of STEM (science, technology, engineering, and mathematics) jobs and have founded or co-founded some of the most successful tech companies in the U.S., including Google, Tesla, and Yahoo. In 2016, a study by the National Foundation for American Policy found that immigrants started more than half of the privately held billion-dollar startup companies in the U.S. These contributions underscore the value of H-1B visas and other work programs that bring skilled immigrants into the country.

- **Tax contributions.** Immigrants—both legal and undocumented—also contribute to federal, state, and local taxes, including Social Security and Medicare. According to a 2017 report by the Institute on Taxation and

Economic Policy (ITEP), undocumented immigrants pay an estimated $11.74 billion in state and local taxes annually. These contributions help support essential public services such as education, healthcare, and infrastructure, while also strengthening the social safety net for all Americans.

Cultural Enrichment and Innovation

America has long been known as a melting pot of cultures, and immigration continues to play a key role in enriching the country's cultural diversity. Immigrants bring new languages, customs, cuisines, and traditions that contribute to the rich tapestry of American society. Cities like New York, Los Angeles, and Miami are celebrated for their vibrant immigrant communities, which enhance the cultural life of these urban centers and create new opportunities for cultural exchange.

- **Cultural diversity.** Immigrants bring fresh perspectives, fostering creativity and innovation. This diversity of thought has been shown to improve problem-solving and drive breakthroughs in business, the arts, and science. Furthermore, immigrant entrepreneurs have started successful businesses in a wide range of industries, from technology to fashion to food services. For example, the rise of food trucks, fusion cuisine, and immigrant-owned restaurants across the U.S. has brought new flavors and culinary traditions to mainstream American culture.

- **Global competitiveness.** Immigration also helps the U.S. maintain its competitive edge in a globalized world. Highly skilled immigrants contribute to cutting-edge research, scientific discovery, and technological innovation, all of which are crucial for keeping the U.S. at the forefront of global progress. The influx of international students to U.S. universities, many of whom stay and work in the country after graduation, plays a crucial role in maintaining America's leadership in research and development.

Moral and Humanitarian Considerations

Another major argument in favor of immigration is the humanitarian responsibility of the U.S. to offer refuge and protection to people fleeing persecution, violence, and hardship. America's long-standing tradition as a destination for asylum seekers and refugees reflects its core values of freedom, justice, and compassion.

- **Refugees and asylum seekers.** The U.S. has a history of offering sanctuary to those fleeing war, violence, and oppression. For example, during and after World War II, the U.S. took in refugees fleeing the Holocaust and other atrocities in Europe. In the modern era, many immigrants come to the U.S. seeking safety from conflicts in places like Syria, Afghanistan, Central America, and Venezuela. Immigration advocates argue that offering protection to these vulnerable populations is a moral imperative and that the U.S. should honor its commitments under international human rights treaties.

- **The American Dream.** Advocates for immigration also emphasize that America's identity is rooted in the idea of the American Dream—the belief that anyone, regardless of where they were born, can achieve success through hard work and determination. Immigration, they argue, is fundamental to this vision of a free and open society, where opportunity is available to all. Restricting immigration, in their view, undermines this foundational aspect of American identity.

The Case Against Immigration

Economic Concerns

While immigration advocates highlight the economic benefits of immigration, critics argue that immigration, particularly undocumented immigration, can harm the U.S. economy and workforce, especially for low-income Americans.

- **Wage depression.** Some argue that an influx of low-skilled immigrants can drive down wages for native-born workers, particularly in sectors like agriculture, construction, and service industries. They contend that employers often prefer to hire immigrants because they are willing to work for lower wages, thus depressing wages for American workers and increasing competition for jobs. According to a 2017 study by Harvard economist George Borjas, low-skilled immigration can have a negative impact on the wages of native-born workers who lack a high school diploma.

- **Strain on public services.** Critics also argue that immigrants, particularly undocumented immigrants, place a significant strain on public resources such as education, healthcare, and social services. While immigrants do contribute to the economy through taxes, some argue that they consume more in public services than they contribute, particularly in states with large immigrant populations. Schools, hospitals, and local governments, especially in border states like California and Texas, often struggle to accommodate the needs of large immigrant populations, which can stretch resources thin.

Security and Border Control

A major point of contention in the immigration debate is the issue of border security and concerns about illegal immigration. Many critics argue that the U.S. must maintain strict control of its borders to protect national security and the rule of law.

- **Illegal immigration.** Critics argue that allowing millions of undocumented immigrants to remain in the country undermines the rule of law and incentivizes further illegal immigration. They contend that the U.S. must enforce its immigration laws more strictly, including by increasing deportations and securing the southern border to prevent illegal entry. The argument here is that lax immigration enforcement sends the message that U.S. borders are open to illegal crossings, which could further encourage people to enter the country without following legal processes.

- **National security.** Another argument against immigration, particularly from conservative voices, centers on the potential security risks posed by an open immigration system. In the post-9/11 era, concerns about terrorism, human trafficking, and drug cartels crossing the U.S.-Mexico border have heightened demands for stronger border security. Some argue that tighter immigration controls are necessary to prevent terrorists or criminals from exploiting the immigration system to gain entry into the country.

Cultural Assimilation and Social Cohesion

Opponents of immigration also raise concerns about the impact of large-scale immigration on social cohesion and national identity. They argue that an excessive influx of immigrants can strain social bonds and challenge the ability of immigrants to assimilate into American culture.

- **Cultural fragmentation.** Critics fear that high levels of immigration, particularly from countries with different languages, religions, and cultural norms, could lead to cultural fragmentation rather than integration. They worry that immigrants may be less likely to adopt American values and instead form insular communities, potentially leading to social divisions. This argument is particularly prevalent among those who believe that English language proficiency and adherence to certain cultural values are key to the successful integration of immigrants into American society.

- **Impact on American identity.** There is also concern that the growing diversity brought by immigration could dilute traditional notions of American identity. Some argue that too much emphasis on multiculturalism and diversity may undermine the shared cultural values that have historically bound Americans together. They fear that rather than becoming part of the American melting pot, new immigrant populations may challenge existing cultural norms and disrupt social harmony.

A Divisive but Crucial Debate

The debate over immigration in the U.S. is shaped by a complex mix of economic, cultural, and security concerns, and it reflects broader questions about the nation's identity and values. Both sides of the argument raise valid points, and finding common ground between them has proven difficult. Advocates of immigration point to the vital contributions immigrants make to the economy, culture, and global standing of the U.S., while critics stress the need for stronger enforcement of immigration laws and safeguards for national security and social cohesion.

As the debate continues, the challenge for policymakers will be to balance the competing interests of economic growth, national security, and humanitarian responsibility, while also preserving the nation's commitment to being a land of opportunity for those seeking a better life. In the following sections, we will explore how immigration intersects with U.S. politics, the human impact of immigration policies, and what the future might hold for this deeply divisive issue.

Immigration and U.S. Politics

Immigration is one of the most politically charged issues in the United States, shaping elections, influencing public opinion, and polarizing the nation along ideological and partisan lines. Over the past few decades, immigration has become a central topic in political debates, with Democrats and Republicans offering contrasting visions for how the country should manage its borders, handle undocumented immigrants, and integrate newcomers into American society.

At the heart of the immigration debate are fundamental disagreements over national identity, economic policy, and security. For some, immigration is seen as a source of vitality, diversity, and innovation; for others, it represents a challenge to economic stability, social cohesion, and national sovereignty. These competing perspectives have led to fierce political battles over immigration policy, with no clear consensus on how to move forward. This section explores how immigration has become a key issue in U.S. politics, examining the role it plays in elections, the contrasting positions of the two major political parties, and the ongoing struggle for comprehensive immigration reform.

Immigration as a Polarizing Political Issue

Immigration has long been a contentious issue in American politics, but the level of polarization surrounding the topic has intensified dramatically in recent years. Public opinion on immigration is deeply divided, often reflecting broader partisan affiliations. According to a Pew Research Center survey conducted in 2021, 88% of Democrats support granting legal status to undocumented immigrants who meet certain conditions, while only 48% of Republicans share that view. Similarly, while 75% of Democrats favor increasing opportunities for legal immigration, only 35% of Republicans agree.

This sharp divide is mirrored in the rhetoric and policies promoted by the Democratic and Republican parties. Democrats generally view immigration as a positive force that enriches the nation culturally and economically, and they advocate for more inclusive policies that prioritize the rights of immigrants, refugees, and asylum seekers. On the other hand, Republicans tend to emphasize the importance of border security, the rule of law, and protecting American jobs, often arguing for stricter immigration controls and enforcement of existing laws.

The divergence between the two parties has made immigration a central issue in elections at all levels of government, from local and state races to presidential campaigns. Candidates on both sides of the political spectrum often use immigration to rally their bases, whether through calls for more humane treatment of immigrants or demands for stronger border enforcement.

Trump Era Policies and Impact

Few presidencies in recent history have had as significant an impact on the immigration debate as that of Donald Trump. Trump's 2016 presidential campaign was built in large part on a hardline immigration platform, with his promise to build a border wall along the U.S.-Mexico border becoming a rallying cry for his supporters. His administration's approach to immigration was characterized by a series of highly controversial policies aimed at reducing both legal and illegal immigration.

The most notable policies under the Trump administration included:

- **The Border Wall.** Trump's push for a physical wall along the southern border became symbolic of his tough stance on immigration. Although some sections of the wall were built, the project was far from completed by the end of his term. Trump's insistence on funding for the wall led to a 35-day government shutdown in 2018-2019, the longest in U.S. history, further highlighting the contentious nature of immigration policy in Washington.

- **Zero-Tolerance Policy and Family Separations.** One of the most controversial aspects of Trump's immigration policy was the zero-tolerance policy, which mandated the criminal prosecution of all individuals caught crossing the border illegally. This policy led to the widespread separation of families, as children were taken from their parents and placed in detention centers. Images and reports of children being held in cages sparked public outrage and widespread condemnation from human rights organizations, religious groups, and international allies.

- **Muslim Travel Ban.** Early in his presidency, Trump issued an executive order that became known as the "Muslim ban", restricting travel from several majority-Muslim countries, including Iran, Syria, and Yemen. The ban was challenged in the courts and revised multiple times before the Supreme Court upheld a version of the ban in 2018. The policy became a flash-point in debates about national security, religious freedom, and America's commitment to being a welcoming nation.

- **DACA and TPS Rollbacks.** Trump also moved to end the Deferred Action for Childhood Arrivals (DACA) program, which provided temporary protection from deportation for undocumented immigrants brought to the

U.S. as children. This move sparked a fierce legal battle, with the Supreme Court ultimately ruling in 2020 that Trump's attempt to end DACA was unlawful. Additionally, the administration sought to end Temporary Protected Status (TPS) for individuals from several countries experiencing crises, such as El Salvador and Honduras, though these efforts were also blocked in court.

Trump's immigration policies divided the nation, with his supporters viewing them as necessary measures to protect American security and sovereignty, while his critics accused him of undermining human rights and demonizing immigrants. The political impact of these policies was profound, helping to galvanize both Trump's base and his opposition. Immigration became a litmus test for candidates running in the 2018 midterms and the 2020 presidential election, with Trump's policies creating a sharp divide between those who favored strict immigration enforcement and those advocating for more humane approaches.

Biden Administration's Approach

Upon taking office in January 2021, President Joe Biden made it clear that his administration would pursue a radically different approach to immigration compared to his predecessor. In his first months in office, Biden moved quickly to reverse or modify many of Trump's immigration policies, reflecting a more progressive stance on the issue. However, his administration has faced significant challenges in managing the complexities of the immigration system and balancing the expectations of advocates on both sides of the debate.

Key actions taken by the Biden administration include:

- **Ending the Border Wall Project.** Biden immediately halted construction of Trump's border wall, redirecting funds toward other security measures and infrastructure projects. This decision was met with approval from immigration advocates but criticism from conservatives, who argued that the border wall was necessary for national security.

- **Reinstating DACA.** Biden restored the DACA program, ensuring that Dreamers—undocumented immigrants brought to the U.S. as children— would continue to be protected from deportation and allowed to work legally in the U.S. He also called on Congress to pass permanent protections for DACA recipients, something that remains stalled in legislative gridlock.

- **Raising the Refugee Cap.** After sharp reductions in the refugee cap under Trump, Biden increased the refugee admissions cap for Fiscal Year 2021 to 62,500, signaling a commitment to welcoming more refugees. However, the administration struggled to meet its target amid logistical and bureaucratic challenges.

- **Handling the Southern Border Crisis.** One of the most difficult challenges for the Biden administration has been managing the influx of migrants at the southern border, including large numbers of asylum seekers and unaccompanied minors. Despite promises of a more humane immigration policy, Biden has faced criticism for continuing some Trump-era policies, including the use of Title 42, a public health law enacted during the COVID-19 pandemic to expedite deportations. Progressives have expressed frustration with Biden's handling of the border crisis, while conservatives argue that his policies have contributed to a surge in illegal immigration.

The Biden administration's immigration approach reflects a broader attempt to strike a balance between security, humanity, and legal order. However, his policies have met resistance from both the left and right, highlighting the difficulty of navigating such a deeply polarized issue.

Immigration Reform Efforts: Stalled Progress

For decades, both Democrats and Republicans have called for comprehensive immigration reform, yet no significant reform has been passed since the Immigration Reform and Control Act of 1986, which granted amnesty to millions of undocumented immigrants. The last serious attempt to pass comprehensive reform occurred in 2013, when the bipartisan Gang of Eight introduced a bill that included a path to citizenship for undocumented immigrants, enhanced border security, and visa system reforms.

Although the 2013 bill passed the Senate with bipartisan support, it ultimately failed in the House of Representatives, largely due to opposition from conservatives who viewed the path to citizenship as "amnesty" for lawbreakers. Since then, efforts to pass immigration reform have repeatedly stalled, with both parties blaming each other for the gridlock.

Some of the key issues in the immigration reform debate include:

- **Path to Citizenship for Undocumented Immigrants.** Democrats generally support providing a pathway to citizenship for the 11 million undocumented immigrants living in the U.S., especially for DACA recipients and those with Temporary Protected Status (TPS). Republicans, however, remain divided, with some favoring stronger enforcement measures before any discussion of legalization, while others oppose a path to citizenship outright.

- **Border Security.** Republicans have long prioritized stronger border security measures, including the expansion of physical barriers and the use of technology to monitor the border. While Democrats acknowledge the need for secure borders, they argue that focusing solely on enforcement ignores the root causes of migration, such as poverty and violence in Central America.

- **Legal Immigration Reform.** Both parties agree that the U.S. legal immigration system is in need of reform, but they differ on how to address the issue. Democrats advocate for modernizing the visa system to reduce backlogs and expand family reunification, while Republicans push for a merit-based system that prioritizes skilled workers over family-based immigration.

Conclusion: Immigration's Role in U.S. Politics

Immigration has become a litmus test in U.S. politics, dividing the nation along partisan lines and shaping the platforms of political candidates at every level. Both Democrats and Republicans recognize that the current immigration system is broken, but finding common ground has proven elusive. The highly charged nature of the debate, coupled with the increasing polarization of American politics, has made comprehensive immigration reform a distant goal, despite widespread acknowledgment of its necessity.

As the immigration debate continues to evolve, it remains clear that any progress will require bipartisan cooperation and a willingness to balance the concerns of security, economic stability, and humanity. Until then, immigration will remain one of the most divisive and consequential issues in U.S. politics, influencing elections, shaping public opinion, and impacting millions of lives. The next section will focus on the human impact of U.S. immigration policies, highlighting the personal stories of immigrants affected by the legal and political battles over immigration reform.

The Human Impact of Immigration Policies

While much of the immigration debate centers on abstract concepts such as national security, economic interests, and policy reform, at its core, immigration is about people. Behind the political battles and rhetoric are the millions of individuals and families who are directly affected by U.S. immigration policies—undocumented immigrants, DACA recipients, asylum seekers, refugees, and mixed-status families. For many, these policies shape their daily lives, dictating whether they can remain in the country they call home, access healthcare and education, or reunite with their loved ones.

This section will explore the human impact of U.S. immigration policies by sharing the personal stories of those caught in the crossfire of immigration debates, highlighting the emotional, social, and economic consequences of current policies. From family separations at the U.S.-Mexico border to the uncertainty faced by Dreamers, these stories illustrate the profound and often heartbreaking effects of immigration laws on individuals and communities.

Stories of Immigrants Affected by U.S. Immigration Policies

The Dreamers: Navigating Uncertainty Under DACA

The Deferred Action for Childhood Arrivals (DACA) program has provided temporary relief for hundreds of thousands of undocumented immigrants brought to the U.S. as children—commonly referred to as Dreamers. While DACA allows recipients to live and work in the U.S. without fear of deportation, it does not provide a pathway to citizenship, leaving Dreamers in a constant state of uncertainty about their futures.

One such Dreamer is Maria, a 26-year-old nursing student who came to the U.S. from Mexico with her parents when she was just 3 years old. Maria has lived almost her entire life in the U.S. and considers it her home. Under DACA, she was able to attend college and pursue a career in healthcare, working as a nurse's assistant to support herself through school. However, despite her hard work and commitment to her community, Maria lives in constant fear that DACA could be repealed and she could be deported to a country she barely remembers.

"I'm terrified that one day I'll lose everything I've worked for," Maria says. "I've grown up here, my family is here, my friends are here, and I love this country. But without DACA, I don't know what my future holds."

Maria's story is not unique—there are approximately 600,000 Dreamers in the U.S., many of whom face the same anxiety about their legal status. While many Americans support granting permanent legal status or citizenship to Dreamers, legislative gridlock has left their futures in limbo. The Supreme Court's 2020 ruling to uphold DACA was a temporary relief, but without congressional action, Dreamers like Maria remain vulnerable to shifting political winds.

Family Separation: The Emotional Toll on Parents and Children

Perhaps one of the most tragic aspects of recent U.S. immigration policy was the family separation crisis that resulted from the Trump administration's zero-tolerance policy at the southern border. Under this policy, thousands of children were separated from their parents when they crossed the border illegally, even when they sought asylum. Images of children held in cages and audio recordings of their cries for their parents sparked national and international outrage, bringing the emotional and psychological toll of these policies into sharp focus.

Juana, a mother from Honduras, fled violence in her home country with her two young daughters, aged 4 and 7. After a harrowing journey to the U.S. border, Juana sought asylum, hoping to find safety for her children. Instead, her daughters were taken from her at a border detention facility, and Juana was placed in an adult detention center while her children were sent to a separate facility hundreds of miles away.

"I thought I would never see them again," Juana recalls through tears. "They were so young, and I had no way of knowing if they were okay. It was the worst moment of my life."

After three months, Juana was finally reunited with her daughters, but the trauma of their separation remains. Both girls suffer from anxiety and nightmares, and Juana fears that the emotional scars will last a lifetime. The family separation policy ended in 2018 following widespread public outcry, but the damage to families like Juana's has already been done. An estimated 5,500 children were separated from their parents under the policy, and the process of reuniting all families has been slow and incomplete.

Asylum Seekers: Facing Danger and Uncertainty

The U.S. has long been a destination for those fleeing violence, persecution, and oppression, but changes to asylum policies in recent years have made it increasingly difficult for asylum seekers to find refuge. Under the Trump administration, the Migrant Protection Protocols (MPP), also known as the Remain in Mexico policy, forced asylum seekers to wait in Mexico while their claims were processed. Many were stranded in dangerous border towns, facing threats of violence, extortion, and kidnapping.

Carlos and his family fled El Salvador after gangs threatened to kill his teenage son for refusing to join their ranks. Seeking safety in the U.S., Carlos and his family presented themselves at the border to apply for asylum. Instead of being allowed to enter the U.S., they were sent back to Tijuana, Mexico, under the Remain in Mexico policy, where they lived in a tent at a makeshift refugee camp for six months.

"Tijuana was dangerous—there were gangs, drug traffickers, and we were constantly living in fear," Carlos says. "We left El Salvador to escape the violence, but it felt like we were trapped in the same danger all over again."

Carlos eventually crossed the border legally and his asylum case is pending, but the experience left his family traumatized. Many asylum seekers face similar challenges, with no guarantee of protection even after enduring the dangerous journey to the U.S. Under President Biden, the Remain in Mexico policy was officially terminated, but the U.S. immigration system continues to face a backlog of asylum claims, and conditions for asylum seekers remain precarious.

Mixed-Status Families: Living in the Shadows

Many immigrant families in the U.S. are mixed-status, meaning some family members are U.S. citizens or legal residents while others are undocumented. This creates a unique set of challenges, as undocumented parents and children live in constant fear of deportation, even while their U.S.-born children enjoy the rights and protections of American citizenship.

Roberto, an undocumented immigrant from Guatemala, has lived in the U.S. for over 15 years. He and his wife, who is also undocumented, have three children, all of whom were born in the U.S. and are American citizens. Despite building a life in the U.S., owning a small business, and contributing to his community, Roberto faces the constant threat of deportation. His children worry that one day their parents could be taken away.

"We've been here for so long, but it feels like we can never fully relax," Roberto says. "Every day, I worry that I'll be stopped by ICE and sent back to a country I haven't seen in years, away from my children. We've tried to live quietly and stay out of trouble, but the fear is always there."

Mixed-status families are a common reality in the U.S., with millions of children growing up with the uncertainty of whether their parents will be deported. This creates emotional stress, mental health challenges, and economic instability for many families, forcing them to live in the shadows despite their long-term presence in the U.S.

The Social and Economic Consequences of Immigration Policies

Beyond the individual stories of hardship, U.S. immigration policies also have broader social and economic consequences. Immigrants—whether documented or undocumented—make up a significant portion of the U.S. workforce and contribute to the country's economic growth. Harsh immigration enforcement policies, such as workplace raids and mass deportations, can have devastating effects on local economies, particularly in sectors like agriculture, hospitality, and construction, which rely heavily on immigrant labor.

The threat of deportation also discourages many undocumented immigrants from accessing essential services, such as healthcare and education, for fear of being reported to immigration authorities. This can lead to negative outcomes not only for immigrants but also for their U.S.-born children, who may struggle to succeed in school or receive adequate healthcare because their parents are afraid to seek help.

Moreover, the ongoing uncertainty surrounding immigration policies creates instability for families and communities. Temporary relief programs like DACA offer only limited protection, leaving recipients vulnerable to political changes and legal challenges. The lack of comprehensive immigration reform means that millions of undocumented immigrants continue to live in legal limbo, with no clear path to citizenship or permanent residency.

The Human Cost of Policy Decisions

The human impact of U.S. immigration policies is profound, affecting millions of people in deeply personal ways. From Dreamers to asylum seekers to families separated at the border, the consequences of these policies are felt in homes and communities across the country. While the political debate often focuses on numbers and abstract concepts, it is important to remember the human faces behind these policies—people who are seeking safety, opportunity, and a better life.

As the U.S. grapples with how to reform its immigration system, finding solutions that balance security with compassion is essential. Immigration is not just a policy issue; it is a matter of human rights, dignity, and justice. The next section will explore how these immigration challenges intersect with broader questions of American identity and national values, and what the future may hold for immigration in the U.S.

Immigration, American Identity, and National Values

The debate over immigration in the United States is not just about policy—it's about the very identity of the nation. America has long prided itself on being a "nation of immigrants," a country where people from around the world can come to seek opportunity, freedom, and a better life. This idea is woven into the fabric of American history, from the Statue of Liberty's inscription welcoming the "huddled masses yearning to breathe free," to the stories of immigrant success that have shaped the country's economy, culture, and society.

However, this identity has always been contested. Throughout history, periods of open immigration have been followed by backlash and restriction, often fueled by concerns about the cultural and economic impacts of immigration. Today, the U.S. is once again at a crossroads, as it grapples with fundamental questions about who belongs in the country, what it means to be an American, and how to reconcile the nation's immigrant heritage with modern challenges around security, diversity, and social cohesion.

In this section, we'll explore how immigration intersects with American identity and national values, looking at how the current debate reflects broader societal tensions. We will examine the tension between embracing diversity and maintaining social cohesion, how immigration policy reflects national values, and the ongoing challenge of balancing humanitarian responsibilities with security concerns.

Defining the Nation of Immigrants

For much of its history, the United States has celebrated its identity as a nation of immigrants. This idea is central to the American narrative, with waves of immigrants—Irish, Italian, Chinese, Jewish, Mexican, and many others—contributing to the economic growth, cultural richness, and social dynamism of the country. From the Industrial Revolution to the modern tech boom, immigrants have been essential to America's progress.

Immigration is also closely tied to the American Dream, the idea that anyone, regardless of their background, can achieve success through hard work and perseverance. Many Americans see immigration as a core part of the country's DNA, a symbol of its openness and opportunities for all. This view is often reflected in how immigrants are portrayed as entrepreneurs, innovators, and contributors to American society, with immigrant-founded companies like Google, Tesla, and eBay standing as proof of this success.

However, this welcoming image of America has always existed alongside fears and anxieties about immigration. Historical policies like the Chinese Exclusion Act of 1882 and the Immigration Act of 1924, which imposed strict quotas on immigrants from certain regions, reflect a long-standing tension between the desire to attract immigrants and the fear that too much diversity could threaten the country's identity or disrupt its social fabric.

In today's debate, supporters of immigration often emphasize this inclusive vision of America, arguing that embracing immigrants strengthens the country both economically and morally. They contend that immigration reflects America's founding values of liberty, equality, and opportunity. However, opponents often frame immigration as a threat to American identity, citing concerns that rapid demographic change could undermine social cohesion or dilute traditional values.

The Debate Over National Identity: Diversity vs. Social Cohesion

One of the central tensions in the immigration debate is the question of how diversity and social cohesion can coexist. Supporters of immigration argue that diversity is one of America's greatest strengths, enriching the country culturally, promoting innovation, and fostering global connections. They point to the success of immigrant communities in cities like New York, Los Angeles, and Houston as examples of how different cultures can coexist and thrive together.

Moreover, they argue that assimilation—the process by which immigrants adopt the customs and norms of their new country—does not necessarily require giving up one's cultural heritage. Instead, they suggest that immigrants can contribute to American society while also maintaining their unique cultural identities. For instance, immigrant communities have brought new foods, languages, and traditions to the U.S., enhancing its cultural landscape. The Latino, Asian, and African immigrant communities have introduced different perspectives and ways of life, which have, over time, become part of the American experience.

However, opponents of large-scale immigration raise concerns that too much diversity, too quickly, could lead to cultural fragmentation. They argue that the increasing number of immigrants from non-European countries—particularly from Latin America and Asia—could strain social unity, creating pockets of communities that may not fully integrate into American society. They point to issues such as language barriers, differences in cultural norms, and varying levels of education and economic success as potential sources of division.

These fears are often framed as concerns about assimilation—whether or not immigrants will adopt American values, learn English, and participate fully in civic life. Critics of current immigration levels argue that in order to maintain social cohesion, the U.S. needs to ensure that immigrants are integrated into society and that immigration levels are controlled to allow for smoother assimilation.

Immigration Policy and American Values

U.S. immigration policy has always reflected broader national values—sometimes emphasizing openness and opportunity, other times prioritizing security and exclusion. Today, the challenge for policymakers is how to craft immigration policies that are consistent with American ideals of freedom, equality, and justice, while also addressing the practical concerns of managing borders, ensuring national security, and protecting the rights of citizens.

One of the core arguments of immigration advocates is that current restrictive policies—particularly those that target asylum seekers, refugees, and undocumented immigrants—violate America's humanitarian commitments and undermine its moral authority on the global stage. The U.S. has long been a refuge for people fleeing war, persecution, and poverty, and immigration advocates argue that turning away those in need is inconsistent with America's values.

For example, the U.S. response to the global refugee crisis—whether in Syria, Afghanistan, or Central America—is seen as a test of the country's moral leadership. Advocates point to the Refugee Act of 1980, which established the U.S. refugee resettlement program, as a reflection of America's commitment to protecting vulnerable populations. However, under the Trump administration, the refugee cap was slashed to historic lows, with critics arguing that the U.S. was abandoning its role as a safe haven for those in need. The Biden administration has sought to reverse this trend by raising the refugee cap, but the issue remains politically divisive.

Additionally, the treatment of undocumented immigrants—including DACA recipients and essential workers—raises questions about how national values like fairness and justice apply to those who live in the U.S. without legal status. Advocates for immigration reform argue that providing a path to citizenship for the 11 million undocumented immigrants living in the U.S. is not only a matter of practical necessity but also a moral imperative. They point to the contributions these immigrants make to the U.S. economy and society, arguing that deporting individuals who have built lives in the U.S. would violate principles of fairness and compassion.

Balancing National Interests with Humanitarian Concerns

One of the most difficult challenges in the immigration debate is balancing national interests—such as economic stability, public safety, and security—with humanitarian obligations to protect refugees, asylum seekers, and vulnerable immigrants. This tension is particularly evident in the debate over border security and the treatment of migrants at the U.S.-Mexico border.

Advocates for stronger border controls argue that the U.S. must prioritize national security and enforce its immigration laws to protect its citizens and maintain the integrity of its borders. They emphasize the need to prevent illegal immigration, combat drug trafficking and human smuggling, and ensure that immigrants who enter the U.S. do so legally. They also argue that a failure to secure the border encourages further illegal crossings and puts pressure on public resources such as schools, healthcare, and housing.

On the other hand, immigration advocates argue that the U.S. has a responsibility to treat migrants humanely and compassionately, particularly those fleeing violence and persecution in their home countries. They point to the harsh conditions faced by asylum seekers who are held in detention centers or forced to remain in dangerous border towns while their cases are processed, arguing that these practices violate basic human rights. The family separation policy, in particular, has been widely condemned as a humanitarian crisis that goes against American values of family unity and justice.

Ultimately, the debate over immigration is a debate over what kind of country America wants to be. Should it remain a beacon of hope and opportunity for those seeking a better life, or should it prioritize protecting its borders and preserving its social cohesion? Can the U.S. find a way to balance security with compassion, and diversity with unity?

Conclusion: The Future of Immigration in America

The debate over immigration in America is as complex as it is divisive, touching on deeply rooted issues of national identity, security, economic interests, and humanitarian values. As the nation grapples with the practical challenges of managing its borders, ensuring national security, and addressing the needs of millions of undocumented immigrants, it also confronts broader questions about what it means to be American in the 21st century. The path forward is uncertain, but finding solutions that balance the competing demands of compassion and pragmatism will be essential for the future of both immigration policy and the country itself.

The Path Forward: Toward Comprehensive Immigration Reform

One of the most pressing challenges is the need for comprehensive immigration reform, something that has eluded policymakers for decades. The U.S. immigration system is widely acknowledged to be broken, with outdated laws and policies that fail to address the realities of modern migration patterns, labor market needs, and humanitarian crises. While there is broad consensus that reform is necessary, deep partisan divisions have made progress difficult.

Comprehensive immigration reform would need to address several key areas:

- **A Path to Citizenship for Undocumented Immigrants.** One of the most contentious aspects of reform is how to handle the 11 million undocumented immigrants currently living in the U.S. Many Democrats and immigration advocates support providing a path to citizenship for these individuals, particularly DACA recipients (Dreamers) and those with Temporary Protected Status (TPS). However, Republicans are more divided, with some opposing any form of legalization, while others argue that legalization should only be considered after significant investments in border security and enforcement.

- **Border Security and Enforcement.** Another key component of reform is border security. Republicans have consistently prioritized stronger enforcement measures, including building physical barriers, increasing personnel at the border, and using technology to monitor crossings. Democrats, while also supporting secure borders, tend to emphasize a more humane approach to enforcement, such as alternative detention programs and community-based monitoring for asylum seekers. The challenge will be finding a middle ground that satisfies concerns about national security while treating migrants with dignity and respect.

- **Reforming the Legal Immigration System.** Reforming the legal immigration system is essential for reducing backlogs, modernizing visa programs, and creating more opportunities for legal migration. This includes updating family-based and employment-based visa systems, expanding H-1B visas for skilled workers, and addressing long waits for green cards. A more flexible, responsive immigration system would help the U.S. meet its labor market needs while providing legal pathways for those seeking to contribute to the American economy.

- **Addressing Root Causes of Migration.** Any long-term solution to immigration challenges must also address the root causes of migration, particularly from countries in Central America. Violence, poverty, and political instability drive many migrants to seek refuge in the U.S. By investing in foreign aid, development programs, and regional partnerships, the U.S. can help reduce the push factors that force people to leave their home countries. This would not only help alleviate pressure on the U.S. border but also contribute to greater stability in the Western Hemisphere.

Public Opinion and Political Will

Public opinion on immigration remains divided, with attitudes often shaped by partisan affiliation, geography, and personal experience. According to recent polling by the Pew Research Center, while a majority of Americans support a path to citizenship for undocumented immigrants and more humane treatment of asylum seekers, there is still significant concern about border security and illegal immigration. The challenge for policymakers is how to craft policies that address these concerns while remaining true to America's values of inclusion and opportunity.

However, political polarization has made compromise difficult. Immigration reform has long been a litmus test for political candidates, and the issue has become deeply entrenched in partisan identity. For Democrats, reform often centers on compassion, inclusion, and the need to reflect America's immigrant heritage. For Republicans, the focus is on law and order, national security, and protecting American jobs.

Finding common ground will require significant political will, as well as a willingness to move beyond partisan rhetoric. This is no small task, but without meaningful reform, the U.S. will continue to face the same challenges— overcrowded detention centers, millions of people living in legal limbo, and a strained immigration system that fails to meet the needs of both the nation and its immigrants.

Immigration and America's Values

At the heart of the immigration debate is a deeper question: What kind of country does America want to be? Immigration forces the U.S. to confront its own values, balancing the desire for security and sovereignty with the ideals of freedom, opportunity, and humanitarianism. As a nation built by immigrants, the U.S. has long been a beacon of hope for those seeking a better life. But it is also a country that has, at various points in its history, enacted exclusionary policies, from the Chinese Exclusion Act to the Muslim Ban, which have limited who can become part of the American fabric.

Immigration touches on some of the most fundamental aspects of the American identity. On one hand, the country prides itself on being a melting pot of cultures and a land of opportunity for all. On the other, there are growing concerns about how to balance diversity with social cohesion, how to integrate new arrivals while preserving what many see as core American values.

The challenge is not just about managing borders or creating more efficient legal pathways for immigrants—it's about reconciling the nation's ideals with its realities. Can the U.S. remain open and welcoming to those fleeing violence and poverty, while also protecting its borders and ensuring that its immigration system works in the best interests of the country as a whole? These questions are not easy to answer, but they are essential to the future of immigration policy.

Global Comparisons: Learning from Other Countries

As the U.S. looks to the future, there are valuable lessons to be learned from other countries that have faced similar immigration challenges. Countries like Canada, Australia, and Germany have implemented immigration policies that balance the needs of the economy with social cohesion, while also addressing humanitarian concerns. For example:

Canada has a merit-based immigration system that prioritizes skilled workers while also maintaining strong refugee protections. The country has managed to integrate large numbers of immigrants without significant social or political backlash, partly due to its emphasis on multiculturalism as a core national value.

Germany has taken in millions of refugees, particularly from the Syrian civil war, and has faced challenges in integrating them into German society. However, Germany's experience highlights the importance of long-term planning and investment in integration programs to ensure that new arrivals can successfully contribute to the economy and society.

Australia has a points-based immigration system that selects immigrants based on skills, education, and work experience. However, Australia has also faced criticism for its strict border control policies, particularly its offshore detention of asylum seekers. The country's experience highlights the difficult balance between security and compassion.

The U.S. can learn from these approaches, adapting successful policies while being mindful of the unique challenges posed by its geographic position and political climate. A balanced immigration system that prioritizes both economic needs and humanitarian responsibilities can help the U.S. remain competitive in the global economy while staying true to its founding values.

The Future of Immigration in America

Immigration will continue to shape the future of the United States, as it always has. The nation's ability to manage immigration will not only impact its economic prosperity but also its moral standing in the world and its social fabric at home. As the debate continues, the path forward must be one of compromise, pragmatism, and compassion—one that balances security and order with the humanitarian values that have long defined America.

In the coming years, the country will face crucial decisions on how to reform its immigration system in a way that reflects the best of its ideals while addressing the practical challenges of the modern world. Whether through comprehensive reform, stronger enforcement, or more inclusive policies, the future of immigration in America will determine not only who enters the country but also who the country chooses to be.

Ultimately, the U.S. stands at a crossroads. Will it remain a beacon of hope and opportunity for the world's huddled masses, or will it turn inward, prioritizing security and exclusion over its long-held image as a nation of immigrants? The choices made today will shape the legacy of immigration in America for generations to come.

Parental Rights vs. School Autonomy in Shaping America's Classrooms

Introduction: The Battle Over Education

Education has long been a cornerstone of democratic societies, tasked with preparing children to become informed, engaged, and capable citizens. Yet, as the United States grapples with social and political polarization, schools have increasingly become battlegrounds in a larger cultural war over who should have the power to shape children's understanding of critical issues like history, race, gender, and citizenship. At the heart of this conflict is a fundamental question: Who decides what is taught in schools—parents or educators?

In recent years, many conservative activists have called for greater parental control over school curriculums, arguing that schools are increasingly teaching politically motivated or progressive ideologies without the consent of parents. They express concern over topics such as Critical Race Theory (CRT), gender identity, and LGBTQ+ issues, arguing that schools are straying from traditional educational content and introducing children to sensitive subjects that should be under parental supervision. Advocates of parental rights assert that as the primary guardians of their children's values and beliefs, parents should have more authority over what their children learn in the classroom.

On the other side of the debate, educators, school administrators, and progressive activists argue that schools must retain autonomy to provide a well-rounded education that prepares students for life in a diverse and evolving society. They contend that critical topics—such as America's history of racism, gender diversity, and sexual orientation—are essential to fostering empathy, understanding, and critical thinking among students. From their perspective, limiting the teaching of such subjects not only censors important ideas but also stifles academic freedom, undermining the educational mission of schools.

This struggle for control has led to fierce battles in school board meetings, state legislatures, and courts across the country. States like Florida, Texas, and Virginia have passed or proposed laws that limit the teaching of controversial topics, while school boards have enacted policies that ban books or restrict discussions on issues such as race and gender. The clash between parental rights and school autonomy has far-reaching implications for American education, raising critical questions about academic freedom, censorship, and the role of public education in a democratic society.

In this essay, I explore both sides of the debate, examining the rise of the parental rights movement and its push for greater control over school curriculums, as well as the perspective of educators who argue that academic expertise and educational standards should guide what is taught in schools. It will also delve into the increasing trend of book bans and curriculum restrictions, analyzing the impact these measures have on students, teachers, and the future of education in America. Ultimately, this conflict is about more than just education; it's about the values, beliefs, and principles that will shape the next generation of American citizens.

Historical Context: The Role of Schools in Society

Schools have always played a fundamental role in shaping the social, cultural, and civic identities of young people in America. From the earliest days of the public education system, schools were seen not just as places to impart academic knowledge, but as institutions designed to prepare children to become informed, responsible citizens. The subjects taught in schools—whether it's history, science, or literature—help to define a society's values and priorities, and over the years, education has reflected and sometimes even driven broader social change.

Schools as Institutions of Civic Education

Since the inception of public education in the 19th century, American schools have been tasked with instilling civic values and fostering national identity. The goal of early public schooling, championed by education reformers like Horace Mann, was to create a literate, disciplined, and unified citizenry capable of participating in a functioning democracy. This often meant emphasizing a shared national narrative that promoted patriotism, hard work, and respect for authority. Schools were seen as vital to shaping the moral character of children and teaching them the principles of good citizenship.

In the 20th century, public education continued to evolve alongside the country's growing diversity. By the mid-1900s, the focus of education expanded to include critical thinking, social awareness, and multicultural understanding. As society became more diverse, schools sought to reflect this diversity in their curriculums, teaching children about different cultures, histories, and perspectives. The goal was to equip students with the knowledge and skills they would need to navigate a complex, pluralistic society.

However, the role of schools in shaping children's understanding of race, gender, and citizenship has long been contested. Just as schools have been sites of social progress, they have also been arenas of resistance and conflict. Battles over school curriculums reflect broader societal debates about what values should be passed on to the next generation, and who gets to decide what those values should be.

Past Tensions: Education as a Site of Cultural Conflict

Education has been a battleground for competing ideologies throughout American history. Religion, race, and science have often sparked some of the fiercest debates about what should be taught in public schools.

One of the earliest and most well-known examples is the controversy over the teaching of evolution in schools in the early 20th century. The famous Scopes "Monkey" Trial of 1925, in which a Tennessee teacher was prosecuted for teaching Charles Darwin's theory of evolution, highlighted the deep divide between religious fundamentalism and modern scientific thought. While the trial ended with a conviction for Scopes, it became a symbol of the growing tension between traditional values and progressive ideas in education.

In the 1950s and 60s, schools became a focal point for the Civil Rights Movement. Following the Brown v. Board of Education decision in 1954, which ruled racial segregation in public schools unconstitutional, schools across the South became battlegrounds for desegregation. Resistance to desegregation led to conflicts that played out in school board meetings, state legislatures, and even on the steps of schools themselves, as federal troops were called in to enforce desegregation orders.

In the 1960s and 70s, debates over sex education and the inclusion of women's rights in school curriculums further fueled tensions between conservative and progressive values. Conservative parents and religious groups argued that schools were introducing children to inappropriate topics that should be left to families, while advocates for more comprehensive education argued that schools had a responsibility to teach children about health, gender equality, and sexuality.

Current Tensions as Part of a Broader Historical Pattern

The debates we see today over the teaching of Critical Race Theory (CRT), gender identity, and sexual orientation are part of a long-standing pattern of conflict over the role of schools in society. Just as previous generations grappled with the role of schools in addressing topics like evolution, civil rights, and sex education, today's parents, educators, and policymakers are debating how schools should approach issues related to race, gender, and sexual identity.

Schools continue to serve as key institutions for promoting not only academic learning but also social values and cultural norms. This dual role often puts them at the center of larger societal debates, especially as the country grows more diverse and divided. While some view schools as necessary platforms for addressing social inequality and fostering understanding, others see them as overstepping their boundaries by introducing children to controversial topics without parental consent.

Shaping Future Citizens

Historically, schools have been charged with the task of preparing students for their roles as citizens in a democratic society. From teaching civic responsibility and critical thinking to addressing controversial topics like race and gender, schools have played a crucial role in shaping how children understand the world and their place in it.

However, this mission has always been subject to contention, as different groups have sought to influence what is taught in schools to reflect their own values and beliefs. The current debates over parental rights and school autonomy are the latest chapter in this ongoing struggle over the role of education in society, reflecting deeper tensions about authority, values, and the future of American democracy.

Parental Rights and Conservative Push-back

In recent years, the conversation about parental rights in education has gained significant momentum, particularly among conservative activists and politicians. Many parents, especially those aligned with conservative values, have expressed growing concerns that schools are introducing topics they find inappropriate or politically charged, such as Critical Race Theory (CRT), gender identity, and sexual orientation. These parents believe that they should have more control over what their children are exposed to in the classroom, sparking a national debate about the role of parental authority versus school autonomy.

The Rise of the Parental Rights Movement

The parental rights movement has its roots in a broader cultural shift in which many parents feel that their traditional values are being undermined by a public education system they perceive as increasingly influenced by progressive ideologies. Advocates of this movement argue that parents—not schools—are the primary guardians of their children's moral and ethical development and, as such, should have the final say in what their children learn, particularly when it comes to sensitive topics like race, sexuality, and gender.

The movement gained national visibility during the COVID-19 pandemic, when virtual learning allowed parents to observe what their children were being taught in real-time. For many parents, this was a wake-up call, as they were confronted with lessons and materials they found objectionable. This led to increased activism at the local level, with parents attending school board meetings, challenging curriculums, and in some cases, demanding the removal of certain books and instructional materials.

Key Issues That Have Galvanized the Parental Rights Movement

- **Opposition to Critical Race Theory.** Many conservative parents are concerned about what they perceive to be the influence of Critical Race Theory (CRT) in schools. CRT is an academic framework developed in the 1980s that examines the role of systemic racism in shaping laws, institutions, and social structures. Although CRT is typically taught at the college or graduate level, critics argue that its principles have filtered down into K-12 education, manifesting in lessons that emphasize racial inequality, privilege, and identity. Opponents of CRT argue that these teachings promote division, foster a sense of victimhood among minority students, and cast white students as oppressors. They contend that schools should focus on teaching children a more patriotic and unifying version of American history, free from what they see as ideological indoctrination.

- **Concerns Over Gender Identity and LGBTQ+ Topics.** Another major focus of the parental rights movement is the teaching of gender identity and LGBTQ+ issues. Many parents believe that schools are exposing children to concepts of gender fluidity and non-binary identities at too young an age. They argue that discussions about transgender rights, sexual orientation, and non-traditional family structures are inappropriate for the classroom, especially in elementary schools. For these parents, such topics should be taught at home, where they can control how and when their children are introduced to these sensitive subjects. Some parents also fear that lessons on gender identity might confuse young children or conflict with religious beliefs about gender and sexuality.

- **Sex Education and Parental Consent.** Sex education has long been a point of contention in the parental rights movement. Many conservative parents are uncomfortable with the way sex education is taught in public schools, particularly lessons that address contraception, sexual orientation, and consent. They argue that parents should have the right to opt their children out of certain lessons or, alternatively, that schools should be required to obtain parental consent before teaching such material. For these parents, sex education should align with their family's moral and religious values, rather than what they see as a progressive agenda to normalize topics they find inappropriate.

Key Concerns of Parents: The Cultural and Moral Dimensions

At the heart of the parental rights movement is the belief that public schools are overstepping their boundaries by teaching content that many parents find politically or morally objectionable. While schools are traditionally viewed as institutions that teach academic subjects like math, science, and language arts, the growing inclusion of topics such as systemic racism, social justice, gender diversity, and climate change has led many parents to believe that schools are promoting an ideological agenda.

Many parents view these topics as inherently political and worry that schools are shifting away from neutral education to a more activist model that seeks to shape students' beliefs and values. This is particularly concerning for parents with conservative or religious backgrounds, who feel that their children are being taught ideas that contradict their own cultural and religious principles.

Some Of the Central Concerns Driving the Parental Rights Movement

- **Political Indoctrination.** Many conservative parents argue that schools are no longer just educating their children—they are indoctrinating them with progressive ideologies. They point to lessons on systemic racism, white privilege, and gender identity as evidence that schools are teaching students to adopt certain political viewpoints, rather than encouraging independent thought or critical thinking. In their view, schools should be neutral spaces for academic learning, not battlegrounds for political and cultural debates.

- **Parental Responsibility.** Another key concern is that schools are usurping the role of parents in teaching children about morality and values. Parents involved in this movement often argue that it is their responsibility—not the school's—to decide when and how their children learn about complex social issues like race, sexuality, and gender. They believe that schools should stick to traditional academic subjects and leave more controversial or sensitive topics to be discussed at home, where parents can offer guidance in line with their family's values.

- **The Erosion of Tradition.** Many parents in the movement see the shift in educational content as part of a larger societal trend toward the erosion of traditional values. They view the growing focus on diversity, equity, and inclusion (DEI) initiatives in schools as part of a progressive effort to reshape society in ways that downplay the importance of patriotism, individualism, and personal responsibility—values they believe are foundational to the American way of life.

The Role of Social Media and Activism

The parental rights movement has been fueled by the rise of social media and grassroots activism, making it easier for concerned parents to organize and mobilize. Platforms like Facebook, Twitter, and YouTube have allowed parents to share information, voice their concerns, and coordinate efforts to challenge school boards and educators. Videos of heated school board meetings, where parents confront administrators over controversial curriculums, have gone viral, further galvanizing the movement and amplifying its reach.

Organizations like Parents Defending Education, Moms for Liberty, and No Left Turn in Education have emerged as powerful advocates for parental rights, providing parents with resources to challenge school curriculums and campaign for greater transparency in education. These groups have been instrumental in pushing for curriculum transparency laws, which would require schools to disclose the content of their lessons and allow parents to have more input in the development of educational materials.

A National Political Movement

What started as a local issue in school board meetings has quickly evolved into a national political movement, with parental rights becoming a key issue in state legislatures, gubernatorial races, and even national politics. Conservative lawmakers in states like Florida, Texas, and Virginia have introduced or passed bills that limit the teaching of CRT, ban discussions of gender identity in certain grade levels, and require more parental oversight in curriculum development.

Florida Governor Ron DeSantis, for example, signed the Parental Rights in Education Act—often referred to as the "Don't Say Gay" bill by its critics—which prohibits discussions of sexual orientation and gender identity in classrooms from kindergarten through third grade. Supporters of the bill argue that it protects children from being exposed to inappropriate material, while opponents view it as an effort to erase LGBTQ+ issues from the classroom.

The 2021 Virginia governor's race was also seen as a referendum on parental control over education, with Republican Glenn Youngkin successfully campaigning on a platform of empowering parents to take back control of their children's education. Youngkin's victory is seen by many as a sign that parental rights will continue to be a major political issue in the years to come.

Parental Rights as a Cultural Flash-point

The parental rights movement reflects a growing anxiety among many parents—particularly those on the right—that public schools are pushing an agenda that is out of step with their values. Whether it's the teaching of CRT, gender identity, or sexual orientation, conservative parents are increasingly seeking to assert control over what their children are taught, seeing it as a matter of protecting their children from what they view as inappropriate or harmful content.

As this movement gains momentum, it raises important questions about who gets to decide what is taught in public schools. Should parents have more say in shaping school curriculums, or should schools and educators maintain autonomy to determine what is best for students' intellectual and social development? In the next section, we will explore the counterargument—school autonomy—and why many educators believe they should retain control over what is taught in the classroom.

School Autonomy: The Educator's Perspective

While the parental rights movement has garnered significant attention, there is a strong counterargument from educators, school administrators, and many education advocates who believe that schools must maintain autonomy in determining what is taught in classrooms. These professionals argue that decisions about curriculums should be guided by academic research, educational standards, and the expertise of teachers who are trained to prepare students for the challenges of an increasingly complex world. They assert that school autonomy is critical to ensuring that students receive a well-rounded, fact-based education, free from political interference.

Academic Freedom and Expertise

Educators contend that they are best equipped to decide what should be taught in classrooms because they have the training, knowledge, and experience necessary to address a wide range of topics effectively. Many teachers undergo years of specialized education to develop skills in pedagogy, curriculum design, and classroom management. They are trained to teach controversial topics—such as race, gender, and sexuality—in an age-appropriate and educationally sound manner.

Moreover, the concept of academic freedom is central to the work of educators. This principle allows teachers to explore a variety of ideas, perspectives, and subjects in their classrooms, free from external political or ideological pressures. Academic freedom is not about promoting any one viewpoint, but rather about exposing students to a broad spectrum of ideas and encouraging them to think critically and form their own opinions. Educators argue that limiting their ability to teach certain topics—whether it's Critical Race Theory or gender identity—not only undermines their professional expertise but also denies students the opportunity to engage with complex and important societal issues.

In defending academic freedom, many educators point out that school curriculums are already subject to rigorous oversight by state education departments, local school boards, and accreditation bodies. These bodies work to ensure that lessons align with state and national standards for educational quality and accuracy. Thus, teachers are not operating in a vacuum but are part of a broader system of accountability designed to ensure that students receive a balanced and evidence-based education.

Curriculum Development Process: How Schools Decide What to Teach

The development of school curriculums is a collaborative and multi-step process that involves input from various stakeholders —educators, school administrators, state boards of education, and curriculum experts. While parents play an important role in shaping the values and beliefs of their children, many educators argue that schools have a distinct educational mission that goes beyond individual family values.

Curriculums Are Typically Created to Meet the Following Objectives

- **Aligning with Standards.** State and national education standards outline what students should learn at each grade level in subjects such as math, science, history, and language arts. These standards are developed by experts in education and are based on extensive research into what knowledge and skills students need to succeed academically and in life.

- **Incorporating Best Practices.** Curriculum development incorporates best practices in education, including the latest research on how students learn and what methods are most effective for teaching complex topics. This might include using inclusive language, teaching critical thinking skills, and encouraging students to engage with diverse perspectives.

- **Adapting to a Changing World.** Schools also have a responsibility to prepare students for the realities of the modern world, which includes understanding issues like climate change, global politics, racial inequality, and gender diversity. Educators argue that avoiding or censoring these topics leaves students ill-prepared to navigate a complex and rapidly changing society.

Educators argue that while parental input is important, school curriculums should be designed by professionals who have the expertise to ensure that students are learning the full range of knowledge and skills they will need to be informed citizens.

Addressing Controversial Topics: Why They Matter

A key argument for school autonomy is that teaching controversial topics—such as race, gender, and sexuality—is necessary for fostering critical thinking, empathy, and social awareness. In an increasingly diverse and interconnected world, students must be prepared to interact with people from a wide variety of backgrounds and perspectives. Educators believe that avoiding difficult subjects or limiting discussions about them does a disservice to students, particularly when these topics are directly relevant to their lives and communities.

- **Critical Race Theory and Racial History.** Although Critical Race Theory (CRT) has become a political flash-point, educators argue that discussing systemic racism and racial inequality is essential for understanding the history and structure of American society. They emphasize that lessons about race are not intended to make students feel guilty or ashamed, but rather to provide them with a more complete and honest picture of U.S. history. Ignoring or whitewashing the country's legacy of slavery, segregation, and discrimination deprives students of the opportunity to learn from the past and address ongoing inequalities.

- **Gender Identity and LGBTQ+ Inclusion.** In many schools, discussions of gender identity and LGBTQ+ issues are part of broader efforts to create an inclusive and safe environment for all students. Educators argue that these lessons help combat bullying, discrimination, and mental health issues faced by LGBTQ+ students. They also point out that students are already exposed to discussions about gender and sexuality in the media and online, making it all the more important for schools to provide accurate, age-appropriate information. Teaching students about gender diversity and LGBTQ+ rights is not about promoting a particular lifestyle, they argue, but about fostering acceptance and understanding in a diverse world.

- **Civics and Citizenship.** Schools have a long-standing responsibility to teach students about citizenship and civic engagement. This includes discussions about democracy, voting rights, social justice, and the role of government. Educators argue that these topics are essential for preparing students to become informed and engaged citizens who can participate meaningfully in democratic processes. Controversial or challenging topics—such as debates over police reform, voting laws, or immigration policy—are part of the civic education process that helps students understand the world around them.

The Slippery Slope of Censorship

One of the most pressing concerns for educators is the potential for curriculum restrictions to lead to widespread censorship. When schools ban certain books or prohibit the teaching of specific topics, it raises concerns about who gets to decide what is appropriate for students to learn. Educators argue that removing controversial or uncomfortable subjects from the curriculum limits students' ability to think critically, challenge ideas, and engage with different perspectives.

Educators warn that book bans and curriculum restrictions can create a slippery slope where more and more topics become off-limits for discussion. For example, banning discussions about gender identity might lead to broader censorship of books or lessons that discuss gender roles, women's rights, or even mental health. Similarly, efforts to restrict discussions of racism might prevent students from learning about important historical events such as the Civil Rights Movement, the Holocaust, or even the history of colonialism.

Many educators view these restrictions as a form of intellectual censorship that prevents students from gaining a full understanding of the world. They argue that schools should be places where students are encouraged to ask questions, explore different viewpoints, and develop their own opinions, rather than being shielded from difficult or controversial topics.

The Role of Schools in a Diverse Society

For educators, the debate over school autonomy versus parental rights comes down to the question of what kind of education best prepares students for the world they will inherit. While parents are undoubtedly critical partners in their children's education, many educators believe that schools must have the freedom to teach honest, fact-based curriculums that reflect the realities of a diverse and interconnected society.

In their view, shielding students from discussions about race, gender, and other sensitive topics does not protect them—it deprives them of the opportunity to engage with the complex issues they will face as adults. Schools, they argue, have a responsibility to prepare students not only for academic success but also for their roles as informed citizens, critical thinkers, and compassionate individuals in a democratic society.

As the debate over school curriculums continues to evolve, it will be essential to strike a balance between respecting parental concerns and ensuring that schools retain the autonomy they need to fulfill their educational mission. In the next section, we will explore the rising trend of book bans and curriculum restrictions, examining the impact these measures have on students, teachers, and the broader goals of public education.

The Rise of Book Bans and Curriculum Restrictions

As debates over school curriculums intensify, a growing number of states, local school boards, and parental advocacy groups have turned to book bans and curriculum restrictions as tools to exert greater control over what is taught in classrooms. These efforts, which often focus on topics like race, gender identity, sexual orientation, and American history, have sparked a national conversation about censorship, academic freedom, and the role of education in shaping young minds. Proponents of these measures argue that they are necessary to protect children from what they view as inappropriate or harmful content, while critics see them as a dangerous form of censorship that undermines intellectual freedom and critical thinking in schools.

Banning Books: A Growing Movement

One of the most visible aspects of this conflict has been the rise in book bans across the United States. Books dealing with racial justice, LGBTQ+ identities, sexuality, and historical oppression have become frequent targets of challenges by conservative parents, activists, and politicians. These individuals argue that certain books contain material that is either inappropriate for children or overtly political in nature, promoting ideologies they believe are divisive or harmful.

Some of the most frequently banned or challenged books include:

- **"Maus" by Art Spiegelman.** A Pulitzer Prize-winning graphic novel about the Holocaust, "Maus" was banned by a school board in Tennessee in early 2022, ostensibly due to its use of profanity and nudity. Critics, however, argue that the ban is part of a broader effort to avoid uncomfortable discussions about historical atrocities like the Holocaust.

- **"The Bluest Eye" by Toni Morrison.** This classic novel, which addresses themes of race, poverty, and sexual violence, has been frequently challenged for its depiction of sexual abuse and racial trauma. Some parents argue that the book's subject matter is too graphic for students, while educators maintain that it is an important work that deals honestly with the legacy of racism in America.

- **"Gender Queer"** *by Maia Kobabe.* A memoir in graphic novel form, "Gender Queer" explores nonbinary identity and has been one of the most challenged books in recent years. Opponents argue that the book's frank discussion of gender and sexual identity, as well as its illustrations, are inappropriate for school-aged children. Supporters argue that it provides valuable representation for LGBTQ+ students.

The trend of banning books is not new in American history, but its recent resurgence has been notable in both its scale and intensity. According to the American Library Association (ALA), there has been a dramatic increase in challenges to books and instructional materials in the past few years. In 2021, the ALA reported 330 book challenges, a 67% increase from the previous year, with many challenges focused on books that address racial justice, gender identity, or LGBTQ+ issues.

Curriculum Restrictions: Limiting Discussions on Race and Gender

In addition to book bans, several states have passed or introduced curriculum restrictions that aim to limit how teachers can discuss topics like race, gender identity, and sexual orientation in the classroom. These efforts have been particularly focused on prohibiting the teaching of Critical Race Theory (CRT) and restricting discussions of LGBTQ+ issues.

The Battle Over Critical Race Theory (CRT)

Perhaps the most contentious issue in recent years has been the debate over Critical Race Theory. CRT is an academic framework that examines how systemic racism is embedded in legal systems and societal structures. Although CRT is primarily taught in law schools and universities, conservative activists argue that its principles are being introduced in K-12 classrooms under the guise of diversity, equity, and inclusion (DEI) initiatives. They claim that CRT teaches students to view American history through the lens of oppression and privilege, and that it promotes division by framing white students as oppressors and students of color as victims.

As a result, several states—including Florida, Texas, Oklahoma, and Idaho—have passed laws banning the teaching of CRT or restricting how teachers can discuss topics like race and racism. These laws often prohibit teachers from suggesting that any race is inherently privileged or oppressive and restrict discussions that might cause students to feel guilt or discomfort because of their race.

For example, Florida's "Stop WOKE Act" prohibits any instruction that suggests individuals are inherently racist, sexist, or oppressive, either consciously or unconsciously, based on their race, gender, or national origin. Proponents argue that the law is necessary to prevent the indoctrination of students and to ensure that children are not being exposed to divisive or harmful ideologies. Critics, however, argue that the law is a form of censorship that whitewashes American history and prevents students from learning about the realities of racism and inequality in the United States.

Restricting Gender Identity and LGBTQ+ Discussions

Similar efforts to restrict curriculum content have focused on gender identity and LGBTQ+ issues. Conservative activists argue that discussions about nonbinary identities, transgender rights, and sexual orientation are inappropriate for school-aged children, particularly in elementary schools. They believe that these topics should be left to parents to discuss with their children, rather than being introduced in the classroom.

One of the most high-profile examples of this is Florida's Parental Rights in Education Act, commonly referred to by critics as the "Don't Say Gay" bill. Signed into law by Governor Ron DeSantis in 2022, the law prohibits classroom discussions about sexual orientation and gender identity in grades K-3 and restricts such discussions in higher grades if they are not deemed age-appropriate. The law also gives parents the right to sue school districts if they believe the law has been violated.

Supporters of the law argue that it is designed to protect young children from being exposed to topics they are not emotionally or cognitively ready to handle. They contend that discussions of gender and sexuality are inherently political and ideological, and that schools should focus on teaching core academic subjects rather than engaging in social engineering. Critics, however, argue that the law is a thinly veiled attempt to erase LGBTQ+ identities from schools and to stigmatize students who are gay or transgender. They contend that such restrictions create a hostile environment for LGBTQ+ students and undermine efforts to promote inclusion and acceptance in schools.

Proponents vs. Critics: Protecting Children or Censorship?

The rise of book bans and curriculum restrictions has sparked a fierce debate between those who view these measures as necessary for protecting children from inappropriate content and those who see them as a form of censorship that undermines academic freedom and critical thinking.

Proponents' Arguments

Proponents of book bans and curriculum restrictions argue that these measures are essential for protecting children from age-inappropriate or ideologically driven content. They believe that parents should have the right to control what their children are exposed to in schools, particularly when it comes to sensitive topics like race, gender, and sexuality. For many parents, this is about ensuring that schools reflect the values and beliefs they want to instill in their children, rather than promoting progressive ideologies that they see as divisive or inappropriate.

Proponents also argue that children should not be forced to confront issues that are beyond their emotional or cognitive maturity. For example, they contend that young children are not ready to understand complex topics like systemic racism or gender identity, and that introducing these concepts too early can confuse or distress them. By banning certain books and restricting curriculum content, proponents believe that schools can create a safe and neutral learning environment that focuses on academics rather than politics.

Critics' Arguments

Critics of book bans and curriculum restrictions argue that these measures amount to censorship and are part of a broader effort to suppress free speech and intellectual freedom in schools. They contend that banning books and restricting discussions on race, gender, and sexuality denies students the opportunity to engage with diverse perspectives and to develop their own critical thinking skills.

Many educators and free speech advocates worry that these measures are creating a climate of fear in which teachers are afraid to address important social issues for fear of backlash or legal consequences. They argue that discussions about race, gender, and sexuality are essential for preparing students to navigate a complex and diverse world. In their view, avoiding or censoring these topics does not protect students—it deprives them of the opportunity to learn about real-world challenges and to develop empathy for people with different experiences and identities.

Critics also point out that many of the books being banned or challenged deal with issues that are directly relevant to students' lives. For example, banning books about LGBTQ+ identities can marginalize LGBTQ+ students and make them feel invisible or unwelcome in their own schools. Similarly, removing discussions of racial injustice from the curriculum prevents students from understanding the full scope of American history and the ongoing struggles for equality and justice.

The Broader Implications of Censorship

The rise of book bans and curriculum restrictions has profound implications for the future of education in America. On one hand, these measures reflect the growing desire of many parents to assert control over what their children learn in school. On the other, they raise serious concerns about censorship, intellectual freedom, and the ability of schools to provide a comprehensive and balanced education.

As this debate continues, it will be critical to consider the long-term effects of limiting students' access to diverse ideas and perspectives. What is the cost of shielding students from difficult conversations about race, gender, and inequality? Will restricting certain books and topics help create a more comfortable learning environment, or will it undermine the very purpose of education by preventing students from grappling with the complex realities of the world?

The Impacts on Teachers and Students

The rise of book bans and curriculum restrictions has far-reaching consequences for both teachers and students. As schools increasingly become the front-lines in America's culture wars, educators are finding themselves under intense scrutiny, while students face the prospect of a more narrowed curriculum that may limit their ability to think critically and engage with complex social issues. These trends have not only led to a climate of fear and self-censorship among teachers but have also raised important questions about the future of public education and the role of schools in fostering informed, empathetic, and civically engaged citizens.

Impact on Teachers: Navigating a Climate of Fear and Self-Censorship

Teachers are at the forefront of implementing and delivering curriculum content, and the growing pressure to comply with state-imposed restrictions on certain topics has left many educators feeling vulnerable and constrained in their professional roles. The increasing prevalence of book bans and restrictions on discussions about race, gender identity, and sexuality has created an environment where many teachers are unsure of what they can and cannot teach.

Fear of Repercussions and Job Security

In states where laws have been passed banning the teaching of Critical Race Theory (CRT) or restricting the discussion of LGBTQ+ issues, teachers face the prospect of disciplinary action, fines, or even job loss if they are found to be in violation of these laws. For example, under Florida's "Stop WOKE Act" and Parental Rights in Education law (often referred to as the "Don't Say Gay" law), educators could face lawsuits from parents or legal consequences for teaching content that violates state guidelines. This has led to a chilling effect, with many teachers choosing to avoid certain topics altogether rather than risk getting in trouble.

Teachers, especially those in states with new restrictive laws, report a heightened sense of anxiety around what they say in class. This self-censorship can undermine the quality of education students receive. Diane Ravitch, a well-known education historian and former U.S. Assistant Secretary of Education, argues that this atmosphere of fear can stifle critical thinking and prevent teachers from engaging students in deep, meaningful discussions about the social, historical, and political realities shaping their world.

Limits on Professional Expertise and Judgment

Educators argue that these restrictions undermine their professional judgment. Teachers are trained to navigate sensitive topics in an age-appropriate way and to foster critical thinking in their students. They believe that it is their responsibility to guide students through challenging issues, such as the complexities of American history, race relations, and gender identity, and to do so in a way that promotes understanding and respect for diverse perspectives.

Many teachers feel that curriculum restrictions prevent them from doing their jobs effectively. Rather than encouraging students to engage with complex issues and come to their own conclusions, teachers may feel forced to sanitize their lessons or stick to sanctioned narratives, which can limit students' exposure to important historical and social realities. For example, avoiding discussions of systemic racism may prevent students from fully understanding the historical context of events like the Civil Rights Movement, the Vietnam War, or the ongoing struggles for racial equality in the United States.

The Emotional Toll on Teachers

In addition to professional concerns, the current climate also takes a significant emotional toll on teachers. Many educators enter the profession out of a deep commitment to helping students learn, grow, and succeed. However, when they are restricted from discussing important topics or when their authority in the classroom is questioned, it can lead to burnout and demoralization.

Teachers who identify as LGBTQ+, or who teach students from diverse racial or gender backgrounds, may feel particularly marginalized by laws that restrict discussions of sexual orientation or gender identity. These restrictions can send the message that their own identities are inappropriate for discussion or validation within the school system, which can lead to feelings of alienation and professional disillusionment.

Impact on Students: Narrowing the Scope of Learning

While teachers feel the immediate pressure of book bans and curriculum restrictions, the long-term consequences of these policies are most profoundly felt by students, who may be deprived of a full and honest education.

Limited Exposure to Diverse Perspectives

One of the most significant impacts on students is the narrowing of the curriculum, which can prevent them from being exposed to a wide range of ideas, histories, and perspectives. When certain books or topics are banned or restricted, students lose access to stories and discussions that might challenge their preconceptions, broaden their horizons, and deepen their understanding of the world.

For example, when books like "The Bluest Eye" by Toni Morrison are removed from the curriculum, students miss out on opportunities to engage with powerful literature that explores themes of racial identity, sexual violence, and the psychological effects of oppression. Similarly, bans on books dealing with LGBTQ+ themes, like "Gender Queer" by Maia Kobabe, can deny students—particularly those who are exploring their own identities—the opportunity to see themselves reflected in literature and to understand that their experiences are valid.

The absence of these diverse perspectives can have a profound impact on students' ability to develop empathy, critical thinking, and an understanding of the complexities of identity and social justice. Exposure to different ideas and viewpoints is a fundamental part of education, helping students develop the tools they need to become informed and engaged citizens. When these perspectives are censored or restricted, students may be left with a more superficial or sanitized view of the world.

Discouraging Critical Thinking

Another concern is that curriculum restrictions and book bans may stifle students' critical thinking skills. Education is not just about memorizing facts—it's about learning to question, analyze, and evaluate information. By confronting students with difficult or controversial issues, teachers encourage them to think deeply and to grapple with the complexity of the world around them.

When students are prevented from discussing topics like racism, gender inequality, or civil rights, they lose the opportunity to engage with real-world issues that are crucial to their understanding of society. Avoiding controversial topics can result in a more passive learning experience, where students are taught to accept information without questioning or challenging it. This can ultimately limit their ability to navigate the complexities of adulthood, make informed decisions, and contribute meaningfully to a democratic society.

Marginalization of Vulnerable Students

For LGBTQ+ students and students of color, curriculum restrictions can be particularly harmful. When schools ban books or restrict discussions about race, gender, or sexuality, it sends a message that these topics—and by extension, these students' identities—are not worthy of discussion or validation. This can contribute to feelings of isolation, alienation, and stigma for students who may already feel marginalized in their school environments.

For example, restricting discussions of gender identity or sexual orientation can make LGBTQ+ students feel invisible and unsupported, particularly if they are grappling with their own identities. These students may feel that their experiences are being erased or dismissed, which can have serious consequences for their mental health and well-being. Studies have shown that LGBTQ+ students who feel supported and affirmed in school are less likely to experience bullying, depression, and suicidal thoughts. By contrast, students who are denied this support may feel that they have no safe space to explore their identities.

Similarly, when schools downplay or ignore discussions of systemic racism, racial injustice, or cultural diversity, students of color may feel that their histories and experiences are not valued. This can perpetuate feelings of exclusion and make it more difficult for students to engage fully in their education.

Impact on the Goals of Public Education

The broader impact of curriculum restrictions and book bans is a shift in the purpose of public education. Schools have traditionally been viewed as spaces where students are exposed to a range of ideas and perspectives, learn to think critically, and are prepared to participate in a diverse and democratic society. However, the growing focus on parental control over curriculums and the rise of censorship may undermine this mission.

Public Education as a Battleground

Public schools are intended to serve the common good, providing all students—regardless of their background—with the tools they need to succeed in life. However, when schools become battlegrounds for political and cultural disputes, this mission can be compromised. If education is increasingly shaped by political ideologies or censorship, students may lose out on the opportunity to engage with the full scope of human knowledge and experience.

As schools navigate the pressure from parents, advocacy groups, and state legislatures, they risk becoming institutions where students are shielded from challenging or controversial topics rather than exposed to them in a way that promotes understanding and growth. This could have significant implications for the future of democratic engagement in the United States, as students who are not taught to think critically about complex social issues may be less prepared to address the challenges of a rapidly changing world.

A New Era of Censorship?

The rise of book bans and curriculum restrictions represents a significant shift in the landscape of American education. As teachers grapple with the constraints imposed by new laws and policies, and as students face a narrowing of the ideas and perspectives they are exposed to, the broader goals of public education may be at risk.

Ultimately, the debate over curriculum control is about more than just what is taught in schools—it's about what kind of society we want to build. Will schools continue to be places where students are encouraged to think critically, engage with diverse perspectives, and explore the full range of human experiences? Or will they become spaces where ideas are censored, and difficult topics are avoided? The answer to these questions will shape the future of education—and the future of democracy—in America.

Parental Control vs. Censorship: Where Is the Line?

The debate over parental control in schools versus accusations of censorship is one of the most significant flash-points in American education today. At its core, this conflict revolves around who should have the ultimate authority over what children are taught in public schools: parents or educators. On one side, proponents of parental rights argue that parents should have more control over their children's education, particularly when it comes to sensitive topics such as race, gender identity, and sexual orientation. On the other side, advocates for academic freedom argue that limiting the scope of what can be taught in schools amounts to censorship, ultimately depriving students of a comprehensive education.

Finding a balance between these competing perspectives is a complex challenge, and the outcome of this debate will have far-reaching consequences for the future of public education in the United States.

Parental Rights: A Call for More Control

The parental rights movement has gained significant momentum in recent years, with many parents arguing that they should have more say over what their children learn in schools. This argument is grounded in the belief that parents, as the primary caregivers and moral guides for their children, have the right to determine how sensitive subjects such as race, gender, and sexuality are addressed.

Parents involved in this movement argue that schools are increasingly pushing progressive ideologies—such as Critical Race Theory (CRT), gender fluidity, or discussions around sexual orientation—without their consent. These parents fear that children are being indoctrinated with political ideologies that conflict with their own family values and beliefs. For example, many conservative parents oppose teaching materials or lessons that they believe portray white students as oppressors or victims of historical or systemic racism, as well as lessons that promote gender fluidity or transgender identities as normal and acceptable.

In their view, schools should focus on neutral academic subjects like reading, writing, math, and science, while leaving more controversial social issues to be addressed by families at home. Proponents of parental rights also support book bans and curriculum restrictions as necessary measures to protect children from content they see as inappropriate or harmful.

Several high-profile legislative efforts reflect this growing parental control movement. For example, Florida's Parental Rights in Education Act gives parents the right to sue school districts that teach students about sexual orientation or gender identity without their consent. Similarly, many states have passed laws prohibiting the teaching of Critical Race Theory, often arguing that these lessons make children feel uncomfortable or guilty based on their race.

Proponents' Core Arguments

- **Parents know best.** Parents argue that, as their children's first educators, they have a right to decide what values and beliefs their children are exposed to in the classroom.

- **Avoiding indoctrination.** They fear that schools are promoting ideologies that undermine traditional family values and conservative principles, with the potential to confuse or mislead students.

- **Protecting children.** Many parents believe that certain subjects— particularly those related to race, gender, and sexuality—are being introduced too early or too aggressively, and that it is their responsibility to protect their children from exposure to content they feel is inappropriate.

Censorship and Academic Freedom: Defending Comprehensive Education

On the other side of the debate, educators, librarians, and advocates for academic freedom argue that book bans and curriculum restrictions constitute censorship and undermine the educational mission of schools. They believe that these measures ultimately harm students by limiting their access to diverse ideas and critical thinking opportunities.

Educators argue that their professional training and expertise equip them to handle sensitive topics in an age-appropriate and thoughtful manner. They also emphasize that public education has always been about more than just teaching academic subjects; it is also about fostering civic engagement, empathy, and an understanding of diverse perspectives. When books are banned or lessons on controversial topics are restricted, educators believe that students are deprived of the opportunity to engage with the full spectrum of knowledge and experiences that shape the world.

Many in this camp warn that curriculum restrictions and book bans are a slippery slope, leading to increasing censorship in the classroom and narrowing the scope of what can be taught. For example, banning a book like "The Bluest Eye" because it discusses race and sexual violence could lead to broader restrictions on literature that explores similar themes. Critics of these bans argue that students need to confront difficult topics—such as racism, gender inequality, and historical injustice—in order to develop the critical thinking skills necessary to become informed and engaged citizens.

Additionally, advocates for academic freedom stress that students—particularly those from marginalized communities—need to see their identities and experiences represented in the curriculum. For example, banning books that discuss LGBTQ+ identities or restricting discussions of gender diversity can leave LGBTQ+ students feeling invisible or excluded. Similarly, removing lessons about systemic racism or racial injustice can prevent students of color from understanding their own history and the ongoing challenges faced by their communities.

Key Arguments from Advocates of Academic Freedom

- **Censorship Harms Students.** Restricting access to diverse ideas and controversial topics prevents students from developing critical thinking skills and limits their understanding of the world.

- **Teachers Are Professionals.** Educators are trained to teach sensitive topics in a thoughtful, age-appropriate way, and their expertise should be respected.

- **Representation Matters.** Students from marginalized communities need to see their identities and experiences reflected in the curriculum to feel included and understood.

Where Is the Line? Navigating the Tension

The central question in this debate is where to draw the line between parental rights and censorship. On one hand, it is clear that parents have a legitimate role in their children's education, and their concerns about how sensitive topics are addressed should not be dismissed outright. On the other hand, educators must have the professional autonomy to design lessons that foster critical thinking, inclusion, and intellectual growth.

Some Possible Approaches to Navigating This Tension

- **Transparency and Communication.** Schools can establish greater transparency about what is being taught in classrooms and why. By engaging parents in the curriculum development process, schools can build trust and ensure that concerns are addressed early on. Some school districts have implemented curriculum transparency laws that allow parents to review instructional materials in advance. While transparency is important, it must be balanced with the need to respect the professional judgment of teachers.

- **Parental Opt-Outs.** One possible compromise is to allow parents to opt their children out of specific lessons they find objectionable. This approach gives parents a degree of control while preserving the ability of schools to offer comprehensive educational programs. However, critics argue that opt-outs could stigmatize students who do not participate in these lessons or who belong to marginalized groups.

- **Broadening Professional Development for Educators.** In order to better navigate sensitive topics, schools could provide teachers with professional development focused on handling controversial issues in the classroom. This could help ensure that teachers are equipped to present balanced, fact-based, and age-appropriate lessons that foster healthy discussions without alienating students or parents.

- **School-Parent Partnerships.** Schools can develop partnerships with parents to create open dialogues about how controversial issues are taught. School boards and educators can host community meetings to explain how sensitive topics will be approached and hear from parents about their concerns. By involving parents early and often, schools can foster a sense of shared responsibility and mutual understanding.

- **Protecting Academic Freedom.** Ultimately, many educators and education advocates argue that it is essential to preserve academic freedom in the classroom. Public education, they contend, is about exposing students to a diverse array of ideas—even those that may challenge their beliefs or make them uncomfortable. Educators believe that without academic freedom, schools will fail to prepare students for the complexities of modern life.

The Broader Impact on Society

The ongoing battle over parental control and curriculum restrictions reflects deeper societal divisions. As the United States becomes more politically and culturally polarized, these debates are likely to continue, with significant implications for the future of public education.

If parental rights advocates succeed in imposing more extensive restrictions on what can be taught in schools, the result may be a more fragmented and segmented education system, where students in different states—or even different school districts—are exposed to radically different sets of knowledge. This could further entrench political and cultural divides, as students grow up learning vastly different interpretations of history, social justice, and identity.

Conversely, if efforts to ban books and restrict curricula are defeated, schools may face backlash from parents who feel that their values are being undermined. This could lead to increased pressure on state and local governments to implement further education reforms—or even more radical changes, such as the expansion of school voucher programs or charter schools, which allow parents greater choice over where and how their children are educated.

Striking a Balance

As the debate over parental rights and censorship continues to evolve, it is clear that finding a balance between these two perspectives is essential. Parents have an important role in their children's education, but schools also have a responsibility to provide students with a comprehensive, fact-based, and inclusive education. The challenge lies in navigating this tension in a way that respects the concerns of parents while upholding the principles of academic freedom and critical thinking that are fundamental to the mission of public education.

The Future of Education: Navigating a Path Forward

The ongoing debates over parental control, curriculum restrictions, and academic freedom reflect the deepening political and cultural divisions in American society. These disputes have placed public education at the center of the nation's culture wars, with far-reaching consequences for students, teachers, and the broader goals of schooling. As schools continue to be battlegrounds for these ideological conflicts, the future of public education in the U.S. is uncertain. Will schools move toward greater parental control, with strict limits on what can be taught, or will they reaffirm their commitment to academic freedom and inclusive education?

This final section explores potential paths forward and what it will take to resolve these conflicts in a way that balances parental concerns, educational autonomy, and the need to prepare students for the complexities of modern life.

The Role of Politics in Shaping Education Policy

One of the clearest trends in recent years is the increasing politicization of education. Historically, public education in the U.S. has sought to maintain some level of neutrality, operating under the belief that schools should be places of learning, not political conflict. However, as debates over race, gender, and history have intensified, politicians at the local, state, and national levels have become heavily involved in education policy, seeking to shape what students learn based on ideological goals.

For example, laws banning the teaching of Critical Race Theory or restricting discussions of gender identity reflect a broader trend of conservative lawmakers responding to their constituencies' concerns by limiting certain topics in classrooms. These actions, in turn, have led to backlash from progressive groups, who see such laws as attempts to whitewash history and suppress the representation of marginalized communities.

This cycle of politicization is unlikely to end soon. As long as education remains a key issue for voters, politicians will continue to use it as a tool to mobilize their base. Moving forward, education policy will likely remain a major point of contention in election cycles, especially at the local and state levels, where school boards and state legislatures hold significant power over curriculum decisions.

Potential Solutions: Bridging the Divide

Despite the heated nature of the current debate, there are ways to navigate these tensions and find a middle ground between the demands for parental control and the need for academic freedom. A few potential solutions include:

No. 1 — Increased Transparency and Parental Engagement

One of the primary complaints of parents advocating for more control over school curriculums is a lack of transparency in what their children are being taught. Schools can address this by providing clearer, more accessible information about lesson plans, reading lists, and curriculum goals. Some districts have already adopted curriculum transparency policies, where teachers are required to post their lesson plans online, allowing parents to see what topics will be covered in advance.

Additionally, schools can take a proactive approach to parental engagement, creating forums for dialogue where parents, educators, and administrators can discuss curriculum concerns and work together to find solutions that respect parental values while upholding academic standards. This engagement process can help parents feel more involved and heard while allowing schools to maintain their educational integrity.

No. 2 — Providing Opt-Out Options for Sensitive Topics

For parents who strongly object to specific lessons—particularly those involving gender identity, sexuality, or racial history—schools could offer opt-out options that allow parents to excuse their children from these lessons. While this solution is far from perfect (as it risks stigmatizing students who do not participate), it provides a compromise that allows parents to maintain control over their children's exposure to certain topics while ensuring that schools can continue to offer comprehensive education on these issues.

No. 3 — Balanced Curriculum Development

A more balanced approach to curriculum development can help schools navigate the tension between competing demands. This means ensuring that curriculums reflect multiple perspectives, particularly on controversial issues, without promoting any single viewpoint. For example, when teaching about American history, curriculums could present both the triumphs of American democracy and the darker chapters of slavery, segregation, and systemic racism, allowing students to engage with the full complexity of the nation's past.

Similarly, schools can teach about gender diversity and LGBTQ+ issues in ways that promote understanding and empathy without necessarily endorsing particular political positions. The goal should be to foster critical thinking, encouraging students to form their own opinions based on a broad array of information.

No. 4 — Expanding Professional Development for Teachers

To help educators navigate these complex issues, schools can invest in more robust professional development programs. These programs can train teachers on how to address controversial topics in ways that are age-appropriate, balanced, and sensitive to diverse student populations. By equipping teachers with the tools they need to manage difficult discussions, schools can reduce the risk of missteps that might fuel backlash from parents or the community.

Additionally, professional development can help educators understand the legal and policy frameworks governing what can and cannot be taught, ensuring that they feel confident and supported as they navigate increasingly restrictive legislation in some states.

The Impact of Private and Charter Schools

As debates over public school curriculums continue to intensify, many parents are turning to private schools or charter schools as alternatives to the traditional public school system. Private schools, particularly those with religious affiliations, often offer curriculums that align more closely with conservative family values, providing an option for parents who are dissatisfied with the direction of public education. Meanwhile, charter schools, which are publicly funded but operate independently of traditional school districts, offer greater flexibility in curriculum design, allowing for more tailored approaches to education.

However, the rise of private and charter schools raises questions about equity and access. While wealthier families may have the resources to send their children to private schools or choose charter schools with specialized curriculums, lower-income families are often left with fewer options, relying on public schools to provide a quality education. As the public school system becomes more fragmented and politically charged, there is a risk that educational inequality will deepen, with students in different districts or states receiving vastly different educational experiences.

Reaffirming the Role of Public Education in a Democracy

At its core, the debate over education is about more than just what is taught in schools—it is about the purpose of public education in a democratic society. Historically, public schools have been seen as a common ground, where children from diverse backgrounds come together to learn not only academic skills but also the values of civic participation, tolerance, and respect for diversity. As these debates unfold, there is a real danger that public schools will become politicized battlegrounds, with different regions or school districts pushing curriculums that reflect their own ideological leanings.

However, public education also has the potential to serve as a unifying force, helping to bridge the divides that are pulling American society apart. By teaching students to engage with difficult ideas, respect different viewpoints, and think critically about the world around them, schools can help foster the kind of informed, engaged citizens that a healthy democracy depends on.

The Path Forward

The future of American education will be shaped by how policymakers, educators, parents, and communities choose to navigate the tension between parental rights and academic freedom. These are not easy issues, and there are no simple solutions. However, the stakes are high: the outcome of these debates will determine what kind of education future generations receive and, by extension, what kind of society the United States becomes.

At its best, education can be a powerful force for empathy, understanding, and democratic engagement. By finding a balance between respecting the legitimate concerns of parents and preserving the academic autonomy of schools, the U.S. can ensure that public education remains a place where all students are empowered to learn, grow, and succeed.

Ultimately, the future of education depends on dialogue, compromise, and a shared commitment to ensuring that schools serve the needs of all students—regardless of their background or beliefs. Whether through increased transparency, professional development for teachers, or balanced curriculum design, the path forward will require thoughtful solutions that respect both parental involvement and educational integrity. In doing so, the U.S. can build a public education system that not only reflects the diversity of its citizens but also equips future generations to thrive in a complex and interconnected world.

Conclusion: The Stakes for Education and Democracy

The debates over parental rights, school autonomy, and curriculum control have brought to the forefront critical questions about the role of public education in American society. These issues are not just about which books are banned or which lessons are taught—they are about the kind of society we want to create and the values we seek to pass on to future generations.

At the heart of the conflict is a fundamental question: What is the purpose of public education? Historically, schools have been seen as spaces for teaching children both academic skills and civic values—places where students learn to think critically, engage with diverse perspectives, and prepare to participate in a democratic society. Yet, as these debates illustrate, there is profound disagreement over how that mission should be carried out, particularly when it comes to teaching controversial topics such as race, gender, sexuality, and history.

As the discussion intensifies, it's clear that the stakes are high. The direction that public education takes will have lasting implications for American democracy, social cohesion, and the future of civil discourse. This concluding section examines the key takeaways from this debate, the long-term implications, and what must be done to find common ground.

324 | AMERICAN CHASMS: THE DIVIDED STATES OF AMERICA

Key Takeaways from the Debate

The fierce debates around book bans, curriculum restrictions, and parental control underscore the deep cultural and political divides within the United States. While parents and educators alike are concerned with what is being taught to the next generation, they often come at the issue from opposing viewpoints.

- **Parental Rights and Values.** Many parents—particularly those in conservative communities—want to exert greater control over what their children learn, especially when it comes to topics that conflict with their religious or cultural values. The parental rights movement emphasizes the importance of safeguarding children from what they view as inappropriate or ideologically biased content. The push for laws like Florida's "Don't Say Gay" bill and the banning of books that deal with race, sexuality, or gender identity reflect this desire for more control.

- **Censorship and Academic Freedom.** On the other side, educators and advocates for academic freedom argue that banning books and restricting certain lessons amount to censorship and prevent students from gaining the full, nuanced education they need to navigate an increasingly diverse world. They believe that teaching about race, gender, and LGBTQ+ issues is essential for fostering critical thinking and empathy and that limiting discussions on these topics undermines the core mission of public education.

- **Political Polarization in Schools.** The increasing politicization of education reflects the growing polarization of American society. Schools have become battlegrounds for ideological conflict, with local school boards, state legislatures, and even national politicians getting involved in deciding what should be taught. This trend threatens to turn education into a partisan issue, with students in different states receiving vastly different curricula based on the political leanings of their communities.

Long-Term Implications for Students and Society

The direction that education policy takes in the coming years will have significant and lasting impacts on both students and society at large. Limiting what students can learn in school—whether through book bans or curriculum restrictions—could have profound implications for the future of democracy, social equality, and civic engagement.

- **Students' Ability to Think Critically.** Education plays a central role in developing students' critical thinking skills. When certain subjects are censored or avoided, students are deprived of the opportunity to engage with difficult and complex ideas. This can leave them ill-equipped to navigate the real-world challenges of racism, sexism, inequality, and democracy. In an increasingly globalized world, where diverse perspectives and cultural literacy are essential, students who are not exposed to a broad range of viewpoints may struggle to adapt and thrive.

- **Marginalized Students.** The impact of curriculum restrictions is particularly significant for marginalized students, including LGBTQ+ youth and students of color. When schools limit discussions about gender identity, sexual orientation, or systemic racism, they send a message to these students that their experiences and histories are not valid or worth discussing. This marginalization can lead to feelings of alienation, depression, and, in extreme cases, higher rates of mental health struggles. By fostering inclusivity and representation in education, schools can help all students feel seen, respected, and supported.

- **A Divided Education System.** The increasing politicization of education could lead to a more divided education system, where students in different states or regions are exposed to drastically different curriculums. In some parts of the country, students might receive a more progressive education that emphasizes diversity, inclusion, and social justice, while in others, they may be shielded from discussions about race, gender, or sexual identity. This fragmentation could exacerbate existing political and cultural divides, making it even harder for Americans to find common ground in the future.

- **The Role of Schools in a Democracy.** Perhaps most critically, the debates over what should be taught in schools raise important questions about the role of education in a democratic society. Public schools have traditionally been seen as leveling the playing field, providing all students—regardless of background—with the knowledge and skills they need to participate meaningfully in civic life. If education becomes increasingly politicized, with different communities teaching vastly different curriculums, the country risks losing this shared foundation. Without a common understanding of history, civics, and social issues, it may become more difficult for future generations to engage in civil discourse, address societal challenges, or work together to solve collective problems.

Finding Common Ground: A Path Forward

Given the high stakes of these debates, it is clear that the country must find a way to navigate the tensions between parental control and academic freedom in a manner that respects the rights of parents while upholding the core mission of public education. Doing so will require a combination of transparency, dialogue, and compromise.

The Future of Public Education and Democracy

The ongoing conflict between parental rights and school autonomy reflects deeper divisions within American society, but it also presents an opportunity for meaningful engagement. By fostering open dialogue, protecting academic freedom, and ensuring that students are exposed to diverse perspectives, the U.S. can build an education system that respects the rights of parents while also preparing students to thrive in a complex, diverse, and interconnected world.

The future of public education in the United States will be determined by how these issues are addressed in the coming years. The stakes are not just about what is taught in classrooms but about the kind of citizens the country will produce and the kind of democracy it will preserve. Ensuring that public education continues to serve the needs of all students—and that it remains a place where open inquiry, critical thinking, and civic engagement are valued—will be essential for the future of both education and American society as a whole.

Final Thoughts: Preserving the Integrity of Public Education

As we reflect on the debates surrounding parental rights, school autonomy, book bans, and curriculum restrictions, it is clear that the American public education system is at a critical crossroads. These issues touch on more than just what students are learning—they delve into the very fabric of American democracy and societal values. The challenge now is to navigate these complex, often polarizing discussions in a way that preserves the integrity of public education while addressing the concerns of various stakeholders.

The Importance of Public Education in a Democracy

At its core, public education is the foundation of a functioning democracy. It plays a crucial role in equipping students with the knowledge and skills they need to participate fully in society—not just as workers, but as citizens. Schools are more than places where students learn to read, write, and solve math problems; they are institutions where students learn to think critically, engage with diverse viewpoints, and develop the ability to contribute meaningfully to democratic life.

The framers of the American education system envisioned public schools as leveling forces—places where students from all backgrounds could come together and learn how to navigate a complex world. In a democracy, where citizens are expected to make informed decisions on everything from voting to community engagement, the role of education is to create critical thinkers, empathetic individuals, and active participants in society.

By engaging with diverse perspectives on history, social issues, and civic responsibilities, students are better prepared to become informed, engaged citizens. They learn to grapple with complexity, to listen to differing viewpoints, and to think for themselves. This is why it is so crucial to preserve the academic freedom of teachers and to ensure that students have access to a broad range of ideas and materials, even when those ideas are challenging or uncomfortable.

The Risk of Censorship and Fragmentation

The rise of book bans and curriculum restrictions represents a troubling trend toward censorship that threatens to limit students' exposure to the full spectrum of knowledge and experience. When certain books are banned or specific topics are deemed off-limits, students lose out on the opportunity to engage with important aspects of history, literature, and society. This can have long-term consequences, not only for their education but for their ability to participate meaningfully in democratic life.

Moreover, the increasing politicization of education threatens to fragment the public school system along ideological lines. As states and school districts impose their own interpretations of what can or cannot be taught, we risk creating a system where students in one part of the country are learning vastly different things than their peers in another. This could exacerbate existing social and political divides, making it even harder for Americans to find common ground in the future.

Striking a Balance: The Path Forward

The key challenge for the future of public education is finding a balance between parental involvement and school autonomy. Both parents and educators play vital roles in shaping children's education, and both perspectives must be respected. Moving forward, it is essential to create policies that allow parents to feel involved in their children's education while still preserving the professional expertise of teachers and the integrity of the curriculum.

Possible Steps Toward Striking This Balance

- **Fostering Open Dialogue.** Schools can create opportunities for parents, educators, and administrators to come together and discuss curriculum decisions. By engaging in open, transparent conversations, schools can build trust with parents and help them understand why certain topics are being taught. This can also provide a forum for parents to voice their concerns and collaborate with educators on solutions that respect both family values and educational standards.

- **Transparency and Access.** Providing parents with greater access to curriculum materials—whether through online platforms or parent-teacher meetings—can help demystify what is being taught in the classroom. Transparency helps build trust and allows parents to feel more involved without compromising the educational goals of the school.

- **Opt-Out Provisions.** In cases where parents have deeply held concerns about specific lessons, providing opt-out provisions for certain classes can be a compromise that respects parental wishes without limiting the educational experience for other students. However, care must be taken to ensure that these opt-outs do not stigmatize students who participate or lead to a diluted curriculum for the majority.

- **Supporting Teachers.** Teachers need support from both policymakers and school administrations to ensure they have the resources, training, and professional autonomy necessary to teach complex subjects effectively. Professional development opportunities can equip teachers with the tools they need to navigate sensitive topics in a way that fosters understanding and empathy, while respecting the diverse backgrounds of their students.

- **Upholding Academic Freedom.** Protecting academic freedom is essential for maintaining the quality and integrity of public education. Schools must remain places where students can explore diverse ideas, ask difficult questions, and engage with the full range of human knowledge and experience. Efforts to ban books or limit discussions on certain topics undermine this mission and risk turning schools into environments of intellectual conformity rather than places of discovery and growth.

Ensuring Equity in Education

As we navigate these debates, it is also crucial to ensure that equity remains at the forefront of education policy. Marginalized students—whether they are students of color, LGBTQ+ students, or those from low-income families—must have access to an education that recognizes and affirms their identities and experiences. Representation matters, and schools must continue to be places where all students feel seen, heard, and valued.

In an increasingly diverse society, education must reflect that diversity—not just in terms of who is in the classroom, but in terms of what is being taught. By providing all students with an education that acknowledges the complexities of history, society, and identity, schools can help foster a more inclusive, empathetic, and just society.

The Future of Public Education

The future of public education in America will depend on our ability to address these challenges in a way that prioritizes the needs of students. While the debates over parental rights, curriculum control, and censorship are likely to continue, it is essential that we find ways to work together in the best interests of children.

Public schools should be places where critical thinking is nurtured, diverse perspectives are embraced, and students are prepared to navigate a complex and ever-changing world. They should be spaces where students learn to engage with difficult ideas, listen to others with empathy, and form their own informed opinions.

If we can preserve these ideals while addressing the concerns of parents and communities, public education in America can continue to serve its foundational role: preparing the next generation of citizens to thrive in a democracy.

At a time when American society is more divided than ever, public education remains one of the few institutions that can bring people together. By ensuring that schools remain places of open inquiry, intellectual freedom, and inclusivity, we can help build a future where all students—regardless of their background—have the opportunity to learn, grow, and succeed.

The road ahead will require compromise, collaboration, and a shared commitment to the ideals of public education. But if we rise to the challenge, we can create an education system that truly serves the needs of all students, while upholding the core values of freedom, equality, and democratic engagement that are the foundation of American society.

Economic Inequality, Wealth Redistribution, and the Battle Between Capitalism and Socialism

Introduction: The Growing Divide

Economic inequality has become one of the defining issues of modern America, with the gap between the rich and the poor widening at an alarming rate. Over the past few decades, the distribution of wealth in the United States has shifted dramatically, leading to a concentration of wealth among the top 1% while the middle and working classes struggle with stagnant wages, rising costs of living, and increasing economic uncertainty. This growing divide has not only affected the lives of millions of Americans but has also reshaped the political landscape, fueling a heated debate over how to address inequality and what role the government should play in redistributing wealth.

The numbers tell a striking story. According to a 2021 report by the Economic Policy Institute, the top 1% of earners in the U.S. now hold more wealth than the bottom 90% combined. This growing disparity is driven by multiple factors, including tax policies that have disproportionately favored the wealthy, the rise of globalization and automation, and the declining power of labor unions. For many Americans, the American Dream—the idea that hard work can lead to upward mobility and financial security—feels increasingly out of reach.

This has led to a deeply polarized political debate. On one side, progressive leaders like Senator Bernie Sanders and Representative Alexandria Ocasio-Cortez argue that the U.S. must implement wealth redistribution policies to address inequality. They propose higher taxes on the wealthy, stronger social safety nets, universal healthcare, and student loan forgiveness as ways to help level the playing field. On the other side, critics, particularly those on the conservative and libertarian wings, warn that such policies could stifle economic growth, discourage entrepreneurship, and lead to excessive government intervention. They argue that a capitalist system rewards innovation and hard work and that government efforts to redistribute wealth would undermine the very engine of economic prosperity.

At the heart of this debate is a fundamental clash of ideologies—capitalism versus socialism. Increasingly, the discussion about economic inequality in America is framed as a choice between these two systems. Progressives advocate for democratic socialism, where the government plays a stronger role in ensuring economic fairness, while conservatives defend free-market capitalism, arguing that individual liberty and market competition are the keys to economic success.

Here, I explore the various dimensions of this debate, examining the historical context of economic inequality in America, the arguments for and against wealth redistribution, and the broader ideological battle between capitalism and socialism. We will also look at the social and political consequences of rising inequality and explore potential solutions for addressing the growing rich-poor divide in a way that balances the need for fairness with the importance of economic freedom.

Historical Context: The Evolution of Economic Inequality in America

Economic inequality in the United States has evolved significantly over the past century, shaped by a complex interplay of historical events, public policies, and economic trends. While inequality has always existed in varying degrees, the current levels of wealth concentration and income disparity are historically unprecedented and reflect deep structural shifts in the American economy.

Economic Inequality Over Time

The U.S. economy has experienced several periods of rising and falling inequality. In the early 20th century, during the Gilded Age, inequality was rampant as industrialists like Andrew Carnegie, John D. Rockefeller, and J.P. Morgan accumulated vast fortunes. Wealth was highly concentrated among a small elite, while factory workers and immigrants faced low wages, poor working conditions, and little economic mobility. During this time, unregulated capitalism allowed for significant exploitation of labor, leading to increased class tensions and social unrest.

The Great Depression in the 1930s, however, shifted the trajectory of inequality in America. In response to the economic collapse, President Franklin D. Roosevelt introduced the New Deal, a series of government programs and reforms designed to stabilize the economy and provide a social safety net for struggling Americans. This included Social Security, unemployment insurance, and significant infrastructure investments that created jobs. Alongside these policies, the government implemented progressive taxation and stronger labor protections, which helped to reduce income inequality and usher in a period of economic growth that was more broadly shared.

The mid-20th century, particularly the years following World War II, is often referred to as the "Golden Age of Capitalism." Between the 1940s and 1970s, the U.S. economy experienced unprecedented growth, and the gains were more evenly distributed than at any other time in American history. A strong manufacturing sector, high union membership, and rising wages meant that the middle class thrived. During this period, income inequality was relatively low, and the gap between the rich and the poor narrowed significantly. The American Dream seemed achievable for many, as homeownership rates rose, and families experienced increasing standards of living.

The Wealth Gap Today

However, starting in the late 1970s, the trend toward greater equality began to reverse. Economic inequality has steadily risen since then, largely due to a combination of policy changes, globalization, and technological advancements. Several key developments during this period contributed to the widening wealth gap:

- **Tax Cuts for the Wealthy.** During the 1980s, President Ronald Reagan championed a series of tax cuts that disproportionately benefited the wealthy. Known as Reaganomics or trickle-down economics, these policies were based on the idea that lowering taxes on the rich and corporations would encourage investment and economic growth, ultimately benefiting everyone. However, critics argue that these tax cuts primarily enriched the wealthiest Americans while leading to rising deficits and cuts to social programs that disproportionately affected the poor and working class.

- **Globalization and the Decline of Manufacturing Jobs.** As the U.S. economy became more globalized in the late 20th century, many manufacturing jobs were outsourced to countries with cheaper labor. This led to the decline of industries that had previously provided good-paying jobs for middle-class Americans, particularly in the Midwest and South. Meanwhile, workers in sectors like finance, technology, and high-skilled services saw their incomes rise significantly, further widening the gap between high- and low-income workers.

- **Technological Advancements and Automation.** The rise of automation and digital technologies has also contributed to economic inequality. While technological advancements have increased productivity and created new industries, they have also displaced many low-skilled workers. Jobs in manufacturing, retail, and clerical work, which once provided stable employment for millions of Americans, have been increasingly automated.

At the same time, highly skilled workers in technology and finance have seen their wages skyrocket, exacerbating the wealth divide.

- **Decline of Labor Unions.** Throughout the mid-20th century, labor unions played a critical role in protecting workers' rights, negotiating for better wages, and ensuring fair working conditions. However, union membership has been in steady decline since the 1980s, due in part to policies that weakened labor protections and empowered employers to resist unionization efforts. As unions have weakened, workers' bargaining power has diminished, contributing to wage stagnation and growing income inequality.

- **Stagnant Wages.** While the wealthiest Americans have seen their incomes rise exponentially in recent decades, wages for most workers have stagnated. The Economic Policy Institute reports that from 1979 to 2020, wages for the top 1% increased by 160%, while wages for the bottom 90% grew by only 26%. As the cost of living has continued to rise, especially in areas like housing, healthcare, and education, many middle- and low-income families have found it increasingly difficult to maintain their standard of living.

The Role of Policy in Widening Inequality

Public policy has played a significant role in shaping the current state of economic inequality. Over the past 40 years, a combination of deregulation, tax cuts for the wealthy, and weakened labor protections has contributed to the growing concentration of wealth at the top.

- **Tax Policy.** The U.S. tax system has become less progressive over time, with significant reductions in the top income tax rate and corporate taxes. The Tax Cuts and Jobs Act of 2017, for example, lowered the corporate tax rate from 35% to 21%, while also reducing taxes for the wealthiest individuals. While proponents of these tax cuts argue that they spur economic growth, critics contend that they exacerbate inequality by primarily benefiting the wealthy and leaving fewer resources for social programs.

- **Wealth and Capital Gains.** In addition to lower income taxes, the wealthy benefit disproportionately from tax breaks on capital gains, which are taxes on profits from investments. Because wealthy individuals derive much of their income from investments, rather than wages, they are taxed at lower rates than middle- and low-income earners, who rely primarily on wages for their income. This creates a system in which the rich can accumulate wealth faster than the average worker.

- **Corporate Influence and Lobbying.** Corporate interests and wealthy individuals wield significant influence over U.S. politics through lobbying and campaign donations. This has led to policies that favor the interests of the wealthy, such as deregulation of industries, tax breaks for corporations, and weakened labor laws. Many progressives argue that this has contributed to a system of crony capitalism, in which wealth and power are increasingly concentrated among a small elite.

The New Gilded Age?

Given these trends, many analysts argue that the U.S. is now experiencing a second Gilded Age—a period characterized by extreme wealth inequality, political corruption, and social stratification. The top 1% of earners in America hold an increasingly disproportionate share of the nation's wealth, while the middle class continues to shrink and poverty rates remain stubbornly high. For many, the gap between the American ideal of equal opportunity and the reality of entrenched inequality has never been wider.

Today, policymakers and activists are grappling with how to address this inequality and what measures are necessary to restore a sense of fairness and opportunity in the American economy. As we move forward, the debate over how to redistribute wealth—whether through higher taxes, expanded social programs, or more radical economic reforms—will play a crucial role in shaping the future of the country.

The Case for Wealth Redistribution

As economic inequality in the United States has reached historically high levels, calls for wealth redistribution have gained momentum, particularly among progressive politicians, activists, and economists. Advocates for redistribution argue that the current system disproportionately benefits the wealthy at the expense of the middle and lower classes, leading to a society where opportunities are increasingly unequal. In response, they propose policies aimed at reducing income inequality, expanding social safety nets, and ensuring that all Americans have access to basic resources like healthcare, education, and housing.

Wealth redistribution is seen by its proponents not as an attack on wealth itself but as a necessary measure to restore fairness in the economy and to address the deep structural inequalities that limit social mobility and economic opportunity for millions of Americans. These advocates point to several key policy proposals that could help close the wealth gap and create a more equitable society.

Progressive Proposals for Redistribution

Higher Taxes on the Wealthy

One of the most prominent and widely debated proposals for wealth redistribution is to increase taxes on the wealthiest Americans and large corporations. Progressives argue that the rich should pay a greater share of their income in taxes to help fund public services and reduce the burden on middle- and lower-income households.

- **Wealth Tax.** Senator Elizabeth Warren has been a leading proponent of a wealth tax on the ultra-rich. Her proposal would impose a 2% annual tax on households with wealth exceeding $50 million and a 3% tax on wealth above $1 billion. Warren's plan is designed to target the assets of the wealthiest Americans, who often accumulate their wealth through investments, real estate, and other assets that are taxed at lower rates than income. She argues that this tax would generate significant revenue that could be used to fund social programs like universal childcare, student debt cancellation, and infrastructure improvements.

- **Income Tax Increases.** Progressives, including Senator Bernie Sanders, have also proposed raising the top marginal tax rate on income for the wealthiest earners. For example, Sanders has advocated for a 52% tax rate on income above $10 million. The idea behind higher income taxes for the rich is to reduce the concentration of wealth at the top and ensure that the wealthiest Americans contribute more to the public good.

- **Corporate Taxation.** Another key element of wealth redistribution involves closing corporate tax loopholes and increasing the tax rate on large corporations. Progressives argue that many of the world's largest corporations, such as Amazon and Apple, pay little to no taxes due to loopholes, offshore tax havens, and tax breaks. Restoring corporate taxes to pre-2017 levels (when the Tax Cuts and Jobs Act significantly reduced corporate tax rates) is seen as a way to ensure that corporations contribute their fair share to society.

Universal Healthcare

Advocates for wealth redistribution often point to healthcare reform as a critical area where inequality manifests. The U.S. is the only wealthy nation without universal healthcare, and this lack of access disproportionately affects low-income Americans, who struggle to afford rising healthcare costs, insurance premiums, and medical bills.

- **Medicare for All.** One of the most popular proposals among progressives is Medicare for All, a universal, single-payer healthcare system that would replace private insurance with government-funded healthcare for all citizens. Senator Bernie Sanders has been the most vocal advocate for this policy, arguing that healthcare is a human right and that no one should go bankrupt or forgo medical care due to an inability to pay. Sanders estimates that a Medicare for All system would significantly reduce administrative costs and ensure that all Americans have access to quality healthcare.

- **Addressing Health Inequality.** The current system exacerbates economic inequality, as wealthy individuals can afford comprehensive healthcare coverage, while low-income individuals often face crippling debt from medical bills. Universal healthcare would reduce the financial burden on working-class families and ensure that everyone, regardless of income, has access to medical services. By redistributing the costs of healthcare through taxation, proponents argue that Medicare for All would improve public health and reduce inequality.

Student Loan Forgiveness

The rising cost of higher education and the resulting student loan debt crisis have become key drivers of economic inequality in America. Progressives argue that the burden of student debt, which disproportionately affects young people and people of color, makes it more difficult for individuals to build wealth, buy homes, or invest in their futures.

- **Student Loan Forgiveness.** Proposals for student loan forgiveness aim to reduce the financial strain on millions of Americans who are struggling to pay off their debt. President Joe Biden has already enacted a partial forgiveness program that cancels up to $20,000 in federal student loans for eligible borrowers. However, progressives like Sanders and Representative Alexandria Ocasio-Cortez advocate for more comprehensive debt cancellation, with Sanders calling for the cancellation of all federal student debt.

- **Free College.** In addition to debt forgiveness, many progressive lawmakers support the idea of free college or at least making public universities tuition-free. This proposal is seen as a way to reduce the long-term inequality generated by student loans and ensure that all Americans have access to higher education without incurring crushing debt. Proponents argue that by investing in education, the U.S. can help close the opportunity gap and create a more economically mobile society.

Expanding Social Safety Nets

Another critical component of the wealth redistribution agenda involves strengthening social safety nets to ensure that all Americans have access to basic resources, regardless of their economic status.

- **Universal Basic Income (UBI).** One of the more radical proposals for wealth redistribution is the introduction of Universal Basic Income (UBI), a policy in which all citizens receive a regular, unconditional cash payment from the government. Andrew Yang, a former presidential candidate, popularized the idea of a UBI during his 2020 campaign, proposing a $1,000 monthly payment for every American adult. Proponents argue that UBI would provide a financial cushion for low-income individuals, helping to reduce poverty and inequality while also boosting consumer spending and stimulating the economy.

- **Enhanced Unemployment Benefits and Minimum Wage.** Progressives have also pushed for policies such as enhanced unemployment benefits, expanded child tax credits, and increases to the federal minimum wage. Many argue that the current federal minimum wage of $7.25 per hour is insufficient for workers to meet basic living expenses, and advocates have called for raising the wage to $15 per hour to ensure that all full-time workers earn a living wage.

Examples from Other Countries

Advocates for wealth redistribution often point to countries with more robust social safety nets, such as the Nordic countries—Denmark, Sweden, and Norway—as examples of how higher taxes and more generous welfare programs can lead to lower inequality without stifling economic growth. These countries have implemented progressive tax systems, universal healthcare, free or heavily subsidized education, and comprehensive social safety nets. As a result, they consistently rank among the top in the world for quality of life, income equality, and social mobility.

The Nordic model demonstrates that it is possible to balance capitalism with social welfare, creating a system in which economic growth and wealth redistribution coexist. Proponents of wealth redistribution in the U.S. argue that these countries prove that government intervention in the economy can promote greater equity without sacrificing economic dynamism.

Challenges and Criticisms

While the case for wealth redistribution is compelling to many, it also faces significant challenges and criticisms. Opponents argue that policies like higher taxes on the wealthy, universal healthcare, and student loan forgiveness could have unintended consequences, such as slowing economic growth, discouraging entrepreneurship, and increasing government debt. Additionally, many conservatives and libertarians view wealth redistribution as an infringement on personal freedom and a move toward socialism, which they believe would harm the free-market economy.

Nevertheless, supporters of redistribution argue that the current system is unsustainable and that addressing inequality is not only a matter of economic justice but also essential for maintaining social cohesion and democratic stability. As the wealth gap continues to grow, they contend that re-distributive policies are necessary to ensure that all Americans have the opportunity to thrive.

The Case Against Wealth Redistribution

While proposals for wealth redistribution have gained traction among progressives, they face significant resistance from conservative and libertarian critics. Opponents of wealth redistribution argue that such policies—whether in the form of higher taxes on the wealthy, universal healthcare, or student loan forgiveness—risk undermining the very foundations of economic growth, personal freedom, and entrepreneurship that have long been central to America's prosperity. They contend that wealth redistribution is not only economically harmful but also morally misguided, as it penalizes success and discourages the hard work and innovation that drive the economy forward.

This section will explore the key arguments against wealth redistribution, focusing on concerns about economic growth, the dangers of government overreach, and the long-term social consequences of expansive welfare programs.

No. 1 — Economic Growth Concerns

One of the most frequently cited arguments against wealth redistribution is that it could stifle economic growth by reducing incentives for investment and innovation. Critics argue that policies like higher taxes on the wealthy or large corporations could discourage the wealthy from investing in new businesses, hiring workers, or taking the financial risks that are essential to economic dynamism.

- **Impact on Investment and Job Creation.** Wealthy individuals and corporations are often the primary drivers of investment and job creation in the economy. By raising taxes on the wealthiest earners, opponents argue, the government risks diverting capital away from productive uses such as building new factories, expanding operations, or funding startups. Critics point out that venture capital and private investment are crucial for financing innovation and growing businesses, which in turn create jobs and spur economic growth. Higher taxes on income or wealth could reduce these investments, leading to slower economic expansion.

- **Trickle-Down Economics.** Many conservatives subscribe to the theory of trickle-down economics, which holds that when the wealthy and businesses prosper, the benefits eventually "trickle down" to the rest of society through job creation, higher wages, and increased consumer spending. They argue that efforts to redistribute wealth by taxing the rich will disrupt this process and hurt the very people wealth redistribution policies are intended to help—workers and the middle class. According to this view, a thriving free-market economy is the best way to lift people out of poverty, not government intervention or wealth redistribution.

- **Innovation and Risk-Taking.** Critics also warn that wealth redistribution could discourage entrepreneurship and risk-taking by reducing the financial rewards for success. High taxes on the wealthy, they argue, undermine the incentive to take risks, start new businesses, and innovate—activities that are essential for driving economic growth. By penalizing success, they contend, the government risks dampening the creative energy and ambition that fuel the economy.

No. 2 — Government Overreach and the Risk of Bureaucracy

Opponents of wealth redistribution often argue that such policies lead to excessive government intervention in the economy, which they believe is both inefficient and counterproductive. In their view, government programs aimed at redistributing wealth—whether through taxation, universal healthcare, or social safety nets—often involve large bureaucracies that are prone to waste, inefficiency, and corruption.

- **Inefficient Bureaucracy.** Critics point to the administrative costs and inefficiencies associated with large government programs as a reason to oppose wealth redistribution. They argue that the private sector is generally more efficient than government agencies at allocating resources, creating jobs, and providing services. When the government becomes too involved in redistributing wealth, it often creates layers of bureaucracy that make programs less efficient and more costly to taxpayers. For example, critics of Medicare for All argue that the program would require a massive expansion of the federal government and could result in long wait times, lower-quality care, and higher taxes for everyone.

- **Government Dependency.** Another concern is that expanding welfare programs could create a culture of dependency on government aid. Critics argue that when individuals rely too heavily on government benefits—such as unemployment insurance, food stamps, or housing subsidies—they may lose the incentive to work, save, or invest in their own futures. In the long term, they believe that this could lead to economic stagnation and a reduction in personal responsibility, as individuals become more dependent on government assistance rather than pursuing economic self-sufficiency.

- **Centralized Control vs. Individual Freedom.** Conservatives and libertarians also view wealth redistribution as an infringement on individual freedom. They argue that re-distributive policies grant the government too much control over the economy, allowing it to pick "winners and losers" and dictate how wealth should be distributed. From this perspective, government redistribution undermines the principles of a free-market economy, where individuals are rewarded based on their skills, effort, and entrepreneurial spirit, rather than government fiat. By centralizing economic decisions, critics warn, wealth redistribution leads to less freedom and more state control over citizens' lives.

No. 3 — The Morality of Wealth Redistribution

Beyond concerns about economic growth and government overreach, critics of wealth redistribution often make a moral argument against such policies. They contend that redistributing wealth from the rich to the poor is fundamentally unjust because it involves taking resources from individuals who have earned them and giving them to others who have not.

- **Penalizing Success.** Opponents argue that wealth redistribution unfairly penalizes success and hard work. In a capitalist system, individuals who succeed financially—whether through entrepreneurship, innovation, or investment—should be rewarded for their efforts. By taxing the wealthy at higher rates or imposing a wealth tax, the government is effectively punishing those who have worked hard to achieve financial success. According to this view, individuals should have the right to keep the wealth they have earned, and it is morally wrong for the government to forcibly redistribute it to others.

- **Rewarding Mediocrity.** Critics also argue that re-distributive policies can create perverse incentives by rewarding individuals for not working as hard or taking as many risks. When the government provides benefits to individuals regardless of their effort—such as through universal basic income or expanded welfare programs—it may reduce the motivation for individuals to strive for success. In the long run, critics warn, this could lead to a less productive society where individuals rely on government handouts rather than contributing to the economy through hard work and innovation.

- **Charity vs. Coercion.** Many conservatives and libertarians argue that helping the poor and disadvantaged is a moral obligation, but they believe that this should be done through voluntary charity rather than government coercion. They contend that private individuals, charities, and religious organizations are better equipped to provide assistance to those in need, as they can do so more efficiently and with a deeper understanding of local needs. Forcing wealth redistribution through taxation, in their view, undermines the voluntary nature of charitable giving and replaces it with a system of coercion, where individuals are compelled to support government programs they may not agree with.

No. 4 — Long-Term Consequences for Society

Critics of wealth redistribution also express concerns about the long-term social consequences of policies aimed at leveling the economic playing field. They warn that wealth redistribution can lead to a culture of entitlement, where individuals come to expect government assistance as a permanent fixture in their lives, rather than as a temporary safety net.

- **Undermining Work Ethic.** One of the primary criticisms is that wealth redistribution policies can erode the work ethic that has historically been a cornerstone of American society. By providing generous social benefits, critics argue, the government may reduce the incentive for individuals to work hard, save, and invest in their future. Over time, this could lead to a less dynamic economy, as individuals become more dependent on government aid and less motivated to improve their own economic situation.

- **Social Tensions and Polarization.** Opponents also warn that wealth redistribution can exacerbate social tensions and lead to greater political polarization. When the government takes wealth from one group to give to another, it can create resentment among those who feel they are being unfairly targeted or punished. This dynamic can contribute to class warfare, with the wealthy and middle-class feeling increasingly alienated from the government and the beneficiaries of redistribution. Critics argue that, rather than fostering social harmony, wealth redistribution may deepen divisions between different socioeconomic groups.

- **European Welfare States as a Cautionary Tale.** Finally, critics often point to the experiences of European welfare states—particularly in countries like Greece, Italy, and Spain—as cautionary examples of the dangers of excessive wealth redistribution. In these countries, high levels of government spending, coupled with generous social programs, have led to debt crises, high unemployment, and slow economic growth. Opponents of wealth redistribution argue that if the U.S. adopts similar policies, it risks falling into the same trap of economic stagnation and fiscal instability.

The Need for Economic Freedom

Critics of wealth redistribution maintain that the solution to economic inequality lies not in government intervention or forced redistribution but in expanding economic freedom and promoting opportunity for all. They argue that by reducing government regulation, cutting taxes, and allowing businesses to thrive, the economy can grow in a way that benefits everyone—rich and poor alike.

In their view, the focus should be on removing barriers to entrepreneurship, improving access to education and training, and encouraging personal responsibility rather than creating a system in which the government redistributes wealth. By allowing individuals to keep more of what they earn and by fostering a dynamic, competitive economy, they believe that economic inequality can be reduced naturally, without the need for government intervention.

No. 5 — The Role of Capitalism in Shaping Wealth Distribution

Capitalism, as an economic system, has been the dominant force shaping the distribution of wealth in the United States for centuries. Proponents argue that capitalism, driven by market competition and private enterprise, is the most efficient way to generate wealth and improve living standards across society. They credit capitalism with fostering innovation, entrepreneurship, and economic dynamism, which in turn has lifted millions of people out of poverty both in the U.S. and globally.

However, critics point to capitalism's role in exacerbating wealth inequality, concentrating wealth in the hands of a small elite while leaving millions behind. As economic inequality rises, the debate over capitalism's merits and flaws intensifies. This section explores how capitalism has shaped wealth distribution, the arguments in favor of capitalism, and the challenges the system faces in addressing today's economic disparities.

Defending Capitalism: The Engine of Wealth Creation

Proponents of capitalism argue that the system is inherently meritocratic— rewarding hard work, risk-taking, and innovation. They claim that capitalism creates a dynamic economy in which individuals have the opportunity to prosper based on their skills, efforts, and ideas.

Wealth Creation through Innovation and Entrepreneurship

At the heart of capitalism is the belief that private ownership and the ability to generate profit encourage innovation and economic growth. The profit motive drives entrepreneurs and businesses to develop new products, technologies, and services that improve people's lives. From Silicon Valley tech startups to Fortune 500 companies, capitalism has produced some of the world's most innovative and successful enterprises, creating millions of jobs and driving progress in industries ranging from healthcare to renewable energy.

Proponents argue that wealth accumulation in this system is a reflection of success. For example, tech entrepreneurs like Elon Musk, Jeff Bezos, and Bill Gates are seen as examples of how capitalism rewards individuals who create products and services that transform industries. Their wealth, critics say, is a byproduct of the economic value they have generated for society.

Market Efficiency and Consumer Choice

Another core argument in favor of capitalism is its ability to efficiently allocate resources through the free market. Unlike centrally planned economies, where the government controls production and distribution, capitalism relies on supply and demand to determine what goods and services should be produced. Consumer choice drives the market, rewarding companies that meet the public's needs and punishing those that fail.

Supporters of capitalism argue that this competitive dynamic not only leads to higher-quality goods and services but also encourages businesses to lower prices, improve efficiency, and innovate in order to stay competitive. In turn, this increases productivity, raises living standards, and helps economic mobility, as people and companies that innovate or provide value to the market are rewarded financially.

Economic Growth and Rising Living Standards

Historically, capitalism has been credited with driving unprecedented economic growth in the U.S. and around the world. The Industrial Revolution and subsequent waves of technological innovation fueled massive increases in productivity, leading to improvements in living standards for many people. For much of the 20th century, the American capitalist system enabled rapid economic expansion, creating millions of middle-class jobs and ensuring that more people had access to education, healthcare, and homeownership.

Advocates argue that even though capitalism creates wealth disparities, it also increases the overall size of the economic pie. They claim that economic inequality is a natural byproduct of this system and that what matters most is ensuring equality of opportunity, not equality of outcomes. According to this view, capitalism creates the conditions for anyone—regardless of background—to succeed through hard work and innovation.

Job Creation and Labor Markets

Capitalism is also seen as the primary driver of job creation, with private businesses employing the majority of the American workforce. Critics of wealth redistribution argue that taxing the wealthy and large corporations at higher rates would reduce the ability of these entities to invest in new ventures and hire workers. In this context, capitalism is viewed as essential for maintaining a dynamic labor market that provides opportunities for employment and advancement.

For example, the rapid growth of tech companies, manufacturing industries, and service sectors has provided millions of jobs. These industries have thrived in a capitalist system that rewards companies for expanding and creating value, which in turn generates employment opportunities across the economy.

Challenges Facing Capitalism: Inequality and Market Failures

While defenders of capitalism highlight its role in creating wealth and driving economic progress, critics argue that the system has significant flaws—particularly when it comes to addressing wealth inequality. The modern capitalist system, they claim, has concentrated wealth and power in the hands of a few, leading to economic disparities that threaten social cohesion.

Concentration of Wealth and Power

One of the primary criticisms of capitalism is its tendency to concentrate wealth at the top. As large corporations and wealthy individuals accumulate more assets, they gain disproportionate influence over the economy and politics. This can lead to monopolies, where a small number of companies dominate entire industries, reducing competition and consumer choice.

For example, the tech giants—Amazon, Google, Apple, and Facebook—have amassed vast market power, allowing them to control large parts of the digital economy and shape public policy through lobbying efforts. Critics argue that this concentration of wealth and power distorts the free market and creates an uneven playing field, where smaller businesses struggle to compete and economic mobility becomes more difficult.

Wage Stagnation and Income Disparities

While capitalism has undoubtedly created wealth, it has not always ensured that this wealth is evenly distributed. In recent decades, wage stagnation has become a major concern, particularly for low- and middle-income workers. Despite rising corporate profits and executive pay, many workers have seen little to no real increase in their wages when adjusted for inflation. This trend has contributed to the growing income gap between the wealthy and the working class.

Critics argue that unregulated capitalism allows corporations to prioritize shareholder profits over the well-being of their employees. For instance, many large companies have engaged in stock buybacks—where profits are used to repurchase shares rather than invest in higher wages or job creation. This practice benefits investors and executives but leaves workers with stagnant wages and limited opportunities for economic advancement.

Market Failures and Externalities

Capitalism's reliance on free markets can sometimes lead to market failures, where the interests of private companies and the public do not align. One example is the issue of environmental degradation and climate change. Many industries, particularly fossil fuel companies, generate profits by externalizing costs onto society, such as pollution, carbon emissions, and resource depletion. Without government regulation, these companies have little incentive to address the long-term consequences of their actions, leading to environmental harm and economic instability.

Additionally, healthcare is often cited as an example of a market failure under capitalism. The U.S. healthcare system, driven by profit, has led to skyrocketing costs, leaving millions of Americans without access to affordable care. Critics argue that capitalism's focus on maximizing profits in the healthcare industry results in unequal access, where the wealthy can afford the best care while the poor are left with inadequate services or crippling debt.

Reforming Capitalism: Addressing Inequality without Abandoning the System

Many argue that capitalism, while imperfect, can be reformed to address its shortcomings and reduce economic inequality. Rather than abandoning the system entirely, some economists and policymakers advocate for market-based reforms that preserve the benefits of capitalism while ensuring that wealth is distributed more fairly.

- **Progressive Taxation and Regulation.** One way to address the excesses of capitalism is through progressive taxation and targeted regulation. By imposing higher taxes on the wealthiest individuals and corporations, the government can generate revenue to fund social programs, infrastructure investments, and public services that benefit the broader population. At the same time, regulations aimed at curbing monopolistic practices, reducing pollution, and protecting consumers can help correct market failures and promote fairness.

- **Corporate Social Responsibility.** In recent years, there has been a growing movement among businesses to embrace corporate social responsibility (CSR), where companies take into account their social and environmental impact. This includes paying fair wages, investing in sustainable practices, and ensuring that workers share in the benefits of economic growth. Advocates of CSR argue that businesses can thrive while also contributing to the well-being of society.

- **Addressing Wage Inequality.** Another potential reform is addressing wage inequality by raising the minimum wage, expanding worker protections, and encouraging companies to share profits more equitably with their employees. Policies such as profit-sharing and employee stock ownership plans (ESOPs) can help workers gain a stake in the companies they work for, aligning their interests with those of shareholders and executives.

Investing in Education and Job Training

Finally, reforming capitalism may require greater investments in education and job training to ensure that all Americans have the skills needed to compete in the modern economy. By improving access to education, particularly for low-income and marginalized communities, policymakers can help bridge the gap between rich and poor, ensuring that more people have the opportunity to succeed in a capitalist system.

Capitalism's Role in Wealth Distribution

Capitalism remains the dominant economic system in the U.S., praised for its ability to create wealth and drive innovation. However, it is clear that capitalism's benefits are not always evenly distributed. While some individuals and businesses amass vast fortunes, others are left behind, struggling with stagnant wages, rising costs, and limited opportunities for economic mobility.

As debates over wealth inequality and wealth redistribution continue, the challenge is finding ways to reform capitalism so that it remains a dynamic engine of growth while ensuring that the benefits of economic progress are shared more broadly. Advocates of capitalism argue that the system can be improved through targeted reforms, rather than abandoned altogether, and that a healthy balance of free markets and government oversight is the key to addressing inequality.

No. 6 — Socialism vs. Capitalism: Ideological Battle Lines

As economic inequality in the United States continues to widen, the debate over how to address this growing divide has increasingly been framed in stark ideological terms. The conversation often pits capitalism against socialism, two opposing economic systems with fundamentally different approaches to wealth distribution, government intervention, and individual freedom. This ideological battle has shaped not only public discourse but also the political landscape, driving polarization as Americans argue over which system offers the best solution to inequality.

Progressive politicians like Senator Bernie Sanders and Representative Alexandria Ocasio-Cortez have brought democratic socialism into the mainstream, advocating for policies that prioritize social welfare and economic justice over the unregulated markets of capitalism. On the other side, conservatives staunchly defend capitalism as a system that rewards hard work, innovation, and individual responsibility, arguing that socialism poses a threat to economic freedom and prosperity.

This section will explore the key ideological arguments in the debate between socialism and capitalism, examining how each side views wealth distribution, government intervention, and the role of the market. It will also look at how this ideological divide has shaped policy proposals and fueled political polarization.

The Rise of Democratic Socialism

In recent years, democratic socialism has gained prominence as a political force in the U.S., particularly among younger voters who are disillusioned with the economic inequality and lack of social mobility under capitalism. Figures like Bernie Sanders and Alexandria Ocasio-Cortez have helped re-frame socialism in a more accessible and less radical way, emphasizing its democratic elements and distinguishing it from authoritarian forms of socialism seen in the past, such as Soviet-style communism.

Democratic socialism, as espoused by these leaders, does not seek to abolish private ownership or market competition entirely. Instead, it advocates for a mixed economy in which the government plays a stronger role in regulating industries, providing universal services, and ensuring that wealth is more fairly distributed. This approach focuses on creating a system that combines the innovation and efficiency of capitalism with the social safety nets and public services typically associated with socialism.

Key Policies of Democratic Socialism

The policy proposals put forward by democratic socialists are rooted in the idea that economic inequality is a systemic problem that requires robust government intervention to correct. Some of the key policies associated with democratic socialism include:

- **Universal Healthcare.** Advocates for Medicare for All argue that healthcare is a human right and that the current profit-driven healthcare system leaves millions of Americans uninsured or under-insured. Under this system, the government would provide comprehensive healthcare to all citizens, eliminating the need for private insurance and significantly reducing the cost of medical care.

- **Free Public Education and Student Loan Forgiveness.** Democratic socialists also support making public universities tuition-free and canceling student debt to give all Americans access to higher education without the burden of crippling debt. They argue that education is essential for social mobility and that no one should be priced out of the opportunity to improve their lives through learning.

- **Progressive Taxation and Wealth Taxes.** Democratic socialists call for higher taxes on the wealthiest individuals and corporations. Proposals such as Elizabeth Warren's wealth tax would impose a tax on households with net worths exceeding $50 million. The revenue from these taxes would be used to fund public services, infrastructure, and social welfare programs.

- **Green New Deal.** In response to climate change, democratic socialists advocate for a Green New Deal, which would involve large-scale investments in renewable energy, sustainable infrastructure, and green jobs. This plan aims not only to combat environmental degradation but also to create millions of jobs and reduce income inequality by prioritizing investments in low-income and marginalized communities.

The Moral Case for Democratic Socialism

At the heart of democratic socialism is a moral argument: that it is unjust for a small minority of people to control the majority of wealth while millions of others struggle to meet their basic needs. Democratic socialists argue that capitalism, left unchecked, leads to exploitation, economic insecurity, and poverty, all of which undermine the social fabric of a democratic society.

From this perspective, wealth redistribution is not about punishing success but about creating a system that ensures everyone has access to the resources they need to live dignified lives. By expanding universal healthcare, affordable housing, and education, democratic socialists aim to create a society in which individuals are not held back by their economic circumstances. In this view, economic justice is a prerequisite for true democracy, as people cannot fully participate in society if they are burdened by poverty or debt.

The Conservative Defense of Capitalism

In contrast, conservatives and free-market advocates see capitalism as the foundation of American prosperity. For them, capitalism is the best system for fostering individual freedom, economic growth, and innovation. Conservatives argue that efforts to expand the government's role in the economy—through wealth redistribution or socialized services—would undermine the incentives that drive people to work hard and create value.

Capitalism as a System of Freedom

For conservatives, capitalism is not just an economic system; it is a reflection of personal liberty. In a free-market economy, individuals have the right to pursue their own economic interests, whether that means starting a business, investing in stocks, or choosing where to work. Private property and free enterprise are seen as essential components of personal freedom, allowing individuals to build wealth, take risks, and innovate without government interference.

In contrast, conservatives view socialism as a system that undermines these freedoms by placing too much power in the hands of the government. They argue that when the government controls major sectors of the economy—such as healthcare or education—it limits individual choice and reduces the efficiency of those industries. For example, conservatives warn that a government-run healthcare system like Medicare for All would result in long wait times, lower-quality care, and higher taxes for everyone, while stifling private-sector innovation in medical treatments and technology.

Rewarding Hard Work and Innovation

Another central tenet of capitalism, according to conservatives, is that it rewards hard work and innovation. In a capitalist system, individuals are free to take risks and reap the rewards of their labor. Entrepreneurs who develop successful businesses can become wealthy, and workers who are highly skilled or industrious can earn higher wages. This system of meritocracy—where people succeed based on their abilities and efforts—creates the conditions for economic growth and upward mobility.

Conservatives argue that wealth redistribution undermines these principles by penalizing success and removing the incentives that drive economic progress. If the government raises taxes on the wealthy to fund social programs, they claim, it reduces the rewards for entrepreneurship and innovation. Similarly, welfare programs that provide financial assistance to low-income individuals can create dependency and discourage people from working or pursuing higher-paying jobs.

The Dangers of Socialism

For conservatives, socialism represents a slippery slope toward government overreach and economic inefficiency. They argue that government-run programs are often bureaucratic and wasteful, leading to higher costs and lower quality than services provided by the private sector. For example, conservatives point to European welfare states—such as Greece and Italy—which have experienced debt crises, high unemployment, and slow economic growth due to their expansive welfare programs and government interventions in the economy.

Moreover, conservatives warn that socialism can lead to the erosion of individual liberty. When the government controls large parts of the economy, it also gains the power to dictate how resources are allocated and how people live their lives. In this view, socialism is not just an economic system but a threat to the freedoms that Americans hold dear.

Polarization of the Debate: Capitalism vs. Socialism in American Politics

The growing divide between those who advocate for democratic socialism and those who defend capitalism has contributed to the broader polarization of American politics. Increasingly, public discourse around economic inequality, wealth redistribution, and government intervention has become deeply ideological, with each side using emotionally charged rhetoric to frame the debate.

Socialism as a Rallying Cry for Progressives

For progressives, socialism has become a rallying cry for addressing the structural inequalities in American society. Leaders like Bernie Sanders and

Alexandria Ocasio-Cortez have galvanized a movement that views capitalism as fundamentally broken, pointing to rising income inequality, unaffordable healthcare, and student debt as evidence of the system's failure. In their view, radical change is necessary to create a more just and equitable society, and democratic socialism offers a path toward that future.

This movement has gained particular traction among younger Americans, who are more likely than previous generations to support socialist policies. According to a 2021 Gallup poll, nearly 40% of Americans now have a favorable view of socialism, with that number rising to 49% among young adults aged 18 to 34. For many in this generation, the economic struggles they have faced—such as student debt, stagnant wages, and the high cost of housing—have made socialism a more appealing alternative to capitalism.

Capitalism as a Conservative Defense

Meanwhile, conservatives have doubled down on their defense of capitalism, framing socialism as a dangerous and un-American ideology. Conservative politicians often invoke Venezuelan-style socialism as a cautionary tale, warning that socialist policies will lead to economic collapse, loss of freedom, and authoritarianism. This narrative has been a central theme in Republican campaigns, where candidates present themselves as defenders of capitalism and limited government.

In the media and public discourse, this ideological divide is often framed as a binary choice between capitalism and socialism, with little room for nuanced discussion of potential reforms or hybrid systems. This framing contributes to the polarization of the debate, as both sides become more entrenched in their positions.

Ideology and Policy in the Wealth Distribution Debate

The ideological battle between socialism and capitalism is not just about economic systems—it's about competing visions for the future of America. On one side, democratic socialists call for government intervention to reduce inequality and ensure that all citizens have access to basic needs like healthcare, education, and housing. On the other, conservatives defend capitalism as a system that rewards hard work, fosters innovation, and upholds individual freedom.

As the debate over wealth distribution continues, it will be shaped by these ideological battle lines, with each side offering a different set of solutions for addressing inequality. However, this binary framing of the debate may also limit the possibility of compromise, as both sides dig deeper into their respective positions. In the next section, we will explore how economic inequality affects society at large and the social and political consequences of a widening rich-poor divide.

No. 7 — The Impact of Economic Inequality on Society

As the gap between the wealthy and the rest of the population grows, the effects of economic inequality ripple across multiple facets of American society. These consequences go beyond financial disparities, impacting social cohesion, political dynamics, public health, and the overall well-being of the country. Economic inequality is not just about the numbers; it influences how people perceive fairness, opportunity, and their ability to achieve the American Dream.

This section explores the wide-reaching effects of economic inequality, highlighting how it impacts social mobility, political polarization, public health, and community trust. It also discusses how a widening divide between rich and poor threatens to destabilize the core values that underpin American democracy.

Erosion of Social Mobility and the American Dream

The idea of the American Dream—the belief that anyone, regardless of background, can achieve success through hard work and determination—has long been a cornerstone of American identity. However, rising economic inequality has raised serious doubts about the attainability of this dream for many Americans.

- **Stagnating Wages and Opportunity Gaps.** In the past, many believed that with dedication and perseverance, they could move up the socioeconomic ladder. But today, wage stagnation, rising living costs, and job automation have eroded the promise of upward mobility for many working- and middle-class families. According to data from the Pew Research Center, real wages for most Americans have barely increased since the 1970s, while the cost of housing, education, and healthcare has skyrocketed. This has made it increasingly difficult for low- and middle-income individuals to improve their financial standing or achieve long-term stability.

- **Intergenerational Inequality.** Economic inequality is also creating intergenerational inequality, where the wealth and opportunities available to individuals are increasingly determined by the economic status of their families. Children born into wealthy households have access to better education, healthcare, and career opportunities, while those from lower-income families face significant barriers to success. As social mobility declines, the notion that anyone can achieve the American Dream becomes less of a reality and more of a myth.

- **Education and the Wealth Gap.** The education system, once seen as a pathway to upward mobility, is also affected by economic inequality. Schools in affluent neighborhoods are often better funded, providing students with more resources, experienced teachers, and extracurricular opportunities. In contrast, underfunded schools in low-income areas struggle to provide even basic educational necessities. This educational inequality perpetuates the cycle of poverty, limiting opportunities for students from disadvantaged backgrounds to compete with their wealthier peers in the job market.

Political Polarization and Social Tensions

The growing divide between the rich and the poor has contributed to a significant increase in political polarization and social tension in the United States. Economic inequality is not just a financial issue—it has become a political battleground, with Americans increasingly divided over how to address it and who is to blame.

- **The Rise of Populism.** Economic inequality has fueled the rise of populist movements on both the left and the right. On the left, populists argue that the government must take drastic measures to reduce inequality, advocating for policies like wealth taxes, universal healthcare, and stronger labor protections. On the right, populist movements often blame globalization, immigration, and government elites for the economic struggles of working-class Americans. Both sides are united in their belief that the current economic system is unfair, but they offer vastly different solutions.

- **Class Warfare and Resentment.** The growing concentration of wealth at the top has led to resentment among those who feel left behind. Many

Americans believe that the wealthy have gained their fortunes through an unfair system, one that prioritizes corporate profits and tax breaks for the rich over the needs of the middle and working classes. This has led to a sense of class warfare, where economic divisions fuel hostility and distrust between different social groups. In an era of increasing polarization, the wealth divide exacerbates existing political divisions, making it harder to find common ground or pursue solutions that benefit everyone.

- **Distrust in Institutions.** Economic inequality also contributes to a growing distrust in institutions, particularly the government. Many Americans believe that the political system is rigged in favor of the wealthy and powerful, with corporate lobbying and campaign finance distorting the democratic process. This perception undermines confidence in democratic institutions and can lead to political instability. A 2018 study by Harvard University found that trust in the U.S. government had fallen to historic lows, with a significant portion of the population believing that the government does not work for ordinary people. When people feel that their voices are not being heard, they are more likely to turn to extreme political movements or disengage from the democratic process altogether.

Public Health and Economic Inequality

Economic inequality has profound effects on public health, with wealth disparities contributing to differences in life expectancy, mental health, and access to healthcare. Research shows that societies with higher levels of inequality tend to have worse health outcomes across the board, regardless of the overall wealth of the country.

- **Life Expectancy and Health Outcomes.** Wealthier individuals typically have access to better healthcare, healthier lifestyles, and the ability to address medical issues early on. In contrast, lower-income individuals are more likely to face chronic diseases, such as diabetes, hypertension, and heart disease, due to a lack of access to affordable healthcare and healthy food options. A 2021 study published in The Lancet found that life expectancy in the U.S. is increasingly divided along economic lines, with people in the wealthiest 1% living up to 15 years longer than those in the poorest 1%.

- **Mental Health and Economic Stress.** Economic inequality also contributes to mental health disparities. Financial stress, job insecurity, and the pressures of living paycheck to paycheck take a toll on mental well-being. Depression, anxiety, and substance abuse are more prevalent in lower-income communities, where individuals face greater economic uncertainty and fewer opportunities for upward mobility. Wealthier individuals, by contrast, have the resources to access mental health care and cope with stress more effectively.

- **Access to Healthcare.** The U.S. healthcare system is one of the most expensive in the world, and millions of Americans, particularly those in lower-income brackets, struggle to afford basic healthcare. Despite the Affordable Care Act expanding coverage, nearly 30 million Americans remain uninsured, and many more are under-insured. Economic inequality exacerbates these disparities, as wealthier individuals can afford top-tier healthcare while poorer individuals delay treatment or avoid medical care due to cost concerns.

Community Trust and Social Cohesion

Economic inequality erodes social cohesion and weakens the trust that binds communities together. When there is a significant gap between the rich and the poor, people tend to become more isolated from each other, both economically and socially.

- **Segregation by Wealth.** Economic inequality often leads to geographic segregation by wealth, where the wealthy live in affluent neighborhoods with better schools, healthcare facilities, and infrastructure, while the poor are concentrated in under-resourced areas. This segregation limits interactions between people from different economic backgrounds, reinforcing stereotypes and perpetuating social divisions. As wealth becomes more concentrated in certain areas, these communities become insulated from the economic realities faced by lower-income neighborhoods, deepening the divide.

- **Loss of Community Trust.** Studies show that societies with high levels of inequality experience lower levels of social trust. When people perceive that wealth and power are concentrated in the hands of a few, they are less likely to trust others and more likely to believe that the system is rigged against them. This erosion of trust makes it more difficult to build strong, cohesive communities and can lead to increased crime, violence, and social unrest.

- **Charitable Giving and Philanthropy.** While wealthier individuals often contribute to charitable causes, critics argue that relying on philanthropy to address inequality is insufficient and can create an imbalance of power. Wealthy philanthropists, like Bill Gates and Jeff Bezos, wield significant influence over public policy through their charitable donations, often dictating which social issues receive attention. Critics contend that while philanthropy can help address specific issues, it cannot replace systemic solutions that address the root causes of economic inequality.

Political Power and Economic Influence

Economic inequality also affects the distribution of political power, with wealthy individuals and corporations exerting disproportionate influence over the political process. This creates a cycle where those with wealth have greater access to policymakers, allowing them to shape laws and regulations in their favor, often at the expense of the broader population.

- **Campaign Finance and Lobbying.** In the U.S., political campaigns are largely financed through private donations, giving wealthy individuals and corporations significant influence over election outcomes. The Citizens United Supreme Court decision in 2010 further expanded the role of money in politics by allowing unlimited corporate spending in elections. As a result, wealthy donors and special interest groups often have more access to politicians and are able to shape policies in ways that benefit their economic interests. This dynamic reinforces economic inequality by creating a feedback loop where the wealthy use their resources to influence policy and protect their own financial interests.

- **Corporate Power.** Large corporations also wield significant political power through lobbying efforts, often pushing for tax breaks, deregulation, and policies that favor their business interests. Critics argue that this concentration of power undermines democratic accountability and makes it more difficult for ordinary citizens to have their voices heard in the political process. When economic policies are shaped by corporate interests, the needs of the broader population—particularly low- and middle-income individuals—are often sidelined.

Inequality's Far-Reaching Effects

Economic inequality is not just an abstract economic issue—it has real and profound consequences for American society. From eroding social mobility to fueling political polarization, economic inequality touches nearly every aspect of life in the U.S. and threatens to undermine the very principles of democracy, fairness, and opportunity that the country was built on.

Addressing economic inequality will require a multifaceted approach that goes beyond simply redistributing wealth. It will involve reforming political institutions, investing in education, addressing healthcare disparities, and finding ways to restore trust and social cohesion in communities across the country.

No. 8 — Potential Solutions to Address Economic Inequality

As economic inequality continues to widen, the search for solutions has become a critical focus for policymakers, economists, and social activists. Addressing this issue requires not only redistributing wealth but also ensuring that the systems responsible for perpetuating inequality are reformed to create long-term economic fairness and opportunity for all. The challenge lies in crafting policies that balance economic growth with social justice, ensuring that efforts to reduce inequality do not stifle innovation or prosperity.

This section will explore a range of policy proposals aimed at addressing economic inequality, including tax reforms, wage increases, education investments, and more radical solutions such as universal basic income. Each of these ideas reflects different strategies for closing the wealth gap while maintaining a dynamic, inclusive economy.

Progressive Tax Reforms

- One of the most frequently proposed solutions to economic inequality is reforming the U.S. tax system to ensure that the wealthiest individuals and corporations contribute a greater share of their income and wealth to public goods and services. Proponents argue that progressive taxation—where higher-income individuals pay a larger percentage of their income in taxes—can help fund programs that benefit the broader population, such as education, healthcare, and infrastructure.

- **Wealth Tax.** A wealth tax has been one of the more high-profile proposals put forward by politicians like Senator Elizabeth Warren and Senator Bernie Sanders. Warren's plan involves a 2% annual tax on households with wealth over $50 million and a 3% tax on wealth above $1 billion. The idea is to target the accumulated assets of the wealthiest Americans, which often escape taxation under the current system. By taxing wealth rather than just income, proponents argue that the government could generate significant revenue for social programs without placing an undue burden on the middle class.

- **Higher Income Taxes for the Wealthy.** Another key aspect of progressive tax reform is increasing the marginal tax rate for the wealthiest earners. For example, Sanders has proposed a 52% tax rate on income above $10 million. The aim of these higher taxes is to ensure that the richest individuals pay their fair share while helping to reduce the concentration of wealth at the top. Historically, the U.S. had much higher tax rates on the wealthy—up to 91% during the Eisenhower administration— which corresponded with strong economic growth and a more equitable distribution of wealth.

- **Corporate Tax Reform.** Many advocates also call for raising taxes on large corporations, especially those that pay little to no federal taxes due to loopholes and offshore tax shelters. Closing these loopholes and raising the corporate tax rate (which was reduced to 21% from 35% by the 2017 Tax Cuts and Jobs Act) could provide additional revenue to fund public services and reduce the tax burden on lower-income households.

Raising the Minimum Wage and Strengthening Worker Protections

Ensuring that workers are paid a living wage is another crucial aspect of addressing economic inequality. Many advocates argue that the current federal minimum wage of $7.25 per hour—unchanged since 2009—is insufficient for workers to meet basic living expenses, particularly in areas with high costs of living.

- **Raising the Federal Minimum Wage.** Progressives have called for raising the federal minimum wage to $15 per hour, a change that would significantly boost incomes for millions of low-wage workers. A higher minimum wage would help reduce poverty and improve economic security for those at the bottom of the income ladder. According to the Economic Policy Institute, a $15 minimum wage would directly benefit 32 million workers, especially women and people of color, who are disproportionately represented in low-wage jobs.

- **Expanding Labor Rights and Union Membership.** Strengthening labor protections and making it easier for workers to unionize is another potential solution. Historically, labor unions played a critical role in negotiating better wages, benefits, and working conditions for employees. However, union membership has declined sharply in recent decades, partly due to anti-union policies and corporate resistance. Reforming labor laws to protect the right to unionize—such as through the PRO Act (Protecting the Right to Organize)—could empower workers to demand higher wages and reduce inequality.

- **Wage Subsidies and Earned Income Tax Credits.** For workers in industries that cannot support a $15 minimum wage, some economists propose alternatives like wage subsidies or expanding the Earned Income Tax Credit (EITC), a refundable tax credit for low- to moderate-income workers. These programs can provide financial support to workers without placing an excessive burden on small businesses that may struggle to afford higher wages.

Investments in Education and Job Training

Education has long been seen as one of the most effective tools for promoting economic mobility and reducing inequality. By improving access to quality education and job training, policymakers can help ensure that more people have the skills needed to succeed in a rapidly changing economy.

- **Universal Access to Higher Education.** Many progressives advocate for tuition-free public colleges and universities, arguing that higher education should be a right, not a privilege. This proposal, championed by figures like Bernie Sanders, would make higher education accessible to all Americans, regardless of their financial background. By reducing the financial barriers to college, the hope is that more students—especially from low-income families—will be able to pursue careers that offer higher wages and greater economic security.

- **Student Loan Forgiveness.** In addition to free college, advocates argue that the government should forgive a portion, if not all, of the existing student loan debt, which now totals more than $1.6 trillion in the U.S. For many borrowers, student loan debt has become a significant financial burden that limits their ability to save, invest, or purchase homes. Forgiving student loans would help reduce wealth disparities, particularly for Black and Hispanic borrowers, who are disproportionately affected by student debt.

- **Job Training and Apprenticeships.** Another critical component of reducing inequality is investing in job training and apprenticeship programs that equip workers with the skills needed for high-demand, high-paying jobs. As industries such as manufacturing and retail become increasingly automated, many workers are being displaced from traditional jobs. Expanding vocational training and re-skilling programs can help workers transition to sectors like technology, healthcare, and renewable energy, where job opportunities are growing.

Universal Basic Income (UBI)

A more radical proposal to address economic inequality is the concept of a Universal Basic Income (UBI), which involves providing all citizens with a regular, unconditional cash payment. Andrew Yang, a 2020 presidential candidate, popularized the idea of UBI in the U.S., proposing a $1,000 monthly payment to every American adult as a way to combat job displacement from automation and ensure a basic standard of living for all.

- **How UBI Works.** Under UBI, every individual would receive a fixed sum of money each month, regardless of their income or employment status. This income could provide a financial cushion for those struggling to make ends meet, reduce poverty, and give people the freedom to pursue education, entrepreneurship, or creative endeavors without the pressure of financial instability.

- **Arguments for UBI.** Supporters argue that UBI could help address the growing economic insecurity faced by many Americans, particularly as automation and artificial intelligence threaten to replace millions of jobs in industries such as transportation, retail, and manufacturing. UBI would provide a guaranteed income floor, allowing people to live with dignity even in the absence of stable employment.

- **Challenges and Criticisms.** Critics of UBI, however, raise concerns about its cost and potential impact on labor markets. Opponents argue that providing unconditional payments could reduce the incentive to work, leading to lower labor force participation. Additionally, the cost of implementing a nationwide UBI would be substantial, potentially requiring tax increases or cuts to other social programs to fund it. Critics also question whether UBI is the most efficient way to address inequality, as wealthier individuals would also receive the payment, even though they may not need it.

Affordable Housing and Anti-Poverty Programs

Ensuring access to affordable housing is another critical component of addressing economic inequality. Rising housing costs in major cities have left many low- and middle-income families struggling to find affordable places to live, exacerbating wealth disparities and contributing to homelessness.

- **Affordable Housing Initiatives.** Proposals to address the housing crisis include expanding the availability of public housing, providing rental assistance, and offering tax incentives for developers to build affordable units. Inclusionary zoning laws, which require a certain percentage of new developments to be set aside for affordable housing, have also been suggested as a way to combat housing inequality and ensure that low-income families have access to desirable areas with good schools and job opportunities.

- **Expanding Anti-Poverty Programs.** In addition to housing, expanding other anti-poverty programs—such as food assistance, childcare subsidies, and unemployment benefits—could help lift millions of Americans out of poverty. Programs like the Supplemental Nutrition Assistance Program (SNAP) and Temporary Assistance for Needy Families (TANF) provide crucial support to low-income households, helping to reduce food insecurity and provide a safety net for families facing economic hardship.

Reforming Campaign Finance and Lobbying Laws

Economic inequality is closely tied to political inequality, with wealthy individuals and corporations wielding disproportionate influence over the political process. Reforming campaign finance laws and lobbying regulations could help reduce the power of money in politics, ensuring that policymakers are more responsive to the needs of the broader population.

- **Public Financing of Elections.** One proposal for reducing the influence of wealthy donors is to implement public financing of elections, where candidates receive government funding for their campaigns, reducing their reliance on private contributions. This would allow candidates to run for office without being beholden to wealthy donors or special interest groups, making the political process more democratic and equitable.

- **Restricting Corporate Lobbying.** Limiting the ability of corporations to influence legislation through lobbying is another potential reform. Many advocates argue that the Citizens United Supreme Court decision—which allows unlimited corporate spending in elections—should be overturned to reduce the influence of money in politics. Strengthening lobbying regulations and requiring greater transparency in corporate donations could help reduce the political power of wealthy interests and ensure that the government works for all citizens, not just the rich.

Building a More Equitable Society

Addressing economic inequality requires a multifaceted approach, balancing wealth redistribution with policies that promote opportunity, economic security, and fairness. Whether through progressive taxation, a higher minimum wage, investments in education, or more radical solutions like UBI, the goal is to create a society where all individuals have the chance to succeed, regardless of their starting point in life.

Implementing these solutions will not be easy. Policymakers will need to navigate political resistance, ensure fiscal sustainability, and find ways to balance economic growth with the need for a fairer distribution of wealth. However, as economic inequality continues to threaten social cohesion and democratic stability, the urgency of addressing these issues has never been greater.

Conclusion: The Future of Wealth Distribution in America

The challenge of addressing economic inequality in the United States is both urgent and complex. The wealth gap between the rich and the poor has reached levels not seen since the Gilded Age, and the consequences of this growing divide are being felt in nearly every aspect of society—economically, socially, and politically. As the wealthiest individuals continue to amass an increasingly disproportionate share of the nation's resources, millions of Americans struggle to make ends meet, find affordable housing, access quality healthcare, and provide for their families.

The future of wealth distribution in America depends on our collective willingness to confront these realities and pursue solutions that balance economic growth with social justice. The question of how to address economic inequality is not just a policy issue—it is a test of the country's values, and it speaks to the kind of society we want to build for future generations.

The Urgency of Addressing Inequality

As we've explored throughout this article, economic inequality poses a serious threat to the social fabric of the United States. The growing concentration of wealth in the hands of a few has created a sense of alienation and disenfranchisement among the broader population, fueling political polarization, eroding trust in institutions, and increasing the risk of social unrest. When large segments of society feel that the system is rigged against them, the very foundations of democracy are put at risk.

Moreover, the impact of inequality on public health, education, and community trust cannot be ignored. Societies with high levels of inequality tend to experience worse health outcomes, greater crime rates, and lower levels of social cohesion. These challenges, if left unaddressed, could lead to a cycle of instability that would make it increasingly difficult for the U.S. to maintain its global leadership and ensure prosperity for all of its citizens.

A Path Forward: Policy and Compromise

The debate over how to address economic inequality is often framed as a binary choice between capitalism and socialism—but the reality is more nuanced. The future of wealth distribution in America likely lies in finding a middle ground—one that preserves the dynamism of a market economy while ensuring that the benefits of growth are shared more equitably.

- **Tax Reforms** that target wealth and corporate profits can help generate revenue for public investments in education, healthcare, and infrastructure without stifling economic innovation. Proposals such as a wealth tax or higher income taxes on the ultra-wealthy could play a pivotal role in reducing inequality and funding social programs that benefit the broader population.

- **Wage Reforms** like raising the minimum wage and expanding worker protections can ensure that all workers earn a living wage and share in the prosperity of the economy. Strengthening labor unions and providing incentives for businesses to adopt profit-sharing models can help reduce wage inequality while maintaining the profitability of companies.

- **Investing in Education and Job Training** remains a critical long-term solution to inequality. By improving access to quality education, reducing student debt, and expanding opportunities for vocational training in high-demand industries, we can empower individuals to rise out of poverty and thrive in a rapidly changing economy.

- **Social Safety Nets** such as universal healthcare, affordable housing, and childcare support are necessary to ensure that all Americans have access to basic necessities, regardless of their economic background. These programs can provide the stability families need to pursue economic opportunities, reduce income volatility, and foster greater social mobility.

Finding the right balance between government intervention and market-driven solutions will require compromise and collaboration across the political spectrum. Policymakers must consider both the short-term impacts and long-term goals of any proposed solution, ensuring that efforts to reduce inequality do not unintentionally hinder growth, stifle innovation, or exacerbate existing divides.

The Role of Technology and Globalization

As we look to the future, it's essential to acknowledge the powerful forces of technology and globalization that continue to reshape the economy. Automation, artificial intelligence, and the digital revolution have the potential to create massive disruptions in labor markets, further exacerbating inequality if proactive policies are not implemented.

Automation is expected to displace millions of workers in industries such as manufacturing, retail, and transportation. Policymakers must prioritize re-skilling and job retraining programs to ensure that workers can transition into new roles in emerging sectors like technology, healthcare, and renewable energy.

Globalization, while it has lifted millions out of poverty around the world, has contributed to job losses in certain sectors of the U.S. economy, particularly for low- and middle-income workers. The U.S. must strike a balance between embracing the benefits of global trade and protecting vulnerable industries and workers from the adverse effects of outsourcing and offshoring.

By recognizing and addressing the challenges posed by these economic forces, the U.S. can ensure that the next generation of workers is better prepared to navigate the global economy and that the benefits of technological progress are shared more equitably.

Restoring Trust and Strengthening Democracy

Perhaps one of the most important aspects of addressing economic inequality is restoring trust in American institutions and strengthening the nation's democratic foundations. As wealth becomes more concentrated, the influence of money in politics grows, creating a system in which the voices of ordinary Americans are often drowned out by wealthy individuals and corporate interests.

Reforming campaign finance laws, limiting the influence of corporate lobbying, and increasing transparency in government decision-making are all necessary steps to ensure that policymakers remain accountable to their constituents and that the political process is not dominated by the wealthy elite.

Addressing economic inequality is not just a matter of enacting new policies—it is about ensuring that all Americans feel that they have a fair shot at success, that their voices are heard, and that their government works for them, not just the wealthy and powerful.

A Vision for a More Equitable Future

While the challenges posed by economic inequality are significant, they are not insurmountable. Throughout American history, the nation has faced and overcome periods of intense inequality and social upheaval, often emerging stronger and more unified on the other side. With the right mix of policies, innovative thinking, and political will, the U.S. can build a more inclusive and equitable economy that offers opportunities for all its citizens.

At its core, the fight against inequality is about reaffirming the ideals of the American Dream—the belief that anyone, regardless of background, can succeed if given the chance. By addressing the structural barriers that perpetuate inequality and investing in the future of all Americans, the nation can renew its commitment to fairness, justice, and shared prosperity.

A Call to Action

The future of wealth distribution in America hinges on the choices we make today. Whether through tax reform, wage increases, education investments, or social safety nets, the U.S. must confront the structural inequities that have left so many behind. In doing so, we have the opportunity to re-imagine and rebuild an economy that works for everyone—one that fosters innovation, protects individual freedoms, and ensures that all Americans have the opportunity to thrive.

The path forward will not be easy, and there will be debates, disagreements, and challenges along the way. But the stakes are too high to ignore. In addressing economic inequality, we are not just shaping the future of our economy—we are shaping the future of our democracy and the kind of society we want to leave for future generations.

As we embark on this journey, it is essential that we approach these challenges with a spirit of collaboration, compassion, and resolve, recognizing that the solutions we seek will require both bold action and shared responsibility. Only by working together can we create a future that truly reflects the values of equity, opportunity, and justice for all.

Navigating the Battle Over Abortion Rights in America

Introduction: The Post-Roe Landscape

The abortion rights debate in America has long been one of the most divisive and emotionally charged issues, and it reached a historic turning point in 2022 with the U.S. Supreme Court's decision in Dobbs v. Jackson Women's Health Organization. This ruling overturned Roe v. Wade, the landmark 1973 decision that had established a constitutional right to abortion. For nearly five decades, Roe provided a national framework for reproductive rights, ensuring that women across the country had access to legal abortions, particularly in the first trimester of pregnancy. With the overturn of Roe, the power to regulate abortion was handed back to the states, setting off a cascade of new laws and policies that has reignited the national debate over abortion rights.

The Dobbs decision has transformed the landscape of abortion rights in the U.S., leading to a patchwork of laws where access to abortion now varies dramatically from state to state. In some states, abortion is nearly completely banned, while others have moved to protect or even expand access. This shift has placed reproductive healthcare in the cross-hairs of political battles, legal challenges, and moral debates, reflecting the broader cultural and political polarization in the country.

At the heart of this debate are two deeply entrenched camps: the pro-choice movement, which advocates for a woman's right to make decisions about her own body without government interference, and the pro-life movement, which argues that life begins at conception and that the rights of the fetus must be protected. Each side is driven by fundamentally different views on life, autonomy, and morality, making compromise difficult and intensifying the national divide.

The overturning of Roe has created new political realities. State governments, rather than the federal government, now play the dominant role in shaping abortion policies, and this has resulted in legal battles and state-level legislation that vary widely. While conservative states have implemented near-total bans on abortion, more liberal states have enacted protections for reproductive rights, positioning themselves as sanctuaries for those seeking abortions. The country is now more divided than ever, with the geography of access heavily influenced by local politics, cultural values, and the power of advocacy groups on both sides of the issue.

This essay explores the complex dimensions of the pro-choice vs. pro-life debate, examining the historical context of abortion rights, the arguments from both sides, the state-level battles that have emerged post-Roe, and the broader impact of this issue on American society. In doing so, it will provide a comprehensive understanding of how abortion has become one of the most polarizing issues in the country and what the future might hold for reproductive rights in a post-Roe America.

Historical Context: Roe v. Wade and the Legal Evolution

The abortion rights debate in America did not begin with Roe v. Wade, but the 1973 Supreme Court decision was a pivotal moment that forever changed the legal and political landscape of reproductive rights in the United States. To understand the current state of the pro-choice vs. pro-life debate, it's essential to explore the historical context that led to the Roe decision, the legal challenges it faced over nearly five decades, and how it ultimately culminated in the 2022 Dobbs v. Jackson Women's Health Organization ruling.

Roe v. Wade (1973): Establishing the Right to Choose

In 1973, the Supreme Court handed down its decision in Roe v. Wade, ruling that a woman's right to choose to have an abortion was protected under the Constitution's implied right to privacy. The case was brought by "Jane Roe" (a pseudonym for Norma McCorvey), a Texas woman challenging the state's strict anti-abortion laws. At the time, many states had laws that either severely restricted or outright banned abortion, forcing women to seek illegal and often dangerous procedures.

The Roe decision, by a 7-2 vote, established a constitutional right to abortion and effectively invalidated restrictive state laws that banned abortion outright. The Court held that the right to privacy, derived from the Due Process Clause of the Fourteenth Amendment, extended to a woman's decision to terminate her pregnancy. However, the ruling also balanced this right against the state's interest in protecting potential life and maternal health, establishing a trimester framework;

- **First trimester.** A woman's right to choose an abortion was largely unrestricted, with minimal state interference.
- **Second trimester.** States could regulate abortion procedures in the interest of the mother's health.

- **Third trimester.** States could restrict or even ban abortion, except when the procedure was necessary to protect the life or health of the mother, as the fetus was considered viable.

This ruling represented a major victory for women's rights advocates and solidified abortion access as a key part of the women's liberation movement. However, it also immediately became a rallying point for those who believed that abortion was morally wrong and that life began at conception, giving birth to the modern pro-life movement.

Challenges to Roe: A Decades-Long Legal Battle

Despite its groundbreaking nature, Roe v. Wade was not the end of the debate— it was only the beginning. In the years following the decision, abortion opponents worked tirelessly to restrict access at both the state and federal levels, setting the stage for decades of legal battles.

- **Planned Parenthood v. Casey (1992).** One of the most significant challenges to Roe came nearly 20 years later in Planned Parenthood v. Casey. In this case, the Supreme Court reaffirmed the core holding of Roe that women have a constitutional right to choose an abortion, but it also made significant changes. The Court abandoned the trimester framework in favor of a new "undue burden" standard, which allowed states to impose restrictions on abortion as long as they did not place an undue burden on a woman's right to access the procedure before fetal viability. This opened the door for states to pass more restrictive abortion laws, such as mandatory waiting periods, parental consent requirements, and informed consent laws, as long as they did not impose significant obstacles.

- **Hyde Amendment (1976).** Another significant post-Roe development was the passage of the Hyde Amendment, which banned federal funding for abortion except in cases of rape, incest, or when the mother's life was in danger. This policy, still in place today, limits access to abortion for low-income women who rely on programs like Medicaid for healthcare coverage.

- **State-Level Restrictions.** Over the years, states, particularly in conservative regions, passed increasingly restrictive laws designed to limit access to abortion, test the boundaries of Roe, and bring the issue back to the Supreme Court. These laws included targeted regulation of abortion providers (TRAP) laws, which imposed strict requirements on abortion clinics, forcing many to close; heartbeat bills, which banned abortion after six weeks of pregnancy; and "person-hood" amendments, which sought to grant legal rights to fetuses.

Dobbs v. Jackson Women's Health Organization (2022): Overturning Roe

The culmination of years of pro-life efforts to overturn Roe came in 2022 with Dobbs v. Jackson Women's Health Organization. This case involved a challenge to a Mississippi law that banned most abortions after 15 weeks of pregnancy, well before the point of fetal viability established in Roe. Mississippi's law directly violated the constitutional protections provided under Roe and Planned Parenthood v. Casey, setting up a direct challenge to those precedents.

In a 6-3 decision, the conservative-majority Supreme Court overturned Roe v. Wade in its entirety, declaring that there is no constitutional right to abortion. The Court ruled that the issue of abortion should be left to individual states, as it was before 1973. Writing for the majority, Justice Samuel Alito stated that Roe had been wrongly decided because the Constitution does not explicitly mention abortion, and therefore, the issue should be decided by the democratic process in each state.

With this decision, the legal landscape for abortion in America was fundamentally altered. Dobbs immediately allowed conservative states to enact total or near-total bans on abortion, while liberal states moved to strengthen and protect abortion rights through new laws and constitutional amendments. The overturning of Roe has led to a patchwork of laws across the country, where access to abortion depends largely on where a woman lives, and the battle over reproductive rights has shifted from the courts to state legislatures.

The Aftermath of Dobbs: A New Era for Abortion Rights

The Dobbs decision marks the beginning of a new era for abortion rights in the United States—one that is even more politically charged than before. With states now holding the power to regulate abortion as they see fit, the country is deeply divided between pro-choice states, which have become sanctuaries for women seeking abortions, and pro-life states, many of which have banned the procedure entirely or imposed severe restrictions.

In the wake of Dobbs, the future of abortion rights in America is uncertain, as advocates on both sides continue to mobilize. Pro-choice advocates are fighting for federal protections to restore abortion rights across the country, while pro-life advocates are working to pass more restrictive laws and, in some cases, pushing for a national abortion ban. At the state level, the legal battles over abortion will likely continue for years, and the issue remains at the forefront of American politics.

The Pro-Choice Perspective: Advocating for Women's Autonomy

At the heart of the pro-choice movement is the belief that women should have the right to make decisions about their own bodies without interference from the government or other external forces. Advocates argue that the decision to have an abortion is a deeply personal one that involves complex considerations about health, family, economics, and individual autonomy. Pro-choice advocates see the ability to access safe and legal abortion as a fundamental part of reproductive rights and gender equality, positioning abortion not just as a medical issue, but as a key aspect of women's liberation and empowerment.

With the overturning of Roe v. Wade in Dobbs v. Jackson Women's Health Organization, the pro-choice movement has mobilized to protect and expand access to abortion, especially in states where reproductive rights are under attack. Central to their arguments are the concepts of bodily autonomy, healthcare as a human right, and the need to address the disproportionate impact of abortion restrictions on marginalized communities.

Bodily Autonomy and Reproductive Rights

The cornerstone of the pro-choice argument is the principle of bodily autonomy—the right of individuals to control their own bodies and make decisions about their reproductive health. Pro-choice advocates argue that forcing a woman to carry an unwanted pregnancy to term violates this fundamental right, effectively placing the government or external authorities in control of her body.

- **Personal and Complex Decisions.** Abortion is not a decision that most women take lightly. It often involves consideration of personal circumstances, such as economic stability, existing family responsibilities, health concerns, or the emotional readiness to raise a child. Pro-choice advocates emphasize that women, not politicians or courts, are best positioned to make these deeply personal decisions based on their own values, circumstances, and needs.

- **The Role of Government.** Pro-choice supporters believe that government intervention in personal medical decisions is a dangerous precedent. They argue that banning or severely restricting abortion infringes on the rights of individuals to make private choices about their own bodies. This, they assert, is a fundamental violation of privacy rights as established in Roe v. Wade. While pro-life advocates emphasize the rights of the fetus, pro-choice advocates maintain that a woman's right to self-determination must take precedence, particularly before the point of fetal viability.

Healthcare and Privacy Concerns

Pro-choice advocates frame abortion as a critical healthcare issue. They argue that access to safe, legal abortion is essential for protecting women's health and well-being, and restricting access only pushes women toward unsafe, illegal procedures, which can lead to serious health complications or even death.

- **Safe and Legal Abortions Save Lives.** Before Roe v. Wade, many women resorted to dangerous, unregulated abortions, often leading to serious injuries or fatalities. According to data from the Guttmacher Institute, unsafe abortions are still a leading cause of maternal death in countries where abortion is heavily restricted. Pro-choice advocates argue that legal access to abortion is essential for preventing a return to these unsafe practices. They highlight that safe abortion procedures, when performed by medical professionals, are among the safest medical procedures, with a low complication rate similar to that of minor surgeries like wisdom tooth removal.

- **Privacy and Medical Autonomy.** Abortion advocates also emphasize that abortion is not just about terminating a pregnancy; it's about maintaining the right to medical privacy. The pro-choice movement frames the abortion decision as part of a broader right to medical autonomy, arguing that the government has no place in deciding what healthcare options should be available to individuals. Reproductive healthcare decisions, they argue, should be made by the patient in consultation with her doctor, not by lawmakers or courts.

Impact on Marginalized Communities

One of the central concerns of the pro-choice movement is the disproportionate impact that abortion restrictions have on marginalized communities, particularly low-income women, women of color, young women, and those living in rural areas. The overturning of Roe v. Wade has exacerbated these disparities, as many of the states that have implemented abortion bans or severe restrictions are the same states where access to healthcare is already limited, and social safety nets are weaker.

Economic Barriers. For many low-income women, accessing abortion has always been more difficult due to the costs associated with the procedure, travel, and time off work. Now that abortion is banned or severely restricted in many states, women in these regions often have to travel hundreds of miles to states where abortion is legal, further increasing the financial burden. Pro-choice advocates argue that these barriers disproportionately harm poor women who cannot afford the time or money required to travel for an abortion, forcing them to either carry unwanted pregnancies to term or seek unsafe alternatives.

Racial Inequities. The racial disparities in healthcare are also a critical issue for the pro-choice movement. Black women and Latinas already face significant challenges in accessing quality healthcare, and they are disproportionately affected by maternal mortality and unintended pregnancies. Research from the Center for Reproductive Rights shows that Black women are more than three times as likely to die from pregnancy-related causes as white women, a disparity that will likely worsen in states that have banned or severely restricted abortion. Pro-choice advocates emphasize that these racial inequities are a public health crisis that will only be exacerbated by restricting abortion access.

Young Women and Vulnerable Populations. The inability to access abortion services disproportionately affects teenagers and young women, who may not have the financial means or family support to travel out of state for an abortion. Additionally, victims of rape and incest are among the most vulnerable groups in the abortion debate, as many of the states with the strictest abortion bans offer no exceptions for these circumstances. Pro-choice advocates argue that forcing these women to carry pregnancies to term is not only cruel but also a violation of their fundamental human rights.

Public Opinion on Abortion Rights

Public opinion in the U.S. regarding abortion is complex and often reflects a nuanced spectrum rather than a simple pro-choice vs. pro-life binary. However, polls consistently show that a majority of Americans support the right to access abortion in some form, particularly in the first trimester.

- **Support for Roe v. Wade.** Before its overturning, Roe v. Wade enjoyed broad public support. According to a Pew Research Center survey conducted in 2021, about 60% of Americans said abortion should be legal in all or most cases, while 39% said it should be illegal in all or most cases. Even among those who identify as "pro-life," many support exceptions for cases of rape, incest, or threats to the mother's health, which are often not included in the most restrictive abortion laws.

- **Complex Views on Timing and Restrictions.** While many Americans support the right to abortion, polls also show that opinions on when and how abortion should be accessed vary. For instance, many people are more supportive of abortion in the first trimester but favor restrictions in later stages of pregnancy unless the mother's health is at risk. This complexity reflects the moral nuances that many Americans feel, even if they support legal abortion. Pro-choice advocates argue that legal protections need to reflect the fact that each pregnancy is unique, and decisions should ultimately be left to the individual woman and her doctor.

Mobilization After the Dobbs Decision

The overturn of Roe v. Wade has galvanized the pro-choice movement, spurring new efforts to protect and expand abortion rights across the country. In the wake of the Dobbs decision, pro-choice advocates have shifted their focus to state-level battles and federal legislative efforts.

- **State-Level Advocacy.** With abortion rights now largely determined by state governments, pro-choice advocates are working to pass legislation in blue states that would enshrine the right to abortion in state constitutions. States like California, New York, and Illinois have passed laws that protect or expand access to abortion, while others, like New Mexico and Colorado, have become safe havens for women from neighboring states with restrictive laws. Pro-choice advocates are also fighting legal battles in purple states where access to abortion is contested, such as Michigan and Pennsylvania.

- **Federal Efforts.** At the federal level, pro-choice lawmakers are pushing for the passage of the Women's Health Protection Act, which would codify the protections of Roe v. Wade into federal law, ensuring that abortion rights are protected nationwide regardless of state laws. However, passing such legislation remains difficult given the partisan divide in Congress.

The Fight for Autonomy and Rights

The pro-choice perspective is grounded in the belief that women have the right to make personal decisions about their reproductive health, free from government interference. Advocates argue that abortion access is a crucial component of gender equality, bodily autonomy, and healthcare rights. With the fall of Roe v. Wade, the pro-choice movement is facing its most significant challenge in decades, but it remains committed to protecting and expanding access to abortion, particularly for those who are most vulnerable to the impacts of restrictive laws.

The Pro-Life Perspective: Defending the Rights of the Unborn

The pro-life movement is rooted in the belief that life begins at conception and that unborn children possess an inherent right to life that must be protected. This perspective views abortion as morally wrong, equating it to the taking of an innocent life. Pro-life advocates argue that the protection of fetal life is a moral duty and that society has an obligation to defend the most vulnerable, even if that means restricting or banning access to abortion.

The overturning of Roe v. Wade in 2022 was seen as a significant victory for the pro-life movement, which had been working for decades to reverse the ruling and return the power to regulate abortion to the states. With the Dobbs v. Jackson Women's Health Organization decision, the battle over abortion has shifted to the state level, with pro-life advocates pushing for total or near-total bans on abortion in many conservative states. This section will explore the key arguments of the pro-life movement, including the sanctity of life, the role of religion and ethics, alternatives to abortion, and the public opinion on restrictions.

Belief in the Sanctity of Life

At the core of the pro-life argument is the belief in the sanctity of human life, which holds that life begins at conception and that every human being, regardless of their stage of development, has an inviolable right to life. For pro-life advocates, abortion is not merely a personal choice; it is the destruction of a living human being who deserves the same protections as any other person.

- **Life Begins at Conception.** The pro-life movement is anchored in the conviction that human life begins at the moment of fertilization. This belief is supported by many religious and philosophical traditions, particularly within Christianity, which holds that all human life is sacred from the moment of conception. Pro-life advocates argue that from this point forward, the fetus is a distinct, living human with a unique set of DNA and the potential to develop into a fully formed person. Thus, terminating a pregnancy at any stage is seen as morally equivalent to taking a human life.

- **Moral Responsibility to Protect the Unborn.** From the pro-life perspective, society has a moral obligation to protect those who cannot protect themselves, including unborn children. Many pro-life advocates frame the issue as one of human rights, arguing that just as society works to protect the rights of other vulnerable groups—such as the disabled, the elderly, or those facing oppression—it must also defend the rights of the fetus. For this reason, the movement seeks to enact laws that restrict or ban abortion and promote policies that affirm the value of life at all stages.

Religious and Ethical Foundations

While not all pro-life advocates base their views on religion, faith plays a central role in shaping the pro-life movement's ethical framework. Many of the most vocal pro-life organizations and individuals come from religious backgrounds, particularly from Catholic and Evangelical Christian communities.

Religious Teachings on Life: Christian doctrine—especially as interpreted by Catholic and Evangelical churches—asserts that life is a gift from God and that every human being is created in the image of God. As such, the destruction of innocent life through abortion is seen as a violation of God's will and a fundamental breach of moral law. The Catholic Church, in particular, has long opposed abortion, teaching that life must be respected and protected from conception until natural death.

- **Ethical Arguments.** Beyond religious beliefs, some pro-life advocates rely on secular ethical arguments to oppose abortion. These arguments often focus on the principle of human dignity, asserting that all humans, regardless of their stage of development, possess an inherent value that society must respect. Pro-life philosophers, such as Robert P. George and Francis Beckwith, have argued that abortion is morally wrong because it violates the rights of the unborn to life, which they consider to be the most fundamental of all human rights.

- **Moral Absolutism.** Many pro-life advocates take a moral absolutist stance on abortion, viewing it as categorically wrong in all cases. They reject the idea that the circumstances of conception—such as rape or incest—or concerns about the mother's financial or emotional readiness justify terminating a pregnancy. From this perspective, the rights of the fetus take precedence over the personal considerations of the pregnant woman, and ending a pregnancy is never an ethical option.

Alternatives to Abortion

The pro-life movement does not only seek to restrict or ban abortion; it also advocates for alternatives that support women facing unplanned pregnancies. Adoption, parental support, and crisis pregnancy centers are central to the movement's efforts to provide women with options other than abortion.

- **Adoption as an Alternative.** Pro-life advocates frequently promote adoption as a compassionate alternative to abortion, offering women the opportunity to give birth and place their child in the care of families who are eager to adopt. Many pro-life organizations run adoption services or provide resources to help connect pregnant women with adoptive families. They argue that adoption not only preserves the life of the unborn child but also provides a solution for women who feel unprepared or unable to raise a child themselves.

- **Parental Support and Counseling.** To address the economic and social pressures that often lead women to seek abortions, the pro-life movement also advocates for providing greater support to pregnant women and new mothers. Crisis pregnancy centers—nonprofit organizations that offer free services such as pregnancy counseling, prenatal care, and parenting classes—are a key component of this strategy. These centers aim to help women navigate the challenges of pregnancy and early motherhood, with the goal of reducing the perceived need for abortion by offering tangible resources and emotional support.

- **Government Policies Supporting Families.** Some pro-life advocates also support policies that provide financial aid and social support for families, including paid parental leave, childcare subsidies, and expanded healthcare access for pregnant women. These advocates argue that creating a pro-family culture and strengthening social safety nets can reduce the demand for abortion by making it easier for women to choose to carry their pregnancies to term.

Public Opinion on Abortion Restrictions

While the pro-life movement seeks to restrict or ban abortion entirely, public opinion on the issue is more nuanced. Surveys consistently show that Americans are divided on abortion, with many supporting restrictions but not outright bans.

- **Support for Restrictions on Abortion.** Many Americans, even those who do not identify as strictly pro-life, support restrictions on abortion after a certain point in pregnancy, particularly in the second and third trimesters. According to a 2021 Gallup poll, 48% of Americans believe abortion should be legal only under certain circumstances, while 32% believe it should be legal in all circumstances, and 19% believe it should be illegal in all circumstances. This indicates that a significant portion of the public favors limits on abortion, particularly later in pregnancy, when the fetus is seen as closer to viability.

- **Exceptions for Rape, Incest, and Health of the Mother.** Many pro-life advocates support exceptions to abortion bans in cases of rape, incest, or when the mother's life is in danger. However, some more absolutist factions of the movement oppose even these exceptions, arguing that all unborn children have the right to life regardless of how they were conceived or the circumstances surrounding the pregnancy. These internal divisions within the pro-life movement reflect broader societal debates about the moral complexities of abortion.

- **Growing Influence of Pro-Life Legislation.** In the wake of the Dobbs decision, many states have passed or are working to pass "heartbeat bills", which ban abortion after six weeks of pregnancy, or even total bans with limited exceptions. These laws are in line with pro-life advocacy for protecting fetal life as early as possible. However, these stringent restrictions have also sparked legal challenges and resistance in states with more pro-choice leanings, highlighting the ongoing legal and cultural battles over abortion.

The Role of Men in the Pro-Life Movement

A unique aspect of the pro-life perspective is the emphasis on the role of fathers and men in the abortion debate. Pro-life advocates argue that men, as fathers, have a responsibility to be involved in decisions regarding their unborn children and to support both the woman and the child.

- **Fatherhood and Responsibility.** Some pro-life organizations focus specifically on promoting responsible fatherhood and encouraging men to support pregnant women by providing emotional, financial, and practical help. They believe that by engaging men in the conversation about pregnancy and abortion, society can promote a more holistic view of family responsibility that emphasizes the role of both parents in raising a child.

- **Men's Rights in Abortion Decisions.** A small but vocal segment of the pro-life movement advocates for the inclusion of men in abortion decisions, arguing that fathers should have a say in whether or not an abortion takes place. While this viewpoint is controversial and not widely accepted, it highlights the broader belief within the pro-life movement that abortion is not solely a women's issue, but one that affects entire families.

Protecting the Unborn

The pro-life perspective is deeply rooted in a commitment to protecting the unborn and upholding the sanctity of life. Advocates argue that society has a moral obligation to defend those who cannot defend themselves, including unborn children, and that abortion is an unjust taking of human life. With the overturn of Roe v. Wade, pro-life activists have gained significant momentum in advancing their agenda, particularly at the state level, where they have successfully passed restrictive abortion laws in many conservative regions of the country.

However, the debate is far from settled. The pro-life movement faces continued opposition from the pro-choice camp, legal challenges to new abortion restrictions, and growing political tensions over how to balance women's rights with the rights of the unborn. As the nation remains divided, the battle over abortion will likely continue to shape the political and cultural landscape for years to come.

State-Level Battles: A Patchwork of Laws

With the Supreme Court's 2022 Dobbs v. Jackson Women's Health Organization decision overturning Roe v. Wade, the legal landscape surrounding abortion in the United States has been reshaped, leading to intense state-level battles over abortion access. The decision returned the power to regulate abortion to the states, resulting in a patchwork of laws across the country. As a result, a woman's ability to access an abortion now largely depends on where she lives. Conservative states have moved swiftly to implement near-total bans or severe restrictions on abortion, while more liberal states have taken steps to protect or even expand abortion access.

These state-level actions have not only reignited political and legal conflicts but also created significant barriers for women seeking abortions in states where the procedure is now heavily restricted or banned. In this section, we explore the diverging state policies, the legal battles playing out across the country, and the regional disparities in abortion access that have emerged in the post-Roe era.

States with Near-Total Abortion Bans

Several states with conservative majorities in their legislatures moved quickly to enact near-total abortion bans or severely limit abortion access once Roe was overturned. Many of these states had trigger laws—pre-written abortion bans that would automatically go into effect if Roe were ever overturned. These states are now at the forefront of the pro-life movement's efforts to restrict or eliminate abortion altogether.

- **Texas.** Texas passed its controversial Senate Bill 8 (SB 8) in 2021, banning abortions after about six weeks of pregnancy, before many women even know they are pregnant. The law was unique in that it relied on private citizens to enforce the ban through lawsuits, allowing anyone to sue a provider or anyone who "aids and abets" an abortion. Following the Dobbs ruling, Texas implemented even stricter abortion bans, allowing the procedure only in cases where the mother's life is at risk.

- **Alabama.** In 2019, Alabama passed a law that banned nearly all abortions, including in cases of rape or incest, with the only exception being to save the life of the mother. This law, which had been blocked by courts while Roe v. Wade was still in effect, immediately went into force after the Dobbs ruling. Alabama's law is one of the strictest in the country, and it has been the subject of significant controversy and legal challenges.

- **Mississippi.** The state at the center of the Dobbs case, Mississippi, enacted a law in 2018 that banned most abortions after 15 weeks of pregnancy. After Dobbs, the state moved to fully enforce the law, with no exceptions for cases of rape or incest. Mississippi has also introduced additional measures to prevent abortion access in the state, aligning with the broader pro-life agenda.

- **Other States.** States such as Louisiana, Arkansas, Oklahoma, and South Dakota have also enacted near-total bans or severely limited access, following the overturning of Roe. Many of these states have criminal penalties for abortion providers and, in some cases, for women who seek abortions, although there are ongoing debates over whether such penalties should be applied to patients.

States Expanding or Protecting Abortion Access

In contrast to the conservative states that have restricted abortion access, several liberal states have acted to strengthen or expand abortion rights in the wake of Dobbs. These states, mostly in the Northeast, West Coast, and some parts of the Midwest, have become safe havens for women seeking abortions, including those traveling from states where the procedure is now banned or severely restricted.

- **California.** California has positioned itself as a leader in protecting abortion rights. Shortly after the Dobbs decision, Governor Gavin Newsom signed a package of laws designed to strengthen access to abortion in the state, including measures to expand funding for abortion services and protect abortion providers from out-of-state legal challenges. The state has also passed a constitutional amendment to guarantee the right to an abortion, ensuring that California remains a safe haven for those seeking reproductive healthcare.

- **New York.** In New York, the Reproductive Health Act passed in 2019 codified abortion rights into state law, protecting access to abortion even if Roe were overturned. Following the Dobbs decision, New York took additional steps to expand funding for clinics, protect out-of-state patients, and safeguard providers from legal action. The state also offers legal protections for abortion providers who are targeted by lawsuits from states with restrictive abortion laws.

- **Illinois.** Illinois has become one of the most abortion-access-friendly states in the Midwest, expanding abortion protections under the Reproductive Health Act of 2019. After the Dobbs decision, Illinois saw an influx of patients from neighboring states with strict abortion bans, leading the state to increase support for providers and ensure that clinics could accommodate out-of-state patients. Illinois' policies stand in stark contrast to neighboring states like Indiana and Missouri, where abortion has been severely restricted.

- **Other States.** States such as Colorado, Washington, Oregon, Vermont, and New Mexico have also taken action to protect abortion access by enshrining it in law or the state constitution, expanding funding for reproductive healthcare, and ensuring that out-of-state patients can access services without fear of legal repercussions.

Legal and Political Fallout

The legal landscape surrounding abortion has become increasingly fragmented as states pass competing laws, leading to legal challenges and ongoing litigation that is reshaping abortion rights across the country. Pro-choice and pro-life groups are locked in fierce battles over the future of abortion access, with each side using the courts and state legislatures to advance their agenda.

- **Legal Challenges to Abortion Bans.** Pro-choice advocates have filed lawsuits in multiple states to challenge trigger laws and near-total bans on abortion, arguing that these laws violate state constitutions or impose undue burdens on women's health. In states like Kentucky, North Dakota, and South Carolina, courts have temporarily blocked abortion bans while litigation continues, creating uncertainty about the future of abortion access in those states.

- **Cross-State Legal Conflicts.** One of the more complex legal issues to arise in the post-Roe era is the question of cross-state legal conflicts. As women travel from states with abortion bans to states where the procedure is legal, some pro-life lawmakers have proposed legislation that would make it illegal for women to cross state lines for the purpose of obtaining an abortion. Additionally, states like Texas have proposed laws that would allow private citizens to sue anyone who helps facilitate an abortion, including providers in other states. These proposals have raised significant constitutional questions and are likely to be the subject of future legal battles.

Impact on Healthcare Providers: The legal environment has also put significant pressure on healthcare providers, particularly in states with strict abortion bans. Many doctors and clinics are unsure of how to navigate the complex and sometimes contradictory laws, leading to fears of legal repercussions even when providing care for pregnancies that threaten the health of the mother. Pro-choice advocates argue that this legal uncertainty is harming women's access to life-saving healthcare and has led to delays in treatment for pregnancy complications.

Cross-State Travel for Abortion Services

One of the most immediate consequences of the post-Roe landscape is the increasing need for women in states with abortion bans to travel to other states to access abortion services. This has created a two-tier system in which access to abortion is largely determined by geography and financial resources.

- **Traveling Long Distances for Care.** In states with near-total bans, women seeking abortions must often travel hundreds of miles to reach a state where the procedure is legal. For example, women in Texas may need to travel to New Mexico or Colorado, while women in Alabama may travel to Illinois or Florida. These journeys often come with significant costs, including travel expenses, time off work, and the logistical challenges of arranging care, particularly for women with children or limited financial resources.

- **Abortion Funds and Support Networks.** To help women navigate these barriers, abortion funds and support networks have expanded their services, offering financial assistance, transportation, and lodging to women traveling out of state for abortion care. Organizations such as the National Network of Abortion Funds (NNAF) play a crucial role in helping women access services they otherwise could not afford. However, these resources are often overwhelmed by the demand, and advocates argue that the need far outstrips the available support.

- **Economic and Racial Disparities.** Pro-choice advocates argue that the increased burden of traveling for abortion care disproportionately affects low-income women and women of color, who already face significant barriers to accessing healthcare. These women may be unable to afford the cost of travel or may not have the time or resources to leave their jobs or families for several days. As a result, the post-Roe landscape has created a situation where wealthier women in restrictive states can still access abortion services by traveling, while poorer women are forced to carry unwanted pregnancies to term.

Polarization and the Future of Abortion Laws

The Dobbs decision has deepened the cultural and political divide in the United States, with red states enacting increasingly restrictive abortion laws and blue states moving to protect or expand access. This polarization is likely to shape the future of abortion laws in America for years to come.

- **Elections and Abortion Policy.** Abortion has become a key issue in gubernatorial and state legislative elections, with pro-choice and pro-life candidates making it a central part of their platforms. In swing states, where public opinion on abortion is more divided, the outcomes of elections could determine the future of abortion access. For example, the 2022 election cycle saw several ballot initiatives related to abortion, such as the successful effort in Kansas to uphold abortion rights in the state's constitution.

- **Potential for Federal Legislation.** While the Supreme Court has returned the regulation of abortion to the states, some lawmakers on both sides of the debate have called for federal legislation to either protect or restrict abortion rights nationwide. Pro-life advocates have proposed a national abortion ban that would limit or prohibit the procedure across all states, while pro-choice advocates are pushing for legislation that would codify Roe v. Wade into federal law, ensuring that abortion rights are protected regardless of state policies. However, the political gridlock in Congress makes it unlikely that such legislation will pass in the near future.

- **A Divided Nation.** The post-Roe landscape in America is defined by regional disparities, legal battles, and intense political polarization. The state-level battles over abortion access have created a situation where a woman's ability to obtain an abortion depends largely on her zip code, with some states enacting near-total bans and others protecting or expanding abortion rights. As legal challenges continue and public opinion remains divided, the future of abortion access in the United States will be shaped by ongoing legislative and judicial actions at both the state and federal levels.

The Broader Cultural and Political Divide

The pro-choice vs. pro-life debate is not just about differing opinions on abortion; it reflects a much deeper cultural and political divide in the United States. Abortion has become a symbolic issue, representing broader conflicts over morality, religion, gender roles, and the proper role of government in regulating private lives. In the wake of the Dobbs decision that overturned Roe v. Wade, these cultural and political divisions have only intensified, further polarizing an already divided nation.

This section will explore how the debate over abortion reflects deeper ideological battles in the U.S., the role of religion in shaping public opinion, the impact on elections and political polarization, and how the fight between women's rights and fetal rights continues to shape the discourse. Ultimately, the abortion debate serves as a lens through which to view the broader cultural tensions that define much of American political life today.

Abortion as a Cultural Issue

Abortion has long been a cultural flash-point in America, symbolizing deeply held beliefs about life, freedom, and personal responsibility. For many people, where one stands on abortion is closely tied to their views on sexual morality, family values, and the role of women in society. The debate often transcends the legal question of whether abortion should be allowed and enters the realm of moral philosophy and social values.

Moral and Ethical Concerns. For the pro-life movement, the abortion debate is about the sanctity of life and the moral duty to protect the unborn. Pro-life advocates argue that society has an ethical obligation to defend the most vulnerable, and they view abortion as a violation of the fundamental right to life. On the other hand, pro-choice advocates frame the issue as one of bodily autonomy and women's rights, arguing that women should have the freedom to make personal decisions about their reproductive health without government interference. This fundamental clash over values makes the abortion debate particularly polarizing, as it taps into deeper moral and philosophical worldviews that go beyond the question of legality.

Gender and Power. The abortion debate is also closely tied to broader questions about gender roles and power dynamics in society. Pro-choice advocates often argue that restrictions on abortion are part of a larger effort to control women's bodies and limit their autonomy, seeing the fight for abortion rights as a critical part of the struggle for gender equality. For many in the feminist movement, the ability to access safe and legal abortion is seen as essential for women's empowerment, allowing them to control their reproductive lives and pursue careers, education, and personal goals on their own terms.

The Role of Religion in Shaping Public Opinion

Religion plays a central role in shaping the views of many Americans on the issue of abortion. For religious conservatives, particularly Evangelical Christians and Catholics, opposition to abortion is often grounded in deeply held beliefs about the sanctity of life and the divine nature of human existence. These communities have been at the forefront of the pro-life movement, driving much of the political and social activism aimed at restricting abortion access.

- **Christian Influence.** The Christian right has been one of the most influential forces in the pro-life movement, mobilizing voters and shaping public policy on abortion for decades. For many Christians, opposition to abortion is based on biblical teachings that affirm the sanctity of life and the belief that all human beings are made in the image of God. Organizations like the National Right to Life Committee, Focus on the Family, and The Catholic Church have been instrumental in framing abortion as a moral issue and advocating for legal protections for the unborn.

- **Religious Diversity of Views.** While many religious communities strongly oppose abortion, it's important to recognize that not all people of faith share the same views. For example, Reform Judaism, Unitarian Universalism, and certain mainline Protestant denominations support abortion rights, emphasizing the importance of individual conscience and the belief that reproductive decisions should be made privately between a woman and her doctor. This diversity of religious views complicates the debate, as both pro-life and pro-choice advocates often invoke their spiritual or moral convictions in defense of their positions.

- **Public Opinion and Religion.** Religious affiliation is one of the strongest predictors of a person's stance on abortion. According to the Pew Research Center, Evangelical Christians and Catholics are far more likely to oppose abortion than those who are religiously unaffiliated. Among white Evangelicals, for instance, over 70% believe abortion should be illegal in all or most cases, while a majority of religiously unaffiliated Americans support access to abortion in most circumstances. This religious divide is reflected in the broader cultural and political landscape, where abortion is often seen as part of a larger battle over America's identity as a secular or Christian nation.

Impact on Elections and Political Polarization

The abortion debate has become a litmus test for many political candidates, playing a significant role in national, state, and local elections. For decades, both Democrats and Republicans have used abortion to mobilize their respective bases, but the stakes have grown even higher following the Dobbs decision.

- **Polarization of the Parties.** The Democratic and Republican parties have become more polarized on the issue of abortion than ever before. While the Democratic Party officially supports access to safe and legal abortion, including efforts to codify Roe v. Wade into federal law, the Republican Party has increasingly moved toward restricting abortion or implementing outright bans. This polarization means that abortion is now one of the most reliable predictors of party affiliation, with few moderates left in either party on this issue.

- **Abortion as a Voting Issue.** For many voters, abortion is a single-issue, driving their political participation and candidate preferences. Pro-life voters have been particularly effective in using abortion as a rallying point, with groups like the Susan B. Anthony List working to elect anti-abortion candidates at all levels of government. Similarly, pro-choice groups like Planned Parenthood Action Fund have focused on electing candidates who will protect abortion access, especially in states where rights are under threat.

- **Key Elections and Ballot Initiatives.** The issue of abortion has played a pivotal role in recent elections, particularly in swing states. For example, in Kansas, a traditionally conservative state, voters rejected a ballot initiative in 2022 that would have allowed the state legislature to restrict or ban abortion. The outcome of this vote was seen as a major victory for the pro-choice movement and demonstrated that even in conservative regions, there is significant public support for keeping abortion legal. Similarly, gubernatorial races in states like Michigan, Wisconsin, and Pennsylvania have hinged on candidates' positions on abortion, with voters making clear that the issue is a top priority.

Women's Rights vs. Fetal Rights: A Moral and Legal Clash

The debate over women's rights and fetal rights lies at the heart of the abortion conflict, and this clash raises difficult questions about how to balance the rights of pregnant women with the rights of the unborn.

- **Women's Rights and Bodily Autonomy.** Pro-choice advocates argue that a woman's right to bodily autonomy is paramount. They maintain that women must have the ability to make personal decisions about their pregnancies, free from government interference, because those decisions directly impact their health, economic well-being, and personal freedom. For pro-choice advocates, forcing a woman to carry an unwanted pregnancy to term is not only an infringement on her personal liberty but also an unjust use of state power to regulate her body.

- **Fetal Rights and Person-hood.** On the other hand, pro-life advocates argue that the fetus, from the moment of conception, is a distinct human being with a right to life that must be protected. The concept of person-hood—the idea that fetuses are legal persons deserving of rights—underpins much of the pro-life movement's legal arguments. Pro-life advocates often contend that the right to life should supersede a woman's right to choose, especially as the fetus develops and becomes viable outside the womb.

- **Viability and Legal Standards.** The issue of viability—the point at which a fetus can survive outside the womb—has been a central factor in how courts have historically approached abortion. Under Roe v. Wade, the Supreme Court allowed for restrictions on abortion after the point of viability, typically around 24 weeks. However, as medical technology advances, the point of viability has moved earlier in pregnancy, raising new legal and ethical questions about when and whether abortion should be allowed. Dobbs shifted this debate back to the states, resulting in a wide range of standards for determining when and how fetal rights should be protected.

The Broader Consequences of Polarization

The intense polarization around abortion reflects a deeper division within American society over fundamental values such as individual freedom, government intervention, and religious beliefs. The broader cultural wars— whether over LGBTQ+ rights, gender identity, race, or education—are often intertwined with the abortion debate, making it a central issue in the ongoing struggle over America's future direction.

Erosion of Civil Discourse. The growing divide over abortion has contributed to a broader erosion of civil discourse in American politics. As both sides become more entrenched in their positions, finding common ground has become increasingly difficult. Pro-choice and pro-life advocates often view each other not merely as political opponents but as adversaries in a moral battle, further deepening the hostility and partisanship that characterizes modern American politics.

Impact on Other Issues. The abortion debate also has significant implications for other issues related to reproductive health, such as access to contraceptives, sex education, and in-vitro fertilization. Pro-choice advocates argue that restricting abortion could lead to broader rollbacks in reproductive rights, while pro-life advocates are increasingly pushing for policies that promote alternatives to abortion, such as adoption and foster care. The broader fight over reproductive rights is likely to continue shaping political and legal debates for years to come.

The Deepening Divide

The cultural and political divide over abortion reflects deeper tensions in American society regarding issues of morality, religion, gender, and government control. In the wake of the Dobbs decision, these divides have only grown sharper, with both pro-choice and pro-life advocates intensifying their efforts to sway public opinion, influence legislation, and shape the future of reproductive rights.

As abortion remains a flash-point in American politics, the broader battle over women's rights, fetal rights, and the role of religion and morality in shaping public policy will continue to be at the forefront of the national debate. Finding common ground on such a deeply emotional and polarizing issue may prove elusive, but the outcome of this debate will have profound implications for the future of reproductive health, civil rights, and American democracy.

The Future of Abortion Rights in America

The overturning of Roe v. Wade in the 2022 Dobbs v. Jackson Women's Health Organization decision has fundamentally changed the landscape of abortion rights in America, but it has not ended the national debate. Instead, the ruling has opened a new chapter in the long-running conflict between pro-choice and pro-life forces, with battles now playing out primarily in state legislatures, courts, and even Congress. As both sides prepare for the future, the legal and political landscape remains uncertain, with potential developments that could further reshape abortion access in the United States.

This section explores the possible future legal battles, the potential for federal legislation, the ongoing efforts by advocacy groups, and the impact of the abortion debate on upcoming elections. It also considers how the fight for reproductive rights might evolve in the years ahead, both in terms of policy and the cultural conversation surrounding abortion.

Potential Federal Responses: The Battle Over National Legislation

One of the most pressing questions in the post-Roe era is whether federal legislation could be enacted to either protect or restrict abortion rights nationwide. With the Supreme Court having handed the issue of abortion regulation back to the states, there are growing calls from both pro-choice and pro-life advocates to take the fight to Congress.

- **Pro-Choice Efforts to Codify Roe v. Wade.** In the wake of Dobbs, many pro-choice lawmakers have pushed for federal legislation that would codify Roe v. Wade into law, ensuring that abortion rights are protected nationwide regardless of state laws. The most prominent effort has been the proposed Women's Health Protection Act, which seeks to guarantee the right to an abortion up until the point of fetal viability and prevent states from enacting laws that impose unnecessary barriers to access. However, passing such legislation faces significant hurdles, particularly in the U.S. Senate, where the filibuster requires a super-majority of 60 votes for most legislation to advance. Given the deep polarization on the issue, it is unlikely that there will be enough bipartisan support to pass such a bill without reforming or eliminating the filibuster.

- **Pro-Life Push for a National Abortion Ban.** On the other side of the debate, some Republican lawmakers and pro-life groups have begun advocating for a national abortion ban that would prohibit the procedure across the country. Proposals vary, with some advocating for bans after 15 weeks of pregnancy (similar to the Mississippi law at the heart of the Dobbs case), while others push for more restrictive measures, including heartbeat bills or total bans. However, like the pro-choice efforts, a national abortion ban would face significant obstacles in Congress, where Democrats currently hold enough power to block such legislation. Nonetheless, the issue remains a rallying cry for conservative activists and will likely be a central feature of future Republican campaigns.

- **Impact of the 2024 Election.** The 2024 presidential and congressional elections will be pivotal for the future of abortion rights in America. Depending on the balance of power in Congress and who occupies the White House, there could be renewed efforts to pass national legislation on abortion. If Republicans gain control of both chambers of Congress and the presidency, the prospect of a national abortion ban could become more realistic. Conversely, if Democrats retain power, they may continue efforts to protect abortion access through federal law.

Ongoing Legal Battles and the Supreme Court's Role

Although the Supreme Court's decision in Dobbs shifted the responsibility for abortion regulation to the states, it is likely that the Court will continue to play a significant role in shaping abortion rights in the future. As new state laws are enacted and challenged in the courts, many expect the judiciary to remain a key battleground.

- **Challenges to State-Level Bans.** Pro-choice advocates have already begun challenging many of the state-level bans and restrictions that have gone into effect since Roe v. Wade was overturned. These lawsuits typically argue that state constitutions protect abortion rights or that certain restrictions impose an undue burden on women seeking abortion care. For example, lawsuits have been filed in South Carolina, Louisiana, and Kentucky, where courts have temporarily blocked enforcement of abortion bans while the legal process unfolds. As these cases make their way through the state and federal court systems, some are likely to return to the Supreme Court, which could issue rulings that further refine the legal framework around abortion.

- **New Legal Questions.** The post-Dobbs landscape has also raised new legal questions that courts may need to address. One key issue is the potential for cross-state legal conflicts, where states with abortion bans may try to restrict residents from traveling to other states to obtain an abortion or target abortion providers in other states who help women from restrictive states. These scenarios could lead to constitutional challenges based on the right to interstate travel and commerce. Additionally, legal battles may arise over the enforcement of medication abortion regulations, especially as demand for abortion pills rises in states with severe abortion restrictions.

- **The Role of the Conservative Supreme Court.** The current conservative majority on the Supreme Court, which played a crucial role in overturning Roe, is expected to remain in place for the foreseeable future. With six conservative justices on the bench, including several who have expressed strong views against abortion rights, it is unlikely that the Court will reverse course on the issue. However, future rulings may further clarify the boundaries of state authority over abortion regulation and could address new legal questions related to fetal rights, viability, and the rights of pregnant women.

State-Level Battles Continue to Intensify

As abortion rights increasingly become a state-level issue, the political and legal battles will likely continue to intensify, with states enacting a wide variety of laws that reflect their ideological leanings. This patchwork of laws will contribute to the geographic disparities in abortion access, creating a two-tier system in which abortion is available in some states but heavily restricted or banned in others.

- **States Expanding Access.** Many blue states are doubling down on their efforts to expand abortion access and protect women seeking abortions from out-of-state legal challenges. For example, California, New York, Illinois, and Oregon have passed or proposed laws that provide legal protections for abortion providers and patients, even if they come from states where abortion is banned. These states have also increased funding for abortion clinics and expanded support networks for women traveling from out of state to seek care. In some cases, state constitutions have been amended to explicitly protect the right to abortion, ensuring that abortion rights remain secure regardless of future Supreme Court decisions.

- **States Restricting or Banning Abortion.** Conversely, many red states are enacting near-total bans on abortion, including states like Texas, Mississippi, Alabama, and Oklahoma, where abortion is now illegal in nearly all circumstances. These states are continuing to refine and strengthen their abortion restrictions, often pushing for even more severe penalties for abortion providers and others involved in the process. Some states have even proposed legislation that would allow private citizens to sue anyone who helps facilitate an abortion, echoing the controversial enforcement mechanism used in Texas' SB 8 law.

- **Ballot Initiatives and Referendums.** In the absence of a national standard, many states will likely turn to ballot initiatives and referendums to let voters decide on abortion policy directly. This was the case in Kansas, where voters in 2022 rejected a proposed constitutional amendment that would have allowed the state legislature to restrict abortion. Similar efforts are expected in Michigan, California, Kentucky, and Montana, where abortion-related ballot measures will let voters weigh in on whether to protect or restrict abortion rights in their respective states.

The Role of Advocacy Groups

Both pro-choice and pro-life advocacy groups will continue to play a crucial role in shaping the future of abortion policy. These groups are heavily involved in lobbying for legislation, supporting political candidates, and mobilizing their supporters at the grassroots level.

- **Pro-Choice Advocacy.** Organizations like Planned Parenthood, the ACLU, and the Center for Reproductive Rights are leading the fight to protect abortion access at both the state and federal levels. These groups are involved in filing lawsuits to challenge restrictive abortion laws, lobbying lawmakers to pass pro-choice legislation, and providing support to abortion clinics and women seeking care. In addition to advocating for legal abortion, many of these groups are expanding their focus to include issues such as contraceptive access, comprehensive sex education, and maternal healthcare, recognizing that the broader landscape of reproductive rights is also under threat.

- **Pro-Life Advocacy.** On the other side of the debate, pro-life organizations such as the Susan B. Anthony List, National Right to Life, and Americans United for Life are continuing their efforts to restrict abortion through legislative action and public outreach. These groups have been instrumental in passing state-level bans and are now focusing on ensuring that these laws are enforced and upheld in court. Pro-life advocacy groups are also pushing for more support for pregnant women and alternatives to abortion, such as adoption services and crisis pregnancy centers. Some groups are even advocating for a national abortion ban, hoping to build on the momentum created by the Dobbs decision.

The Cultural Conversation and Changing Public Opinion

The cultural conversation surrounding abortion is likely to evolve in the coming years, as both sides work to shift public opinion in their favor. Polling data shows that while a majority of Americans support the right to an abortion in some circumstances, there is significant division over when and how abortion should be regulated.

Generational Divides. One of the key factors that could shape the future of abortion policy is the generational divide in public opinion. Younger generations, particularly Millennials and Generation Z, tend to be more pro-choice than older Americans. According to a Pew Research Center survey, around 70% of adults under 30 support legal abortion in all or most cases, compared to 50% of those aged 65 and older. As these younger generations become more politically active, their views could influence future abortion policy and potentially lead to more widespread support for abortion rights.

Cultural Shifts. In addition to generational changes, the broader cultural conversation around abortion is likely to shift as social movements and media continue to influence public attitudes. The growing visibility of issues like reproductive justice, which emphasizes the intersection of race, class, and gender in discussions about reproductive health, is likely to play a significant role in shaping how the public understands abortion. Similarly, the rising popularity of telemedicine and medication abortion could change the practical realities of abortion access, particularly in states where in-person clinics are heavily restricted.

Uncertain But Pivotal Future

The future of abortion rights in America remains deeply uncertain, with the Dobbs decision marking just the beginning of a new era of legal, political, and cultural battles. Both sides of the debate are highly mobilized, and the coming years will see continued efforts to shape policy, public opinion, and the legal landscape.

While some states will continue to serve as safe havens for abortion access, others will enforce near-total bans, creating a deeply divided country where a woman's right to an abortion depends largely on where she lives. The ongoing state-level battles, coupled with the potential for federal legislation and Supreme Court interventions, will keep the abortion debate at the forefront of American politics for years to come.

As both pro-choice and pro-life advocates gear up for the next phase of this struggle, one thing is clear: the fight over abortion rights is far from over, and its outcome will have profound implications for reproductive freedom, women's rights, and American society as a whole.

Conclusion: A Nation Divided and the Path Forward

The debate over abortion rights in America is one of the most deeply entrenched and emotionally charged issues the nation has faced, and the Dobbs v. Jackson Women's Health Organization decision of 2022, which overturned Roe v. Wade, has only intensified this division. With the power to regulate abortion now resting in the hands of state governments, the U.S. has entered an era where access to reproductive healthcare varies dramatically depending on geography, political control, and cultural attitudes.

This decision has ignited both the pro-choice and pro-life movements, setting the stage for a new phase of legal battles, political campaigns, and cultural conflict. While some states have moved swiftly to ban or restrict abortion, others have acted to protect and expand access. This has created a patchwork of abortion laws that, in many ways, reflect the broader cultural and political polarization in the United States.

A Deepening Divide

The Dobbs ruling has deepened the divide between red and blue states, urban and rural areas, and those who view abortion as a matter of women's rights versus those who see it as a question of fetal rights. In conservative states, legislatures are passing increasingly restrictive laws, emboldened by the new legal environment. In contrast, more liberal states are positioning themselves as sanctuaries for abortion access, providing legal protections for women and providers and expanding services to accommodate those traveling from more restrictive states.

This geographic disparity means that a woman's access to abortion is now highly dependent on where she lives, creating a two-tier system that has disproportionately impacted low-income women, women of color, and those living in rural areas. Wealthier women in restrictive states can often afford to travel to states with more permissive laws, while poorer women are left with fewer options, facing the potential for unwanted pregnancies and increased risks to their health and economic well-being.

The Ongoing Legal and Political Battles

The post-Roe landscape has led to an explosion of state-level legal battles, as both sides of the debate seek to solidify their positions. Pro-choice advocates are challenging restrictive abortion laws in court, arguing that they violate state constitutions or impose undue burdens on women seeking healthcare. Meanwhile, pro-life groups are pushing for stronger enforcement mechanisms and are considering new strategies to curb abortion access, such as targeting medication abortion and exploring ways to prevent women from traveling out of state for procedures.

At the federal level, the future of abortion rights will likely hinge on the 2024 elections and beyond. Both parties are preparing for a high-stakes battle over control of Congress and the White House, recognizing that the outcome could determine whether federal legislation on abortion—either to protect it or to restrict it—moves forward. While pro-choice advocates are pushing to codify Roe v. Wade into law through measures like the Women's Health Protection Act, pro-life groups are increasingly vocal in their calls for a national abortion ban, potentially starting with a ban on abortions after 15 weeks or even earlier.

The Broader Cultural Implications

Beyond the legal and political battles, the abortion debate reflects deeper cultural tensions that have long shaped American society. At its core, the conflict is about more than just reproductive rights—it touches on fundamental questions of individual freedom, morality, and the role of government in regulating private lives.

For pro-choice advocates, the right to abortion is central to women's autonomy and their ability to participate fully in society. They argue that restrictions on abortion are part of a broader effort to control women's bodies and undermine their rights, emphasizing that reproductive freedom is essential for gender equality.

For pro-life advocates, abortion is viewed as a moral issue concerning the sanctity of human life. They believe that the government has a duty to protect unborn children, who they view as vulnerable human beings deserving of legal rights. This perspective is often deeply rooted in religious convictions and a belief that life begins at conception.

These opposing worldviews have only become more entrenched, making it difficult to find common ground. The abortion debate is now a central issue in the broader culture wars, alongside other divisive topics such as LGBTQ+ rights, gender identity, and racial justice. As both sides continue to mobilize, the battle over abortion will remain a defining issue in American politics and culture for years to come.

The Path Forward: Finding Common Ground?

Despite the polarization, there may be opportunities for compromise and consensus in some areas of the debate. For instance, polling shows that a majority of Americans support some form of abortion access, particularly in the early stages of pregnancy, but also favor restrictions on abortion in the third trimester or after fetal viability. There is also broad support for efforts to reduce unintended pregnancies through greater access to contraception, comprehensive sex education, and family planning services.

Contraceptive Access. Expanding access to contraception and emergency contraception could help reduce the number of unintended pregnancies and, by extension, the demand for abortion. Pro-choice and pro-life advocates might find common ground in promoting policies that ensure affordable contraception is available to all women, particularly those in low-income communities or rural areas where healthcare access is limited.

Support for Families. There is also potential for collaboration on policies that provide greater support for pregnant women and families, such as expanded paid parental leave, childcare subsidies, and healthcare access. By addressing the socioeconomic factors that lead some women to seek abortions, both sides may be able to work toward solutions that reduce the need for abortion while supporting women's choices.

However, finding common ground will require a willingness to engage in civil discourse and a recognition that the debate over abortion is deeply complex, with no easy solutions. It is unlikely that the cultural and political divide over abortion will be bridged entirely, but there may be opportunities to pursue practical policies that protect both women's health and the rights of the unborn, while also reducing the divisiveness of the debate.

Looking Ahead: Uncertain, But Critical

The future of abortion rights in America remains highly uncertain, but the stakes are incredibly high. The pro-choice and pro-life movements are both deeply committed to their causes, and the legal, political, and cultural battles over abortion will continue to evolve in the coming years. The next phase of this fight will likely play out in state legislatures, courtrooms, and voting booths, as Americans grapple with the implications of a post-Roe world.

What is clear is that abortion will remain a defining issue in American life, one that cuts to the heart of how the country views freedom, morality, and justice. As both sides continue to mobilize, the path forward will require difficult conversations, policy innovation, and, perhaps most importantly, a commitment to listening to the diverse perspectives that shape this complex and deeply personal issue.

In the end, the question of how to balance women's rights with fetal rights, individual autonomy with societal responsibility, and legal protections with personal freedom will continue to challenge the country—and it will require ongoing dialogue, debate, and a willingness to explore new ways to protect the health and dignity of all people involved.

The fight over abortion in America is far from over. The Dobbs decision may have changed the legal landscape, but the cultural, political, and moral debates surrounding abortion will continue to shape the nation's future for generations to come. As the battle moves forward, it is essential for all sides to engage in thoughtful dialogue and work toward solutions that respect the complexity of the issue while striving to protect the rights and well-being of women, children, and families across the country.

Balancing Access and Security

Introduction: The 2020 Election and the Renewed Debate Over Voting Rights

The 2020 U.S. presidential election was a turning point not only for the future of American politics but also for the long-standing debate over voting rights and election integrity. In the aftermath of the election, claims of widespread voter fraud—despite being thoroughly debunked—led to a wave of legislative efforts aimed at tightening voting regulations. These efforts, predominantly led by Republican-controlled state legislatures, have sparked a highly contentious national conversation about the balance between election security and voter access.

For those advocating for stricter voting laws, the changes are necessary to protect the integrity of elections, ensure that only eligible voters can participate, and prevent fraud, which, while rare, is seen as a serious threat to public confidence in the democratic process. These advocates point to the need for measures like voter ID laws, limits on mail-in voting, and more stringent rules for voter registration as ways to safeguard elections. While widespread fraud has not been proven in U.S. elections, supporters of these laws argue that preventative measures are essential for maintaining public trust in election results.

On the other side of the debate, critics of these new laws argue that they amount to voter suppression, particularly for minority communities, low-income voters, the elderly, and young voters—groups that often face greater challenges in accessing the necessary documentation or transportation to comply with new requirements. Civil rights advocates and many Democrats argue that these laws disproportionately affect voters of color and are designed to reduce Democratic voter turnout in key battleground states, thereby undermining the principle of universal suffrage.

The introduction of these laws has revived the national debate on voting rights, leading to the introduction of federal legislation such as the For the People Act and the John Lewis Voting Rights Act, which aim to protect and expand access to the ballot box. However, these proposals have faced stiff opposition from Republicans, who argue that such laws would federalize elections and take away states' rights to regulate their own voting procedures.

In this essay, I explore the key elements of the ongoing debate, analyzing the arguments on both sides and the broader implications for the future of voting rights in America. The conflict between voter suppression and election security has become a defining issue in the modern political landscape, and understanding the nuances of this debate is critical to ensuring the integrity and inclusivity of American democracy.

Election Security Concerns: Arguments for Stricter Voting Laws

The push for stricter voting laws has been a defining feature of the political landscape since the 2020 presidential election, driven by concerns over election security and the integrity of the democratic process. Advocates for these laws, predominantly from Republican-led states, argue that these measures are essential to protect elections from fraud, restore public trust in the electoral process, and prevent any irregularities—no matter how small—that could call election results into question. Though widespread voter fraud has not been proven in modern U.S. elections, these proponents argue that preventive measures are necessary to ensure that all votes are legitimate and counted fairly.

The Context: The 2020 Election and Claims of Voter Fraud

The aftermath of the 2020 election saw a surge in allegations of voter fraud, largely promoted by then-President Donald Trump and his supporters, despite there being no significant evidence to support these claims. Multiple court cases, recounts, and audits across key battleground states reaffirmed the integrity of the election, and non-partisan agencies, including the Cybersecurity and Infrastructure Security Agency (CISA), described the 2020 election as "the most secure in American history." However, the lingering narrative of election fraud created a deep mistrust of the electoral system among a substantial portion of voters, particularly in conservative circles.

To address these concerns, Republican lawmakers in states like Georgia, Texas, Florida, and Arizona introduced a wave of new legislation aimed at tightening voting rules. These bills, proponents argued, were designed to prevent potential future fraud and irregularities that could undermine the legitimacy of election outcomes.

Common Measures in Stricter Voting Laws

Stricter voting laws generally fall into a few key categories, each intended to increase oversight and reduce the possibility of fraudulent or improper votes being cast. Some of the most common measures include:

- **Voter ID Requirements.** One of the most widely debated aspects of stricter voting laws is the introduction or strengthening of voter identification requirements. Proponents argue that requiring voters to present a government-issued ID at the polls ensures that only eligible individuals can cast ballots, preventing impersonation or ineligible voting. They liken it to needing an ID for other essential activities, such as boarding a plane or buying alcohol, and argue that it is a simple measure to maintain the integrity of elections.

- **Restrictions on Mail-In Voting and Absentee Ballots.** The expansion of mail-in voting during the 2020 election, driven by the COVID-19 pandemic, led to increased scrutiny. Stricter voting laws in several states now limit the availability of mail-in or absentee voting, requiring stricter criteria for eligibility (such as proof of disability or absence from the state) and reducing the number of drop boxes for returning ballots. Supporters argue that restricting mail-in voting reduces opportunities for fraud, such as ballot harvesting (when third parties collect and submit mail-in ballots) and ensures that mail-in ballots are only used when necessary.

- **Reduced Early Voting Periods.** Many of the new voting laws have also sought to shorten early voting periods, limit weekend voting, or reduce the availability of 24-hour voting options. Proponents argue that early voting, while convenient, opens up more opportunities for logistical errors or fraud, and by narrowing the window, election officials can better manage and secure the process.

- **Restrictions on Voting Assistance.** In some states, laws have been passed that limit who can provide assistance to voters, especially for those casting mail-in ballots. This includes restrictions on third-party ballot collection and stricter oversight of who can help elderly or disabled voters fill out their ballots. Proponents of these restrictions argue that limiting outside influence reduces the chance of coercion or ballot tampering.

- **Cleaning Voter Rolls.** Another common element of these laws involves efforts to regularly clean or purge voter rolls to remove names of deceased individuals, those who have moved, or ineligible voters. Supporters argue that maintaining accurate voter rolls helps prevent errors and potential fraud, such as ineligible individuals accidentally or intentionally voting under the wrong name.

Proponents' Arguments: Ensuring Election Integrity

Those advocating for stricter voting laws believe that these measures are necessary to maintain public confidence in the electoral system and ensure that every vote cast is legitimate. While they acknowledge that cases of widespread fraud have not been proven, proponents argue that the perception of potential fraud—whether real or not—has eroded trust in elections, and these laws are a way to restore that trust.

- **Restoring Public Confidence.** One of the core arguments made by advocates of stricter voting laws is that the American public's confidence in the electoral system must be restored after the contentious 2020 election. They argue that even if fraud did not occur on a large scale, the perception that it could have happened weakens democracy. By implementing more stringent controls, states can demonstrate that they are serious about preventing even the smallest chance of irregularities.

- **Preventing Future Fraud.** While voter fraud is statistically rare, proponents argue that even a small number of fraudulent votes could sway the results of a tight election. They point to local and state-level races that have been decided by razor-thin margins and suggest that stricter laws would reduce the risk of fraud affecting those outcomes.

- **Protecting the Integrity of Every Vote.** Proponents believe that the value of an individual's vote is diminished if ineligible votes are cast. They argue that stricter voting laws help ensure that every eligible vote counts and that illegitimate votes do not dilute the results. From this perspective, election security measures are framed as protecting the fundamental rights of voters, rather than restricting access.

A Broader Trend: Election Integrity as a Political Issue

In the wake of the 2020 election, election integrity has become a major political issue, particularly for Republican voters. Polls have shown that a significant portion of the Republican electorate believes that election fraud occurred during the 2020 election, despite the lack of evidence supporting these claims. As a result, many Republican lawmakers have made election security a priority in state legislatures, positioning themselves as defenders of free and fair elections.

Election integrity laws are often framed as being about protecting democracy rather than limiting voting access. Many Republican lawmakers and supporters argue that these reforms are not designed to suppress voters but to ensure that every vote is fair, secure, and accounted for. However, this approach has drawn sharp criticism from Democrats and voting rights advocates, who see these laws as a reaction to false narratives and as an effort to limit the voting power of certain groups.

Voter Suppression or Security? The Critics' Perspective

While proponents of stricter voting laws argue that these measures are necessary to ensure election integrity, critics contend that these laws amount to voter suppression, disproportionately affecting minority communities, low-income voters, young people, and urban dwellers—groups that are often more likely to vote for Democratic candidates. For these critics, the push for more stringent voting requirements is less about protecting elections and more about limiting voter turnout, particularly among people of color and other marginalized groups who already face obstacles to voting.

Critics argue that these laws undermine the principles of universal suffrage and equal access to the ballot, turning voting into an unnecessarily complicated and burdensome process for certain groups. In this section, we will examine the key arguments from the perspective of voting rights advocates and those who oppose these new restrictions, highlighting concerns about how these laws may negatively impact democracy and voter participation.

Impact on Marginalized Communities

One of the primary criticisms of stricter voting laws is that they disproportionately affect voters of color and low-income Americans, who are more likely to face the logistical and financial barriers imposed by new restrictions. Critics argue that these measures will have a discriminatory impact, creating more obstacles for these communities and discouraging voter turnout.

- **Voter ID Laws.** While proponents of voter ID requirements argue that these laws are a simple and fair way to verify voters' identities, critics point out that they disproportionately burden minority voters. According to a 2019 study by the Brennan Center for Justice, people of color are significantly less likely than white voters to possess government-issued IDs due to a range of factors, including the costs of obtaining IDs, lack of transportation, and difficulties accessing DMV offices, particularly in rural and inner-city areas. This is especially true for Black, Latino, and Native American voters, who may also face additional hurdles, such as having no birth certificate or needing to navigate complicated bureaucratic processes to obtain identification.

- **Restrictions on Mail-In Voting.** Many states expanded mail-in voting during the COVID-19 pandemic to ensure that people could safely vote from home. Critics argue that restrictions on mail-in voting—such as requiring excuses for absentee ballots, limiting the number of drop boxes, or reducing the availability of early voting—disproportionately harm voters who cannot easily make it to the polls, such as elderly, disabled, or low-income individuals who work long hours or cannot take time off from their jobs. These restrictions make voting less accessible, particularly for those who rely on the flexibility of mail-in voting due to their personal or professional circumstances.

- **Reduced Early Voting Periods.** Cutting down on early voting days or limiting access to weekend voting disproportionately affects working-class voters, especially those who rely on early voting to cast their ballots due to rigid work schedules or transportation challenges. In particular, the reduction of Sunday voting, often associated with "Souls to the Polls" events in Black communities, has been seen by critics as an attempt to suppress Black voter turnout, as these church-organized efforts have long been a significant part of African American political participation.

- **Longer Wait Times and Poll Closures.** Another significant concern is the impact of polling place closures and reduced voting hours, which critics argue disproportionately affect urban and minority voters. For example, many of the areas that have seen polling place reductions are predominantly minority communities, leading to longer wait times on election day. Voters in these areas may be discouraged from voting because of the inconvenience of waiting in line for several hours—particularly if they have jobs, childcare responsibilities, or other commitments that make it difficult to stay at the polls for an extended period.

The Historical Context of Voter Suppression

Critics of the new wave of voting restrictions point to the long history of voter suppression in the United States, particularly in Southern states that enacted Jim Crow laws aimed at disenfranchising Black voters. Tactics such as literacy tests, poll taxes, and intimidation were once used to systematically block African Americans from voting, and while such overt forms of voter suppression are no longer legal, many argue that modern voting restrictions are simply subtle iterations of these past tactics.

The Voting Rights Act of 1965 was a landmark piece of legislation that sought to combat this history of racial disenfranchisement by requiring states with a history of voter suppression to get federal approval before changing their voting laws. However, in 2013, the Supreme Court struck down the preclearance provision in Shelby County v. Holder, arguing that it was outdated and no longer necessary. Since that ruling, many states have enacted voting laws that critics claim would not have been possible under the previous federal oversight, leading to concerns that these new laws represent a return to discriminatory practices that disproportionately affect minority voters.

Voter Suppression or Election Integrity? The Debate over Intent

At the heart of the debate over stricter voting laws is the question of intent: are these laws genuinely designed to protect election integrity, or are they meant to suppress voter turnout among groups that tend to favor Democratic candidates?

- **Disproportionate Impact on Democratic Voters.** Critics argue that many of the new laws target Democratic-leaning constituencies, such as urban residents, minorities, young people, and low-income voters. These groups are more likely to vote for Democratic candidates, and by placing more restrictions on how, when, and where they can vote, critics say that these laws are an effort to reduce their overall turnout. This argument is supported by research showing that, historically, voter ID laws and other restrictive measures disproportionately reduce turnout among minority and low-income voters—demographics that typically lean Democratic.

- **Questioning the Evidence of Voter Fraud.** Critics also point to the lack of substantial evidence supporting claims of widespread voter fraud, the main justification used for many of these laws. Numerous studies and investigations, including by Trump's own Department of Justice and various state election audits, have found no evidence of large-scale fraud that would have changed the outcome of the 2020 election. For many, this raises the question: if fraud is not a widespread issue, why introduce new restrictions? From the perspective of voting rights advocates, the lack of substantial fraud cases indicates that these laws are not truly about securing elections but rather about disenfranchising specific groups of voters.

- **The Role of Partisan Politics.** Finally, critics argue that the push for stricter voting laws is politically motivated, driven by Republican efforts to retain power in key battleground states where changing demographics are making elections more competitive. With minority populations growing and urban areas increasingly voting Democratic, critics argue that Republican lawmakers see these restrictions as a way to tilt the electoral scales in their favor by reducing turnout among groups more likely to vote against them.

Legal Challenges and Federal Legislative Efforts

In response to the wave of new voting restrictions, voting rights advocates have launched a series of legal challenges and are pushing for federal legislation to protect access to the ballot.

- **Legal Challenges.** Civil rights organizations, such as the American Civil Liberties Union (ACLU) and the NAACP Legal Defense Fund, have filed lawsuits against many of the new voting laws, arguing that they violate the Constitution and disproportionately disenfranchise minority voters. In several states, these legal battles have temporarily blocked the implementation of certain laws, such as Georgia's new voting law, which faced multiple legal challenges based on claims that it unfairly targets Black voters and reduces access to absentee ballots.

- **The For the People Act and the John Lewis Voting Rights Act.** At the federal level, Democrats have proposed legislation aimed at protecting and expanding voting rights. The For the People Act seeks to standardize voting procedures across the country, expand mail-in voting, and ensure that all states offer at least two weeks of early voting. The John Lewis Voting Rights Act aims to reinstate the preclearance provisions of the original Voting Rights Act, requiring states with a history of discrimination to get federal approval before making any changes to their voting laws. However, both pieces of legislation have faced fierce opposition from Republicans, who argue that they amount to federal overreach and undermine state sovereignty in managing elections.

A Battle Over the Future of Voting in America

The debate over stricter voting laws is not just a legal or political issue—it is a fight over the very future of American democracy. While proponents argue that these laws are necessary to maintain the integrity of elections and prevent fraud, critics view them as a modern form of voter suppression that threatens to disenfranchise millions of voters, particularly in minority communities.

As legal battles continue and the push for federal voting protections intensifies, the question remains: can the U.S. find a balance between election security and voter access, or will the country become further divided over this fundamental aspect of democracy?

Key Legislation in the Debate: Federal Proposals

As the debate over voting rights and election integrity intensifies, two major pieces of federal legislation have emerged at the center of the fight: the For the People Act and the John Lewis Voting Rights Act. These proposals aim to address the growing concerns around restrictive state voting laws by creating national standards for voting access and ensuring protections against discriminatory practices. However, both bills have faced significant opposition, particularly from Republicans, who argue that the measures would federalize elections and undermine state sovereignty. In this section, we will explore the key provisions of each bill, the arguments for and against them, and the broader implications for the future of voting rights in the United States.

The For the People Act: Expanding Access and Ensuring Transparency

The For the People Act (also known as H.R. 1 in the House of Representatives) is a sweeping election reform bill introduced by Democrats in response to concerns about state-level voting restrictions and the broader issue of election transparency. It seeks to create a uniform set of federal standards designed to expand access to the ballot, reduce the influence of money in politics, and safeguard democracy from foreign interference. The bill has become a focal point in the national debate over voting rights, with progressives viewing it as essential to protecting democracy, while conservatives argue that it represents an overreach of federal power.

Key Provisions of the For the People Act

- **Automatic Voter Registration (AVR).** One of the most significant components of the For the People Act is its proposal for automatic voter registration. Under this system, individuals would be automatically registered to vote when interacting with government agencies, such as the Department of Motor Vehicles, unless they actively opt out. Proponents argue that AVR would greatly increase voter participation, particularly among young people and minorities, who are often underrepresented in voter rolls.

- **No-Excuse Mail-In Voting.** The bill also seeks to standardize mail-in voting by requiring all states to offer no-excuse absentee voting, meaning that voters can request a mail-in ballot for any reason. This provision builds on the expansion of mail-in voting during the COVID-19 pandemic, which saw a significant increase in voter participation due to the convenience of voting by mail. The Act also mandates the use of drop boxes for voters to submit ballots securely.

- **Early Voting and Election Day as a Federal Holiday.** Another key provision includes a requirement for states to provide at least two weeks of early voting, including weekends, which would ensure more flexible voting options for people who have difficulty making it to the polls on Election Day. Additionally, the bill proposes making Election Day a federal holiday to increase voter turnout and give all citizens an equal opportunity to participate in elections.

- **Restoring Voting Rights to Felons.** The For the People Act includes provisions to restore voting rights to individuals convicted of felonies who have completed their sentences. This would significantly impact millions of formerly incarcerated individuals, many of whom are disproportionately people of color, by re-enfranchising them and ensuring their right to vote.

- **Campaign Finance and Transparency Reforms.** Beyond expanding voting access, the bill aims to address the outsized influence of money in politics. It includes measures to increase transparency in campaign finance, such as requiring disclosure of large donors and dark money contributions, and seeks to reduce the influence of super PACs and corporate interests in elections.

Supporters' Arguments

- **Expanding Voter Access.** Proponents of the For the People Act argue that the bill is essential to ensuring that every eligible American has the opportunity to vote. They emphasize that the bill addresses many of the barriers that disproportionately affect minority voters, low-income voters, and young people, who often face challenges in registering to vote, accessing polling places, or taking time off work to cast a ballot. Supporters see the bill as a crucial tool to expand democratic participation and strengthen voting rights at a time when many states are moving in the opposite direction by enacting restrictive laws.

- **Addressing Voter Suppression.** For advocates of the bill, the For the People Act is a direct response to what they view as a coordinated effort by Republican-led states to suppress voter turnout, particularly among Democratic-leaning constituencies. They argue that federal action is needed to counter these efforts and protect the fundamental right to vote, especially in light of recent state laws that restrict mail-in voting, limit early voting, and impose strict voter ID requirements.

- **Reining in Special Interests.** Supporters also praise the bill's campaign finance reforms, which they argue will help reduce the influence of big money in politics and give ordinary citizens a stronger voice in the electoral process. By increasing transparency and limiting the role of corporate money in elections, proponents believe the bill will help restore public trust in the political system and reduce corruption.

Opponents' Arguments

- **Federal Overreach and State Sovereignty.** Critics, particularly Republicans, argue that the For the People Act represents a federal takeover of elections, infringing on states' rights to set their own voting laws and procedures. They maintain that elections should be managed at the state level, in keeping with the Constitution, and that the bill undermines this principle by imposing one-size-fits-all standards on states with different voting systems and needs.

- **Undermining Election Security.** Opponents also express concerns that provisions like automatic voter registration and no-excuse absentee voting could weaken election security and increase the risk of fraud. While evidence of widespread voter fraud is minimal, critics argue that expanding mail-in voting and loosening requirements for voter registration could open the door to potential abuse, undermining the integrity of elections.

- **Disincentivizing Local Innovation.** Some argue that the bill's national standards could prevent states from experimenting with innovative solutions to election challenges. Critics maintain that local governments are better equipped to understand the specific needs of their populations, and they worry that the federal government's involvement could lead to inefficiencies or the imposition of inappropriate policies in states with different demographics and political environments.

The John Lewis Voting Rights Act: Restoring Federal Oversight

The John Lewis Voting Rights Act (also known as H.R. 4) is another key piece of legislation aimed at protecting voting rights, particularly for minority communities. Named in honor of the late civil rights icon John Lewis, the bill seeks to restore the protections of the Voting Rights Act of 1965, which were significantly weakened by the Supreme Court's 2013 decision in Shelby County v. Holder. The ruling in that case struck down the preclearance provision of the Voting Rights Act, which required states with a history of discriminatory voting practices to obtain federal approval before changing their election laws.

Key Provisions of the John Lewis Voting Rights Act

- **Restoring Preclearance.** The central feature of the John Lewis Voting Rights Act is the restoration of preclearance, but with updated criteria for determining which states and localities would be subject to federal oversight. States that have a recent history of voting discrimination would need to seek approval from the federal government—either through the Department of Justice or a federal court—before making changes to their voting laws, such as redistricting or altering voter registration rules.

- **Modernized Criteria for Oversight.** The Act introduces new criteria for determining which states should be subject to preclearance, taking into account recent cases of voter discrimination rather than relying on data from the 1960s and 70s. This updated approach seeks to address the Supreme Court's ruling in Shelby County, which argued that the original formula was outdated and no longer reflective of current voting conditions.

- **Federal Intervention in Discriminatory Practices.** In addition to preclearance, the bill allows the federal government to step in and block state voting laws that are shown to have a discriminatory impact on minority voters, even if the intent behind the law is not explicitly discriminatory. This provision is designed to address what voting rights advocates see as modern-day voter suppression tactics that disproportionately affect Black, Latino, and Native American voters.

Supporters' Arguments

- **Preventing Voter Discrimination.** Supporters argue that the John Lewis Voting Rights Act is essential to preventing racial discrimination in voting, particularly in states with a history of suppressing minority votes. By restoring federal oversight, they believe the Act will ensure that any changes to voting laws are thoroughly vetted to ensure they do not disproportionately harm voters of color.

- **Addressing Modern Suppression Tactics.** Voting rights advocates see this legislation as critical in combating modern-day voter suppression efforts, such as restrictive voter ID laws, gerrymandering, and voter roll purges, which may disproportionately affect minority voters. By reinstating federal preclearance, the Act would prevent states from implementing these laws without proper oversight.

Opponents' Arguments

- **State Sovereignty and Federal Overreach.** Opponents of the John Lewis Voting Rights Act argue that it infringes on state sovereignty by subjecting certain states to heightened scrutiny and federal control. They maintain that states should have the right to manage their own election processes without interference from the federal government, especially since the original conditions that led to the Voting Rights Act of 1965 have changed significantly.

- **Outdated and Unnecessary.** Critics also argue that the bill is unnecessary, claiming that the discriminatory practices that prompted the Voting Rights Act's original passage in 1965 are no longer prevalent in the same way. They contend that the preclearance formula is outdated and unfairly targets certain states based on past behavior, rather than addressing modern electoral challenges.

Federal Action and the Future of Voting Rights

The For the People Act and the John Lewis Voting Rights Act represent two distinct approaches to expanding voting access and protecting the integrity of elections. Both bills aim to counter the wave of restrictive state voting laws, but they have faced significant opposition from Republicans who see these measures as an infringement on states' rights. As the debate continues, the future of these bills—and the broader issue of voting rights—will likely play a key role in shaping the 2024 presidential election and beyond.

State-Level Voting Laws: A Patchwork of Policies

Since the Dobbs v. Jackson Women's Health Organization decision that overturned Roe v. Wade, the U.S. has entered an era where access to certain rights—including voting—varies significantly from state to state. This reality is reflected in the growing patchwork of voting laws that differ widely based on whether a state is controlled by Republicans or Democrats. The result is a divided nation, with some states enacting laws that expand access to the ballot, while others impose new restrictions that critics argue disproportionately affect voter turnout among minority groups, low-income individuals, and younger voters.

As state legislatures continue to pass new voting laws, the implications for future elections and democratic participation in America are profound. This section will explore how these laws vary across the country, examine examples from both Republican-led and Democratic-led states, and consider how the differences in state voting laws are shaping the political landscape.

Republican-Led States: Restricting Voting Access

In the wake of the 2020 presidential election, many Republican-controlled states have passed new laws aimed at tightening voting rules, often citing concerns over election security and voter fraud. These laws generally focus on limiting access to early voting, mail-in ballots, and same-day voter registration, measures that supporters argue are necessary to protect election integrity. Critics, however, contend that these laws are part of a broader effort to suppress voter turnout, particularly among Democratic-leaning constituencies such as people of color, young voters, and urban residents.

Georgia

Georgia, a key battleground state in the 2020 election, passed SB 202 in 2021, a sweeping voting law that has become a flash-point in the national debate over voting rights. The law introduced a number of restrictions, including:

- **ID Requirements for Absentee Voting.** Voters are now required to provide a copy of their state-issued ID when applying for an absentee ballot.

- **Reduced Drop Boxes.** The law limits the number of ballot drop boxes, restricting them to early voting sites and making them only accessible during business hours.

- **Shortened Absentee Voting Period.** Georgia reduced the time frame for requesting absentee ballots, making it harder for voters to navigate the process if they miss the window or face delays.

- **Limitations on Offering Food and Water to Voters in Line.** A controversial provision of the law makes it illegal for volunteers or activists to provide food or water to voters waiting in line, a common practice in urban areas where long lines at polling places are common.

Supporters of the law, including Georgia Republicans, argue that it is necessary to restore confidence in elections following unproven claims of widespread fraud during the 2020 election. They assert that requiring voter ID for absentee ballots and reducing the availability of drop boxes will ensure that elections are secure and that only eligible voters participate.

However, critics, including voting rights advocates like Stacey Abrams and groups like the NAACP, argue that the law disproportionately affects Black voters and other marginalized groups, who are more likely to rely on absentee voting and face longer wait times at polling places. The provision banning the distribution of food and water has been especially criticized as a voter suppression tactic, particularly in areas where voter turnout has historically been high but logistical challenges, such as long lines, persist.

Texas

Texas, another Republican stronghold, has also passed a series of voting restrictions aimed at tightening election security. Senate Bill 1 (SB 1), passed in 2021, includes several provisions that restrict access to voting:

- **Restrictions on 24-Hour Voting.** SB 1 prohibits 24-hour voting, a measure that was used during the 2020 election in Harris County (home to Houston) to accommodate voters who work late-night shifts or have irregular schedules.

- **Ban on Drive-Thru Voting.** The bill also bans drive-thru voting, a method that was popularized in 2020 as a way to protect voters from COVID-19 exposure while still participating in elections.

- **Increased Scrutiny on Mail-In Voting.** Like Georgia's law, Texas' SB 1 requires voters to provide ID when requesting and returning mail-in ballots. It also gives partisan poll watchers greater access to voting areas, allowing them to observe more closely, which critics argue could lead to intimidation.

Governor Greg Abbott and other Republican lawmakers defended the legislation as a way to "ensure that every eligible voter gets to vote, and that only eligible votes are counted." They argue that eliminating methods like drive-thru voting and limiting 24-hour voting prevents potential abuses and standardizes the voting process across the state.

Opponents, including Democrats and voting rights groups, argue that the law specifically targets Democratic voters in large urban areas like Houston, where

Black and Latino voters make up a significant portion of the electorate. These voters, critics argue, are more likely to benefit from flexible voting methods such as drive-thru voting and extended hours, and removing these options constitutes an effort to reduce their turnout.

Democratic-Led States: Expanding Voting Access

In contrast to Republican-led states, many Democratic-controlled states have moved in the opposite direction, passing laws designed to expand access to voting and make it easier for people to participate in elections. These laws typically focus on expanding early voting, promoting mail-in voting, and making voter registration more accessible.

California

California, one of the most liberal states in the country, has been at the forefront of efforts to expand voting rights and increase voter participation. The state passed a series of reforms aimed at making it easier for residents to vote, including:

- **Permanent Mail-In Voting.** All registered voters in California now automatically receive a mail-in ballot for every election. This change was made permanent after the 2020 election, when mail-in voting surged in popularity due to the COVID-19 pandemic.

- **Extended Early Voting.** California offers early voting for up to 11 days before Election Day, ensuring that voters have multiple opportunities to cast their ballots without facing long lines or crowded polling places.

- **Same-Day Voter Registration.** California also allows same-day voter registration, meaning residents can register to vote and cast a ballot on the same day during early voting or on Election Day.

Proponents of these laws, including Governor Gavin Newsom, argue that they are essential to increasing voter participation and making voting as accessible as possible, especially for people who may have difficulty getting to the polls on Election Day. They also point to the success of mail-in voting during the 2020 election as proof that expanding access can be done without sacrificing election integrity.

However, critics, including some Republicans, argue that automatically mailing ballots to all voters increases the potential for fraud and raises concerns about ballot security. They contend that expanding access to mail-in voting could lead to more administrative errors, such as ballots being sent to outdated addresses or misused by third parties.

New York

New York, another Democratic stronghold, has also made efforts to expand access to the ballot, particularly through initiatives aimed at early voting and voter registration:

- **Early Voting.** New York established early voting for the first time in 2019, allowing voters to cast ballots during a nine-day period before Election Day. This measure was designed to reduce long lines on Election Day and make voting more convenient for busy residents.

- **Automatic Voter Registration.** In 2020, New York passed legislation to implement automatic voter registration (AVR), meaning that eligible residents are automatically registered to vote when interacting with state agencies such as the Department of Motor Vehicles unless they opt out.

- **No-Excuse Absentee Voting.** New York also temporarily expanded no-excuse absentee voting during the COVID-19 pandemic, allowing all voters to request mail-in ballots. Efforts are underway to make this change permanent through a state constitutional amendment.

Supporters of these efforts, including Governor Kathy Hochul, argue that making it easier to vote is essential for protecting democracy and ensuring that all eligible citizens can participate in the electoral process. They emphasize that expanded access has not led to any credible evidence of fraud and that more inclusive voting laws reflect the diversity of the state's population.

Opponents, however, argue that certain reforms, such as automatic voter registration, may create administrative challenges and potentially increase errors in voter rolls. They also express concerns that measures like no-excuse absentee voting could lead to issues with ballot integrity if not carefully managed.

Polarization of Voting Laws and Political Implications

The growing divide between Republican and Democratic states in terms of voting access is reshaping the political landscape in the U.S. In states where voting access is expanding, Democrats are likely to benefit from higher turnout among young voters, minorities, and urban residents, all of whom tend to support the party. In contrast, in states with new restrictions, Republicans may benefit from lower turnout in these same groups, which could help the GOP maintain control in key swing states.

This patchwork of laws is creating two very different electoral experiences depending on where Americans live. In Republican states, voters may face more hurdles to casting ballots, especially if they rely on absentee voting or live in areas with fewer polling places. In Democratic states, voters are likely to find it easier to access the ballot, with more opportunities for early voting, mail-in voting, and same-day registration.

Impact on Future Elections

The impact of these varying state laws will likely be seen in upcoming midterm and presidential elections, with turnout disparities between states becoming more pronounced. Battleground states, where election outcomes are often decided by small margins, are of particular interest, as changes in voting laws could sway election results by either increasing or decreasing turnout in key constituencies.

The divergent approaches to voting access are also fueling broader legal battles, with many restrictive voting laws facing court challenges on the grounds that they violate the Constitution or federal voting rights laws. The future of these laws—and the larger question of how voting rights will evolve in the U.S.—will likely be determined in the courts and through continued political pressure at both the state and federal levels.

The Impact on Voter Turnout and Democracy

The growing polarization in state-level voting laws is already having a profound impact on voter turnout and the overall health of American democracy. With some states passing legislation to restrict voting access while others expand it, the ability of citizens to participate in elections is becoming increasingly unequal, based largely on geography and political control at the state level. This division is reshaping the American electorate, potentially disenfranchising millions of voters and raising serious questions about the future of democratic participation.

In this section, we explore the potential long-term effects of these laws on voter turnout, the implications for democratic legitimacy, and the broader consequences of creating a two-tier voting system in the United States.

Disparities in Voter Turnout

One of the most significant consequences of the current patchwork of voting laws is the creation of stark disparities in voter turnout between states with restrictive voting policies and those that promote greater access. Historically, voter turnout has varied based on socioeconomic factors, with low-income voters, people of color, and young people participating at lower rates. The new wave of voting restrictions exacerbates these disparities, making it even harder for vulnerable populations to vote.

Lower Turnout in Restrictive States

States that have enacted stricter voting laws—including new voter ID requirements, limitations on early voting, and restrictions on mail-in ballots—are likely to see a drop in turnout among voters who rely on more flexible voting options. For example:

Voter ID laws disproportionately affect voters who lack access to government-issued identification, such as low-income individuals, minorities, and elderly citizens. In states with strict voter ID laws, studies have shown a measurable decline in turnout among these groups.

Restrictions on mail-in voting and absentee ballots, especially in states like Texas and Georgia, may lead to lower participation among voters who have limited ability to travel to polling locations, such as those who are disabled, elderly, or live in rural areas. This is particularly concerning in areas where polling places are far apart or where public transportation is limited.

Reduced early voting periods disproportionately affect working-class voters, who may find it difficult to vote on Election Day due to work schedules, childcare responsibilities, or long wait times at the polls.

In these states, minority voters are often the most affected by these restrictions. For instance, a study by the Brennan Center for Justice found that in North Carolina, after the introduction of strict voter ID laws and cuts to early voting, Black voter turnout fell by nearly 9% in the 2016 presidential election compared to 2012.

Higher Turnout in States Expanding Access

Conversely, states that have moved to expand voting access—by implementing same-day voter registration, automatic voter registration, and no-excuse absentee voting—are likely to experience higher turnout, particularly among underrepresented groups. For example:

Automatic voter registration (AVR) systems, now in place in states like Oregon and California, have been shown to significantly increase voter participation. In Oregon, after the state adopted AVR in 2016, voter registration rates surged, leading to a 4% increase in turnout in the 2016 presidential election.

Mail-in voting has proven to be especially popular in states like Colorado, California, and Oregon, where every voter receives a mail-in ballot by default. Studies have shown that mail-in voting increases participation among groups that are traditionally underrepresented, such as young voters and people of color.

In states with expansive voting laws, voters have more options and flexibility, which increases overall participation and reduces barriers that typically prevent some voters from casting their ballots.

The Erosion of Democratic Legitimacy

The growing disparity in access to voting raises concerns about the legitimacy of the electoral process. When entire groups of people are disproportionately affected by restrictive laws, it undermines the principle of universal suffrage—the idea that every citizen should have an equal opportunity to participate in democratic elections.

Disenfranchisement of Minority Communities

The disenfranchisement of minority voters is particularly concerning. Historically, efforts to suppress the voting rights of Black, Latino, and Native American communities have been a persistent issue in American democracy. The introduction of laws that limit access to absentee voting, reduce polling places, or impose stringent voter ID requirements echoes the discriminatory practices of the past, such as Jim Crow laws that were explicitly designed to disenfranchise Black voters.

If certain communities consistently face higher barriers to voting, it creates a two-tier system where the voices of wealthier and whiter voters are amplified, while marginalized groups are left out of the political process. This imbalance threatens the legitimacy of election outcomes, as it raises questions about whether the results truly reflect the will of the people or whether they are skewed by unequal access to the ballot.

Loss of Public Confidence in Elections

Public confidence in the fairness and integrity of elections is also at risk. Widespread claims of voter fraud—despite the absence of evidence to support such claims—have already eroded trust in the electoral system. Adding restrictive voting laws to the mix could exacerbate this issue by giving the appearance that elections are being manipulated to favor one political party over another.

When voters, particularly those from minority groups, feel that their access to the ballot is being restricted, it weakens trust in democracy itself. This could lead to further disengagement from the political process, lower voter turnout, and an increased sense of disenfranchisement among those who feel their votes do not count.

A Two-Tier Voting System: A National Divide

The rise of a two-tier voting system—where access to the ballot depends on where a person lives—has profound implications for the future of democratic participation in the United States.

Unequal Access Based on Geography

The stark differences between states that restrict voting and those that expand it are creating a situation where voters in Republican-led states face more significant barriers to voting than those in Democratic-led states. This uneven access to the ballot could deepen existing political divisions between red and blue states and create a landscape where geography plays an outsized role in determining voter turnout and electoral outcomes.

For example, voters in states like California and Colorado have relatively easy access to mail-in ballots and early voting, while voters in Georgia, Texas, and Arizona must navigate stricter rules that make it more difficult to cast a ballot. This divide raises questions about equality and fairness in the democratic process, particularly as national elections hinge on turnout in key battleground states.

Implications for Political Representation

The two-tier system could also impact political representation, especially in federal elections where voter suppression in one state could tip the balance of power in the House, Senate, or Electoral College. For example, if voting restrictions in swing states like Georgia or Arizona reduce turnout among Democratic-leaning constituencies, it could shift the outcome of elections in favor of Republicans, regardless of national sentiment.

The unequal distribution of voting rights also exacerbates issues of political inequality and could lead to policy outcomes that do not reflect the preferences of the majority of Americans. When certain groups are systematically prevented from voting or face higher barriers to participation, the resulting policies may favor those who have greater access to the ballot.

Legal Challenges and the Future of Voting Rights

The future of voting rights in America will likely be shaped by ongoing legal challenges to restrictive state laws, as well as the push for federal legislation aimed at protecting and expanding access to the ballot.

Legal Battles Over State Voting Laws

Many of the restrictive voting laws passed in Republican-controlled states are currently facing court challenges from civil rights groups, including the American Civil Liberties Union (ACLU), the NAACP Legal Defense Fund, and the League of Women Voters. These lawsuits argue that the new laws violate the Voting Rights Act and the U.S. Constitution by disproportionately affecting minority voters and creating unnecessary barriers to voting.

The outcome of these legal battles will have a significant impact on future elections, particularly as courts weigh the balance between state sovereignty in regulating elections and the need to protect the right to vote.

Federal Legislation: A Potential Solution?

At the federal level, proposals such as the For the People Act and the John Lewis Voting Rights Act aim to address the growing divide in voting access by establishing national standards that would protect voter rights across all states. However, these bills face significant opposition in Congress, particularly from Republicans who argue that they represent federal overreach and infringe on state control of elections.

Whether or not federal legislation is passed, the national debate over voting rights is likely to continue, with advocates on both sides pushing for reforms that reflect their vision of democracy. The stakes are high: the future of voter access, election integrity, and the legitimacy of American democracy itself hang in the balance.

Election Integrity vs. Access: Finding Common Ground

The debate over election integrity and voter access has become one of the most polarizing issues in American politics. On one side, advocates for stricter voting laws argue that such measures are essential to prevent voter fraud, ensure the accuracy of election results, and restore public confidence in the democratic process. On the other side, critics argue that these laws disproportionately disenfranchise minority groups, young voters, and low-income Americans, effectively restricting their access to the ballot box. The result is a deeply divided political landscape, with different states enacting laws that either tighten or expand voting access depending on the party in power.

Despite these entrenched positions, there is growing recognition that compromise and common ground may be possible. Election reform does not have to be a zero-sum game. There are bipartisan solutions that could improve both election security and voter access, ensuring that elections are both fair and inclusive. In this section, we explore potential avenues for compromise, look at successful examples of bipartisan election reforms, and consider how these efforts could shape the future of voting rights in the United States.

Balancing Security and Access

The challenge in the voting rights debate is finding ways to ensure secure elections without creating barriers to voting, especially for vulnerable populations. Many experts and advocates argue that security and access are not mutually exclusive, and that election systems can be designed to protect against fraud while also promoting higher voter turnout. Several potential reforms offer a path forward:

Voter ID with Accessibility Provisions

One of the most contentious issues in the debate over voting rights is the requirement for voter ID. Proponents argue that requiring a government-issued ID helps prevent voter fraud by ensuring that only eligible voters can cast ballots. However, critics contend that strict voter ID laws disproportionately impact minority groups and low-income voters who may not have easy access to the required identification.

A potential compromise could involve creating voter ID laws that include provisions to make obtaining an ID more accessible. For example, states could offer free voter IDs to anyone who needs one, provide mobile ID units that travel to under-served communities, or allow a broader range of identification to be used at polling places, such as student IDs, utility bills, or tribal identification cards. These measures would address concerns about voter fraud while ensuring that no eligible voter is disenfranchised due to the lack of an ID.

Automatic Voter Registration (AVR) Paired with Enhanced Security Measures

Automatic voter registration (AVR) is a reform that has been shown to increase voter participation by registering eligible citizens to vote when they interact with government agencies, such as the Department of Motor Vehicles. Under AVR, individuals are automatically registered unless they choose to opt out. This reform has been implemented in several states, including Oregon and California, where it has led to significant increases in voter registration and turnout.

Critics of AVR often express concerns about voter roll accuracy and the potential for ineligible voters to be mistakenly registered. A possible compromise would involve pairing AVR with enhanced security measures, such as regular voter roll maintenance to ensure that voter lists are kept up to date and cross-checking voter registrations with state and federal databases to prevent duplicate registrations or ineligible voters from being registered. This approach would maintain the benefits of increased voter participation while addressing concerns about election integrity.

Expanded Early Voting with Uniform Standards

Another area where compromise could be found is early voting. Expanding early voting allows voters more flexibility to cast their ballots at a time that is convenient for them, reducing long lines on Election Day and making it easier for those with demanding schedules to participate in elections. However, some states have significantly reduced early voting periods, arguing that it can increase administrative costs and create opportunities for errors or fraud.

A possible solution could involve expanding early voting while also establishing uniform standards to ensure that early voting is conducted securely. For example, states could set minimum security protocols for early voting sites, such as video surveillance of polling places and secure storage of ballots. By creating standardized procedures for early voting, states could make it easier for voters to participate while maintaining election security.

Successful Examples of Bipartisan Election Reforms

Despite the partisan divide, there have been successful examples of bipartisan election reforms in several states that could serve as models for the rest of the country. These efforts show that it is possible to address concerns about election security and access without alienating one side or the other.

Colorado: A Model for Mail-In Voting

Colorado is widely regarded as a national model for mail-in voting. Since 2013, the state has conducted all elections by mail, sending every registered voter a ballot that can be returned by mail or dropped off at a secure drop box. Colorado also offers in-person voting for those who prefer it, and the state has robust security measures in place to protect against fraud, including signature verification, ballot tracking, and secure ballot storage.

Both Democrats and Republicans in Colorado have praised the system for increasing voter turnout while ensuring election integrity. The state has seen consistently high turnout rates since implementing mail-in voting, and there have been no significant issues with fraud. Colorado's success suggests that mail-in voting, when combined with strong security measures, can be an effective way to make voting more accessible without compromising election security.

Utah: A Republican State Embraces Vote-by-Mail

Utah, a deeply Republican state, has also embraced vote-by-mail as a way to increase voter participation. Like Colorado, Utah automatically mails ballots to all registered voters, who can then return them by mail or drop them off in person. The state has implemented several security measures, including signature verification, secure ballot drop boxes, and post-election audits to ensure the accuracy of the results.

Utah's vote-by-mail system has been popular among voters of both parties, with Republicans and Democrats alike benefiting from the convenience and accessibility of the system. The state has demonstrated that mail-in voting can work in conservative states, providing a potential road-map for other Republican-led states looking to expand voter access while maintaining election security.

The Importance of Voter Education

In addition to reforming voting laws, a key part of balancing security and access is ensuring that voters understand the rules and procedures for participating in elections. Voter education is critical to ensuring that all eligible citizens know how to register, where to vote, and what identification or documentation they may need. Effective voter education programs can help prevent confusion at the polls and reduce the likelihood of voters being disenfranchised due to misunderstandings about the voting process.

Investing in Voter Outreach

States and local governments can invest in voter outreach programs that educate the public about their voting options, including mail-in voting, early voting, and Election Day voting. These programs can be especially helpful for first-time voters, young people, and immigrants, who may be unfamiliar with the voting process.

Outreach efforts should include targeted campaigns for marginalized communities, such as minority voters, non-English-speaking populations, and low-income voters, to ensure that these groups have the information they need to participate in elections. By providing clear, accurate information about the voting process, states can help reduce barriers to voting and increase turnout.

Simplifying the Voting Process

In addition to voter education, states can also work to simplify the voting process by making registration easier and streamlining election procedures. For example, offering online voter registration allows citizens to register to vote from their homes, making the process more convenient and accessible. States can also offer multilingual voting materials and voter assistance hot-lines to help ensure that all voters, regardless of language or ability, can participate in elections without unnecessary difficulties.

Bipartisan Efforts for Reform

Although the current political climate makes compromise on voting rights difficult, there is evidence that bipartisan coalitions can come together to pass meaningful reforms. In Nevada, for instance, Democrats and Republicans worked together to pass legislation that expanded early voting and improved election security measures. Similarly, in Kentucky, the Republican-controlled legislature passed a bill to make it easier for voters to request absentee ballots and vote early while also implementing voter ID requirements that included provisions for voters to obtain free IDs.

These examples show that it is possible for lawmakers from both parties to find common ground when it comes to protecting the integrity of elections while also making it easier for citizens to vote. By focusing on reforms that address the needs and concerns of both sides, states can implement policies that ensure secure, fair, and accessible elections for all Americans.

A Path Forward

The debate over election integrity and voter access is unlikely to be resolved anytime soon, but there is room for compromise and common ground. By pursuing reforms that balance the need for secure elections with the goal of expanding voter access, the United States can strengthen its democracy and ensure that all eligible citizens have the opportunity to participate in the electoral process.

As states continue to pass new voting laws, lawmakers, advocates, and citizens must remain committed to finding solutions that promote both security and access. The future of voting rights in America depends on the ability to navigate these complex challenges while protecting the fundamental right to vote for all.

The Road Ahead: What's Next in the Voting Rights Debate?

The future of voting rights and election integrity in the United States is deeply uncertain, with the debate showing no signs of slowing down. The 2020 presidential election and its aftermath have entrenched a polarized landscape in which states are pulling in opposite directions—Republican-controlled states enacting stricter voting laws, while Democratic-controlled states expand access to the ballot. As this division grows, the future of the country's electoral system will be shaped by a combination of state-level battles, federal legislative efforts, and likely, Supreme Court intervention.

This section will explore what might lie ahead for voting rights, touching on the legal challenges, the potential for federal legislation, the role of grassroots movements, and the impact of these ongoing struggles on future elections, particularly the 2024 presidential race.

Legal Battles Over State-Level Voting Laws

As states continue to enact a wide range of voting laws, both expanding and restricting access, legal challenges are already making their way through the courts. Many restrictive voting laws passed by Republican-led states face lawsuits from civil rights groups and voting rights advocates, who argue that these laws violate the Constitution and federal voting rights protections.

Constitutional Challenges

Many of the new voting restrictions, such as voter ID requirements, limits on mail-in voting, and the reduction of early voting days, are being challenged on the grounds that they disproportionately affect minority voters, low-income individuals, and young people, potentially violating the Equal Protection Clause of the Fourteenth Amendment and the Voting Rights Act of 1965. For example, lawsuits have been filed against Georgia's SB 202 and Texas' SB 1, arguing that these laws amount to modern-day voter suppression and should be overturned.

In some states, courts have temporarily blocked parts of these laws from going into effect, while other cases continue to work their way through the judicial system. The ultimate fate of these laws may be decided by the U.S. Supreme Court, which could issue rulings that set new national standards for voting rights and the balance of state and federal authority over election regulations.

Potential Supreme Court Intervention

The conservative majority on the Supreme Court, reinforced during the Trump administration, is likely to play a critical role in the future of voting rights. The Court's 2013 decision in Shelby County v. Holder, which weakened the Voting Rights Act by eliminating the preclearance requirement, opened the door for states to pass more restrictive voting laws without federal oversight.

The question now is whether the Court will take further action to limit or expand federal protections for voting rights. In Brnovich v. Democratic National

Committee (2021), the Court ruled in favor of an Arizona voting restriction, signaling that the Court may continue to defer to states in setting election laws. However, as more legal challenges arise, the Court may be forced to reconsider its stance on issues like voter ID, gerrymandering, and ballot access—all of which could reshape the electoral landscape for years to come.

Federal Legislation: A Continuing Fight in Congress

Despite the significant state-level activity around voting laws, much of the focus remains on efforts to pass federal legislation that would protect voting rights across the country. Two major pieces of legislation—the For the People Act and the John Lewis Voting Rights Advancement Act—have been at the center of the voting rights debate, but both have faced significant obstacles in Congress.

For the People Act (H.R. 1)

The For the People Act, introduced by Democrats in response to the wave of restrictive voting laws, aims to expand voter access, reform campaign finance laws, and limit gerrymandering. It would set national standards for elections, including automatic voter registration, same-day registration, no-excuse absentee voting, and at least two weeks of early voting. The bill also includes measures to combat voter suppression and increase election security by preventing interference and modernizing election systems.

However, the bill has faced stiff opposition from Republicans, who argue that it represents a federal overreach that undermines state sovereignty in managing elections. The bill passed the House of Representatives but stalled in the Senate, where the filibuster has prevented it from moving forward. With the current 50-50 split in the Senate, overcoming the filibuster would require either 60 votes or a change to filibuster rules, both of which appear unlikely in the near future.

John Lewis Voting Rights Advancement Act (H.R. 4)

The John Lewis Voting Rights Advancement Act seeks to restore key provisions of the Voting Rights Act of 1965, including the preclearance requirement that was struck down by the Supreme Court in 2013. This would require certain states, particularly those with a history of voter suppression, to obtain federal approval before making changes to their voting laws. Supporters argue that the

Act is essential to preventing discriminatory voting practices and ensuring that all Americans have equal access to the ballot.

Like the For the People Act, this legislation faces an uphill battle in the Senate, where Republicans have opposed it on the grounds that it infringes on states' rights. The bill passed the House but has been stalled in the Senate due to the filibuster. Without significant changes in the makeup of the Senate, passing the John Lewis Voting Rights Advancement Act remains a challenge.

Grassroots Movements and Voter Mobilization

While the fight for voting rights continues in the courts and Congress, grassroots movements are playing an increasingly important role in protecting and expanding voter access. Voter mobilization efforts, particularly those led by organizations in communities of color and civil rights groups, have been critical in pushing back against restrictive voting laws and encouraging turnout in key elections.

Voter Registration Drives

In response to restrictive laws, organizations such as Fair Fight Action, founded by Stacey Abrams in Georgia, and Vote.org are ramping up their efforts to register voters, particularly in minority communities and low-turnout areas. These groups are working to ensure that voters are aware of their rights, understand the voting process, and have access to the resources they need to cast their ballots.

These efforts were particularly successful in the 2020 election, where voter mobilization efforts in Georgia, Arizona, and Michigan helped deliver key victories for Democratic candidates. As more states implement restrictive voting laws, grassroots organizations will likely continue to play a pivotal role in countering voter suppression and ensuring that all eligible citizens have a chance to vote.

Litigation and Advocacy

In addition to voter mobilization, civil rights groups are actively pursuing litigation to challenge restrictive voting laws. Organizations such as the ACLU, the NAACP Legal Defense Fund, and the Southern Poverty Law Center have filed lawsuits in multiple states to block laws that they argue disproportionately affect Black, Latino, Native American, and low-income voters. These legal challenges aim to preserve access to the ballot and prevent states from enacting measures that disenfranchise voters.

At the same time, these groups are engaging in advocacy efforts to push for federal voting rights legislation and to raise public awareness about the importance of voting access. They are also working to provide direct support to voters, including helping them navigate voter ID requirements, access absentee ballots, and deal with long wait times at polling places.

Impact on the 2024 Presidential Election and Beyond

The ongoing debate over voting rights is likely to have a profound impact on the 2024 presidential election and future elections at all levels of government. As states continue to pass new voting laws, the ability of citizens to register, vote by mail, and vote early will vary widely based on where they live. In battleground states like Georgia, Arizona, Pennsylvania, and Wisconsin, where elections are often decided by narrow margins, these changes could be decisive in determining the outcome of the next presidential race.

Battleground States

Many of the most contentious voting laws are being implemented in battleground states, where both parties are fighting for control. In states like Georgia and Arizona, where new voting restrictions have been enacted, lower turnout among Democratic-leaning voters could tilt the scales in favor of Republican candidates. Conversely, in states like Michigan and Pennsylvania, where voting access has been expanded, increased turnout among young voters and people of color could benefit Democrats.

The next few years will likely see intense efforts by both parties to mobilize voters, with Republicans focusing on election integrity and Democrats emphasizing the need to protect voter access. As voting laws continue to evolve, the outcomes of key elections will hinge not just on the candidates but on the rules of the game—and who is able to cast a vote.

A Critical Moment for American Democracy

The battle over voting rights and election integrity represents a critical moment for the future of American democracy. The country is at a crossroads, with the potential for significant changes to how elections are conducted, who gets to vote, and how votes are counted. As legal battles continue, federal legislation stalls, and grassroots movements ramp up their efforts, the question of whether the United States can find a balance between election security and voter access remains unresolved.

The 2024 presidential election will be a key test of the country's electoral system, as new state laws take effect and voters grapple with an increasingly complex and divided voting landscape. In the years ahead, the fight for voting rights will continue to shape the political, legal, and cultural landscape of the nation, determining whether America's democracy remains accessible, inclusive, and fair for all.

Conclusion: The Future of Voting Rights and Election Integrity

The debate over voting rights and election integrity is at the forefront of America's political and cultural divide, with significant implications for the future of democratic participation in the United States. The fallout from the 2020 presidential election, and the contentious claims of voter fraud, has driven a deep wedge between those advocating for stricter election laws and those fighting to protect and expand voter access. This conflict has led to a patchwork of state laws that vary widely, creating two vastly different voting experiences based on where one lives. As these battles continue to intensify at the state level, in Congress, and through legal challenges, the future of voting rights in America hangs in the balance.

A Divided Nation: Two Americas for Voting Rights

The U.S. is rapidly evolving into two distinct electoral systems, with Republican-controlled states tightening restrictions and Democratic-controlled states expanding access. In states like Georgia, Texas, and Arizona, new laws have made it more difficult to vote, especially for minority communities, low-income voters, and young people. These laws include provisions like stricter voter ID requirements, limits on absentee voting, fewer drop boxes, and reductions in early voting days. Supporters argue these measures are necessary to safeguard elections from fraud and increase public confidence in the integrity of the electoral process.

On the other hand, blue states such as California, New York, and Colorado are moving in the opposite direction, implementing laws to broaden voter access. These states have enacted reforms like automatic voter registration (AVR), no-excuse absentee voting, and same-day voter registration, all aimed at making it easier for people to participate in elections. These measures are seen as vital to ensuring universal suffrage, particularly for marginalized groups that have historically faced barriers to voting.

This polarization is not only shaping the way elections are conducted but also deepening the cultural and political divide across the country. As access to the ballot becomes increasingly dependent on geography, the risk grows that certain populations will be disenfranchised, leading to elections that do not reflect the true will of the American people.

Legal Challenges and the Role of the Courts

The battle over voting rights is far from settled, and the courts will play a crucial role in shaping the future of American elections. Many of the restrictive voting laws passed by Republican-led states are already facing legal challenges, with lawsuits arguing that these laws violate the Constitution and federal voting rights protections, particularly the Voting Rights Act of 1965.

In recent years, the Supreme Court has shown a willingness to defer to states on election-related issues, as evidenced by its ruling in Shelby County v. Holder (2013), which effectively dismantled the preclearance provisions of the Voting Rights Act. This decision opened the door for many of the restrictive laws we see today. The Court's more recent rulings, including Brnovich v. Democratic National Committee (2021), have further narrowed the scope of federal protections for voters, making it more challenging to fight discriminatory laws.

However, future legal challenges may still shape the landscape of voting rights, especially as cases continue to work their way through the lower courts. The potential for Supreme Court intervention looms large, and the outcomes of these cases could redefine the balance between state sovereignty and federal protections for voters, either solidifying current restrictions or opening the door for more expansive voting rights protections.

The Stakes for American Democracy

The ongoing fight over voting rights and election integrity is not just a legal or political issue—it is a question of the very future of American democracy. The stakes are incredibly high. At its core, this debate is about who gets to participate in the democratic process and how accessible that process should be. Voter suppression—whether through restrictive laws, long wait times, or confusing voting rules—undermines the legitimacy of elections and diminishes the power of the people to choose their representatives.

The risk is that, as more states pass restrictive laws, millions of Americans will find it harder to cast their ballots, particularly those in marginalized communities. These voters, many of whom are Black, Latino, Native American, disabled, or low-income, have historically faced the greatest barriers to participation. If they are systematically disenfranchised, the political power of these groups could be weakened, leading to policies and elected officials who do not truly reflect the diversity of the electorate.

At the same time, concerns about election security cannot be ignored. Although widespread voter fraud is rare, it is essential that elections are perceived as fair and trustworthy by all Americans. If large segments of the population lose faith in the legitimacy of the electoral process, it could lead to further political instability and civic unrest, as seen in the aftermath of the 2020 election.

Federal Legislation: A Path Forward?

Efforts to pass federal voting rights legislation remain critical to addressing the growing disparities in voting access across the country. The For the People Act and the John Lewis Voting Rights Advancement Act both aim to establish national standards for elections, preventing states from enacting laws that suppress the vote or discriminate against minority groups. However, both bills have faced significant hurdles in Congress, particularly in the Senate, where the filibuster has blocked their passage.

Without meaningful federal action, the future of voting rights will largely be determined by the courts and the states, creating further fragmentation in election laws. Advocates for voting rights continue to push for changes to filibuster rules or other mechanisms that could enable these bills to pass, but the political landscape remains deeply divided.

The 2024 presidential election will likely be a pivotal moment for the future of voting rights. Both parties will fight to mobilize voters, but the rules governing who can vote and how they vote will play a decisive role in determining the outcome. The next few years will see intense efforts by Republicans to reinforce election security measures and by Democrats to protect and expand access to the ballot.

Grassroots Efforts: Protecting the Right to Vote

Amid these legal and political battles, grassroots organizations remain on the front-lines of the fight to protect voting rights. Groups like Fair Fight Action, the American Civil Liberties Union (ACLU), and the NAACP Legal Defense Fund are working to ensure that all eligible voters have the resources and information they need to cast their ballots. These organizations are also providing legal support, challenging restrictive voting laws in court, and advocating for policy changes at both the state and federal levels.

Voter registration drives, voter education campaigns, and efforts to increase turnout among minority and low-income voters will be crucial in future elections. These grassroots movements played a critical role in the 2020 election, particularly in battleground states like Georgia, where voter mobilization efforts helped flip the state in favor of Democrats. Moving forward, grassroots activism will continue to be a powerful force in countering voter suppression and ensuring that every American has a voice in the democratic process.

A Fragile Democracy at a Crossroads

The future of voting rights and election integrity in America remains uncertain, but one thing is clear: the battle for control over how elections are conducted and who gets to participate is far from over. The next few years will be decisive in determining whether the country moves toward a more inclusive and accessible electoral system or whether restrictive voting laws will create a two-tiered democracy, where access to the ballot is increasingly unequal.

As legal battles continue, federal legislation stalls, and grassroots efforts intensify, the nation stands at a crossroads. The outcomes of these struggles will shape the future of American democracy—not just for the 2024 election, but for generations to come. Protecting the right to vote remains one of the most critical challenges of our time, and the road ahead will require vigilance, commitment, and a collective effort to ensure that every voice is heard and that every vote counts.

Reality or Fiction?

Introduction: The Climate Change Debate in Modern America

Climate change has emerged as one of the most urgent and contentious issues of the 21st century, shaping both global and national policy debates. In the U.S., discussions around climate change often focus on competing visions for the country's environmental future, with intense disagreement about the scale of the problem, the role of government intervention, and the potential economic costs of addressing the crisis. While the scientific consensus overwhelmingly points to the need for immediate action to mitigate the effects of global warming, the political response remains divided.

The primary fault line in this debate lies between those who advocate for rapid government intervention to curb greenhouse gas emissions and those who caution against hasty decisions that could disrupt economic stability, especially in industries dependent on fossil fuels. As environmentalists push for investments in clean energy and stricter regulations, conservatives emphasize the continued importance of oil, coal, and natural gas to the U.S. economy, warning of the potential risks of a sudden transition away from these energy sources.

Adding to the complexity of the debate is the persistence of climate skepticism. Despite the overwhelming consensus among scientists that human activity is driving climate change, a significant portion of the population remains skeptical or opposed to aggressive measures to address the crisis. These skeptics often frame climate action as economically disruptive or based on exaggerated projections of future impacts.

Here, I discuss the key aspects of the climate change debate, examining the conflict between fossil fuels and green energy, the role of government regulation versus market-driven solutions, and the ongoing influence of climate denialism. By exploring these dimensions, we can better understand the stakes involved and the potential paths forward in the fight against climate change.

The Urgency of Climate Change: Scientific Consensus vs. Political Debate

The urgency of addressing climate change is supported by a wide-ranging scientific consensus, with countless studies concluding that human activities, particularly the burning of fossil fuels like coal, oil, and natural gas, are leading to a rise in global temperatures and contributing to more frequent and severe weather events. The Intergovernmental Panel on Climate Change (IPCC), a body of leading climate scientists, consistently report that without immediate and large-scale reductions in greenhouse gas emissions, the world will face catastrophic consequences, like rising sea levels, more intense heatwaves, prolonged droughts, and increased frequency of extreme weather events such as hurricanes and floods.

Scientific Consensus: The Evidence for Urgency

A vast majority of climate scientists—97% according to several major studies—agree that human activities are the primary cause of global warming. Reports from the IPCC and other scientific bodies provide clear evidence of the rapid warming of the planet over the past century, largely driven by carbon dioxide (CO_2) emissions from burning fossil fuels. The latest IPCC report warns that if the world fails to limit warming to 1.5°C above pre-industrial levels, the impacts of climate change could become irreversible and devastating.

The environmental consequences of global warming are already becoming evident:

- Melting polar ice caps are contributing to rising sea levels, threatening coastal cities and communities.
- Increased frequency of wildfires, particularly in places like California and Australia, is devastating ecosystems and human settlements.
- Heatwaves are becoming more common and more severe, posing public health risks, especially for vulnerable populations.
- Coral bleaching and other climate-related events are causing widespread damage to marine ecosystems.

Furthermore, scientists argue that climate change disproportionately affects the world's poorest regions, exacerbating issues such as food insecurity, water scarcity, and forced migration. The need for immediate action, they warn, is paramount if the world is to avoid the most severe impacts of global warming.

Political Divides: Climate Change as a Partisan Issue

Despite the overwhelming scientific consensus, the issue of climate change remains deeply politicized in the U.S. The debate often reflects broader ideological divides, particularly between progressive and conservative viewpoints.

Progressives and Environmentalists

Progressives and environmental advocates tend to emphasize the moral and practical necessity of taking urgent action to mitigate climate change. They argue that delaying action will only increase the economic and human costs of global warming in the future. Proposals like the Green New Deal, which advocates for a comprehensive overhaul of the U.S. energy sector, seek to move the country toward 100% renewable energy by mid-century, while simultaneously addressing issues like social inequality and job creation in green industries.

Environmentalists point to the economic opportunities embedded in the fight against climate change, including the potential for millions of jobs in solar, wind, and other renewable energy sectors. They argue that a transition away from fossil fuels is not only necessary for the health of the planet but also offers a chance to restructure the economy in a more sustainable and equitable way. For these advocates, the costs of inaction far outweigh the challenges of implementing comprehensive climate policies.

Conservative and Skeptical Perspectives

On the other hand, conservatives often express concerns about the economic impact of rapid transitions away from traditional energy sources. While few conservatives outright deny the existence of climate change today, many question the urgency or severity of the crisis as presented by climate scientists and environmentalists. They argue that aggressive action to phase out fossil fuels could disrupt key industries, lead to significant job losses, and cause energy prices to spike, disproportionately affecting working-class Americans who rely on affordable energy.

For many conservatives, the solution lies in market-driven innovations rather than government mandates. They advocate for gradual transitions that allow the free market to incentivize the development of cleaner energy technologies without sacrificing economic stability. This perspective prioritizes maintaining energy independence and ensuring that the U.S. economy remains competitive globally, especially as countries like China and India continue to rely heavily on fossil fuels.

Bridging the Gap: Balancing Economic and Environmental Needs

While the scientific consensus is clear about the urgency of addressing climate change, the political debate remains focused on how to balance the economic costs with the environmental necessity of taking action. Many policymakers on both sides of the debate are grappling with how to address climate change in a way that both protects the planet and supports economic growth.

One area of potential compromise could involve expanding research and development for green technologies, particularly in areas like carbon capture, nuclear energy, and energy efficiency, while also providing support for workers in fossil fuel industries to transition to new careers in the green economy. This approach could satisfy both environmentalists' desire for aggressive action and conservatives' concerns about economic disruption.

The Need for Consensus

The debate over the urgency of climate change reflects broader disagreements about science, economics, and the role of government regulation. However, as the evidence for the real-world impacts of climate change continues to mount, it is becoming increasingly clear that some level of action is inevitable. The challenge for policymakers is to find a way to bridge the gap between the competing priorities of economic growth and environmental sustainability, ensuring that the U.S. plays its part in the global effort to combat climate change while also protecting the livelihoods of its citizens.

Fossil Fuels vs. Green Energy: Economic and Environmental Trade-offs

The debate over fossil fuels versus green energy lies at the heart of the climate change discussion, with major implications for both the U.S. economy and the global environment. On one side, advocates for traditional energy sources such as coal, oil, and natural gas emphasize their central role in powering the economy, maintaining energy security, and supporting millions of jobs. On the other side, environmentalists and proponents of renewable energy argue that transitioning to clean energy is essential to combating climate change and ensuring a sustainable future. This section explores the arguments on both sides, highlighting the economic and environmental trade-offs involved in the shift from fossil fuels to renewable energy sources.

The Role of Fossil Fuels in the Economy

For over a century, fossil fuels have been the foundation of the global energy system, driving economic growth and industrialization. In the United States, coal, oil, and natural gas have provided affordable and reliable energy, powering industries, transportation, and households.

Economic Importance of Fossil Fuels

Supporters of fossil fuels emphasize their critical role in the U.S. economy:

- **Job Creation.** The fossil fuel industry supports millions of jobs across the country, particularly in states like Texas, Wyoming, West Virginia, and North Dakota. These jobs range from coal mining and oil drilling to related fields like transportation, refining, and manufacturing.

- **Energy Independence.** The U.S. energy boom over the past two decades, driven by the discovery of vast shale oil and natural gas reserves, has allowed the U.S. to become a net exporter of oil and gas, reducing dependence on foreign energy sources. Many conservatives argue that this energy independence is vital for national security and economic stability, as it shields the country from global energy price fluctuations and geopolitical instability in oil-rich regions.

- **Affordable Energy.** Fossil fuels, especially natural gas, have played a key role in keeping energy prices low, benefiting consumers and businesses alike. Industries such as manufacturing, transportation, and agriculture rely on cheap energy to maintain competitiveness and minimize costs. Critics of a rapid transition to renewable energy warn that it could lead to higher energy costs, disproportionately affecting low-income households and industries that depend on affordable energy.

Natural Gas: A "Bridge" Fuel?

Some advocates for fossil fuels view natural gas as a bridge fuel that can help transition the economy toward cleaner energy while maintaining reliability. Natural gas emits significantly less carbon dioxide (CO_2) than coal when burned for electricity, making it a cleaner alternative within the fossil fuel category. This view suggests that natural gas can serve as a short- to medium-term solution while renewable energy infrastructure is developed and scaled up.

However, environmentalists argue that relying on natural gas delays the necessary transition to fully carbon-neutral energy sources, pointing out that methane—a potent greenhouse gas—often leaks during natural gas extraction and transportation, undermining its environmental benefits.

The Case for Renewable Energy

On the other side of the debate, environmentalists and advocates for renewable energy argue that transitioning away from fossil fuels is essential to mitigate climate change and promote sustainability. Renewable energy sources, such as solar, wind, hydro-power, and geothermal, offer a clean alternative to fossil fuels, emitting little to no greenhouse gases.

Environmental Benefits of Renewable Energy

The most significant argument for renewable energy is its potential to drastically reduce greenhouse gas emissions, which are the primary driver of climate change. According to the International Energy Agency (IEA), transitioning to renewable energy could prevent billions of tons of CO_2 emissions each year, helping to limit global warming to 1.5°C above pre-industrial levels—a key goal of the Paris Agreement.

Beyond emissions reductions, renewable energy has other environmental benefits:

- **Reduced Air and Water Pollution.** Fossil fuel extraction and combustion produce significant air pollution, contributing to respiratory diseases, smog, and acid rain. In contrast, renewable energy sources, particularly solar and wind, produce no air pollution. Similarly, renewable energy has a far smaller impact on water resources, as fossil fuel production often involves large-scale water use and contamination.

- **Energy Sustainability.** Unlike fossil fuels, which are finite resources, renewable energy is virtually inexhaustible. The sun will shine, the wind will blow, and rivers will flow regardless of how much energy is consumed, making renewable energy a sustainable solution for long-term energy security.

Economic Opportunities in Clean Energy

While opponents of green energy often focus on the potential job losses in fossil fuel industries, advocates argue that the renewable energy sector has the potential to create millions of new jobs. Investments in solar, wind, and energy efficiency technologies are already creating jobs in manufacturing, installation, maintenance, and research and development. According to the U.S. Bureau of Labor Statistics, jobs in renewable energy fields like solar panel installation and wind turbine service are among the fastest-growing occupations in the country.

- **Solar Energy.** Solar power has become one of the fastest-growing energy sources in the U.S., with the cost of solar panels dropping by nearly 90% over the past decade. As a result, solar installations have surged, creating new opportunities for workers in panel manufacturing, installation, and system maintenance.

- **Wind Power.** Wind energy has also expanded rapidly, particularly in states like Texas, Iowa, and Oklahoma. Wind turbines now generate nearly 10% of U.S. electricity, and the industry continues to grow as new offshore wind projects come online.

Advocates for green energy also point to the potential for energy independence through renewable energy. Unlike fossil fuels, which must be extracted and transported (often over long distances), solar and wind power can be generated domestically, reducing reliance on foreign energy sources and insulating the U.S. from global energy market volatility.

Economic Costs and Transition Challenges

Despite the environmental and economic benefits of renewable energy, the transition away from fossil fuels presents significant economic challenges.

Job Losses in Fossil Fuel Industries

One of the most significant concerns is the potential for job losses in traditional energy sectors like coal mining, oil drilling, and natural gas extraction. Many communities, particularly in Appalachia and the Midwest, are economically dependent on the fossil fuel industry. A rapid transition away from fossil fuels could devastate these regions, leading to widespread unemployment and economic dislocation.

Fossil fuel workers and industry advocates argue that any transition to renewable energy must include provisions for job retraining, economic diversification, and support for displaced workers. This is a key sticking point in the political debate, with some policymakers arguing that government programs are necessary to ensure a just transition that does not leave fossil fuel workers behind.

Reliability and Infrastructure

Another challenge is the question of energy reliability. Renewable energy sources like solar and wind are intermittent—the sun doesn't always shine, and the wind doesn't always blow. Ensuring a stable and reliable energy supply will require significant investments in energy storage technologies, such as batteries, and improvements to the electrical grid to accommodate the variability of renewable power generation.

In addition, transitioning to renewable energy will require large-scale investments in new infrastructure, including the construction of new solar farms, wind turbines, and grid upgrades. While these investments are necessary for the long-term shift to clean energy, they come with significant upfront costs, which some argue could lead to higher energy prices for consumers in the short term.

Long-Term Economic and Environmental Outlook

The long-term outlook for both the economy and the environment will depend on the choices made in the coming years. While fossil fuels will likely continue to play a role in the energy mix for the foreseeable future, the global transition to clean energy is already underway. Countries around the world, including the U.S., are increasing their investments in renewable energy, recognizing the need to address climate change and promote sustainability.

However, balancing the economic costs of this transition with the urgent need to reduce emissions remains a major challenge. Policymakers will need to carefully consider how to manage this transition in a way that both protects the environment and supports economic growth.

Government Regulation vs. Market Solutions: Who Should Drive the Change?

The debate over how to combat climate change and transition from fossil fuels to clean energy often revolves around the role of government regulation versus the reliance on market-driven solutions. Environmentalists tend to advocate for stronger government intervention through policies such as carbon taxes, emission limits, and large-scale public investments in renewable energy infrastructure. Conversely, opponents of strict regulation, particularly conservatives and free-market proponents, argue that private sector innovation, not government mandates, should drive the transition, warning that excessive regulation could stifle economic growth and innovation.

This section will explore both sides of the argument, examining the respective roles of government and market forces in shaping America's response to climate change.

Government-Led Initiatives: The Case for Regulation

Many proponents of aggressive climate action argue that government intervention is essential to tackling climate change, as the issue is too complex, large-scale, and urgent to leave solely to the private sector. They believe that comprehensive climate policies are necessary to incentivize change, regulate harmful practices, and ensure that carbon emissions are reduced in time to prevent the worst impacts of global warming.

A Comprehensive Regulatory Approach

Environmentalists and many progressive policymakers support wide-reaching regulations to reduce carbon emissions and encourage the adoption of clean energy.

A Government-led Approach Might Include

- **Carbon Pricing.** Many advocates push for a carbon tax or a cap-and-trade system that puts a price on carbon emissions, forcing companies to either reduce their emissions or pay for the right to pollute. A carbon tax would place a set fee on each ton of carbon dioxide emitted, while a cap-and-trade system would set an overall limit on emissions and allow companies to buy and trade emissions permits.

- **Emission Standards.** Regulations like the Clean Power Plan (introduced during the Obama administration) aimed to set strict limits on carbon emissions from power plants, especially those using coal. Such regulatory standards are designed to force industries to cut their emissions, or face penalties, pushing them to adopt cleaner technologies.

- **Subsidies for Clean Energy.** Governments can promote renewable energy by offering subsidies, tax credits, and grants for wind, solar, geothermal, and other clean energy technologies. By lowering the cost of investment, these policies encourage companies and utilities to shift toward greener energy sources.

- **Green New Deal.** The most ambitious proposal for government intervention is the Green New Deal, championed by progressive Democrats. This plan calls for a rapid transition to 100% clean, renewable energy by 2050, alongside large-scale investments in infrastructure, jobs, and social justice measures that support workers and communities affected by the shift away from fossil fuels.

Supporters' Arguments: Urgency and Public Good

Proponents of government regulation argue that the market alone will not respond quickly enough to address the scale of the climate crisis. They believe that without regulation, companies will continue to prioritize profits over environmental protection, delaying the transition to clean energy.

Key Arguments For Government Intervention

- **The Urgency of Action.** Climate change is accelerating faster than markets are adapting. Without government-enforced limits on carbon emissions, the planet is on track to exceed the 1.5°C temperature rise, leading to catastrophic environmental consequences. Regulations ensure that all sectors contribute to emission reductions.

- **Market Failures.** The market has historically failed to account for negative externalities like pollution. Without a price on carbon, there's no financial incentive for companies to reduce emissions. Government regulation can correct this market failure by imposing carbon pricing or emission limits.

- **Equitable Transition.** Advocates argue that market forces alone could lead to an unequal transition, where vulnerable communities, workers in fossil fuel industries, and low-income households bear the brunt of the economic shift. Government-led initiatives, such as job retraining programs or support for affected regions, can ensure a just transition that leaves no one behind.

Market-Based Approaches: The Case for Innovation and Deregulation

Opponents of strict government regulation, particularly free-market advocates and conservative policymakers, argue that market-based solutions are more effective and economically sound ways to combat climate change. They emphasize the role of private innovation, competition, and consumer demand in driving the transition to cleaner energy without the need for heavy-handed government interference.

The Power of Private Sector Innovation

Many free-market proponents argue that technological innovation—driven by the private sector—has the potential to solve many of the world's environmental challenges. Examples include:

- **Advances in Clean Technology.** They point to innovations in solar, wind, and battery storage technologies, which have already brought down the cost of renewable energy through market competition and economies of scale. As the cost of renewables continues to fall, many argue that consumers and companies will naturally transition away from fossil fuels.

- **Carbon Capture and Storage (CCS).** Another promising market-driven technology is carbon capture, which could allow for the continued use of fossil fuels while capturing and storing the carbon emissions underground. Companies and energy producers are investing in this technology as a way to balance energy demand with environmental concerns.

- **Electric Vehicles (EVs).** The electric vehicle market is a clear example of how innovation can drive down costs and increase accessibility. As demand for EVs grows, competition between manufacturers is expected to further accelerate the decline in EV prices, making them more affordable for the average consumer.

Supporters' Arguments: Efficiency, Growth, and Consumer Choice

Those who oppose heavy government regulation believe that the market, left to its own devices, will produce more efficient and innovative solutions than government mandates could. They argue that regulation can stifle innovation, create bureaucratic inefficiencies, and raise the cost of energy for consumers.

Key Arguments Against Government Regulation

- **Economic Growth and Jobs.** Critics argue that strict environmental regulations, like those proposed in the Green New Deal or the Clean Power Plan, could hurt the economy by raising energy prices, shutting down industries, and leading to widespread job losses—particularly in fossil fuel-dependent regions. They argue that a market-based approach would allow for a gradual transition that minimizes job losses and economic disruption.

- **Innovation through Competition.** Free-market proponents contend that the best way to foster innovation is through competition, not government mandates. In their view, private companies are better equipped to develop the next generation of clean technologies, and government subsidies or regulations distort market signals, leading to inefficiencies.

- **Consumer Choice.** Many also argue that consumers should be allowed to choose their energy sources, whether fossil fuels or renewables, based on price, reliability, and preference. By imposing regulations that favor renewables, the government could raise energy prices and reduce choices for consumers, especially in rural or lower-income areas where renewable infrastructure may not yet be fully developed.

Hybrid Approaches: Combining Government and Market Forces

Some argue that the best path forward involves a hybrid approach, combining the strengths of both government intervention and market forces. Under this model, the government would play a critical role in setting standards and providing initial funding for renewable energy infrastructure, while the private sector would drive innovation and investment in clean technologies.

Public-Private Partnerships

A common proposal is to encourage public-private partnerships in which the government provides incentives for the private sector to invest in renewable energy while maintaining a light regulatory touch. For example:

- **Research and Development (R&D) Grants.** The government can fund R&D for emerging clean energy technologies such as advanced battery storage, hydrogen fuel cells, and nuclear fusion, which may be too risky for private investors to fully fund on their own. Once these technologies mature, private companies can bring them to market.

- **Tax Incentives.** Rather than imposing strict regulations, the government could provide tax credits and deductions for companies that reduce their emissions or adopt renewable energy. Allowing businesses to adopt greener practices voluntarily, without mandating specific technologies or business models.

Balanced Regulation and Innovation

A hybrid approach would also include balanced regulation, where the government sets basic environmental standards (such as a carbon tax or clean energy targets) but allows companies the flexibility to determine how they meet those standards. This approach would incentivize innovation, ensuring that emission reductions are met.

Conclusion: Navigating the Trade-offs Between Regulation and the Market

The debate over government regulation versus market-based solutions reflects broader disagreements about the role of government in addressing climate change. While environmentalists argue that bold, top-down regulation is necessary to meet the urgency of the climate crisis, free-market advocates believe that innovation and private enterprise should lead the way, with the government playing a minimal role.

In reality, both sides offer valuable insights. A combination of regulation and market incentives may be the most practical way forward, ensuring that emissions are reduced while maintaining economic growth and fostering innovation. Finding the right balance between these two approaches will be critical to shaping the future of energy policy and the fight against climate change.

Climate Denialism: The Roots and Impact of Skepticism

Despite the overwhelming scientific consensus on climate change, skepticism persists, particularly within certain political and ideological groups. This climate denialism has played a significant role in shaping public opinion and policy, slowing the urgency of government action and stoking debates over the economic costs of climate initiatives. While the scientific community agrees that human activity, primarily the burning of fossil fuels, is driving global warming, a significant portion of the American public remains skeptical of this consensus.

This section explores the origins of climate change skepticism, the influence of misinformation and lobbying efforts, and the broader impact of denialism on U.S. environmental policy.

The Roots of Climate Change Skepticism

Climate change skepticism did not arise in a vacuum; it has deep political, economic, and cultural roots. Several factors have contributed to the persistence of climate denialism, even in the face of overwhelming evidence.

Economic Interests and Fossil Fuel Lobbying

A major driver of climate skepticism has been the fossil fuel industry, which has a vested interest in maintaining the status quo. Major oil, gas, and coal companies have spent decades funding organizations, think tanks, and media outlets that cast doubt on climate science. By promoting narratives that question the extent or severity of climate change, these companies have sought to delay regulatory actions that would curtail their profitability.

- ExxonMobil and other large fossil fuel companies have been documented as knowing about the risks of climate change as early as the 1970s. Despite this, these companies funded campaigns that discredited climate science, often comparing the tactics to those used by the tobacco industry to deny the health risks of smoking.

- Lobbying efforts and political donations from the fossil fuel sector have helped shape the stance of conservative politicians, particularly in regions that are economically dependent on fossil fuels. By funding political candidates who support deregulation and oppose aggressive climate policies, the fossil fuel industry has ensured skepticism remains a mainstream political position.

Political Ideology and the Role of Government

Climate change denialism also intersects with broader political ideologies, particularly in the conservative and libertarian movements. Many climate skeptics are driven by a deep suspicion of government intervention in the economy, viewing climate policies as an excuse for increased regulation, taxation, and government overreach.

- For many on the political right, climate action is framed as a threat to individual freedom and economic prosperity. Skeptics often argue that the environmentalist movement is a front for socialism, with climate policies like the Green New Deal seen as attempts to redistribute wealth and limit personal freedoms.

- Libertarians and conservatives who oppose big government are particularly resistant to climate policies that involve significant federal intervention, such as carbon taxes, emission limits, or large-scale public investments in renewable energy. This ideological opposition to government regulation has become a core aspect of climate skepticism.

Cultural and Religious Factors

Cultural factors also play a role in shaping climate change skepticism. In some conservative circles, particularly among evangelical Christians, there is a belief that human dominion over the Earth justifies the exploitation of natural resources. Additionally, some religious groups downplay the significance of climate change, believing that natural disasters are part of God's plan rather than the result of human activity.

In many rural and economically conservative communities, climate skepticism is often tied to concerns about the economic disruption that climate policies could cause. Coal miners, oil workers, and others in fossil fuel-dependent industries may feel personally threatened by the shift to renewable energy, which contributes to resistance to the scientific consensus on climate change.

The Role of Misinformation and Media Influence

The persistence of climate change skepticism has been heavily influenced by the spread of misinformation and disinformation in media and online platforms. Over the past few decades, misleading information about the causes, consequences, and severity of climate change has been promoted by a range of sources, from fossil fuel-funded think tanks to right-wing media outlets.

Think Tanks and Pseudo-Science

Several think tanks and policy organizations, funded in large part by the fossil fuel industry, have been at the forefront of promoting climate skepticism. Groups such as the Heartland Institute and the Competitive Enterprise Institute have published reports that question the science of climate change, downplay its potential effects, or argue that the costs of climate action outweigh the benefits. These reports, while not based on credible scientific evidence, have been widely cited by conservative politicians and media outlets.

- The Heartland Institute, for example, has held annual conferences that feature speakers who question mainstream climate science. These events often attract attention from right-wing media, further amplifying the message that climate change is exaggerated or misunderstood.

- Some of these think tanks and advocacy groups focus on casting doubt about climate models and predictions, often arguing that uncertainty in the science justifies delaying action. By emphasizing areas where climate models are still developing, they contribute to the false notion that the science is unsettled.

Right-Wing Media and Social Media

The influence of right-wing media, particularly Fox News, talk radio, and conservative online platforms, has been instrumental in spreading climate skepticism to a broader audience. These outlets often feature commentators who frame climate change as a hoax, a liberal conspiracy, or a ploy for government control.

- High-profile conservative media figures like Rush Limbaugh and Tucker Carlson have repeatedly questioned the validity of climate science, arguing that environmental regulations harm American businesses and infringe on personal liberties. These narratives are reinforced by frequent misrepresentation of scientific studies or cherry-picked data that suggest climate change is less severe than the consensus indicates.

- Social media platforms have also played a major role in spreading climate denialism. Platforms like Facebook, YouTube, and Twitter have been criticized for allowing misinformation to spread unchecked. Algorithms that prioritize engagement often amplify sensationalist or misleading content, allowing climate denialist views to reach millions of users.

The Impact of Climate Denialism on Policy

The influence of climate denialism on U.S. environmental policy has been significant, particularly under Republican administrations. Climate skepticism at the political level has delayed the implementation of aggressive climate action, weakened environmental regulations, and led to the rollback of climate policies at the federal level.

Trump Administration and Policy Rollbacks

The most prominent example of climate denialism influencing policy was during the Trump administration (2017-2021). President Donald Trump and many of his appointees openly questioned the severity of climate change, and this skepticism shaped the administration's environmental policies.

- The Trump administration withdrew the United States from the Paris Climate Agreement, arguing that the international accord would hurt the American economy and impose unfair burdens on the U.S. while allowing countries like China and India to continue polluting.

- Trump's Environmental Protection Agency (EPA), under Administrator Scott Pruitt, moved to roll back key climate regulations, including the Clean Power Plan, which was designed to limit carbon emissions from power plants. The administration also weakened fuel efficiency standards for vehicles, undermining one of the key policies aimed at reducing transportation emissions.

- The administration promoted the expansion of oil and gas drilling, including opening up public lands and offshore areas for fossil fuel extraction. This was in line with Trump's broader "energy dominance" agenda, which prioritized fossil fuel production over environmental protection.

Delaying Climate Action

The persistence of climate denialism has had a direct impact on the pace of action in the U.S. For decades, debates over whether climate change is real, or whether human activity is responsible, have delayed legislative action at the federal level. While many other countries have moved forward with ambitious climate policies, the U.S. has often lagged behind due to political gridlock fueled by climate skepticism.

Even as climate denialism becomes less politically tenable in the face of more extreme weather events and growing public awareness of climate change, it continues to shape the public discourse, limiting the scope and ambition of proposed solutions. Many policymakers are hesitant to propose aggressive climate policies for fear of backlash from conservative voters and the fossil fuel lobby.

The Persistent Influence of Climate Denialism

Climate denialism remains a powerful force in American politics, despite the mounting evidence of global warming and its devastating impacts. The roots of climate skepticism run deep, driven by economic interests, political ideologies, and the spread of misinformation. As long as a significant portion of the public—and key political leaders—continues to question the severity of climate change, the U.S. will struggle to enact the bold policies necessary to combat the crisis.

The challenge for the climate movement will be to overcome the influence of denialism and misinformation by building broad-based coalitions that can push for meaningful action. In the next section, we will explore how other countries have tackled climate change and what the U.S. might learn from their approaches to environmental policy and energy transition.

Global Comparisons: How Other Countries Are Handling Climate Policy

As the U.S. continues to debate the balance between economic concerns and the urgent need for climate action, many other countries have moved forward with ambitious climate policies. These international efforts demonstrate various approaches to balancing environmental goals with economic realities, providing both challenges and potential models for the U.S. to consider. From the European Union's comprehensive Green Deal to Canada's carbon pricing, nations around the world are taking steps to curb emissions, invest in renewable energy, and create sustainable economic opportunities. Moreover, international agreements such as the Paris Climate Accord aim to bring countries together under a unified vision for addressing the global climate crisis.

International Approaches: How Countries Are Tackling Climate Change

Countries around the world have taken different paths to address climate change, with varying levels of ambition and success. Many nations have set ambitious carbon reduction goals, and their strategies often involve a mix of regulatory measures, market-based mechanisms, and public investments in clean energy.

The European Union: The European Green Deal

The European Union (EU) has taken a leading role in global climate policy with its ambitious European Green Deal. Introduced in 2019, the Green Deal aims to make Europe the first climate-neutral continent by 2050. Its goals include reducing net greenhouse gas emissions by at least 55% by 2030, compared to 1990 levels, and achieving carbon neutrality by mid-century. To achieve these targets, the EU has implemented a wide range of policies:

- **Emissions Trading System (ETS).** The EU operates the world's largest carbon market, the Emissions Trading System (ETS), which caps emissions from the energy, industrial, and aviation sectors. Companies that exceed their emissions caps must purchase additional permits, creating a financial incentive to reduce emissions.

- **Renewable Energy Targets.** The EU has set ambitious renewable energy goals, with a target for 40% of the EU's energy to come from renewable sources by 2030. Countries like Germany and Denmark have been global leaders in wind and solar energy, significantly reducing their reliance on fossil fuels.

- **Circular Economy Initiatives.** The Green Deal also emphasizes creating a circular economy, where products are reused, repaired, and recycled, reducing waste and conserving resources. This holistic approach aims to integrate climate goals into all sectors of the economy.

The EU's strategy exemplifies a comprehensive, multi-sector approach to addressing climate change while fostering economic growth through innovation in clean technology and sustainability.

Canada: Carbon Pricing as a Climate Solution

Canada has adopted a robust carbon pricing system to reduce emissions while encouraging innovation in clean energy. The federal carbon tax, introduced in 2019, places a price on carbon pollution, starting at $20 per ton and increasing annually, reaching $170 per ton by 2030. This pricing mechanism encourages businesses and individuals to adopt more sustainable practices by making fossil fuel consumption more expensive.

- **Revenue Recycling.** A key aspect of Canada's carbon tax is that the revenue generated is returned to households through rebates, ensuring that lower-income families are not disproportionately affected by the increased cost of energy. By refunding the majority of carbon tax revenue, the policy maintains public support while still encouraging a shift to cleaner energy.

- **Provincial Flexibility.** Canada's federal carbon tax applies in provinces that do not have their own equivalent carbon pricing systems. However, several provinces, including British Columbia and Quebec, have implemented their own carbon pricing mechanisms, either through carbon taxes or cap-and-trade programs.

Canada's experience highlights the effectiveness of market-based solutions like carbon pricing in reducing emissions while preserving economic stability. By using tax revenue to fund clean energy projects and support vulnerable households, Canada balances economic concerns with the need for climate action.

China: The Largest Emitter and Largest Investor in Clean Energy

As the world's largest emitter of greenhouse gases, China plays a crucial role in global climate policy. While China remains heavily dependent on coal for electricity, it has also become the world's largest investor in renewable energy. China's climate policies reflect a complex balancing act between sustaining economic growth and reducing emissions.

- **Renewable Energy Investments.** China is the global leader in the production and deployment of solar panels, wind turbines, and electric vehicles (EVs). In 2020, China installed more than 70 gigawatts of solar capacity, and it has ambitious plans to continue scaling up its renewable energy production.

- **National Carbon Market.** In 2021, China launched its national carbon market, the largest in the world by volume of emissions. While still in its early stages, the market covers major polluting industries and is intended to gradually reduce emissions intensity across the economy.

- **Long-Term Goals.** China has committed to peak emissions by 2030 and to achieve carbon neutrality by 2060. While critics argue that these goals are not aggressive enough given China's status as the world's largest emitter, the country's significant investments in renewable energy are reshaping the global energy market.

China's approach demonstrates the possibility of simultaneously growing a massive industrial economy while investing heavily in clean energy. However, the country's reliance on coal and the pace of its transition to renewables remain subjects of global scrutiny.

International Agreements: The Role of the Paris Climate Agreement

The Paris Climate Agreement, signed in 2015, is the cornerstone of international efforts to combat climate change. The agreement unites nearly 200 countries under a common goal of limiting global warming to well below 2°C, with efforts to limit the temperature increase to 1.5°C above pre-industrial levels. Each country commits to Nationally Determined Contributions (NDCs), which outline their plans for reducing emissions.

The U.S. Rejoining the Paris Climate Agreement

The U.S. played a key role in brokering the Paris Agreement, but in 2017, the Trump administration announced its withdrawal from the accord, citing concerns that it would disadvantage American industries. The decision to exit the agreement was seen as a blow to global climate efforts, particularly as the U.S. is the world's second-largest emitter.

However, upon taking office, President Joe Biden quickly moved to rejoin the Paris Agreement as one of his administration's first acts. By reentering the accord, the U.S. signaled its commitment to global climate cooperation, pledging to cut U.S. emissions by 50-52% by 2030 and achieve net-zero emissions by 2050.

Rejoining the Paris Agreement also restores the U.S. as a leader in international climate diplomacy, a role that is critical in urging other countries to increase their climate commitments. As part of this renewed leadership, the U.S. has committed to working with allies to mobilize financial and technical support for developing nations, ensuring that climate solutions are equitable on a global scale.

Economic and Political Trade-offs in Other Nations

Countries implementing climate policies face significant economic trade-offs as they transition away from fossil fuels. While many nations are embracing green energy to meet climate goals, they must also balance the need for economic competitiveness and energy security. This balance often leads to varied approaches to climate policy, with some nations opting for carbon taxes, while others invest heavily in subsidizing renewable energy industries.

Carbon Taxes and Subsidies for Green Energy

Countries like Sweden and Finland have introduced some of the world's highest carbon taxes, making fossil fuels more expensive and incentivizing businesses to shift to clean energy. Meanwhile, nations like Germany and Denmark have focused on renewable energy subsidies, creating favorable market conditions for wind, solar, and biomass industries. These policies have made Germany a global leader in wind energy and Denmark a pioneer in offshore wind farms.

However, the costs of transitioning to a low-carbon economy are significant. Governments must manage the economic impact on traditional energy sectors, address the social costs of displaced workers, and ensure affordable energy prices for consumers. These trade-offs are particularly pronounced in countries that rely heavily on fossil fuels for economic growth, such as China and India, which continue to balance economic development with environmental commitments.

Lessons for the U.S.

The U.S. can draw several lessons from the experiences of other countries:

- **Carbon Pricing Works.** The success of carbon taxes in Europe and Canada demonstrates that market-based mechanisms can effectively reduce emissions while supporting economic growth. Introducing a national carbon tax or cap-and-trade system in the U.S. could help align the country's economic incentives with its climate goals.

- **Investing in Innovation.** Countries like Germany and China show the importance of government investment in clean energy technologies to ensure that industries remain competitive on the global stage. The U.S. can increase investments in research and development to advance technologies like battery storage, electric vehicles, and hydrogen energy.

- **Supporting Vulnerable Workers.** As seen in Canada, governments must protect workers and communities dependent on fossil fuels by offering job retraining programs and investing in the green economy. Policies that ensure a just transition can maintain political support for climate action while addressing economic disparities.

Geopolitical Stakes of Climate Policy

The race to dominate the clean energy industry has significant geopolitical implications. Countries that lead in developing and exporting renewable energy technologies—such as solar panels, electric vehicles, and batteries—are likely to shape the global energy market and wield significant economic power. The U.S. faces competition from China, which has invested heavily in these industries, positioning itself as a major player in the green energy transition.

For the U.S., maintaining global competitiveness in the clean energy market will require substantial public and private investments in innovation, infrastructure, and education. The geopolitical stakes of climate policy are clear: nations that lead in renewable energy will not only reduce their carbon footprints but also secure economic and political advantages in the decades to come.

The Path Forward: Balancing Economic and Environmental Priorities

The transition to a clean energy economy presents both challenges and opportunities. While it is clear that climate action is necessary to address the growing threat of global warming, there remains an ongoing debate about how to balance the environmental urgency of reducing carbon emissions with the economic realities of maintaining jobs and supporting industries reliant on fossil fuels. Finding a path forward that considers both environmental sustainability and economic stability is crucial for achieving long-term success in mitigating climate change. This section explores potential middle-ground solutions that aim to address the needs of both the economy and the environment.

Finding Common Ground: Economic and Environmental Solutions

To achieve the goal of reducing carbon emissions without causing undue economic hardship, policymakers need to consider strategies that bridge the gap between environmental advocates and industries dependent on fossil fuels. The focus should be on ensuring that climate policies do not disproportionately harm workers or communities dependent on traditional energy sectors while also accelerating the transition to a more sustainable future.

Investment in Clean Energy Infrastructure

One potential area of compromise lies in investing in clean energy infrastructure while also supporting workers from the fossil fuel industry. Large-scale investments in solar, wind, and battery storage can provide new economic opportunities and create millions of jobs in renewable energy industries. Governments can incentivize the construction of green energy projects through subsidies, tax credits, and public-private partnerships. At the same time, it is essential to ensure that these investments also support regional economies that have historically relied on coal mining, oil extraction, and natural gas production.

The key is to pair investments in clean energy with programs that offer job retraining and financial assistance to fossil fuel workers. For example, the creation of retraining programs for former coal miners or oil workers would allow them to transition into the renewable energy sector—whether as technicians, engineers, or other roles that align with their skills and experience. A comprehensive approach to workforce transition is critical to maintaining economic stability in communities heavily reliant on fossil fuels.

Supporting Vulnerable Communities

In both the U.S. and globally, vulnerable populations—such as low-income communities, rural areas, and developing nations—are often the most affected by climate change, yet they have the least capacity to adapt. Policymakers must ensure that these communities are not left behind during the shift to a green economy. For example, communities that are heavily reliant on traditional energy sources, such as Appalachia in the U.S., should receive targeted support through economic diversification programs and investments in local green infrastructure.

Internationally, developing countries face unique challenges in adapting to the impacts of climate change while growing their economies. Wealthier nations have a responsibility to provide financial support to help these countries invest in clean energy and adopt sustainable practices without sacrificing economic growth. Programs like the Green Climate Fund, which supports climate adaptation in the developing world, can help ensure that global climate action is equitable.

The Role of Technology and Innovation

Another crucial element of balancing climate action with economic priorities is the role of technology in enabling a smooth transition. Technological advancements in clean energy have the potential to mitigate climate change while creating significant economic opportunities. Both the public and private sectors will need to collaborate to accelerate the development and widespread adoption of these technologies.

Advances in Energy Storage and Electric Vehicles

One of the biggest hurdles to scaling up renewable energy is the intermittent nature of sources like solar and wind power. However, recent breakthroughs in energy storage technologies, particularly in battery storage, are addressing this challenge. Efficient and scalable battery systems can store excess energy generated by renewables and release it when needed, ensuring a more reliable energy grid.

Electric vehicles (EVs) are another area of significant progress. EVs produce zero emissions at the point of use and, when paired with renewable energy sources, can drastically reduce transportation-related emissions. The EV market is growing rapidly, driven by consumer demand and supportive policies. Governments can accelerate this trend by expanding charging infrastructure and offering incentives for both manufacturers and consumers. The widespread adoption of EVs will not only reduce emissions but also create jobs in manufacturing, charging network expansion, and research and development.

Hydrogen Energy and Carbon Capture

Hydrogen energy is another promising technology that can contribute to decarbonizing sectors that are hard to electrify, such as heavy industry and long-distance transportation. Hydrogen can be produced from renewable energy sources and used as a clean fuel. Several countries, including Japan and Germany, have made significant investments in hydrogen technology, which could play a critical role in the global energy transition.

In addition, carbon capture, utilization, and storage (CCUS) technologies offer a way to reduce emissions from existing fossil fuel plants and heavy industries. While carbon capture does not eliminate the need for a broader transition to renewables, it can serve as a bridge solution, helping to reduce emissions while renewable technologies continue to scale. By capturing carbon emissions and storing them underground or using them in industrial processes, CCUS can help reduce the overall carbon footprint of industries that are difficult to fully decarbonize.

Public-Private Collaboration

The development and deployment of these technologies will require close collaboration between the public and private sectors. Governments can support innovation by funding research and development (R&D), offering tax incentives for clean tech companies, and creating policies that encourage the adoption of green technologies. At the same time, the private sector can leverage these incentives to drive competition and innovation, helping to lower costs and increase the efficiency of new technologies.

Public-private partnerships will be critical to scaling up technologies like hydrogen energy, battery storage, and carbon capture. These collaborations can help speed up the transition to a low-carbon economy while creating economic opportunities across sectors.

A Balanced Path Forward

The path forward for addressing climate change will require a careful balance between environmental priorities and economic considerations. By encouraging investment in clean energy infrastructure, supporting vulnerable communities, and leveraging technological innovation, policymakers can create a framework that both reduces carbon emissions and promotes economic growth.

Ultimately, a successful climate strategy will need to prioritize the long-term sustainability of the planet while ensuring that the transition to a green economy is equitable and inclusive. Through smart policies that support innovation, invest in communities, and bring together public and private sector resources, the U.S. and the global community can meet the challenge of climate change while creating a future that is both environmentally sustainable and economically prosperous.

Conclusion: The Stakes for the Future

The debate over climate change reflects one of the most significant challenges of our time, and it is fundamentally about balancing long-term environmental sustainability with short-term economic considerations. At its core, this discussion pits the immediate economic impacts of transitioning to clean energy—including potential job losses in traditional industries and the costs of new infrastructure— against the urgent need to mitigate global warming and prevent irreversible damage to the planet. While the challenges are complex, the consequences of inaction are clear: rising temperatures, more frequent extreme weather events, and severe threats to both ecosystems and human societies.

Summing Up the Debate: Economic vs. Environmental Considerations

The economic arguments against rapid climate action often center on the potential disruption of industries tied to fossil fuels—sectors that provide millions of jobs and play a key role in powering the global economy. Opponents of swift transitions to green energy worry about rising energy costs, loss of livelihoods, and diminished energy security. On the other hand, environmental advocates argue that these short-term economic costs pale in comparison to the long-term consequences of unchecked climate change. Without significant action, the world faces disastrous outcomes—from sea-level rise and food insecurity to increasingly severe storms and widespread displacement of people.

In the long run, addressing climate change could also spur economic growth by creating millions of jobs in the renewable energy sector, promoting technological innovation, and avoiding the immense costs of climate-related disasters. The key to resolving this debate lies in finding a balanced approach that promotes both economic stability and environmental health, ensuring that the transition to a green economy benefits all.

Urgency of Action

As scientific evidence continues to mount, it becomes harder to ignore the growing impact of climate change on the planet. The Intergovernmental Panel on Climate Change (IPCC) has consistently warned that without immediate and large-scale reductions in carbon emissions, global temperatures will continue to rise, surpassing the critical 1.5°C threshold that scientists have identified as a tipping point. The effects of climate change are already being felt across the globe—from more intense wildfires and hurricanes to droughts and flooding that are displacing entire communities.

These growing risks highlight the urgency of comprehensive action. Climate change is not a distant problem—it is already happening, and the longer governments delay taking significant measures, the more severe and costly the impacts will become. The time for incremental, slow-moving policies has passed; instead, the world needs immediate, bold action that tackles both the environmental and economic dimensions of the crisis. This means massive investments in clean energy infrastructure, job retraining programs for displaced workers, and international cooperation to ensure that all nations contribute to global solutions.

A Global and Generational Challenge

Climate change is not confined to any one country—it is a global issue that transcends borders and affects every continent and every community. The nature of the crisis requires international cooperation, as the actions taken (or not taken) by one country can affect the entire planet. Multilateral agreements such as the Paris Climate Accord are crucial frameworks for ensuring that nations work together toward common climate goals, but these agreements must be backed by concrete actions and ambitious targets to be truly effective.

Moreover, climate change is a generational challenge. The choices made by today's leaders and societies will determine the quality of life for future generations. Younger generations are already leading the charge for more aggressive climate policies, recognizing that they will bear the brunt of the environmental damage if action is not taken now. The movement toward sustainability is not just about protecting the environment for the next few decades, but about ensuring a livable, thriving planet for centuries to come.

Intergenerational equity—the idea that current generations have a responsibility to future generations—is central to the climate debate. What we do today to combat climate change will shape the world for our children, grandchildren, and beyond. The stakes could not be higher: this is a defining moment for human civilization, and the world must rise to meet it.

The Choice for the Future

The path forward is clear: we must adopt policies that balance economic and environmental priorities, promote innovation, and foster global cooperation. The future of our planet depends on the choices we make today. While the economic impacts of transitioning to clean energy may seem daunting, they are far outweighed by the long-term benefits of avoiding the catastrophic consequences of climate inaction. By investing in sustainable technologies, supporting vulnerable communities, and fostering international collaboration, we can build a future that is both prosperous and environmentally sustainable.

The challenge of climate change is both a national and a global struggle, one that requires urgent and unified action from policymakers, businesses, and citizens alike. Only by working together—across party lines, sectors, and nations—can we hope to meet the demands of this moment and ensure a better future for all.

A Nation Divided Over Reform and Public Health Policy

Introduction: Healthcare at the Crossroads

Healthcare in the United States has long been one of the most contentious and politically divisive issues. As a nation, we are deeply divided on how best to structure a system that balances quality care, affordability, and accessibility. On one end of the spectrum, there are calls for Medicare for All or other forms of universal healthcare, seen by many as the most effective way to ensure that every citizen has access to medical care, regardless of their financial situation. On the other end, proponents of market-based solutions argue that healthcare should remain largely private, with competition driving innovation and quality, and that government-run systems lead to inefficiency, higher taxes, and a decline in the standard of care.

The debate over healthcare reform was already heated before 2020, but the onset of the COVID-19 pandemic added a new layer of complexity, sparking fierce disagreements over public health mandates, vaccines, and lock-downs. The pandemic has not only exposed deep weaknesses in the U.S. healthcare system, but also underscored just how divided we are as a society on issues of public health and government intervention. While many saw the roll-out of vaccines and health mandates as crucial tools to protect public safety, others viewed them as government overreach and a violation of personal freedoms.

There are two major issues that have fueled healthcare debates in recent years: the ongoing battle over healthcare reform and the deep divisions surrounding COVID-19 policies. This essay explores both. By examining both the ideological and practical aspects of these issues, we can better understand why healthcare remains such a divisive topic in American politics and consider how the nation might move forward.

The Debate Over Healthcare Reform: Medicare for All vs. Market-Based Approaches

The U.S. healthcare system has been a topic of heated debate for decades, with healthcare reform being a focal point of political discourse. At the core of this debate are two competing visions: one that advocates for universal healthcare or Medicare for All, and another that supports a more market-driven approach focused on private insurance and competition. The stark contrast between these approaches highlights broader philosophical divides over the role of government in American life, and it has become one of the most polarizing issues in modern politics.

Background of the U.S. Healthcare System: The Role of Private Insurance

The current U.S. healthcare system is a hybrid model that combines private insurance with government programs such as Medicare (for seniors) and Medicaid (for low-income individuals). Most Americans under 65 obtain health insurance through their employers, while others purchase private plans on the individual market. However, this model leaves tens of millions uninsured or under-insured, contributing to a system where access to care is unequal and often tied to one's employment status.

In 2010, the Affordable Care Act (ACA), commonly known as Obamacare, was passed in an effort to reduce the number of uninsured Americans and expand access to care. The ACA included provisions such as subsidies for low-income individuals, an expansion of Medicaid, and the creation of online marketplaces for insurance plans. However, it stopped short of providing universal coverage, and its implementation has faced fierce opposition, particularly from conservatives who see it as government overreach and an unnecessary expansion of federal power.

Medicare for All and Universal Healthcare Models

In response to the limitations of the current system, many progressives have rallied around the idea of Medicare for All, a form of single-payer healthcare in which the government would provide health insurance for all Americans, effectively replacing the private insurance industry. Under this model, the government would cover most, if not all, healthcare costs for everyone, eliminating co-payments, deductibles, and premiums.

Proponents of Medicare for All argue that it would solve many of the problems in the current system by ensuring universal access to healthcare, regardless of a person's income, job status, or health condition. They point to other countries with single-payer or universal systems, such as Canada and the United Kingdom, where healthcare is provided as a right and where overall costs are lower due to the absence of administrative overhead and profit-driven motives.

Supporters also emphasize that a universal healthcare system would lead to better public health outcomes by providing preventive care and treatment to all, reducing the burden on emergency rooms, and eliminating the financial ruin that often accompanies major medical expenses. According to a 2020 study by The Lancet, implementing Medicare for All could save the U.S. more than $450 billion annually in healthcare costs and prevent more than 68,000 deaths a year by ensuring broader access to care.

Opposition to Government-Run Healthcare

Despite its growing popularity among progressives, Medicare for All faces strong opposition from conservatives, libertarians, and even some moderates. Critics argue that a government-run healthcare system would lead to higher taxes and longer wait times for medical services. They also claim that the quality of care would decline under a system where doctors, hospitals, and providers have fewer financial incentives to deliver innovative, high-quality treatments.

Many opponents point to the bureaucratic inefficiencies that can plague government-run programs, arguing that a single-payer system would inevitably result in rationing of care, with patients facing delays for routine procedures and limited access to cutting-edge treatments. They also highlight the potential for massive tax increases to fund the program. According to estimates from the Urban Institute, Medicare for All could cost the federal government over $34 trillion over 10 years, leading critics to argue that it would be economically unsustainable.

Opponents also emphasize the importance of choice in healthcare. Many Americans value the ability to choose their own doctors, hospitals, and insurance plans. A single-payer system would eliminate these options, forcing everyone into the same government-run system, which some argue would reduce competition and innovation in the healthcare industry.

Political Battles Over the ACA

Since its passage in 2010, the Affordable Care Act has been the subject of repeated attempts at repeal and modification, especially from Republicans who argue that it represents an unacceptable expansion of government involvement in healthcare. The most notable effort came in 2017, when the Trump administration and Republican-controlled Congress attempted to repeal the ACA, though they ultimately failed to gather enough votes to do so.

Critics of the ACA argue that it has driven up the cost of premiums for those who don't qualify for subsidies and has placed an undue burden on small businesses, which are required to offer health insurance to employees. Supporters, however, counter that the ACA has successfully expanded healthcare coverage to more than 20 million previously uninsured Americans, provided important protections for individuals with preexisting conditions, and slowed the overall growth of healthcare costs.

The political battle over the ACA highlights the deeper ideological divide over healthcare: Should healthcare be treated as a basic human right, guaranteed by the government, or as a commodity that individuals should be responsible for purchasing in the private market?

Case Studies: Lessons from States and Other Countries

Several U.S. states have experimented with healthcare reform on a more localized level, providing case studies for both sides of the debate. For instance, Massachusetts implemented a state-run health insurance mandate in 2006 under Governor Mitt Romney, which became a model for the ACA. The state has achieved one of the highest rates of insured residents in the country but continues to face challenges with rising healthcare costs.

Meanwhile, states like Vermont have tried to implement single-payer systems but faced financial obstacles. Vermont's attempt at single-payer healthcare was abandoned in 2014 due to concerns about the tax increases necessary to fund the program, showing that even well-intentioned reforms can face significant hurdles.

Internationally, countries like Canada and Germany offer insights into different models of healthcare reform. Canada's single-payer system provides universal coverage with no out-of-pocket costs for most services, though it faces criticism for long wait times for elective procedures. Germany, on the other hand, uses a system of competing non-profit insurers and a public option, providing universal coverage while maintaining some level of market competition.

A Continuing Battle Over the Future of Healthcare

The debate over healthcare reform in the U.S. is far from settled. Medicare for All continues to gain support on the left, while conservatives and moderates remain committed to preserving market-driven healthcare that emphasizes choice and competition. Both sides bring valid concerns to the table, and finding a compromise that balances universal access, affordability, and quality of care remains a daunting challenge.

As the COVID-19 pandemic has further exposed the flaws in the U.S. healthcare system, the urgency of addressing these issues has only increased. The next section will delve into how the pandemic has amplified divisions not just over healthcare reform, but also over public health policy, particularly with regard to vaccines, mask mandates, and the tension between individual rights and public safety.

COVID-19 Vaccines and Mandates: A Deepening of Political Divides

The COVID-19 pandemic brought an unprecedented global health crisis, and with it, a profound shift in how Americans view public health, government mandates, and personal freedoms. What began as a unifying effort to curb the spread of a deadly virus quickly morphed into a highly politicized battle over vaccines, mask mandates, lock-downs, and the appropriate role of government in managing public health. As COVID-19 spread, the response to vaccines and mandates became a reflection of the broader cultural and political divides that have come to define modern American society.

While many Americans viewed vaccines and public health mandates as critical tools to protect the most vulnerable and restore societal normalcy, others saw them as an infringement on individual rights, sparking fierce debates over personal freedom, government overreach, and trust in science. The pandemic, in many ways, has deepened the existing fault lines in American politics, with COVID-19 responses becoming a litmus test for where one falls on the ideological spectrum.

Initial Response to the Pandemic: Lock-downs, Masks, and the Politics of Public Health

When COVID-19 first began to spread in the United States in early 2020, state and federal governments responded with a series of lock-downs, stay-at-home orders, and mask mandates aimed at slowing the transmission of the virus. These measures, which had strong support from public health officials and epidemiologists, were initially seen as necessary to prevent overwhelming the healthcare system.

However, as the pandemic wore on, the public health response quickly became a flash-point for political division. Conservative voices increasingly pushed back against the restrictions, arguing that they caused significant economic harm, disrupted personal freedoms, and represented an unacceptable expansion of government control. For many, especially those in more rural and conservative areas, mask mandates and lock-downs came to symbolize government overreach and top-down control from political elites.

On the other hand, those who supported these measures emphasized the importance of collective action to protect public health. They argued that mask-wearing and social distancing were simple, effective measures to reduce the spread of the virus and protect vulnerable populations, especially in the absence of a vaccine. These supporters viewed resistance to mandates as selfish and anti-science, accusing their opponents of undermining efforts to combat the pandemic for political or ideological reasons.

Vaccines: Public Health Tool or Government Overreach?

The development and roll-out of COVID-19 vaccines in late 2020 and early 2021 were initially heralded as a triumph of science and a pathway out of the pandemic. Vaccines, developed by companies like Pfizer, Moderna, and Johnson & Johnson, were rolled out at record speed, with emergency use authorizations granted by the FDA in a matter of months. Public health officials and political leaders urged Americans to get vaccinated to achieve herd immunity, prevent severe illness, and eventually restore normalcy.

However, despite the broad availability of vaccines, the U.S. quickly encountered a new political divide—between those who embraced vaccination as a civic responsibility and those who viewed it with suspicion. While many Americans lined up to receive the vaccine as soon as it became available, a significant portion of the population, particularly in conservative and rural areas, expressed vaccine hesitancy or outright refusal.

Pro-Vaccine Arguments

- **Public Health and Collective Responsibility.** Proponents of vaccination stressed the importance of vaccines in achieving herd immunity and protecting vulnerable populations, such as the elderly and immunocompromised. They viewed widespread vaccination as a necessary step to ending the pandemic, reopening businesses, and returning to normal life.

- **Scientific Consensus.** Public health officials emphasized the overwhelming scientific consensus around the safety and efficacy of COVID-19 vaccines, pointing to clinical trials and data showing that vaccines dramatically reduced the risk of severe illness, hospitalization, and death.

- **Moral and Civic Duty.** Many saw getting vaccinated as a moral obligation, not just for personal protection but for the protection of the community. By getting vaccinated, individuals contribute to the broader effort to control the virus and save lives.

Vaccine Opposition and Skepticism

On the other side of the debate, a significant portion of the population viewed the push for vaccination with deep skepticism. Opposition to COVID-19 vaccines often overlapped with broader political and cultural concerns, including mistrust of government, big pharma, and the medical establishment.

- **Mistrust of Government and Institutions.** Many vaccine skeptics cited a lack of trust in the government's handling of the pandemic. They questioned the rapid development of the vaccines, feared potential long-term side effects, and expressed doubts about the accuracy of public health messaging.

- **Personal Freedom.** For many Americans, particularly those who identify as libertarians or conservatives, the notion of a vaccine mandate—whether imposed by the government or private employers—was seen as a violation of individual rights. They argued that individuals should have the freedom to make their own healthcare decisions without coercion or government intervention.

- **Misinformation and Conspiracy Theories.** The rise of misinformation on social media platforms played a significant role in fueling vaccine hesitancy. Conspiracy theories about vaccines being used for population control, microchips, or other nefarious purposes spread rapidly online, contributing to a growing anti-vaccine movement that aligned itself with broader anti-government sentiment.

Mandates and Personal Freedom: The Vaccine Mandate Controversy

As the pandemic dragged on, federal, state, and local governments, along with private businesses, began to implement vaccine mandates for certain sectors, including healthcare workers, government employees, and, in some cases, the general public for access to public venues. These mandates sparked intense backlash from those who saw them as a gross infringement on personal freedom and bodily autonomy.

For many on the left and in the public health community, mandates were viewed as necessary for achieving high vaccination rates and protecting public health. They argued that the collective good outweighed individual objections, particularly in the context of a global pandemic. The Supreme Court upheld some vaccine mandates, ruling that they were a legitimate use of government power to protect public health, especially for front-line workers in industries like healthcare and education.

On the other hand, opponents of mandates saw them as a step too far—an authoritarian overreach that set a dangerous precedent for future government interventions. Some conservative leaders framed the mandates as a violation of constitutional rights, arguing that the government should not be able to force individuals to receive a medical treatment they do not want. This resistance was particularly strong in states like Florida and Texas, where governors issued executive orders banning vaccine mandates and framing their opposition as a defense of personal liberty.

The Role of Misinformation in Deepening Divides

One of the most troubling aspects of the COVID-19 vaccine and mandate debate has been the spread of misinformation. Social media platforms, such as Facebook, Twitter, and YouTube, became breeding grounds for conspiracy theories and false information about the virus, vaccines, and public health measures. Misinformation often blurred the lines between legitimate concerns about vaccine safety and outlandish claims that undermined trust in the scientific community.

Public health officials and scientists have faced an uphill battle in countering this flood of false information, and the consequences have been severe. In communities where vaccine hesitancy is high, hospitals saw higher rates of hospitalization and death from COVID-19, particularly during the Delta and Omicron variant waves. The spread of misinformation not only deepened the political divide over COVID-19 but also highlighted the fragility of public trust in institutions of authority.

Legal and Cultural Consequences of the COVID-19 Divide

The legal battles over vaccine mandates and mask requirements have led to a series of court challenges and Supreme Court rulings. In some cases, courts upheld vaccine mandates, especially in sectors like healthcare, citing the government's right to protect public health. In other cases, mandates were struck down, particularly when applied to private businesses, adding further complexity to the ongoing debate.

Culturally, the pandemic has further entrenched the urban-rural divide, with urban areas more likely to embrace public health measures and rural areas showing greater resistance. This divide is often tied to broader cultural identities— liberal, urban voters who trust in government and scientific institutions versus conservative, rural voters who prioritize personal freedom and skepticism of centralized authority.

The Lasting Impact of COVID-19 on Public Health

The COVID-19 pandemic has not only exposed the vulnerabilities of the American healthcare system but also deepened existing political and cultural divides. What began as a public health crisis has transformed into a symbolic battleground over personal freedom, trust in government, and the appropriate role of public institutions in shaping citizens' lives. The debates over vaccines and mandates have not only impacted health outcomes but have also left a lasting imprint on the nation's political and social fabric.

As we move forward, the challenge will be finding a way to balance public health priorities with individual liberties, while rebuilding trust in the institutions that are meant to protect and serve the public. The pandemic has shown that when public health becomes politicized, it becomes harder to implement the policies necessary to keep people safe. It has also demonstrated the need for better communication, science literacy, and the importance of addressing misinformation in a way that fosters unity rather than furthering division.

The Intersection of Politics, Public Health, and Culture

As the debate over healthcare reform and COVID-19 mandates continues, it's clear that the issues at hand go far beyond questions of policy or public health. The pandemic has exposed the deep cultural, political, and regional divides in American society. What began as a debate over how to manage a global health crisis has evolved into a larger conversation about individual freedom, government authority, and the role of expertise in shaping public life.

COVID-19 highlighted how deeply ingrained political and cultural identities are in shaping views on public health measures, and how health decisions became political litmus tests. At the same time, the healthcare reform debate—whether about expanding Medicare or preserving private insurance—has become symbolic of larger ideological battles about the proper role of government and the free market. As these two issues intersect, they reveal how healthcare has become not just a policy issue, but a reflection of America's broader cultural divisions.

Healthcare as a Political Identity Marker

Healthcare, like many other issues, has become a political identity marker in the U.S. A person's stance on Medicare for All, for instance, can reveal not just their views on healthcare, but their broader political philosophy. Those in favor of universal healthcare often view it as a human right, a moral obligation to ensure that all citizens, regardless of income, have access to necessary medical services. For these individuals, supporting government-led healthcare is consistent with a worldview that emphasizes collective responsibility and the idea that the state should play a role in protecting the vulnerable.

Conversely, those opposed to government-run healthcare tend to emphasize individual freedom and market-based solutions. They believe that private competition fosters innovation and quality of care, and they fear that a government takeover would lead to inefficiency, higher taxes, and a decline in the quality of service. For these individuals, resisting Medicare for All is part of a larger resistance to big government and a belief in personal responsibility.

This divide over healthcare reflects broader political alignments. Progressives tend to support more government intervention in healthcare, while conservatives and libertarians generally prefer private sector solutions. In recent years, this ideological divide has widened, with both sides seeing their healthcare preferences as part of a broader vision for how society should be structured. As such, healthcare reform has become a proxy battle for the deeper ideological struggles that shape American political life.

Cultural and Regional Divides: The Urban-Rural Split

The COVID-19 pandemic brought the urban-rural divide in America into sharp focus, particularly in terms of how public health measures were perceived and enacted. Generally speaking, urban areas—which tend to lean more liberal—were quicker to adopt and enforce lock-downs, mask mandates, and vaccination campaigns. In cities, where population density increases the risk of virus transmission, there was a strong push for collective measures to mitigate the spread. Public health authorities in urban areas often found support for these mandates, which were framed as necessary for the greater good.

In contrast, many rural areas, which lean more conservative, resisted these public health measures. For people in these communities, particularly in states like Texas, Florida, and South Dakota, mask and vaccine mandates were seen not as public health tools, but as government overreach that infringed on personal freedoms. The lower population density and differing cultural attitudes in rural areas contributed to a belief that individual responsibility—rather than government mandates—was the appropriate response to the pandemic.

This urban-rural divide is not new, but the pandemic has exacerbated it. Public health policies became symbolic battlegrounds for larger cultural issues. For urban residents, adherence to mandates represented a sense of collective responsibility and trust in science, while for rural residents, resisting mandates symbolized a commitment to personal liberty and skepticism of centralized authority. This divide extends to healthcare more broadly, where urban areas are more likely to support expanded government involvement in healthcare, while rural areas often favor private sector solutions.

The Role of Trust in Government and Institutions

At the heart of both the healthcare reform debate and the COVID-19 response is a question of trust—trust in government, trust in public institutions, and trust in scientific expertise. Over the past few decades, trust in these institutions has been steadily declining, particularly among conservatives, who often view government as inefficient and overreaching.

This erosion of trust was magnified during the pandemic. The government's handling of the COVID-19 crisis—ranging from initial missteps in communication to the politicization of public health measures—left many Americans questioning the competence and motivations of federal and state authorities. This skepticism extended to public health agencies like the Centers for Disease Control and Prevention (CDC), with critics accusing these institutions of flip-flopping on key issues like mask-wearing and vaccine efficacy, further fueling mistrust.

In contrast, many liberals and progressives maintained high levels of trust in these institutions and were more likely to follow the guidance of public health experts. They viewed the scientific consensus as authoritative and saw compliance with public health measures as not only necessary but a moral obligation. For these individuals, the rejection of public health guidance by some conservatives was seen as anti-science and irresponsible.

This partisan divide in trust has had profound consequences for public health outcomes. Areas with higher levels of trust in government and scientific institutions were more likely to see widespread vaccine uptake and adherence to public health guidelines, resulting in lower rates of COVID-19 transmission and deaths. Conversely, areas with lower levels of trust often experienced higher rates of hospitalization and death, particularly during the Delta and Omicron waves of the pandemic.

Healthcare, Public Health, and the Culture Wars

The intersection of healthcare reform and COVID-19 has also become part of the broader culture wars that dominate American political life. For many, debates over vaccines, masks, and lock-downs are not just about public health—they are part of a larger ideological struggle over the role of individual freedom versus collective responsibility.

This cultural clash has been exacerbated by the media landscape, where polarized news outlets and social media platforms reinforce existing beliefs and provide echo chambers for both sides. The right-wing media ecosystem frequently highlights stories of government overreach, portraying vaccine mandates and mask requirements as threats to personal liberty. Meanwhile, left-leaning media tends to emphasize the science behind public health measures and paints opposition to these mandates as reckless and irresponsible.

COVID-19 and healthcare debates have also taken on symbolic meanings. For many, wearing a mask or getting vaccinated became a symbol of solidarity and care for others, while for others, refusing to comply became a symbol of defiance against what they saw as an overreaching government. This cultural symbolism only deepened the polarization, making it harder for public health officials to craft policies that would be widely accepted across the political spectrum.

A Society Divided Along Cultural Lines

The intersection of politics, public health, and culture during the COVID-19 pandemic has revealed just how divided America has become. Healthcare reform—whether in the form of Medicare for All or the preservation of private insurance—is not just a policy debate, but a reflection of deeper philosophical differences over the role of government in our lives. Similarly, responses to the pandemic—whether in support of vaccines and mask mandates or opposition to them—are shaped by broader cultural values, including attitudes toward individual freedom, collective responsibility, and trust in institutions.

The pandemic has acted as a catalyst, deepening long-standing cultural divides and turning issues of public health into political identity markers. Where one stands on healthcare reform or COVID-19 mandates often reflects not just views on these specific issues, but a wider worldview that encompasses beliefs about freedom, government intervention, and the role of science in shaping public policy.

This growing polarization makes it difficult to find common ground, as both sides become increasingly entrenched in their positions. Those who support universal healthcare see it as a moral imperative to protect the vulnerable, while those who oppose it fear the loss of personal choice and the expansion of big government. Similarly, public health measures intended to combat COVID-19— measures that were initially seen as temporary—have become enduring points of contention, with one side viewing them as necessary for the public good, and the other seeing them as an affront to personal liberty.

Ultimately, these divisions reflect a deeper cultural and political rift in American society, one that goes beyond healthcare or public health. The challenge moving forward will be finding a way to address these issues in a manner that respects both the need for public safety and the importance of individual rights. Without bridging these divides, it will be difficult to craft healthcare policies or public health strategies that have broad support across the political and cultural spectrum.

The Future of Healthcare Reform in a Post-COVID World

The COVID-19 pandemic exposed many of the weaknesses and inequities in the U.S. healthcare system, further intensifying the already heated debate over healthcare reform. From the overwhelmed hospital systems in some regions to the stark disparities in access to care between different socioeconomic and racial groups, the pandemic brought into sharp focus the flaws in how healthcare is provided, funded, and accessed in America. As the country begins to transition into a post-COVID world, the questions surrounding healthcare reform have become even more urgent. The pandemic has demonstrated the need for a system that can better respond to public health crises, provide equitable care, and ensure that no one falls through the cracks.

This section will explore how the pandemic experience has reshaped the healthcare debate and what the potential paths forward might look like. Whether through incremental changes or bold reforms like Medicare for All, the future of healthcare in America is at a crossroads, and the decisions made in the coming years will have lasting impacts on the nation's health, economy, and society.

Post-Pandemic Reflections on the Healthcare System

The strain that COVID-19 placed on the U.S. healthcare system revealed critical weaknesses in the nation's ability to respond to public health emergencies. In the early days of the pandemic, hospitals in some areas, particularly in New York City, were overwhelmed by the influx of patients, with ICUs reaching capacity and ventilator shortages becoming a dire concern. At the same time, the pandemic also exposed deep racial and economic disparities in healthcare access. Communities of color and low-income populations were disproportionately affected by the virus, facing higher rates of infection, hospitalization, and death.

These disparities underscored the need for a more equitable healthcare system— one that ensures everyone, regardless of race, income, or geography, can access the care they need. The pandemic also highlighted the importance of public health infrastructure, which had been underfunded for decades, leaving the U.S. ill-prepared to manage a crisis of this magnitude. Public health experts have pointed to the need for greater investment in preventive care, community health initiatives, and emergency preparedness.

Additionally, the pandemic shone a light on the fragmentation of the U.S. healthcare system, where responsibility for care is split between public programs like Medicare and Medicaid, private insurers, and out-of-pocket spending by individuals. This patchwork system left millions of people uninsured or under-insured when they needed care the most, further intensifying the calls for healthcare reform.

Re-imagining Healthcare After COVID-19: Policy Proposals and Reforms

In the wake of the pandemic, there is growing momentum for re-imagining healthcare in the U.S. Many policymakers, public health officials, and advocates see the pandemic as a turning point that could catalyze significant changes to the system. While opinions differ on the exact nature of these reforms, a few key ideas have gained traction in the post-pandemic landscape:

- **Medicare for All.** The proposal for a single-payer healthcare system, where the government provides health coverage to all citizens, has gained renewed interest in the aftermath of the pandemic. Supporters argue that a universal system would have been better equipped to handle a public health emergency, ensuring that all Americans could access care without worrying about cost or insurance coverage. Senator Bernie Sanders and other progressives have pointed to the success of universal healthcare systems in countries like Canada and Germany as models the U.S. could follow. However, as discussed in earlier sections, the proposal faces strong opposition from conservatives and moderates who fear it would lead to higher taxes, inefficiencies, and decreased quality of care.

- **Public Option.** For those who are wary of a full-scale single-payer system, the idea of a public option has emerged as a middle-ground solution. Under this model, individuals would have the option to buy into a government-run health insurance plan (similar to Medicare) while still allowing private insurers to operate. Advocates see this as a way to expand coverage and reduce costs without fully eliminating the private insurance market.

President Joe Biden campaigned on the promise of introducing a public option, and it could serve as a more politically feasible alternative to Medicare for All.

- **Strengthening the Affordable Care Act (ACA).** Another potential path forward is the continued strengthening and expansion of the Affordable Care Act. The ACA, passed in 2010 under the Obama administration, expanded access to healthcare by providing subsidies for private insurance and expanding Medicaid in many states. The Biden administration has signaled its intent to reinforce the ACA, including expanding subsidies, increasing the number of Americans eligible for Medicaid, and reducing the cost of coverage for middle-income families. While this approach avoids the political and economic challenges of Medicare for All, it may not address some of the deeper systemic issues in U.S. healthcare, such as the rising cost of prescription drugs and the administrative complexity of private insurance.

- **Telemedicine and Healthcare Technology.** One of the more positive changes brought about by the pandemic has been the rapid expansion of telemedicine. As lock-downs forced people to stay home, healthcare providers shifted to virtual consultations for many types of care. Telemedicine has proven to be an effective way to increase access, particularly for rural and under-served communities. The success of telemedicine during the pandemic has sparked discussions about how to integrate it more permanently into the healthcare system. However, policymakers will need to address issues of broadband access, insurance reimbursement, and privacy to ensure that telemedicine is a viable option for all Americans.

Learning from Other Countries: A Global Perspective on Healthcare Reform

As the U.S. considers its next steps in healthcare reform, there are important lessons to be learned from other countries that have navigated the challenges of providing universal care. Countries like Canada, Germany, and the United Kingdom each have different models of healthcare, but all ensure that every citizen has access to care without the financial barriers present in the U.S.

- **Canada's Single-Payer System.** Canada's healthcare system is frequently cited as a model for single-payer healthcare. While it provides universal coverage for all citizens, critics often point to the long wait times for certain procedures and a perceived lack of access to specialized care as potential drawbacks. However, during the pandemic, Canada's centralized system allowed for a more coordinated response to the virus, and the government's ability to guarantee healthcare for all citizens eliminated many of the inequities seen in the U.S.

- **Germany's Hybrid Model.** Germany's healthcare system provides a compromise between public and private systems, with both government-funded and private health insurance options available to citizens. This hybrid model allows for universal coverage while maintaining a level of competition between insurers, which some argue leads to higher quality care. Germany's response to the pandemic was bolstered by its robust public health infrastructure and widespread access to healthcare. Its hybrid approach could offer valuable insights for the U.S., especially as policymakers consider a public option that works alongside private insurance.

- **The United Kingdom's National Health Service (NHS).** The NHS is a fully government-funded and government-operated healthcare system that provides comprehensive care to all UK citizens. During the COVID-19 pandemic, the NHS played a critical role in ensuring that healthcare was accessible and free at the point of service, allowing the country to roll out mass testing and vaccination campaigns without the complexities of private insurance billing. However, the system has faced significant funding shortages and staffing challenges, leading to concerns about the long-term sustainability of such a model, especially in light of increasing demands on the system.

Each of these countries presents different models of healthcare, but they all share one important feature: the recognition that healthcare is a right, not a privilege. The U.S. could benefit from studying these systems, adapting their strengths, and avoiding their weaknesses as it seeks to reform its own healthcare model in the wake of the COVID-19 pandemic.

Balancing Public Health and Individual Rights in the Future

As the country moves forward, a key challenge will be finding a balance between the collective good of public health and the individual rights of citizens. The pandemic has shown that public health crises require coordinated action to protect the most vulnerable, but it has also sparked intense debates over personal freedom and the limits of government intervention. These debates will continue to shape healthcare reform discussions in the years to come.

For example, while vaccine mandates and mask requirements were central to controlling the spread of COVID-19, they were also seen by many as government overreach. Moving forward, policymakers will need to carefully navigate the tension between ensuring public safety and respecting individual autonomy. This challenge extends beyond COVID-19 and applies to future public health crises, as well as broader discussions about healthcare access and affordability.

A New Chapter in Healthcare Reform

The COVID-19 pandemic has provided an opportunity for the U.S. to re-evaluate its healthcare system and consider meaningful reforms that could improve access, quality, and affordability. The weaknesses exposed by the pandemic — from overcrowded hospitals to unequal access to healthcare services — have ignited a new sense of urgency to fix the systemic problems that have plagued the U.S. healthcare system for decades. Whether through expanding Medicare, implementing a public option, or pursuing more incremental changes to the Affordable Care Act, the time is ripe for serious discussions about how to create a system that works for everyone.

COVID-19 has also reshaped how we think about public health infrastructure, emphasizing the need for more robust investment in preventive care, emergency preparedness, and healthcare technology. The rapid expansion of telemedicine during the pandemic offers a glimpse into what the future of healthcare could look like, particularly if digital health solutions can be made more accessible to rural and under-served communities.

Most importantly, healthcare reform in the post-COVID era must address the stark disparities in healthcare access and outcomes for marginalized communities. The pandemic has laid bare the disproportionate toll it has taken on low-income populations, people of color, and rural residents. Any future reform must focus on creating a more equitable healthcare system that ensures these vulnerable populations are not left behind.

In the end, the future of U.S. healthcare reform depends on political will, public pressure, and a willingness to compromise. While the divisions over universal healthcare, government mandates, and personal freedoms remain deep, the lessons learned from the pandemic provide a unique opportunity to move toward a more resilient, fair, and efficient healthcare system. The path forward won't be easy, but if the U.S. can harness the momentum for change, it has the potential to transform its healthcare system in a way that benefits all Americans — and that can withstand the challenges of the next public health crisis.

The Path Forward in a Politically Polarized Nation

The debate over healthcare reform and COVID-19 policies has exposed and deepened existing divisions in American society. On one side, there is growing support for universal healthcare, such as Medicare for All, as a way to guarantee access to care for all Americans and address the inequities that the pandemic has made more visible. On the other side, opponents of government-led healthcare argue that such systems are inefficient, expensive, and limit personal choice. Similarly, debates over COVID-19 vaccines, mask mandates, and lock-downs have pitted concerns over public health against the defense of individual freedoms.

These key points of contention — the role of government in healthcare, the balance between public safety and personal liberty, and the long-term sustainability of the healthcare system — have made it difficult to find common ground. However, the urgency created by the pandemic has forced the nation to confront these issues head-on. COVID-19 exposed the weaknesses of the U.S. healthcare system, from overburdened hospitals to the millions left uninsured or without adequate care. It also highlighted the disparities that exist across racial, economic, and geographic lines, further intensifying the need for reform.

The pandemic has added a sense of immediacy to the conversation, pushing both policymakers and the public to recognize that change is necessary. Whether the solution is incremental improvements to the Affordable Care Act, the adoption of a public option, or more radical reforms like Medicare for All, the U.S. must now decide how to ensure that quality healthcare is accessible to everyone while addressing the financial sustainability of the system.

Moving forward, the challenge will be finding common ground. The healthcare debate, like the response to COVID-19, does not need to be defined by polarization. There is room for compromise in areas such as telemedicine expansion, improving access for under-served communities, and building a more resilient public health infrastructure. Any viable path forward will need to balance the need for public safety with respect for personal freedoms, ensuring that measures to protect public health do not undermine individual rights, and vice versa.

In conclusion, the future of healthcare reform and public health policy in America will depend on our ability to engage in nuanced, thoughtful discussions that rise above political polarization. Only by recognizing the importance of both personal freedom and the collective good can the U.S. move toward a more equitable and effective healthcare system. The lessons learned from the pandemic, as well as the examples set by other nations, provide a road-map for what is possible — if we are willing to work together.

For The United States of America

America stands at a crossroads. The deep divisions that we face—whether political, social, or cultural—are undeniable. From debates over fascism and authoritarianism, to battles surrounding gender identity, religion, and climate change, we find ourselves in a time of intense polarization. Our conversations are often fragmented, driven by sound bites and social media echo chambers, which have eroded our ability to communicate thoughtfully and respectfully. It would be easy to look at our current moment with a sense of despair, to see only the divisions and conflicts that tear us apart.

But this is not the full story of America. America has always been a land of hope, a land where the idea of a brighter future has driven us forward through adversity. While we face real and serious challenges today, we must remember that this is not the first time our nation has been divided. From the Civil War to the Civil Rights Movement, from economic depressions to world wars, we have faced dark and uncertain times before—and we have always found a way forward.

The Hope in Our History

America's history is one of resilience, rebirth, and the capacity to overcome even the most bitter divisions. From the very beginning, the United States was founded on ideals of freedom, democracy, and equality—ideals that, even when imperfectly applied, have been the guiding light that draws us through periods of strife and turmoil. Throughout our history, we have faced seemingly insurmountable challenges, yet time and again we have emerged stronger, not because our path was easy or smooth, but because we chose to persevere, to reflect on our shortcomings, and to grow from them.

The American Revolution: A Nation Built on Hope

The very birth of our nation was a radical experiment fueled by hope. The American colonies faced overwhelming odds when they declared independence from the world's most powerful empire in 1776. The Revolutionary War was not a guaranteed success; in fact, it was an almost impossible fight against a much larger and better-equipped British army. But it was the hope for self-determination, for a society free from tyranny, that fueled the fight. Ordinary men and women, united by a shared vision of freedom and democracy, risked everything for a chance to build a new kind of nation—a nation where individual liberty was the cornerstone.

In the face of hardship, sacrifice, and seemingly endless conflict, the founding generation persisted. And out of that struggle, America emerged not just as a new country, but as a symbol to the world that people could govern themselves, that they could create a society rooted in the radical idea that all men (and eventually, all people) are created equal. That founding moment was more than a military victory; it was the embodiment of hope in the face of overwhelming challenges.

The Civil War: Healing the Nation's Greatest Wound

The Civil War stands as perhaps the darkest chapter in American history—a time when the nation was literally and figuratively torn in two. The conflict over slavery, state rights, and the very definition of freedom divided the country along geographical, political, and moral lines. Brothers fought brothers, families were split, and the very future of the Union was in doubt.

Yet even amid the bloodshed and chaos, hope endured. The hope that this young nation could emerge from the horrors of war with a renewed commitment to its founding principles—that all men, regardless of race, were indeed created equal— was the guiding force behind Abraham Lincoln's leadership. Lincoln, through his Emancipation Proclamation and his Gettysburg Address, reminded the nation of its higher purpose. He urged us to look beyond the immediate devastation and to recommit ourselves to the promise of the Declaration of Independence.

When the Union finally emerged victorious, the task of reconstruction was monumental. The wounds of war, both literal and figurative, would not heal overnight. But through the Reconstruction Amendments—the 13th, 14th, and 15th Amendments—the nation took significant steps toward realizing the promise of equality and justice for all. The hope that America could transcend its original sin of slavery fueled these efforts, even as new challenges arose.

It is easy to forget how fragile the Union was during that time, how close we came to dissolving as a nation. But it was the belief that America could still fulfill its promise—a belief in hope—that carried us through.

The Great Depression and World War II: Overcoming Global and Domestic Crises

In the early 20th century, America faced back-to-back crises that tested the very fabric of the nation: the Great Depression and World War II. The Great Depression devastated the American economy, with unemployment skyrocketing, banks collapsing, and millions of families plunged into poverty. Yet even in this time of desperation, hope was not lost.

Franklin D. Roosevelt, through his New Deal programs, became a beacon of hope for a suffering nation. His famous words, "The only thing we have to fear is fear itself," became a rallying cry for Americans to persevere, to believe that things could and would get better. The New Deal wasn't just about economic recovery; it was about restoring the American people's faith in government, in each other, and in the future. Through programs like Social Security, public works projects, and financial reforms, the government took an active role in pulling the country out of despair. More importantly, Roosevelt's leadership rekindled the hope that the American Dream was still alive, even in the face of staggering hardship.

No sooner had the U.S. begun to recover from the Depression than it was thrust into the global conflict of World War II. Once again, America faced overwhelming odds, now not only fighting for its own survival but for the survival of democracy and freedom worldwide. The Greatest Generation—ordinary men and women— answered the call to defend those ideals, sacrificing on the battlefields of Europe, the Pacific, and North Africa. The war effort demanded unprecedented unity, determination, and resilience at home and abroad.

Yet again, hope was the driving force. The belief that America could rise to meet the challenge, that it could play a leading role in defeating tyranny, propelled the nation to victory. And in the aftermath of the war, America emerged not only as a military superpower but as a global leader committed to the principles of freedom, democracy, and human rights. This hope for a better, more just world led to the creation of institutions like the United Nations and the Marshall Plan, which sought to rebuild war-torn Europe and prevent future conflicts.

The Civil Rights Movement: A Renewed Fight for Justice

The Civil Rights Movement of the 1950s and 1960s was yet another defining moment where America was forced to confront its deep-seated divisions—this time, over the issue of racial equality. Despite the promises of freedom and equality laid out in the Constitution, African Americans were still subjected to segregation, discrimination, and violence. Once again, the nation was at a crossroads, forced to reckon with its failure to fully extend the promises of liberty and justice to all its citizens.

The leaders of the Civil Rights Movement, most notably Martin Luther King Jr., embodied the hope that America could be better. King's vision of a "beloved community," where people of all races, creeds, and backgrounds could live together in peace and equality, captured the spirit of hope that has always been central to the American experiment. King and others, through nonviolent protest, civil disobedience, and moral courage, forced the nation to confront its contradictions and take meaningful steps toward racial justice.

The passage of the Civil Rights Act of 1964 and the Voting Rights Act of 1965 were monumental achievements—hard-fought victories that came not from despair but from the belief in change, the belief that America could live up to its ideals. These laws were not just legislative triumphs; they were symbols of hope—hope that the nation could overcome its legacy of racial oppression and move toward a more just and equal society.

A Legacy of Overcoming

Throughout each of these periods—whether it was the fight for independence, the battle to preserve the Union, or the struggle for civil rights—hope has been our constant companion. America's greatness has always been found in its ability to learn, to grow, and to evolve. We are not perfect, and we have never been. But the American story is not one of perfection; it is one of progress. We are a nation that has continually pushed forward, even in the face of adversity.

And so, as we look at the divisions that face us today—political, social, racial, and economic—we must remember that this is not the first time we have faced such challenges. We have overcome deep divides before, and we will again. Hope, paired with action, will guide us.

In the past, we chose hope over despair, unity over division, and progress over stagnation. That is the legacy we must carry forward today.

The Promise of Tomorrow

Our history proves that America is resilient. We've been here before—facing seemingly insurmountable challenges—and yet, we've always found a way to persevere. But overcoming these challenges requires more than mere optimism; it requires leadership, compassion, and a collective will to build a better future. We've done it before, and we can do it again. If we commit to our founding principles and embrace the hope that has always been at the heart of the American spirit, we will rise to meet the challenges before us and come out stronger, more united, and more just.

A Hopeful Path Forward

As we look toward the future, it's clear that the divisions we face today—whether political, cultural, economic, or social—are deep and complex. But while these challenges are daunting, they are not insurmountable. The very fabric of America is woven with the thread of hope—the belief that we can be better, that we can rise above our current struggles, and that we can create a future where unity and progress triumph over division and stagnation. The hope for a better tomorrow has driven us through some of our darkest days, and it will carry us forward once again.

The path forward is not an easy one. It requires an honest reckoning with our past and our present, but it also demands a deep faith in what we are capable of achieving together. If we embrace the challenges we face with courage, and if we commit to addressing our divisions with compassion and understanding, there is no limit to what we can accomplish as a nation.

Confronting Our Divisions with Compassion and Understanding

The first step on this hopeful path forward is to acknowledge and understand the divisions that exist in our society. We are polarized—on issues ranging from gun control and immigration to race relations, gender identity, and climate change. These divisions are real, and they have left many Americans feeling isolated, unheard, and disenfranchised.

But as deep as these divisions may be, they are not new. America has always been a country of diverse opinions, cultures, and ideologies. What sets us apart, however, is our ability to overcome these divides by finding common ground and building a shared vision for the future. That vision starts with compassion and understanding—a willingness to listen to those we disagree with, to seek out commonality in the midst of conflict, and to recognize the humanity in one another.

We must resist the temptation to demonize those who hold different views. Instead of further entrenching ourselves in our ideological corners, we need to approach our differences with curiosity and a genuine desire to understand the concerns, fears, and hopes of our fellow citizens. The path forward begins with dialogue, not confrontation; with empathy, not hostility. In the end, we all want similar things—a country where freedom, justice, and opportunity are available to everyone, where safety and security are guaranteed, and where dignity and respect are extended to all.

This doesn't mean that compromise will come easily or that we should abandon our principles. It means that we must be willing to engage in hard conversations, to listen even when it's uncomfortable, and to look for solutions that benefit the greater good. In doing so, we will find that there is more that unites us than divides us.

Leadership Grounded in Hope, Not Fear

The leaders we need for the future are those who are guided by hope, not by fear or vengeance. In recent years, we have seen too many leaders who thrive on divisiveness, who exploit our differences for political gain, and who stir up anger and resentment instead of inspiring unity and progress. But this is not the kind of leadership that will carry us forward.

We need leaders who embody the best of America—leaders who call on our better angels, who elevate kindness, compassion, and empathy as the guiding values of our national life. We need leaders who will not appeal to our basest instincts, but who will instead challenge us to be better, to rise above pettiness and partisanship, and to pursue the common good with purpose and integrity.

These leaders must inspire us to believe in the promise of America, just as Lincoln, FDR, and King did during their respective eras of crisis. They must show us that hope is not just a feeling, but a strategy for action—that by working together, we can overcome even the most significant obstacles. And they must lead by example, demonstrating through their actions and words that unity is stronger than division, that kindness is more powerful than hatred, and that justice is not a distant ideal but a practical reality we can achieve.

Importantly, the kind of leadership we need extends beyond the halls of government. We need leadership in our communities, in our schools, in our workplaces, and in our homes. Every American has the potential to lead by fostering dialogue, by bridging divides, and by working to solve problems in ways that bring people together rather than push them apart. The future of this nation depends not only on our elected officials but on all of us taking up the mantle of leadership, wherever we find ourselves.

Recommitting to Our Core Values

As we move forward, we must also recommit ourselves to the core values that have always defined America. Our nation was founded on principles of freedom, equality, and justice—values that are enshrined in our Constitution and that have guided us through generations of turmoil and triumph. These values are not relics of the past; they are the foundation upon which we can build a brighter future.

We need to reclaim our commitment to free speech, not as a weapon to wield against others, but as a tool for understanding and growth. We need to reaffirm our belief in equal opportunity, ensuring that every American, regardless of race, gender, religion, or background, has a fair shot at achieving the American Dream. And we must never lose sight of our obligation to justice—to ensure that every person, in every corner of this country, is treated with fairness and dignity under the law.

These values are not just ideals; they are practical tools for building a better society. When we lean into them, when we make decisions guided by freedom, justice, and equality, we create a country where everyone can thrive. And when we live out these values, we remind the world what America truly stands for.

Strengthening Our Role as Global Leaders

As we heal and unite at home, America must also reclaim its role as a leader on the global stage. For decades, the United States has been a beacon of democracy, freedom, and human rights around the world. But to lead effectively abroad, we must first lead by example here at home.

Our strength as a nation has always been our moral leadership. In times of global crisis—whether through two world wars, the fight against fascism, or the struggle to end apartheid and promote civil rights—America has led not only with its military power but with its values. We are at our best when we export not just economic opportunity, but the ideals of freedom, justice, and human dignity.

By addressing our own challenges—by strengthening our democracy, fighting for racial justice, and taking bold action on climate change—we will once again be in a position to lead the world. We cannot shy away from our global responsibilities. The world looks to America not only for its innovation and prosperity but for its vision of what a just and free society can achieve.

By reclaiming this role, we will inspire hope not only within our borders but around the globe. We will stand as an example of what is possible when diverse people, united by common values, work together toward a better future.

Building a Future Together

The future of America depends on all of us. It requires each of us to take responsibility for the health of our democracy and the well-being of our fellow citizens. It means recognizing that while we may disagree on policy, we share a commitment to the American experiment—to the belief that people from different backgrounds, different perspectives, and different walks of life can come together to build a more perfect union.

Building a future together means embracing the idea that unity does not require uniformity. We can have passionate debates about the issues of the day—whether it's the economy, healthcare, immigration, or gender rights—while still respecting the inherent dignity of those with whom we disagree. Healthy discourse and democratic debate are the lifeblood of our republic, and they are how we will find solutions to the challenges we face.

Ultimately, hope is not just about seeing a brighter future—it's about building it. And building that future requires all of us to participate, to contribute, and to believe that through hard work and collective effort, we can create a nation where justice, freedom, and opportunity are not just words on a page, but lived realities for every person.

The Leaders We Need for the Future

As America navigates its way through a time of deep division, uncertainty, and unprecedented challenges, the question of leadership becomes more critical than ever. Who will guide us through the tumult of our polarized politics, racial tensions, economic disparities, and the daunting threat of climate change? The leaders we need for the future are not those who stoke the flames of division, nor those who seek personal gain or power by exploiting the fears and frustrations of a weary populace. Instead, we need leaders grounded in kindness, empathy, wisdom, and a commitment to the common good.

The path forward requires leaders who can unite rather than divide, who can offer a vision for the future that transcends the rancor and pettiness of today's political discourse. In an era where too many political figures have leaned into hatred, vindictiveness, and revenge, we must demand something more—leaders who appeal to our better angels, who see their role not as wielders of power but as stewards of a shared responsibility to make America a more just, compassionate, and united nation.

Kindness and Compassion as Leadership Imperatives

Too often, political leadership has been defined by a display of force, bravado, and ruthlessness. But true leadership is not about projecting power over others; it is about serving others. The leaders we need for the future must be driven by a deep sense of compassion—a genuine concern for the well-being of all Americans, especially the most vulnerable among us. Compassionate leadership does not see opponents as enemies to be defeated but as fellow citizens with different perspectives to be understood and engaged with respectfully.

In times of crisis, whether economic, social, or environmental, it is leaders with kindness and empathy who will bring people together. Think of the leaders who have inspired us in the past—figures like Abraham Lincoln, Martin Luther King Jr., or Nelson Mandela. These were leaders who understood that healing and reconciliation required empathy for those on all sides of an issue. They did not shy away from hard truths or moral courage, but they also approached their adversaries with grace and a desire to unify rather than further divide.

In a political landscape often dominated by toxic rhetoric and dehumanizing language, we need leaders who can restore decency to public life. Leaders who speak not just to their political base, but to the entire nation. Leaders who understand that to truly lead is to listen—to the concerns, hopes, and fears of all Americans, regardless of their party affiliation, race, class, or background.

Leaders Who Build Bridges, Not Walls

The divisions we face today—whether racial, political, economic, or cultural—are real, but they are not insurmountable. The leaders we need for the future must be bridge builders—those who seek to close the gaps between opposing sides rather than widen them. They must be individuals who can facilitate dialogue, not monologue; leaders who prioritize collaboration over domination, and compromise over conflict.

To bridge these divides, leaders must reject the zero-sum mentality that dominates much of today's politics. Too often, political leaders present every issue as a battle between winners and losers, where success for one side means defeat for the other. But the problems we face as a nation are too complex for such binary thinking. Whether it's healthcare, education, immigration, or gun control, real solutions will only emerge when leaders are willing to work across the aisle, to find common ground, and to understand that progress requires the willingness to listen and the humility to learn.

Bridge-building is not an easy task, and it requires great political courage. It demands that leaders resist the pressures of their own party's extremes, and instead focus on bringing together a broad coalition of Americans who are invested in finding solutions rather than perpetuating division. This type of leadership is not about ideological purity but about pragmatism, patience, and a commitment to long-term change rather than short-term political victories.

Integrity and Accountability in Leadership

At a time when trust in institutions and political leaders is at an all-time low, the future of American leadership depends on a return to integrity and accountability. Too many of today's leaders have been caught up in scandals, corruption, or cynical manipulation of the truth, further eroding the public's faith in government and democracy itself. For democracy to flourish, we need leaders who demonstrate an unwavering commitment to honesty, transparency, and accountability.

Integrity in leadership means telling hard truths, even when they are unpopular or politically costly. It means making decisions based on what is best for the country as a whole, not just what will satisfy the demands of the most vocal constituents or the biggest donors. Leaders with integrity are willing to own their mistakes, to admit when they are wrong, and to correct course when necessary. They are not afraid of being held accountable, because they understand that their power is derived from the people they serve.

This kind of leadership is especially important in a time when disinformation and misinformation are rampant. Leaders must be committed to truth-telling—grounding their policies in facts and evidence, rather than in conspiracy theories or partisan echo chambers. They must resist the urge to pander to the extremes and instead work to elevate the level of discourse, setting an example for how public figures should engage with their constituencies and each other.

Visionaries with a Long-Term Focus

The challenges America faces today—from climate change to economic inequality, from healthcare reform to racial justice—are not problems that will be solved overnight. The leaders we need for the future must be visionaries—individuals who can see beyond the next election cycle and work toward long-term solutions that will benefit future generations.

Visionary leaders are those who recognize that the greatest accomplishments often require time, persistence, and collaborative effort. Think of John F. Kennedy's vision for putting a man on the moon—not because it was easy, but because it was hard, and because it inspired Americans to dream bigger and aim higher. We need that same kind of bold leadership today, especially in areas like green energy, technology, and infrastructure. Visionary leaders are willing to take political risks in the short term to ensure long-term success for the country.

These leaders must also focus on the next generation—on what kind of country we will leave for our children and grandchildren. They must prioritize investments in education, healthcare, and the environment to ensure that the future is brighter, more just, and more sustainable than the present. Leadership is not just about managing today's crises; it's about laying the groundwork for tomorrow's opportunities.

Courage to Face Challenges with Optimism

Above all, the leaders we need for the future must have the courage to face the immense challenges of our time with optimism and resolve. Cynicism, fatalism, and despair have no place in leadership. While it is true that the problems America faces are serious—deep political divisions, systemic racism, a climate crisis, economic disparities—effective leaders must maintain hope in the possibility of progress.

This does not mean ignoring or downplaying the gravity of these issues. Instead, it means believing that we can find solutions, that we can build bridges, and that we can move forward as a stronger, more united nation. Optimism is not naivety—it is a refusal to succumb to the idea that our divisions are too great to overcome. It is the belief that we are capable of more and that the best days of America are still ahead.

A Call for Leadership

The leaders of the future will not emerge by accident. They will be chosen by us, the American people. It is up to each of us to demand better from our elected officials, to support those who embody the values of kindness, integrity, and vision, and to hold accountable those who fail to live up to these ideals.

Leadership is about more than policy positions and political affiliations—it's about character. It's about how leaders treat the people they serve, how they navigate conflict, and how they inspire hope in the face of adversity. The leaders we need are not those who will tear us further apart, but those who will bring us together. They are not those who will manipulate us with fear and anger, but those who will inspire us with compassion and courage.

As we look to the future, let us demand leaders who believe in the promise of America—leaders who will guide us not through fear or vengeance, but through hope and unity. Let us find and support those who will lead us forward, not just for today, but for generations to come. In their hands, and in ours, lies the future of this great nation.

Recommitting to Our Core Values

At the heart of the American experiment lies a set of enduring values—freedom, equality, justice, and democracy. These values are enshrined in our Constitution and our founding documents, and they have served as the moral compass guiding us through the triumphs and trials of our history. Yet, in times of deep division and polarization, it can be easy to lose sight of these core principles. As we chart a path forward, we must recommit ourselves to these values, ensuring that they remain at the center of our national life.

The challenges we face—whether they relate to racial justice, economic inequality, free speech, or the rule of law—are not just political problems; they are also moral questions. They ask us to reflect on who we are as a people and what kind of country we want to be. By reaffirming our commitment to the values that have always defined America, we can begin to heal the divisions that have torn us apart and move toward a future rooted in justice, equity, and opportunity for all.

Freedom: The Foundation of Our Democracy

At the core of the American identity is the value of freedom—the idea that individuals have the right to determine their own lives, to speak their minds, and to pursue their dreams without undue interference from the government or other powerful forces. Freedom is the foundation upon which our democracy is built, and it has been the driving force behind our greatest achievements as a nation.

However, freedom does not mean the absence of responsibility. It does not give us the right to infringe upon the freedoms of others, nor does it absolve us of the duty to use our liberty wisely. The First Amendment, for example, grants us the right to free speech, but it also places upon us the responsibility to use that speech in ways that enrich our public discourse rather than degrade it. As we face the challenges of the 21st century, we must find ways to balance our individual freedoms with the common good.

Reaffirming our commitment to freedom means fighting for the rights of all Americans—whether that means defending the freedom of the press, protecting the right to protest, or ensuring that voter rights are upheld. But it also means recognizing that freedom is not a zero-sum game. Your freedom does not diminish mine, and we must work together to ensure that the freedoms we enjoy are extended to every citizen, especially those whose rights have historically been denied or infringed upon.

Freedom also comes with a collective responsibility to defend our democracy. This means protecting the integrity of our elections, ensuring that every citizen's vote counts, and resisting any efforts to undermine the rule of law. In recent years, we've seen how fragile democracy can be, and we've learned that the freedom we hold dear must be vigilantly defended.

Equality: The Ongoing Struggle for Justice

Equality is another core American value—one that we have often struggled to live up to, but which has always been a central part of our national identity. From the Declaration of Independence's assertion that "all men are created equal" to the Civil Rights Movement of the 20th century, the fight for equality has been one of the defining narratives of American history. Yet, despite the progress we've made, we still face profound inequalities in our society, particularly when it comes to race, gender, sexual orientation, and economic status.

Recommitting to equality means recognizing the disparities that exist in our society and taking concrete steps to address them. This does not mean ignoring or erasing our differences, but rather ensuring that those differences do not result in discrimination, exclusion, or marginalization. Whether it's ensuring equal access to education, healthcare, and employment opportunities, or fighting against systemic inequalities in the criminal justice system, the pursuit of equality must remain a central focus of our national agenda.

Racial justice, in particular, must be a priority as we move forward. The legacy of slavery, segregation, and systemic racism continues to shape the experiences of Black Americans and other marginalized groups. The Black Lives Matter movement has brought renewed attention to these issues, but the work of achieving true racial equality is far from finished. We must continue to fight for police reform, voting rights, and economic justice to ensure that all Americans are treated equally under the law.

Gender equality is another area where progress has been made but challenges remain. While women have made significant strides in areas like education and the workforce, gender disparities persist in wages, leadership roles, and access to reproductive healthcare. The Me Too movement highlighted the pervasiveness of sexual harassment and assault, and it's clear that more needs to be done to ensure that women are able to live free from fear and discrimination.

Achieving true equality will not happen overnight. It requires a sustained effort to dismantle the barriers that prevent people from reaching their full potential, whether those barriers are legal, economic, or social. But by recommitting to the value of equality, we affirm our belief in the inherent worth and dignity of every person and our determination to build a society where opportunity is not limited by race, gender, or background.

Justice: Ensuring Fairness for All

Justice is the moral backbone of a society, and the American legal system is designed to ensure that justice is blind and that everyone is equal before the law. But as recent events have made clear, this ideal remains far from reality for many Americans. Police violence, mass incarceration, and racial profiling are just a few of the ways in which the justice system disproportionately affects people of color, particularly Black and Latino Americans. Economic inequality has also led to a system where those with financial means can often buy better legal representation, further skewing justice in favor of the privileged.

Recommitting to justice means taking bold steps to reform our criminal justice system so that it truly serves all Americans, not just the wealthy or the well-connected. We must address mass incarceration, which has disproportionately affected communities of color and left millions of Americans trapped in a cycle of poverty and disenfranchisement. Rehabilitative justice—focusing on rehabilitation rather than punishment—should be at the core of our approach to reform, ensuring that those who make mistakes are given the opportunity to reintegrate into society.

It also means addressing the systemic inequalities that have kept racial minorities from fully participating in the economic and social life of our country. This includes ensuring that justice is applied equally to all, whether in the courts, the workplace, or the voting booth. It is not enough to say that we believe in justice; we must work to create a system that is truly fair, equitable, and just for all.

Environmental justice is another crucial aspect of the broader justice conversation. Communities of color and low-income neighborhoods have disproportionately borne the brunt of pollution, toxic waste, and environmental degradation. Recommitting to justice means ensuring that all Americans, regardless of where they live, have access to clean air, safe drinking water, and a healthy environment.

Democracy: Protecting the People's Voice

Democracy is the bedrock of our political system. It is the mechanism by which we choose our leaders, express our preferences, and hold our government accountable. But democracy is not a given; it must be actively maintained and defended. In recent years, we have seen the erosion of trust in our democratic institutions, with widespread concerns about voter suppression, gerrymandering, and foreign interference in our elections.

Recommitting to the value of democracy means taking concrete steps to protect voting rights, ensure election integrity, and restore faith in our political system. Every American, regardless of their race, income, or political affiliation, deserves the right to participate in our democracy, free from obstacles or intimidation. We must resist efforts to undermine the voting process, whether through restrictive voter ID laws, partisan gerrymandering, or attempts to delegitimize elections with baseless claims of fraud.

At the same time, we must work to restore civility and dialogue in our political discourse. Democracy thrives on healthy debate and the exchange of ideas, but too often, our political conversations have devolved into name-calling, finger-pointing, and echo chambers that prevent real understanding. Reaffirming our commitment to democracy means fostering a political culture that encourages open dialogue, respectful disagreement, and compromise.

Democracy also means accountability. Those who are entrusted with public office must be held accountable for their actions, and our democratic system must be structured in such a way that it promotes transparency and ethical governance. When public officials act in their own interest rather than the public good, they undermine the very principles that democracy stands for.

A Call to Re-commitment

In these challenging times, it is easy to lose sight of the values that have guided America for more than two centuries. But it is precisely in moments like these that we must recommit ourselves to those values, ensuring that they continue to shape our national life. Freedom, equality, justice, and democracy are not abstract ideals; they are the foundation of our shared identity, the principles that have allowed America to weather its greatest storms and emerge stronger.

Recommitting to these values means more than simply paying lip service to them. It means living them out in our policies, our institutions, and our personal lives. It means recognizing that the fight for freedom, equality, justice, and democracy is ongoing and that it requires constant vigilance and renewed effort.

If we can do this—if we can come together around these core values and work to make them a reality for every American—then there is no limit to what we can achieve as a nation. The path forward is challenging, but it is also full of promise. Let us move forward with hope, with determination, and with a renewed commitment to the values that make America truly great.

A Call to Reclaim America's Role in the World

As we look inward to address our divisions, we must also look outward to reclaim our role as leaders of the free world. For generations, the United States has stood as a beacon of democracy, freedom, and hope to nations across the globe. We have been a guiding light in moments of darkness, offering the world a vision of liberty, human rights, and justice. But as we grapple with internal challenges—

political polarization, social unrest, and economic inequality—we must recognize that our ability to lead internationally is deeply tied to our ability to heal and unite as a nation.

America's strength has never been based solely on its military might or economic power; it has always been rooted in its moral leadership. When we have led the world, it has been because we stood for principles that transcended borders and ideologies. The values of democracy, freedom of expression, human dignity, and equal justice under the law are not just American values—they are universal aspirations. And it is this commitment to higher ideals that has allowed America to stand as a global leader throughout its history.

The Importance of Strong, Stable Leadership

Today's world faces a number of global challenges—from climate change to geopolitical tensions, from the rise of authoritarianism to the threats posed by cybersecurity breaches. These problems require strong, stable, and principled leadership from the United States. But before we can effectively lead the world, we must first heal the fractures that exist within our own borders. America cannot champion democracy abroad if it allows the erosion of democratic norms and institutions at home. We cannot call for human rights internationally if we fail to address racial injustice or economic inequality in our own society.

Reclaiming our role as global leaders begins with an inward reflection—an honest assessment of where we stand as a nation. The world looks to us not only for economic stability and military strength, but for the moral compass we provide. Our leadership on the world stage is contingent on our unity, justice, and compassion at home. If we want to lead the world toward sustainability, peace, and prosperity, we must first take bold steps to lead ourselves in the same direction.

Leading on Climate and Environmental Policy

One of the most pressing global challenges is climate change, and America must once again take up the mantle of leadership in the fight for a sustainable future. The effects of climate change—rising sea levels, extreme weather, wildfires, and environmental degradation—are already being felt around the world. The impacts are most severe in vulnerable communities, both in the U.S. and globally, where natural disasters, droughts, and floods displace millions and exacerbate poverty and inequality.

In this context, America must act as both an example and a driving force for international efforts to combat climate change. By rejoining the Paris Climate Agreement under the Biden administration, the U.S. took an important first step toward re-engaging with the global community on climate action. But much more is required. We need to lead by example, implementing policies that aggressively reduce our own carbon emissions, invest in clean energy, and protect the environment. At the same time, we must work to ensure that developing nations are supported in their own transitions to sustainable energy and climate resilience.

Our leadership on climate change will not only help safeguard the planet for future generations but will also solidify our role as a global leader in one of the most important arenas of international cooperation. The world needs a United States that is committed to the health of the planet and willing to invest in innovation and technology that will benefit all.

Embracing Diplomatic Leadership

In a world that is becoming increasingly multi-polar, with rising powers like China and Russia challenging the U.S.'s influence, America must recommit to diplomatic leadership as a means of shaping a stable and peaceful international order. For decades, the U.S. has been a champion of multilateralism, fostering international cooperation through organizations like the United Nations, NATO, and the World Trade Organization. These institutions were built on the principles of collective security, international law, and human rights, all of which America has historically promoted.

Yet, in recent years, we have seen a retreat from this kind of leadership, marked by a rise in isolationism and protectionism. We must reverse this trend. America is strongest when it is actively engaged with the world—when it builds alliances, strengthens partnerships, and works with others to address shared challenges. Diplomacy, not force, must be our first tool of choice in dealing with international disputes, whether they concern nuclear proliferation, regional conflicts, or human rights abuses.

A renewed commitment to diplomacy means re-engaging with our traditional allies while seeking new partnerships with emerging powers, and leading global efforts on issues like pandemic preparedness, trade agreements, and cybersecurity. The global challenges we face cannot be solved by any one country alone, and America's role must be to bring nations together in pursuit of common solutions.

Reaffirming Democratic Values and Human Rights

At the core of America's global leadership has always been our commitment to democratic values and human rights. From our role in defeating fascism and totalitarianism during World War II to our support for decolonization movements and democratic uprisings throughout the 20th century, America has long been a champion of freedom, self-determination, and human dignity.

But in recent years, we have seen the rise of authoritarian regimes and illiberal democracies across the globe. Countries like Russia, China, and Hungary have embraced policies that restrict free speech, undermine the rule of law, and concentrate power in the hands of a few. These regimes often position themselves as alternatives to Western liberal democracy, offering a model of governance based on control, surveillance, and repression.

The world needs a strong defender of democracy, and the United States must step into that role once more. But to do so, we must first ensure that our own democracy is healthy and vibrant. We must demonstrate to the world that democracy is not only viable but essential for a free and just society. This means ensuring free and fair elections, protecting voting rights, and promoting equal justice under the law. It means standing firm against the forces of disinformation and authoritarianism, both at home and abroad.

Moreover, America must continue to be a voice for human rights on the global stage. Whether it's advocating for the rights of women and minorities, LGBTQ+ rights, or fighting against genocide and ethnic cleansing, our commitment to human dignity must remain unwavering. The United States cannot be silent in the face of oppression, nor can we ignore the plight of those who suffer under repressive regimes.

Rebuilding Our Moral Leadership

Ultimately, America's influence in the world has always stemmed from more than just its military or economic power—it has come from its moral leadership. The world has looked to the United States as a country that, despite its flaws, has strived to build a society where freedom, justice, and equality are paramount. We have been a symbol of what is possible—a place where people of all backgrounds and beliefs can come together to build a better life and a better world.

But in recent years, that moral leadership has been diminished. The rise of polarization, the erosion of democratic norms, and the persistent inequalities within our society have weakened our standing in the international community. To reclaim our role as global leaders, we must first rebuild the foundations of trust at home.

This means addressing the divisions that have fractured our society. It means committing ourselves to a higher standard of justice and ensuring that our domestic policies reflect the values we seek to promote abroad. Moral leadership does not come from force or fear; it comes from integrity, a commitment to the common good, and the belief in human dignity.

The world is watching America. And as we face our internal challenges, the international community looks to us not only for our power but for our moral example. We have been leaders before, and we can be leaders again. But it will require us to rise above our current divisions, reaffirm our core values, and recommit to the ideals that have always defined our greatness.

A Vision for the Future

Reclaiming America's role in the world is not just about restoring what was lost; it is about re-imagining what leadership can look like in the 21st century. The challenges we face—from climate change to economic inequality, from pandemics to rising authoritarianism—require bold, innovative solutions and a commitment to global cooperation. The United States must be at the forefront of these efforts, not as a dominant superpower dictating terms, but as a collaborative leader working with other nations to achieve shared goals.

This vision for the future requires a new kind of leadership—one that embraces diversity, innovation, and compassion. It requires a recognition that the greatest challenges we face are global in nature, and that our ability to solve them depends on our willingness to work together, both within our borders and beyond them.

The world needs an America that leads with hope rather than fear, with justice rather than vengeance, and with a commitment to building a better future for all. We have been that America before, and we can be that America again. The path forward is not without obstacles, but with unity, vision, and moral courage, we can reclaim our role as leaders of the free world—not just for ourselves, but for the generations to come.

The Pride and Responsibility of Being American

To be an American is to hold both a deep pride and an immense responsibility. We are part of a nation with a legacy that stretches back to the boldest of ideals—freedom, equality, and self-determination. Our founding principles were revolutionary, a beacon of hope for the world, and they remain as important today as they were when this nation was born. Yet, with that inheritance comes the responsibility to ensure that the American experiment—this grand, ongoing pursuit of a more perfect union—continues to grow and evolve for future generations. We are stewards of its future, and with that comes a duty to confront the hard truths about where we are today and how we can build a better tomorrow.

America is not just a place; it is an idea—an idea that transcends borders, backgrounds, and circumstances. The American Dream is the belief that anyone, regardless of where they come from, can find freedom, opportunity, and justice in this land. It is the belief that through hard work, perseverance, and a commitment to the common good, anyone can rise and contribute to a society where the pursuit of happiness is not just a promise but a reality. That idea has been tested time and again throughout our history. It has faced moments of deep division, conflict, and turmoil. But each time, we have found a way to recommit to our core values and overcome the challenges before us.

The Duality of Pride and Responsibility

Pride in being an American is natural. We live in a nation that has accomplished incredible things—leading the world in scientific innovation, fostering artistic creativity, expanding the boundaries of civil rights, and standing as a global defender of freedom. From landing on the moon to liberating Europe during World War II, America's achievements have long been a source of collective pride, not only for what we've done, but for the spirit that has driven us—ingenuity, courage, and a relentless pursuit of progress.

But pride alone is not enough. Along with that pride comes an equally important sense of responsibility. We are the custodians of a democratic tradition that is fragile and requires constant nurturing. It is our responsibility to protect the freedoms we cherish, to uphold the rule of law, and to defend the rights of all people, especially those whose voices have been marginalized or silenced. As Americans, we are called upon not only to celebrate our achievements but also to learn from our mistakes—to confront the ways in which we have fallen short of our ideals and to work tirelessly to close the gap between our aspirations and our reality.

Being an American means owning both our triumphs and our failures. It means recognizing that the promise of America—the idea that we are all created equal and entitled to life, liberty, and the pursuit of happiness—remains unfulfilled for many. Our history is one of both light and shadow, of both monumental achievements and grievous wrongs. From the horrors of slavery and Jim Crow to the continued struggles for racial justice, from the exclusion of women from public life to the fight for LGBTQ+ rights, America's story is one of both progress and setbacks. Yet, through it all, we have moved forward because we have embraced the responsibility of making this country better—not just for ourselves, but for future generations.

Confronting Our Divisions with Integrity

If we are to fulfill our responsibility as Americans, we must first be willing to confront the hard truths about our divisions. It is easy to look at the state of our political and social discourse today and feel discouraged. The lines that divide us—red and blue, urban and rural, liberal and conservative—seem more entrenched than ever. But division is not new to America. We have faced times of great discord before—times when the very foundation of our union seemed at risk of collapsing under the weight of partisan strife, racial tensions, and economic inequality.

Yet each time, we found a way to rise above those divisions, not by ignoring them, but by confronting them with honesty and integrity. We debated, we struggled, and we eventually reached compromise because we understood that the American idea was worth fighting for. Today, we are called to do the same. We must not shy away from the difficult conversations about race, justice, economic opportunity, and human rights. We must be willing to acknowledge the wounds of our past and the inequalities that persist today, all while holding onto the belief that progress is possible.

Confronting our divisions means more than simply identifying the issues that separate us; it means listening to one another with a genuine desire to understand different perspectives. It means engaging in civil discourse rather than retreating into ideological echo chambers. And most importantly, it means recognizing that the values we share—freedom, equality, and justice—are far stronger than the divisions that threaten to tear us apart.

Embracing the Promise of Unity

As we face these divisions, we must also embrace the promise of unity. Unity is not about sameness—it is not about erasing our differences or pretending that we all share the same views. Instead, unity is about recognizing that, despite our differences, we are bound together by a shared commitment to the ideals that have defined America since its founding. Unity is about finding common ground in our shared humanity and shared purpose.

The American identity is not monolithic. It is, in fact, defined by its diversity. We are a nation of immigrants, of different faiths, cultures, and languages. The beauty of America lies in its ability to bring together people from all walks of life, people who hold different beliefs and come from different backgrounds, and yet are united by the belief in freedom and opportunity. This is the promise of America: that regardless of who you are or where you come from, you have a place here, and you have a voice in shaping the future of this country.

Unity, however, does not mean the absence of conflict. Disagreement and debate have always been essential to the American democratic process. But what we must remember is that healthy debate requires a foundation of respect, mutual understanding, and a shared commitment to the greater good. If we are to move forward as a nation, we must learn to disagree without dehumanizing one another, to debate without dividing ourselves into irreconcilable factions.

The American Idea: A Beacon of Hope

America is not just a country; it is a beacon of hope—an idea that has inspired people across the globe for more than two centuries. The American Dream has drawn millions to our shores, seeking freedom from tyranny, persecution, and poverty. This idea—that through hard work and perseverance, anyone can build a better life—has been the foundation of our national identity.

The world still looks to America as a symbol of what is possible when people come together in pursuit of freedom and justice. But this idea is not self-sustaining. It requires each generation to recommit to the principles that make it possible. It requires us to be vigilant in protecting democratic norms, in upholding the rule of law, and in ensuring that the opportunities of America are available to all, not just the privileged few.

Being an American means believing in the power of hope—hope that we can always improve, that we can always be better, that we can live up to the ideals upon which this country was founded. It means recognizing that while we are imperfect, we are constantly striving toward a more perfect union. It means believing that the best days of America are not behind us, but ahead of us.

The Legacy We Leave for Future Generations

The responsibility of being American is not limited to the present moment—it extends to the legacy we leave for future generations. The choices we make today will shape the America of tomorrow. Will we be a nation that turns inward, focused only on our own self-interests? Or will we be a nation that embraces its role as a leader on the global stage, standing for democracy, human rights, and freedom?

Our responsibility is to ensure that the next generation inherits a nation that is not only prosperous but also just, equitable, and sustainable. This means confronting the climate crisis with the urgency it demands, ensuring that future Americans have a healthy planet to live on. It means continuing the work of expanding civil rights so that every child born in this country can grow up knowing that they are valued and protected under the law. It means defending the institutions of democracy, so that future generations can enjoy the freedoms that have been passed down to us.

The American story is not just about the past; it is about the future we are building together. We must remember that we are the authors of that story, and we have the power to shape it in ways that reflect our highest ideals. The pride we feel as Americans comes from knowing that we are part of something bigger than ourselves—something that has the potential to lift up not just our own people, but people around the world.

Rising to the Challenge

In these challenging times, we are called to remember the pride and responsibility that come with being American. We are the inheritors of a bold and audacious experiment in democracy and self-governance, and it is our duty to ensure that this experiment not only endures but thrives. To do so, we must confront the divisions that threaten to tear us apart, embrace the unity that has always been our greatest strength, and recommit ourselves to the values of freedom, equality, and justice.

The American idea is as powerful today as it was when it was first conceived. But it is up to us to keep that idea alive, to pass it on to future generations, and to ensure that it remains a beacon of hope for all. As long as we hold onto the values that make us who we are—as long as we remain committed to liberty, equality, and hope—we will find a way to overcome the challenges before us and build a future that is worthy of the American Dream.